42-9

THE JUDICIAL PROCESS

AN INTRODUCTORY ANALYSIS

OF THE COURTS

OF THE UNITED STATES,

ENGLAND, AND FRANCE

New York

THE
JUDICIAL
PROCESS

HENRY J. ABRAHAM

University of Pennsylvania

Oxford University Press   1962

To Philip

PREFACE

When my *Courts and Judges: An Introduction to the Judicial Process* appeared in 1959, I begin its Preface by pointing tó the general absence of even the most rudimentary knowledge of the judicial process on the part of the vast majority of students of Political Science entering elementary or even advanced courses, and observed that equally striking was the unavailability of accessible materials providing basic data in the field. The measure of success my small book has enjoyed encouraged the writing of the present volume, which is far more ambitious in scope than its predecessor.

This new book is a selective comparative introduction to the judicial process, and seeks to analyze and evaluate the main institutions and considerations affecting the administration of justice under law. The rather extensive coverage of certain significant features and elements of comparative judicial processes was prompted not only by several helpful suggestions by users of the earlier book, but by the continued neglect of these processes in basic textbooks.

An important segment of this work is thus devoted to the judicial process in England and Wales, and France, and—to a necessarily considerably lesser extent in this context—the Soviet Union. Other states are included whenever appropriate, especially in connection with the doctrine and practice of judicial review. Nonetheless, at least half of the material deals with the judicial process in the United States.

The detailed Table of Contents obviates capsule explanations of the substance of each chapter in this volume. I have compiled numerous graphs, figures, and c'iarts, all designed to facilitate comprehension. There are two indexes, one general, one for cases. And there are four extensive bibliographies dealing with (1) works in general on American Constitutional Law; (2) biographies and autobiographies of and by justices of the United States Supreme Court; (3) Comparative Constitutional Law; and (4) Civil Liberties.

Although I have endeavored to be objective in analysis and presentation throughout, in some circumstances it is neither possible nor desirable to shun value judgments; I have thus stated frankly my own opinions where it seemed appropriate to do so.

Once again I express my profound appreciation to the many colleagues who stimulated and urged me on in the writing of this book and whose generous suggestions were so helpful. I am especially grateful to Professors William M. Beaney, David Fellman, Wallace Mendelson, Jewell Cass Phillips, and R. J. Tresolini. Above all, I owe a particular debt of gratitude to Mr. James Wellwood, M.A., of Gray's Inn, Barrister-at-Law, Lecturer in Law at King's College, University of London, for his unselfish counsel and essential criticism on the sections on England and Wales. As they have been throughout my pleasant association with the Oxford University Press, Mr. Byron S. Hollinshead, Jr. and Miss Leona Capeless have been delightful and invaluable co-workers. Mrs. Helen White performed the thankless but so essential task of typing the entire manuscript cheerfully and efficiently. Whatever errors remain are mine. My wife, Mildred, gave me the kind of constant encouragement and confidence that only a devoted partner can provide.

And the book is happily dedicated to one who also helped in his own way.

Wynnewood, Pennsylvania   H. J. A.
February 1962

CONTENTS

THE JUDICIAL PROCESS

I

INTRODUCTION:
THE LAW AND COURTS

Respect for the law is one of the select group of principles which we have come to regard as essential to the effective and equitable operation of popular government. As a democratic principle it is recognized as binding on both the governed and those who govern.

In fostering this principle the role of the judiciary is crucial, for, in the words of Mr. Justice Arthur T. Vanderbilt:

> it is in the courts and not in the legislature that our citizens primarily feel the keen, cutting edge of the law. If they have respect for the work of the courts, their respect for law will survive the shortcomings of every other branch of government; but if they lose their respect for the work of the courts, their respect for law and order will vanish with it to the great detriment of society.[1]

This is true, whether the judicial branch be technically separated from the other two branches of government, as in the United States; partly fused with them, as in France; or largely fused, as in the United Kingdom of Great Britain and Northern Ireland. The law will be respected as long as it is interpreted and applied within the structures of justice as accepted by the majority of society—in the long run, if not always in the short run. It is, after all, the expressed will of those who rule society.

But the law, in its procedural as well as its substantive aspects, is essentially made and administered by men whose views and

[1] *The Challenge of Law Reform* (Princeton: Princeton University Press, 1955), pp. 4–5.

interpretations are buffeted by the winds of change through the years, so that it has become "a truism that the quality of justice depends more on the quality of the men who administer the law than on the content of the law they administer." [2] Judicial activity, observed Roscoe Pound in one of his lectures, is really the creative element in law. Accordingly, if man's great interest on earth is justice, as Daniel Webster put it, then perhaps a more immediate interest is the securing of the most highly qualified individuals to administer justice impartially with a minimum of chicanery and obfuscation. It follows logically that judges must be assured of an optimum degree of independence and relative freedom from pre-judicial pressures from forces both inside and outside of government. Moreover, they must be able to function in a hierarchical structure that is effectively conducive to the performance of the basic task at hand—the impartial administration of justice under law.

They pursue this task through the medium of a court, an institution, as Carl Brent Swisher noted concisely, that along with such other characteristics as it may incidentally possess:

> determines the facts involved in particular controversies brought before it, relates the facts to the relevant law, settles the controversies in terms of the law, and more or less incidentally makes new law through the process of decision. Over the centuries of Anglo-American history our judiciary has been developed and geared to this process so that it has an integrity or integratedness peculiar to its own. In particular it has a mode of informing the minds of the responsible officers —in this instance the judges—which is unique and which must be kept in sharp focus in any attempt to estimate the capacity of a judiciary to perform competitively in the gray areas which lie between it and institutions which are primarily legislative or executive.[3]

---

[2] Evan Haynes, *The Selection and Tenure of Judges* (National Conference of Judicial Councils, 1944), p. 5, as quoted in Jewell Cass Phillips, *State and Local Government in America* (New York: American Book Co., 1954), p. 237.

[3] Presidential Address, delivered before the American Political Science Association, New York City, September 8, 1960. (Reprinted in 54 *American Political Science Review* 879–80, December 1960.)

THE NATURE OF LAW

For at least twenty-five centuries, and perhaps longer, men have discussed the nature of law.[4] In one way or another, it touches every citizen of every nation. The contact may be pleasant or unpleasant, tangible or intangible, direct or indirect, but it is nonetheless a constant force in the lives of people everywhere on the globe. It is essential that we have some understanding of its nature and of the human beings who interpret and administer it.

"What is Law?" has been asked by priests and poets, philosophers and kings, by masses no less than by prophets. A host of answers might be given, yet the answer to the question remains one of the most persistent and elusive problems in the entire range of thought. For one may well view the entire gamut of human life, both in thought and in action, as being comprised within the word Law.[5]

It may seem strange that the true essence of such a ubiquitous phenomenon as law should be beyond the grasp of general human understanding. Since law deals with human conduct, in order to grasp its nature it would appear necessary merely to distinguish it from the other factors relating to that conduct: religion, science, morals, ethics, custom. Yet herein lies the difficulty, so ably stated by James Coolidge Carter more than half a century ago:

> Law, Custom, Conduct, Life—different names for almost the same thing—true names for different aspects of the same thing —are so inseparably blended together that one cannot even be thought of without the other. No improvement can be effected in one without improving the other, and no retrogression can take place in one without a corresponding decline in the other.[6]

There is but little doubt that law has much in common with all these other aspects of human conduct, yet it is nonetheless true that it also possesses at least one unique characteristic lacking in all others: its sanction is applied exclusively by organized political government.[7]

[4] William A. Robson, *Civilization and the Growth of Law* (New York: The Macmillan Co., 1935), p. 3.   [5] Ibid.

[6] *Law: Its Origin, Growth and Function* (New York and London: The Knickerbocker Press, 1907), p. 320.

[7] William Seagle, *The Quest for Law* (New York: Albert K. Knopf, 1941), p. 7.

Three Historical Categories. Although it may be stretching the definition somewhat, some kind of law has always existed—however inadequate or even absent both legal organization and enforcement machinery may have been. First came *primitive* law, based chiefly on primitive custom and lacking even rudimentary machinery and organization. Prevailing among some of the early Indian, Oceanic, and Asiatic tribes, it was and is the law of those "preliterate" peoples who have not yet developed but have nevertheless recognized social rules, and have discovered means of coping with social conflict. The earliest known system of written law was the Code of Hammurabi, so named in honor of its founder, the fabled King of Babylonia. It was promulgated about 2050 B.C. and contained a statement of the existing rules and customs of the land. It personified the idea that justice was man's inherent right, sanctioned by supernatural forces rather than by royally bestowed favor.

Archaic law, featuring some manner of courts and officialdom—institutions that are basic to every legal system—and introducing certain codes of procedure and substance, arrived on the scene during the days of Rome and feudalism and among the primitive Germanic and African tribes. However, Moses' *Pentateuch,* given in the fifteenth century B.C., may well lay an earlier claim. Certainly the *Great Sanhedrin,* the supreme council of the Jewish nation in Greco-Roman days, was a judicial body that stated and interpreted the law of the Hebrews.

Mature Law appeared in the twelfth century of the Christian era in England; it heralded the professionalization of the law under the guide of professional lawyers. It fathered the law we know today.

POSITIVE AND NATURAL LAW

The above-mentioned three kinds of law are prongs of *positive law,* the type of law with which we have been and will be concerned throughout this book. It is held to derive from man for the purpose of ruling man; it is a command based upon the relationship between ruler and ruled; its primary nature is that it is *man made.* It springs from no source higher than the human will.

This is what John Chipman Gray alluded to when he defined a man's legal rights as:

> power which he has to make a person or persons do or refrain from doing a certain act or . . . acts, as far as the power arises from society.[8]

In other words, according to the tenets of positive law—as defined by John Austin, who in turn was inspired by the French social theorist Auguste Comte—law consists of definite rules of human conduct with appropriate sanctions for their enforcement, both of these being prescribed by duly constituted human authority.

Natural Law. But in the eyes of many there is another category of law—*natural law,* which is viewed by its adherents as governing human relations in the absence of positive law, and as either standing above positive law or at least as a supplement to it. Its theory was originated by the Stoics. Since this book necessarily deals only with the application and interpretation of positive law, the intriguing concept of natural law must be treated rather summarily here. One of the most significant statements of natural law— which is regarded as discoverable by human reason—came from the Roman statesman and theorist, Cicero, who, in defining law, was explicit in indicating his concept of its essence as follows:

> Law is the highest reason, implanted in Nature, which commands what ought to be done and forbids the opposite . . . the origin of justice is to be found in law, for law is its natural force; it is the mind and reason of the intelligent man, the standards by which justice and injustice are measured.
>
> I shall seek the root of justice in nature. . . .[9]

Law here is seen as an organic whole with the universe and held together by a supreme rationality, which inheres in both man and

[8] *The Nature and Sources of Law* (New York: Columbia University Press, 1916), p. 19.
[9] Cicero, "The Laws," in Francis William Coker, *Readings in Political Philosophy,* rev. ed. (New York: The Macmillan Co., 1955), pp. 145–6.

the universe. The thread of rationality not only holds the system together but gives a definite order to it:

> . . . the universe obeys God; seas and lands obey the universe, and human life is subject to the decree of supreme law.[10]

It would seem that natural law thus stands on two assumptions: first, the rationality and intelligence of man; second, the existence of a higher *rational* order of things. Since man is presumed to be intelligent, he can hence readily "find" the law, that is, to understand the higher rational order.

Without endeavoring to prove or disprove this theory and estimate of man, the latter's history at least places the issue in doubt. At best, it appears that man is equally as capable of capricious action based upon passion as he is of rational action based upon intelligence. If man's intelligence is placed in doubt, so is his ability to understand a higher rational order. Indeed, the belief in a higher order or a universal law of justice is equally difficult to accept because of the wide discrepancies between belief and action in real life—as pointed out by Carmeades so many years ago.

Nonetheless, today natural law is identifiable with the abiding sense of justice that pervades the community of man—regardless of its changing substance. But it is positive law that governs us as law-abiding members of the body politic of organized society.

COMMON LAW AND STATUTORY LAW

For our purposes, then, law—broadly speaking—represents the rules of conduct that pertain to a given political order of society, rules that are backed by the organized force of the community. As it has evolved through the centuries, law may be made either by the political representatives of the people—sometimes rather inaccurately styled "bar-made" law—or it may be "bench-made" by judges and justices. The former type is generally known as *statutory law*, the latter as *common law*. Both will bear close examination, but, at the risk of some oversimplification, the crucial distinction between the two is that between codified written law and unwritten law based on custom and tradition. (The terms "bar-

[10] Ibid. p. 151.

made" and "bench-made" are never used in England, where the two types are simply categorized as "statutory" and "judge-made.")

COMMON LAW

Utilized by most English-speaking states, *common law* is variously known also as *English, Anglo-Saxon,* or *Anglo-American* law. Despite its conceptualization by Lord Coke as "the perfection of reason," it is indeed a vast and complex instrument of justice. Although at first glance it may well seem chaotic and abstruse, on closer examination it is readily possible to discern a logic which binds the many diverse components that comprise it into a comprehensive and comprehensible entity.[11]

Common law is judge-made, bench-made, law rather than a fixed body of definite rules such as the modern civil law codes. In Roscoe Pound's words, it is a "mode of judicial and juristic thinking, a mode of treating legal problems." [12] He might have added "a mood." Often based on precedents, it personifies continuity of binding the present with the past. Since it thus necessarily grew, and still grows, by virtue of judicial decisions, it is best to explain and analyze it historically.

Historical Background. With the decline and fall of Rome came the growth of Christianity and Christian philosophy. The concept of the state as the highest form of society began to be questioned with the rise of the Christian Church. Concurrent with the Norman invasion of the British Isles "precise and orderly methods into the government and law of England" were introduced.[13] Thus began under the Norman and Angevin monarchs of the eleventh and twelfth centuries the gradual growth of a central administration and the development of the courts of law. The term "common law" was used for the law developed in the King's Courts and was generally employed in order to distinguish between it and that of the ecclesiastical courts. In effect, the concept "common law" was adopted from the *canon law* of the Christian Church, which was

---

[11] For an excellent description see F. H. Lawson, *The Rational Strength of English Law* (Stevens, 1951).

[12] Roscoe Pound, *The Spirit of the Common Law* (Boston: Little, Brown and Co., 1921), p. 1.

[13] Theodore F. T. Plucknett, *A Concise History of the Common Law*, 5th ed. (Boston: Little, Brown and Co., 1956), p. 9.

the common law of Christendom. The common law of the King's Courts was made by the royal justices from the mass of customary law of the realm and became the common law of England. Basically, in its origin the latter was hence merely the customs recognized by the royal courts.

There were three great courts of common law: *King's Bench, Exchequer,* and *Common Pleas.* As the routine of these royal courts became firmly established, it was possible to forecast their decisions in terms of similar cases decided by them in the past. However, according to Theodore F. T. Plucknett,[14] the concept of basing decisions upon precedent was not adopted as a conscious policy, but was instituted merely to enable all existing courts to function with a minimum of trouble.

In many respects the common law reflects the feudal structure whence it was derived. Over a period of centuries the law defining the relationship between the Anglo-Norman monarchs and their tenants-in-chief became the law that was applicable to all Englishmen. At first this dealt solely with private law, but it was gradually extended to cover public law as well. The core of the feudal law was the concept of fealty which long prevailed after the passing of feudalism. Ruler as well as subject was bound—theirs were well-defined rights and obligations to be adhered to by all parties. Private rights of freemen were not subject to arbitrary change, and the primary task of the monarch was to preserve and protect the law.

But the groups whose rights the monarch had to acknowledge were limited to the nobility, the landed gentry, and some segments of the rising bourgeoisie. Hence it is hardly astonishing that the common law—which was essentially a law of property, in particular landed property—was "regarded by the politically influential class . . . as its shield." [15] Ordinary freemen had access to the King's Courts only in exceptional circumstances. However, during the twelfth and thirteenth centuries the practice of issuing *royal writs* was introduced, although these covered merely a few classes of civil cases. But early in the reign of Henry II (1154–89)

[14] Ibid. p. 342.
[15] Sir Charles Ogilvie, *The King's Government and the Common Law: 1471–1641* (Oxford: Basil Blackwell, 1958), p. 6.

an ordinance proclaiming that no man could be denied his freehold without a royal writ rendered centralization in a royal court inevitable. This was followed by several writs which continued the trend and culminated in the *Assize of Novel Disseisin of 1166,* which ordained that anyone who was denied his freehold could seek a remedy in the King's Court. (The Assize also provided for a jury of one's neighbors in questions of fact.) Thus, by 1166 the King was firmly established as the protector of the freehold.

By 1178 the work load of the King's Court had become more than King and Council could handle, and five full-time judges were appointed, some of whom would travel about the countryside, settling disputes in each locality according to the prevailing mores. They attended to the bulk of the cases although the monarch and his Council still disposed of "novel and difficult" matters. This arrangement ultimately led to the schema of legal proceedings based on writs, which were promulgated in ever increasing numbers. They were stereotyped and came to be sold to the litigants at a fixed price. Until the middle of the thirteenth century the King issued new writs to deal with a host of new problems. However, the barons became increasingly jealous of his power to make law, and in 1258 the King was forbidden to issue writs without the specific consent of his Council. In the absence of a new writ the thirty or forty writs then extant were interpreted and stretched in order to deal with problems with which often they were not designed to cope.[16]

With the founding of the Inns of Court unofficial reports of cases commenced to be published in annual *Year Books.* These books were records of court proceedings dealing mainly with procedural points for the benefit of practitioners rather than full reports of "casebook law" in the modern sense. Nevertheless, they did quite naturally come to serve as a gradually mounting source of precedents and were frequently referred to by those practitioners in the courts. *Stare decisis*—let the decision stand—began to have genuine meaning as a matter of judicial policy. According to Charles Ogilvie, the first inkling of the future English system of

---

[16] Ibid. p. 13.

case law may be found in the *Dialogues de Scaccario,* written by Richard Fitz-Nigel between 1177 and 1179:

> "There are," he said, "cases where the courses of events, and the reasons for decisions are obscure; and in these it is enough to cite precedents." [17]

Thus were laid the bases from which the common law grew. As society became more complex, so did the law. At first it was made by the royal courts, but from the thirteenth century on it was always accepted as the supreme and fundamental law of the land. The divine right of kings was a sixteenth-century idea, not a medieval one. Bracton (Henry of Bratton), writing in the thirteenth century, stated that the King was "under God and the law." And the great Sir Edward, later Lord, Coke—Attorney-General, Leader of Parliament, and Chief Justice of the Court of Common Pleas—when called before his King, echoed Bracton in declaring that the monarch should also be bound by law. When the King told him that he could not be subject "to any man," Coke replied that, agreed, the King "is not subject to any man, but to God and the Law." It was Lord Coke who, more than any other individual of his time, compiled and analyzed precedents at common law and who was largely responsible for the then increasingly accepted practice of reporting cases fully. From these he drew a set of maxims and rules, later to be amplified and explained precisely by the famed Sir William Blackstone. The latter's monumental work, *Commentaries on the Law of England,* ultimately became the bible of practically all legal schooling in both England and America.

No matter what the stripe or agency of absolutism, actual or nascent, any notion that the judges are to serve the popular majority was and is utterly wrong. For under the tenets of the common law, while recognizing the authority of King, Parliament, and People, all must bow to the law and act within its limits. England's judges have ever abided by their judicial oath to "administer the law without fear or favor."

Various attempts were made to displace common law in England by civil law—to no avail. Common law not only proved victorious, but over the years it was exported to such countries as

[17] Ibid. p. 17.

Canada, Australia, New Zealand, India, Pakistan, and Israel, and taken to the United States by the colonists. An interesting exception is itself a member of the United Kingdom of Great Britain and Northern Ireland, that is, Scotland, where the existing legal system was derived, as were the Continental systems, from Roman law; but it has been greatly influenced by the common law.

Characteristics. As has already been pointed out, common law is predominantly *judge-made law*. Under it the judge is the creator, interpreter, and modifier of laws. Even when he merely "interprets" law, he may well be creating it. To that extent, statutory law, the law enacted by legislative bodies, is tentative. Discussing the benefits of judge-made law, Mr. Justice Cardozo pointed out that the judge can use "free scientific research" when analyzing a problem. By "free" he meant that the common law removes the judge to a very real extent from action by positive authority; by "scientific" he referred to the objective element in the judge's decision. Thus he may come closer to the just and the true, for law under the common law system develops by "judicial experience in the decision of cases." [18]

Another significant characteristic of common law is the doctrine of *precedent*, under which the judges refer to a previous decision or decisions in order to adjudicate the case presently at issue. The importance of precedent varies with individual judges, for although common law has a rule demanding the recognition of precedent, the judges may distinguish between various precedents in evolving the new law. Moreover, times and conditions change with changing society, and, true to the thought that "every age should be mistress of its own law," an era should not be hampered by outdated laws. It is this ready ability of the common law to discard that which does not serve the public which has contributed to its survival and its adoption, wholly or partly, in so many lands. Nevertheless, although Mr. Justice Cardozo applauded this elasticity and timeliness, he cautioned that while a judge may discard the old and adopt the new, he must remember that the past is often a reflection of the present and he must know and understand it, "for the depths are the foundation of the heights." [19]

[18] Pound, loc. cit. p. 216.
[19] Margaret E. Hall (Ed.), *Selected Writings of Benjamin Nathan Cardozo* (New York: Fallon Law Book Company, 1948), p. 78.

Because common law as such is uncodified, it is generally described as *unwritten law*. However, case-precedents really are not unwritten; they are derived from the principles of law embodied in the judgments of cases which are decided and reported. Presumably most courts keep records, although they are not all required to do so. An example is the average Justice of the Peace on the level of the several states in America, who, in contrast to his English counterpart, must follow the precedent of decided cases.

In summary, the common law appears to have three distinct characteristics that together have enabled the system to develop and expand. The first is its *vitality and capability to sustain change*. It does not impress its own peculiarities upon any other law; it only aids in the systematic development of a richer and presumably more just law. The second is its *practical quality*. It is unwilling to accept anything a priori and follows the notion that ideally all laws ought to be tested at the bar of courts. Thus, rules and regulations are treated as working hypotheses, continually retested in what Mr. Justice Cardozo called "those great laboratories of the law, the courts of justice." Third is its *rendition of law as a moral obligation to be obeyed*. The results of the laboratory tests of the law are accepted as valid and everyone is obliged to obey them. After all, in the famous words of Mr. Justice Oliver Wendell Holmes, Jr.:

> The common law is not a brooding omnipresence in the sky, but the articulate voice of some sovereign or quasi-sovereign that can be identified.[20]

And as the great jurist put it both so well and hauntingly in his *The Common Law* in 1881:

> The life of the law has not been logic; it has been experience. The felt necessities of the time, the prevalent moral and political theories, intuitions of public policy, avowed or unconscious, even the prejudices which judges share with their fellow-men, have had a good deal more to do than syllogism in determining the rules by which men should be governed. The law embodies the story of a nation's development through many centuries,

[20] *Southern Pacific Co. v. Jensen*, 244 U. S. 205 (1916), at 222.

and it cannot be dealt with as if it contained only the axioms and corollaries of a book of mathematics.[21]

EQUITY

A branch of Anglo-American jurisprudence, born hundreds of years ago, and closely related to the common law, *equity* is actually a supplement to the common law. Although the *Court of Chancery* did not appear until the fifteenth century, equity courts arose in England in the fourteenth century—apparently as early as 1340—as a result of a practice that permitted a disappointed litigant at common law to lay his plight before his sovereign. That is, he could petition the King to "do right for the love of God and by way of charity," the king being empowered to mold the law for the sake of "justice," to grant the relief prayed for as an act of grace, when the common law gave no, or no adequate, remedy.

Chancellor and Chancery. The monarch, on the other hand, habitually referred these petitions to his Chancellor. This member of his Council, who until the Reformation was always a cleric became known as the "Keeper of the King's Conscience." He was the Council's most important member and the Keeper of the Great Seal, an office to which considerable powers were attached. It was he who could, for example, issue a writ of *subpoena,* the well-known writ commanding a person to appear before a duly constituted legal authority. From many points of view the Chancellor was second in power only to his monarch. Ultimately, the volume of these cases brought about the establishment of a separate court, known as the *Court of Chancery.* This was the early court of equity. It maintained its separate existence until 1875, when it was merged in the Supreme Court of Judicature by the Judiciary Act of 1873. Its jurisdiction is now mainly exercised by the Chancery Division of the High Court of Justice, but all courts now administer both common law and equity.

The United States of America never had *separate* courts of equity on the federal level. But several states retain such separate courts. In others, the same jurist doubles as law judge and equity judge, sitting one day as the former and one as the latter! In

---

[21] (Boston: Little, Brown and Co., 1881), p. 1.

again others, no separate equity courts exist at all [22]—the same courts that decide matters at common and statutory law also administer equity.

Defining Equity. But what is equity? We noted that it is a "supplement" to the common law, thus apparently the "conscience" of the law. It is a supplement to the common law in the sense that the principles of equity—which are now part of the fabric of the common law—were developed by the Court of Chancery as an addition to the principles of the medieval common law. Equity began where the law ended, and it is in that role that we know it today. It thus created and continues to create precedents. It takes the form of a *judicial decree,* not of a judgment of "yes" or "no." Equity leaves the judge reasonably free to order *preventive* measures—and under some circumstances even *remedial* ones—usually in the form of a writ, such as an *injunction,* or restraining order, designed to afford a remedy not otherwise obtainable, and traditionally given upon a showing of peril. The judge in the original Court of Chancery exercised his discretion, since remedies in equity were discretionary—and so they are today. A few illustrations may serve to clarify the practice at issue.

For instance, in equity an injunction may be issued by a judge to prevent members of a local of the United Steel Workers of America from going out on strike without having banked the furnaces of the Jones and Laughlin Steel Corporation, despite the inapplicability of the permissive injunctive provisions of the Norris-LaGuardia Act in this case, and despite the fact that they had given due notice to strike in accordance with the requirements of the Taft-Hartley Act. True, the steel firm involved could probably recover monetary compensation for resultant damages from its insurance company, or from the U.S.W. if it should be found that a contractual provision had been violated by the action of the workers. However, the company here is not interested in such money; its sole aim is to prevent its furnaces from the certain destruction that would result from a failure to bank them. Hence the demand for an equity decree in the form of an injunction against the union.

Another illustration, although considerably less in the realm

---

[22] Frederick G. Kempin, Jr., *Development of the Common Law* (Philadelphia: Lecture Note Fund, University of Pennsylvania, 1959), I-4-7.

and nature of immediate peril, might be Mr. John Miller's lovely old virgin copper beech on the edge of his private property, directly in the path of a future highway to be built by the Commonwealth of Pennsylvania. The latter has every right to chop down the tree under its power of *eminent domain,* provided only that it does so for a public purpose—which a state public highway certainly is—and further that it grant just compensation, which it usually does quite liberally in these circumstances. But Mr. Miller is not interested in financial compensation, either; he wants to continue to enjoy the beauty and the shade of the magnificent tree and the sentimental attachments that go with it—he proposed to his wife under it; his children and grandchildren climbed it with relish for years. Thus he, too, may appeal to the courts for equity. His chances for success are undoubtedly considerably less than were those of the steel firm mentioned above, but judges are human beings, not automatons.

A final example deals with the satisfaction of written or oral contracts when, through negligence or accident, one party cannot fulfill his part of such a contract. Thus, let us assume that George Brown takes his good shoes to cobbler Fred Long for resoling. Prominently displayed in Long's neat shop is a sizable sign reading "Not Responsible for Goods Left After Thirty Days." After some 20 days have passed, Brown is suddenly called out of town on an emergency, and has no time either to stop in the Long shop for the shoes or arrange to have someone else call for them. When he returns two weeks later, he immediately goes to the cobbler to pick up his shoes—alas! they are missing and nowhere to be found. Long claims that inasmuch as fully 35 days have passed since Brown left the shoes, and since the sign clearly advised him of the cobbler's lack of responsibility after 30 days, Long is not legally responsible. But Brown insists that he be given either his shoes or adequate compensation for them and, upon Long's firm refusal, asks for equity in court.

Although it is hazardous to predict the outcome of the case— almost any case, for that matter—it is likely that the judge would find for Brown because of the extenuating circumstances that prevented him from calling for his shoes "on time." Since Brown had committed no genuine fault, Long would either have to produce or replace the shoes. Indeed, in the State of Connecticut, for one, the 30-days-responsibility signs do not relieve the shop owner of responsibility under any conditions that are not deemed grossly unfair to him. In the latter category, however, would be a claim for merchandise left for repairs several years ago; but a claim within a reasonable period of time—which has been construed to be several months in the case of a piece of jewelry—must be honored, regardless of the warning sign. Small wonder that the English equity courts used to be referred to as "Keepers of the King's Conscience"!

STATUTORY LAW

Despite the fact that *statutory law*—variously known as *code* law, *written* law, *Neo-Roman* or *Roman* law, or *civil* law—comes to us from ancient Rome, the question of its broader application is essentially a modern one. Whereas the common law has dealt traditionally with matters of a private character, the relations between individuals, statutory law is concerned more frequently with society as a whole. It is law that originates with specifically designated, authoritative lawmaking bodies—presumably legislatures, but it also embraces executive-administrative decrees and ordinances, treaties and protocols, all of which are committed to paper.

Historical Background. Statutory law developed in and from the homogeneous city-state, exemplified by the Codes of Emperor Justinian I (527–65), the *Corpus Juris Civilis,* which was promulgated about A.D. 535. Hence it is frequently referred to as Roman law and, to confuse teachers and students alike, as *civil* law—which has nothing whatever to do with civil jurisdiction (see below). In contrast to diversified England, with its manifold customs that veritably seemed to cry out for some sort of common law, Rome in its glory lent itself ideally to the development of a statutory system, one that could be readily written down, codified. Statutory law had—and has, of course—the advantages of preciseness, simplicity, and clear-cut applicability, although it still remains subject to interpretation by administrators as well as judges.

Enacted by legislative and/or executive-administrative bodies of government, codified and spelled out in writing by the legal profession, the Bar itself, clearly and readily available for all to see—

statutory law has survived as the generally accepted law for most of the states of continental Europe, Russia, Latin America, and many of the newly emergent African nations. Justinian's Code had been initially introduced into Western Europe in 544 when the Eastern Empire reconquered Italy. But it did not assume genuine significance for the West until the systematic study of Roman law was revived at the Italian universities in the twelfth century.[23] One of its most famous codifiers was Napoleon I, whose Civil Code was published in 1804, a Code of Civil Procedure in 1807, and others subsequently. Indeed, the *Code Napoleon* has been far more enduring than most of the colorful Emperor's famed military triumphs.

"Mixing" Common and Statutory Law

England and the United States today have legal systems based on the common law that readily and naturally found its way across the Atlantic Ocean from the Mother Country to the Colonies. But although it must be categorized as a common law system, the Anglo-American legal framework in effect now consists of a mixture of common *and* statutory law. A great deal of contemporary law is necessarily statutory; it is coded. However, this is a relatively recent development, for statutes as a basis of Anglo-American law played no really significant role until the second quarter of the nineteenth century.

The mixture came into its own largely, although certainly not exclusively, as a result of the perpetuating conservatism of the common law, particularly in the realm of the sanctity of private property, based on the overriding concept of economic *laisser faire*. With the advent of a rising spirit of common social consciousness and responsibility, and a gradual movement toward the service or welfare state on both sides of the ocean, legislative bodies everywhere—but considerably more slowly in the United States than in the United Kingdom—commenced to change or even displace the age-old concepts and practices of the common law in favor of what were viewed as primary considerations of necessary public interest.

Nonetheless, common law remained as an important basis of

[23] A. T. von Mehren, *The Civil Law System* (Englewood Cliffs, N. J.: Prentice-Hall, Inc., 1957).

legislative motivations and actions, and often an enacted statute would—as indeed it still does today—simply spell out the grand sweep of certain aspects of common law. Furthermore, no legislative body—and sometimes not even the executive—is consistently, or even largely, capable of pinpointing in writing all the aspects and ramifications of a statute or order, nor would that necessarily be desirable, even if it were possible. The result is interpretation, usually first by administrative units, then often by the courts, and —as we shall have ample opportunity to observe in Chapters V to IX—when courts interpret they cause statutes to grow and/or contract. This interpretation becomes part of the statutes and orders, thus giving them meaning in the spirit and application of the common law. Truly, England and America resort to a framework of law that is a generally wholesome blend of common, statutory, and equity law.

Of course, there are certain areas of statutory law where little, if any, discretionary element remains for the judge. The United States Criminal Code, for example, represents a compendium of laws that prescribe what shall constitute a crime and what the penalties therefor shall be. A judge may have a modicum of leeway regarding the former, but the sole substantive discretion left to him in the realm of the latter is one specifically written into the code. Thus, a particular law may conceivably permit him to exercise his considered judgment as to the severity of a sentence which he is called upon to impose for a given criminal infraction, but this discretion will be strictly limited by the minimum and maximum penalties as provided in it. Moreover, it may well be limited by the nature of the verdict of the jury. Indeed, *criminal law* is becoming more and more codified everywhere among the common law lands, hence statutory. The same applies to *public law* generally, although the great bulk of *private* law is still common law. A few words of explanation about these two and some additional legal concepts are in order.

SOME ADDITIONAL
LEGAL DEFINITIONS AND CONCEPTS

Without in any way attempting even to half cover, let alone exhaust, the vast and sometimes exasperating ranges and spaces of legal terms and concepts, a few which deal with notions that play a part in these pages must be elaborated upon, however briefly. A host of others will be treated throughout the book. (A standard legal dictionary, e.g. *Black's Law Dictionary*,[24] will readily supply answers to any others that may occur to the inquiring reader.) We begin with a distinction between the two types of law into which *municipal law*—the law that applies within a state—is normally divided, namely *private* and *public* law.

Private law governs the relationship between private citizens or persons; it regulates the relations of individuals with each other. It is concerned with the definition, regulation, and enforcement of rights in cases where both the person in whom the right inheres and the person upon whom the obligation devolves are private individuals. Obvious examples of private law are the law governing contracts between individuals or corporations and that pertaining to marriage and divorce. In the sense that infractions of the legal obligations inherent in these areas are subject to adjudication by courts, the state is involved, of course, but it is neither the subject of the right nor the object of the duty.

Public law, on the other hand, is a branch or department of law which is very much concerned with the state in its political or sovereign capacities—including the important two subheadings of administrative and constitutional law (to be described presently). Public law is concerned with the definition, regulation, and enforcement of rights in those cases where the state *is* viewed as the subject of the right or the object of the duty, including criminal law and criminal procedure. In other words, it is that portion of law that is concerned with political conditions and situations— with the powers, rights, duties, capacities, and incapacities that are characteristic of and peculiar to both supreme and subordinate political superiors.

Public law applies to and affects the entire people of a nation or state that adopts or enacts it—in contrast with private law, which affects and applies to only one or a few individuals—for it regulates both the relations between individuals and the state and the relations between the branches of the government. Thus, the vast majority of legislation enacted by Congress is in the category

---

[24] The definitions used in this section are based in part on its 3rd ed. (St. Paul: West Publishing Co., 1933), pp. 1419, 1416, 411, and 59.

of public law—and its statutes are codified, preceded by the term "Public Law_____ [Number]." Social welfare, defense appropriations, subversive activities control, farm subsidies, all these areas of legislation represent illustrations of the vast and diversified content of public law.

Administrative law, which has quite naturally achieved ever increasing prominence over the past few decades, consists of those rules and regulations that are promulgated by the sundry administrative agencies of government that have been empowered to deal with the operation of government under the delegated rule-making authority of the legislative body. That branch of public law prescribes in detail the activities of the agencies involved—such as those concerned with the collection of revenue; regulation of competitive practices; coinage; public health, welfare, safety, and morals; sanitation; regulation of the armed forces; and a host of others.

Constitutional law is the other great branch of public law. It determines the political organization of a state and its powers while also setting certain substantive and procedural limitations on the exercise of governing power. Because of its position and nature it stands legally above all other types of municipal law, public as well as private. In the United States, with its written Constitution, constitutional law consists of the application of fundamental principles of law based on that document, as finally interpreted by its highest judicial organ, the Supreme Court of the United States. A fairly recent example is the famous *Steel Seizure Case.*[25] Believing himself invested with the power to do so in his capacity as Commander-in-Chief, coupled with what he and his advisers viewed as "inherent" authority, President Truman seized the steel mills on April 8, 1952, in order to forestall a nation-wide strike in the midst of the Korean War. The owners filed a writ to enjoin him, charging the absence of both constitutional and legislative authority for his actions. After a series of dramatic skirmishes in the lower federal courts, the United States Supreme Court received the case for adjudication—clearly a matter in the realm of constitutional law. On June 2, 1952, the Court rendered its decision, featured by seven different opinions! But six of the nine justices did agree on *one* crucial point: that by *usurping legislative power*

[25] *Youngstown Sheet and Tube Co. v. Sawyer,* 343 U. S. 579 (1952).

President Truman had violated the Constitution, and that the seizure of the steel mills was hence *ultra vires*—particularly so since Congress had expressly refused to enact a suggested amendment to the Taft-Hartley Act authorizing such governmental seizures in an emergency.

In brief, constitutional law prescribes generally the plan and method under which the public business of the political organ, known as the state, is conducted. And it differs further from the other types of law we have seen in that it is both enacted and changed either in an extraordinary manner by ordinary legislative bodies or by extraordinary bodies, such as a constitutional convention, constituted especially for that purpose.

In the United States changes in the letter of the fundamental document are based on the special constitutional amendment provisions of its Article V, which combine extraordinary federal with extraordinary state action. In the United Kingdom, where no formal written constitution and no power of judicial review exist, Parliament is supreme and may effect changes in the constitutional law of the land by ordinary legislation. But it is highly unlikely to tamper with the great cornerstones of its unwritten Constitution— that intriguing British concept consisting of the heritage of the common law, great statutes, important documents, decisions of the courts (other than judicial review), and customs and conventions, that combined constitute the very life blood of the realm. In France the written Constitution of the Fifth Republic may be altered only by extraordinary action of Parliament with the co-operation of the President of France, either with or without ratification by a popular referendum, depending upon the procedure invoked by the President in the course of the initiating stages. And in Switzerland, constitutional alterations not only call for mandatory ratification by popular referenda, but the Swiss citizens may take the initiative directly by drawing up a proposed constitutional amendment and submitting it for direct popular referendum approval.

CIVIL AND CRIMINAL LAW

Another basic distinction of considerable importance which confronts the observer of the judicial and legal processes is that between *civil* and *criminal* law (the former not to be equated here with the concept of "civil law" when used as a synonym for statutory or Roman law; here the reference to it is in connection with the subject matter governing in a particular case). Whether a particular offense is of a civil or criminal nature determines not only the severity of the punishment that may be invoked, but frequently also the type of tribunal before which the case at issue will be heard. As we shall see in subsequent chapters, some courts are empowered to hear cases involving *both* types of law, as in all three major federal constitutional courts of the United States; but in many instances the judicial hierarchy provides for a separate set of criminal and civil courts, as is true, to a greater or lesser extent, of both England and France—although some of the English judges may be used interchangeably.

Civil Law. A case at *civil law* is normally one between private persons and/or private organizations, for civil law governs the relations between individuals and defines their legal rights. A party bringing suit under it seeks legal redress in a *personal* interest, such as for a breach of contract, a divorce action, a defamation of character, the use of a copyrighted story without permission. Yet while suits at civil law far more often than not are suits among private persons, as indicated, the government, too, may conceivably be involved. For example, under the Sherman Anti-Trust Act of 1890, as amended, the federal government in the United States is empowered to bring either civil or criminal action against an alleged offender. It has much more frequently brought civil than criminal actions under that statute; one of the reasons for this is that they are not so difficult to win and that they cause less of an uproar in the interested community. Also, cases at civil law are often more difficult for courts to dispose of, for as a rule they neither lend themselves to ready "guilty" or "not guilty" judgments, nor do they commonly involve the verdict of a trial jury— whatever the merits of that institution may be.

Criminal Law. A case at *criminal law* is invariably brought by and in the name of the government, no matter at what level— national, state, or local—it may arise. Chiefly statutory in the United States, criminal law defines crimes against the public order and provides for appropriate punishment. Prosecution brought under it by the proper governmental authority involves an accusation that the defendant has violated a specific provision of a law, an infraction for which a penalty has normally been provided by statute. Criminal cases comprise such felonies or major crimes as homicide, espionage, sabotage, rape, and perjury, to name but a few. The coverage is as extensive as the lawmakers choose to make it. Since the prosecuting authority in a criminal case is necessarily an agent of the sovereign, the latter's name appears in its title. Hence, assuming one Brown's indictment for murder in Pennsylvania, the case would be docketed for trial as either *The Commonwealth of Pennsylvania v. Brown* or as *People v. Brown.* Moving to the federal level, one of the cases brought under the membership clause of the Smith Act of 1940 read *United States v. Scales.*[26] However, by far the largest volume of criminal law is still enacted at the state level in the United States, and thus is enforced by state officials under state law. Unitary countries, such as France and the United Kingdom, are not confronted with that jurisdictional problem.

But in all cases and at all levels it is the jurists who render the decisions. To them, their fascinating and significant tasks, and the hierarchical framework in which they perform their duties, we now turn.

[26] 367 U. S. 203 (1961).

II

STAFFING THE COURTS

SELECTION

What principles should govern the selection of the men—and women as well—who dispense justice? To raise this question brings us face to face with moral as well as political questions of the greatest importance. However awe-inspiring their functions may be or seem, our judges are still human beings. As such they make the ultimate decisions in the judicial process. In essence, there are just two basic methods of selection: *appointment* and *election*— no matter who does the actual appointing or electing—although, as we shall see below, a compromise between the two modes has been devised and is practiced on certain levels of the judiciary in some jurisdictions. A collateral question is whether judges should be members of a career service as in France and, to a lesser degree and in a different vein, in England, or essentially political appointments, no matter how well qualified and however endorsed professionally, as in the United States. Practices of selection differ in large measure in accordance with the traditions and needs of the country concerned. A crucial consideration here is the very position of the judiciary in the framework of government that provides the rationale for the particular mode adopted and adhered to. Under the Roman law tradition of the Continent, the judiciary is a part of the over-all administrative hierarchy and, as such, represents a separate position and profession than that of the ordinary lawyer. Under the common law system, on the other hand, the judges are drawn exclusively from the ranks of the legal profession. Nevertheless, in evaluating the guiding principles for the selection and tenure of the judiciary in the three countries that concern us most here—the United Kingdom, France, and the United States—a commonly held ideal is evident: judges are expected to be impartial and hence must be given assurance of independence, security, and dignity of tenure. When these are present, the fact that different techniques attend selection in these lands is hardly of great significance. Nevertheless, these techniques must be studied and understood.

THE TWO CHIEF METHODS

With the important exception of many state and local courts in the fifty constituent states, the *appointive* method is employed predominantly in the United States. It is used exclusively at the federal level of the government, regardless of whether the tribunal concerned is a constitutional or legislative court (a distinction that will be described in detail in Chapter IV). Britain and France use appointment exclusively.

Appointment. In the *United States* all federal judges are appointed by the President, subject to confirmation by simple majority vote of the Senate, on a more or less political basis. Depending upon the Chief Executive involved, the President's heavy responsibility has often been largely delegated to the Attorney-General and, in practice, to the Deputy Attorney-General. This was noticeably true during the later years of the Administration of President Eisenhower when the selection of members of the federal judiciary was left almost exclusively to Attorney-General William P. Rogers and Deputy Attorney-General Lawrence E. Walsh. But two other important factors enter here. One is the obvious need for consultation with the United States Senator(s) and/or other seats of political power in the home state of the candidate for judicial office—provided these political figures are of the same party as the appointing authority. At the very least, care must be taken that the appointee is not "personally obnoxious" to the home state Senator, on pain of having the Senator invoke the age-old, almost invariably honored, custom of "senatorial courtesy"—a certain death-knell to the candidacy at the bar of the Senate. The custom is based on the assumption that the President will, as a matter of political patronage practice and courtesy, consult with the appointee's home state Senator(s) prior to the former's designation —provided that the Senator is a member of the President's party.

If the President fails to adhere to the custom, the aggrieved Senator's colleagues will, on his call for the nominee's defeat, support him as a matter of fraternal courtesy. The other factor that has played an increasingly significant role in the appointive process of the federal judiciary in the United States, especially since the Truman Administration, is the American Bar Association's Committee on the Federal Judiciary, long headed by a distinguished Philadelphia attorney, Bernard G. Segal.

That committee, which was widely utilized subsequently during President Eisenhower's terms of office—a practice continued under President Kennedy—has generally produced good results with its work and is understandably popular with the legal profession, although there is no unanimity on that evaluation. There are those who believe deeply that the selection of the members of the judicial branch of the government must rest in fact, as well as in name, with the executive branch, its head being specifically charged to do so under the judiciary article of the Constitution (Article III); and that the apparent delegation of that authority to a private body, no matter how qualified and how representative —a crucial point—is at best questionable, and at worst a dereliction of duty. Moreover, the Bar is not free from political biases. Had President Wilson, for one, heeded the advice of the A.B.A., Mr. Justice Brandeis would never have been nominated. Whatever the merit of this demurrer, the committee has become a prestigious and respected vehicle in the nominating process. After an investigation customarily lasting from six to eight weeks, it reports to the Justice Department on the qualifications of the prospective nominee, and rates him in one of four ways: Exceptionally Well Qualified, Well Qualified, Qualified, or Not Qualified. In a number of cases the Eisenhower Administration discontinued the consideration of nominees for the federal bench after the A.B.A.'s Committee had found them less qualified than others, and its reports even enabled the Department to rule out certain names recommended by the home state Senator(s).

To illustrate, in September 1961, the Senate confirmed 60 lower court federal judges of whom 52 had been rated by the A.B.A. Nine had been rated "Exceptionally Well Qualified," 27 "Well Qualified," 14 "Qualified," and two "Not Qualified." Yet these two—one, James R. Browning the Clerk of the S.S. Supreme Court, the other an Oklahoman, Luther Bohanan—had sufficiently powerful support to be confirmed.

On occasion, it has even been proposed that various bar associations run their own candidates for judgeships if the political parties fail to choose "properly qualified candidates," as did Presiding Justice Bernard Botein of the Appellate Division for Manhattan and the Bronx in a speech to the New York State Bar Association in July 1961. Nor would an affirmative response to this appeal have constituted a novelty: both in 1906 and 1932, the Bar sponsored independent nominees on the "Judiciary Nominators Republican" ticket, but both were defeated by Democrats slated by Tammany Hall, in the first instance by 190,000 to 113,000 votes, in the second by 585,000 to 293,000. The losers thus polled a respectable total, yet lost nonetheless.

Considerably more will be said on the point later, but it should be re-emphasized here that in selecting his nominees no alert and prudent Chief Executive of the United States and his entourage would nowadays attempt to designate members of the judiciary *purely* on the basis of political considerations. Too much is at stake in matters of policy and public awareness, and the American Bar Association is a powerful factor in the selection process. Yet, granted the sundry and largely salutary needs and drives for appointments on the basis of over-all merit and excellence, the political pressures must nevertheless be reckoned with and are disregarded only at the appointing authority's peril. Moreover, a federal judgeship is viewed as such a "plum" by all concerned that it represents a potent patronage-whip in the hands of the executive vis-à-vis state politicians as well as Congress.

Both the problem and its flavor are suggested rather nicely and candidly by the following passage in Senator Joseph S. Clark's newsletter of August 11, 1961, to his constituents in Pennsylvania:

> I have forwarded to the Attorney General recommendations to fill additional Judgeships recently authorized by Congress in the United States District Courts in Pennsylvania, and one vacancy in the Court of Appeals for the Third Circuit. I regret that, by custom, Senators have the obligation of making these recommendations after appropriate consultation with their State political leaders. I believe the selection of judges should

be entirely nonpartisan and should be made by the Attorney General and the President without Senatorial intervention. Nevertheless, I must live with the rules as they exist until they are changed. After consultations with Governor Lawrence, Democratic State Chairman Otis Morse II, Congressman William J. Green, Jr., and others, I am satisfied that the recommendations made for existing vacancies are men of ability and integrity. The Attorney General and the President will make the final decisions on these Judgeships of course, and may disregard our recommendations if they wish.

In *Britain*—we are here again almost exclusively concerned with England and Wales, for convenience hereafter referred to as England, since Scotland and Northern Ireland, the two other members of the United Kingdom of Great Britain and Northern Ireland, operate separate court systems—judges are designated by the Crown with little or no surrender to politics. Practically speaking, this means that they constitute the choices of the Lord Chancellor, the senior law member of the government, who is the Queen's chief adviser on the selection—but, since the Lord Chancellor is chosen by the Prime Minister, the latter does have at least an indirect voice in the selection of judges, especially on the middle and higher levels. Among these are the Lords of Appeal in Ordinary (the Law Lords), the Lord Chief Justice, the Master of the Rolls, the President of the Probate, Divorce, and Admiralty Division of the High Court of Justice, and the Lord Justices of the Court of Appeal. But it must be clearly understood that it is the Queen who actually issues the commission of appointment.

The Lord Chancellor himself, however, is the politically designated head of the judicial hierarchy of the United Kingdom. In addition he advises on the appointment to judicial office from the rank of Justice of the Peace and Recorder to the higher offices of the English Judiciary. He sits on the Woolsack and presides over the House of Lords; is a member of the Cabinet; and as head of the Judiciary combines in his person the threefold function of executive, legislator, and jurist—a complete refutation of the principle of separation of powers so dear to the Baron de Montesquieu. Since the group of barristers from whose ranks the Lord Chancellor chooses judges is small and select, he knows a good many of them, and when members of the Opposition would seem to give promise as competent judges, he will certainly not hesitate to cross party lines to make appointments. If he does not personally know or know of a candidate, he will consult with the head of the division to which the judge is to be appointed and obtain his views—but *not* his prior approval. Incidentally, barristers must resign from the bar when they go on the bench.

No letters of recommendation are accepted, and efforts to put political pressure upon the Lord Chancellor are scouted strongly. R. M. Jackson, Reader in Public Law and Administration in the University of Cambridge, in his excellent study on the machinery of justice in England,[1] contends that political considerations have hardly entered the process of judicial selection since 1907—although they died a slower death in the case of the office of Lord Chief Justice; and he insists that, as a consequence, there has been no apparent connection between the "political antecedents" of the judges and their decisions in over a century.[2] However, members of the House of Commons may be appointed to county-court judgeships and also to the High Court. Yet, to this day, because of the fear of executive interference with the administration of justice, no Ministry or Department of Justice exists in the United Kingdom.

In *France,* and in many other countries on the Continent, the trained judges are appointed to, rise in, and are promoted from a type of career service which is an adjunct of the general civil service. The de Gaulle Constitution of 1958 specifically makes a point of the time-honored concept that an ideal judge is an impartial judge. There is a Ministry of Justice, but the judges of France do not really feel its authority, although the Minister is part of the appointing process. Political patronage plays scarcely a role in their selection; they have all been schooled as judges or have had experience as such, and they enter the judicial service on the basis of passing competitive examinations.

Theoretically, the President of the Republic, who is charged by the Constitution to be "the guarantor of the independence of judicial authority," [3] selects the judges; actually, they are chosen

[1] Richard M. Jackson, *The Machinery of Justice in England,* 3rd ed. (Cambridge: University Press, 1960), p. 236.

[2] Ibid. p. 237.   [3] Title VIII, Article 64.

either by the eleven-member *Conseil Superieur de la Magistrature* (High Council of the Judiciary) in the case of the *Cour d'Appel* and the *Cour de Cassation,* or by the Minister of Justice, who may consult with or receive advice from the High Council, in the case of the lower courts. The High Council consists of the President of the Republic (as *le président*), the Minister of Justice (as vice-president), and nine persons with legal background chosen by the President for a term of four years, partly on the recommendation of the *Cour de Cassation* and the *Conseil d'État,* as follows: one from the latter; three from the former; three from other courts; and two selected for their general legal knowledge and competence. In any event, the selecting authorities have but little choice—considerably less than in England and infinitely less, of course, than in the United States.

The assets and liabilities of the appointive versus the elective method are rather obvious. In general, the main argument in favor of appointment hinges on the contention that a candidate for a judicial post who is obliged to run on a partisan ballot cannot possibly serve as an *impartial* judge, and that he is selected, as Al Smith once put it, "by an electorate who are not really in a position to pass upon the legal and other abilities of the individual." [4] On the other hand, the champions of election on a partisan ballot argue that appointment by a political executive contains even worse features of political beholdenness than election. As is so often the case, neither side of the argument is *ipso facto* correct on all counts; both contain some merit, and it is easy to over-simplify. Someone, however, has to assume responsibility for staffing the courts; it might as well be the executive, who not only possesses the expertise and has access to all pertinent data, but who is fairly well known to the populace at large on almost all levels, and, in fact, is usually the sole officer of government with an all-embracing constituency. At least in theory, the people are always in a position to hold him accountable in a free society. To make him responsible for unfortunate judicial appointments is more meaningful and more palatable to the electorate than an arrangement that requires the latter not only to submerge judges into the political arena but to become intimately familiar with

[4] As quoted by Arthur T. Vanderbilt, "Brief for a Better Court System," *The New York Times Magazine,* May 5, 1957, p. 9.

their adjudicatory record. Whatever the ramifications of this balancing of scales, executive appointment of judges has proved to be the preferred method of selection in England, France, and the United States (with notable exceptions). Although compromise arrangements of the type illustrated below may well move onto the scene here and there, there is no chance that election will supplant appointment for the selective process of judges in the vast majority of countries in the free Western world.

Election. Nevertheless, election of members of that branch of the government is not unknown, even at the national or federal level of governments. In Switzerland, a major exception to the *federal* appointment principle, judges are elected by the two federal chambers—the *Nationalrat* and the *Ständerat*—sitting jointly as the *Bundesversammlung* (National Assembly). However, re-election is so usual that to all intents and purposes permanent tenure of office is the logical result of the practice. In a drastically different category, the Soviet Union, too, practices the elective method exclusively, but (a) the victorious candidates serve for short terms only and (b) they have been approved by the political hierarchy of the state in advance of their candidacy—the mark of a dictatorial society.

Election of judges in the Western world is most widespread at the level of the several states in the United States, where it may be by either the electorate (e.g. Florida) or the legislature (e.g. the higher judges in South Carolina) for at least some of the members of the judicial hierarchy in all but a handful (e.g. Hawaii). True, judges *sometimes* appear on bipartisan tickets (e.g. Pennsylvania), even on a nonpartisan one (e.g. Minnesota) on occasion, but loyal service in partisan politics tends to be a prerequisite for nomination—in line with Jacksonian tradition. True also that while the elective term of office is on the average but six years, it extends to life for certain judgeships in some states (e.g. Supreme Court of Rhode Island), and to rather lengthy periods in others (e.g. twenty-one years, nonrenewable, for the post of Supreme Court Justice in Pennsylvania). In a few states the concept of supporting the sitting judge has been adopted when he is up for re-election, but this theoretically laudatory practice has been honored almost as much in the breach as in the observance. Moreover, the mitigating factors that are inherent in the deviations from the straight, partisan, short-term ballot election are found in but a few states, and even in these they are usually confined to the upper echelons of the judiciary. Other practices worthy of note in this general connection are those of gubernatorial appointment subject to some legislative consent (e.g. the Delaware Senate) and direct selection of some by the legislature itself (e.g. the presiding justices of the Supreme Court and county courts of Vermont); some by courts (e.g. trial judges in county courts, and juvenile or domestic relations court judges by the judges of the circuit or corporation courts of Virginia).

A Compromise?

An intriguing attempt at a compromise between the elective and appointive methods of choosing state judges in America has been advanced and popularized, in somewhat different versions, by the states of California, Missouri, Alaska, and Kansas. It is designed to minimize political influence and provide a degree of security of tenure, while retaining an element of popular control. Although repeatedly and even enthusiastically supported by leading spokesmen of the legal profession and knowledgeable laymen alike, it has not been widely adopted by the states—chiefly due to powerful political opposition, which views this compromise as a genuine threat to the patronage aspects of judicial selection, as well it might. California and Missouri were the pioneers in the compromise movement and it is their plans that command our attention here.

The California Plan. The first well-known original attempt at a solution to the vexatious problem of judicial selection was the *California Plan,* adopted by referendum vote of that state's electorate in 1934. A vigorous campaign for ratification of the plan had begun two years earlier by the California State Bar Association, encouraged by its national parent body, closely allied with the California Chamber of Commerce. The two powerful state groups had become convinced of the inadequacy of the system under which California then operated—judicial appointment by the Governor with subsequent popular approval, which in their eyes constituted little more than public rubber-stamping of the appointing authority's rank political designations.

Under the California Plan, which applies to the judges of the Supreme Court and District Courts of Appeals only, the Governor nominates *one* person to the Commission on Qualifications. This body is composed of the Chief Justice of the State Supreme Court, the Presiding Judge of the District Court of Appeals of the area concerned, and the Attorney-General. If the commission approves the Governor's nominee, the latter is deemed appointed for the duration of *one year only*. At the end of that year he must offer himself for popular election for a full twelve-year term of office—his name being the only one on the nonpartisan ballot. The sole question appearing on the ballot in connection with the nominee's candidacy is "Shall _____ be elected to the office for the term prescribed by law?" There are no limits on the number of terms to which a successful candidate may aspire. Should the electorate's response to the question on the ballot be in the negative, his successor will be designated by the Governor in the same manner, ultimately to go before the electorate as well. In any event, the burden of approval is on the people, who must familiarize themselves with his record—or at least they should do so.

The first test of the plan returned the sitting judges by a 2:1 affirmative vote, a not overly impressive record which, however, has been greatly improved since that time. Appraisals of the California Plan have been generally favorable, but some have criticized as inadequate what in their view is the essentially negative restriction placed on the Governor's power by the commission. To refuse to confirm a gubernatorial appointment takes a certain amount of courage—not inevitably demonstrated by the commission. There have also been doubts voiced concerning the wisdom of placing a measure of control over judicial appointments, however negative, into the hands of the chief law officer of the state, the Attorney-General. Nonetheless, the plan has worked well and has been favorably received by the vast majority of those concerned.

Both Ohio and Michigan after considerable investigation developed plans patterned upon that of California. Both plans were submitted to their respective electorates in 1938, yet they were resoundingly defeated. Although they aided in the plans' conceptualizations, the bar associations of the two states did little to further their adoption by the voters, who were bombarded by opposition propaganda, sponsored chiefly by labor and farm groups, who were suspicious of what they viewed as the "elitist" connotations inherent in the plans.

The Missouri Plan. Desirous of adopting a modified version of the California Plan, and learning a tactical lesson from its Waterloo in Ohio and Michigan, the supporters of the *Missouri Plan* waged a much more vigorous and enlightened campaign, headed by both professional and lay groups. The movement for its adoption was spearheaded by the Missouri Institute for the Administration of Justice, an educational corporation composed one-third of lawyers and two-thirds of laymen, who successfully enlisted the active support of civic, labor, farm, and business organizations. They explained to the electorate the true purpose of the plan: to secure an intelligent and impartial selection of personnel for the bench, to eliminate as much as possible the haphazard results of the elective system, and to relieve the judges of the pressures of political campaigning. And the supporters of the plan pointed out prudently that neither the California nor the Missouri Plan was designed to supplant the elective method entirely—that this was clearly a compromise between appointment and election. Characterized by the American Bar Association as the "most acceptable substitute available for direct election of judges," the plan became law in the form of an amendment to Missouri's Constitution in 1940.

The Missouri Plan is mandatory for the judges of the Missouri Supreme Court, all other state appellate courts, the circuit and probate courts in St. Louis and in Jackson County, and the St. Louis Court of Corrections. It is optional, subject to popular referenda, in the 38 other circuits of the state. Thus, judges of a number of courts, especially those of the lower levels, may well remain outside the compromise plan, as is true of California. Under the Missouri version, nonpartisan nominating boards known as the Missouri Appellate Commissions, and operating on different court levels, select *three* candidates for every vacant judgeship. For the Supreme Court and the appellate courts, the commission consists of the Chief Justice of the State Supreme Court as chairman; three lawyers, elected by the state bar, one from each of the three courts of appeals; and three citizens *not* members of the bar, appointed by the Governor, again on the basis of one from each of the three appellate districts. The commissions for the circuit and other lower court judges comprise the presiding judge of the court of appeals district in which the circuit happens to be situated; two members of the bar elected by its own members residing in the circuit involved; and two similarly resident nonbar citizens appointed by the Governor. The members of all these nonsalaried commissions are designated for staggered six-year terms of office, with changes taking effect in alternate years. Since the Governor has a four-year term and cannot succeed himself, it is thus impossible for him to appoint all of the lay members. To ensure an additional degree of impartiality, commissioners are permitted to hold neither public office nor an official position in a political party.

The Governor of Missouri is obliged to choose *one* of the three individuals selected by the Appellate Commission and appoint him for *one* year, as under the California Plan. After this probationary period, the appointee must offer himself to the electorate for a full 12-year term (in the appellate courts) or six-year term (in the trial courts), running unopposed on a separate, nonpartisan judicial ballot at the time of the general election. The question on the ballot, very similar to that of California, is "Shall Judge . . . of the . . . Court be retained in office? Yes ( ) No ( ) (Scratch one)."

Generally deemed to be the most adult and most commendable system of judicial selection extant in the various states, the Missouri Plan embraces a number of commendable features. It combines the democratic notion of accountability to the electorate with an intelligent method of selecting qualified candidates for judicial office. The necessity of facing the electorate on his record provides the judge with an incentive of judiciousness, and the fact that he runs on his own record rather than against that of an opponent allied with a specific political party goes far toward taking the courts out of the more crass aspects of politics. On the other hand, a case could be made for the contention that the awareness of establishing a "good record" for the electorate's eyes and ears may lead to timid and/or "popular" judgments. The results of the Missouri Plan in action, however, do not generally support that theory.

An examination of the election returns for a number of years demonstrates the over-all acceptance of the plan by Missouri's electorate. In 1942 the state went Republican, but two judges of the Supreme Court, both Democrats, were retained by a vote of 2:1; six circuit court judges in St. Louis were similarly returned for new full terms in that same election. In 1944 Missouri went Democratic, yet two judges of the Supreme Court, one a Republican and one Democratic, received the same proportion of the popular vote. In 1946 St. Louis went Republican, but retained its ten circuit judges, all Democrats (!), seven of these by 4:1 majorities. In 1948 the state went Democratic, yet of the two judges retained by Kansas City by an identical vote of 5:1, one was a Democrat and one a Republican. In St. Louis, in the same general election, five Democratic and one Republican circuit judge were returned for full terms of office, the Republican and two Democrats receiving 4:1 votes, the other three Democrats 3:1.[5]

From November 1940 through March 1960 a total of forty-four appointments were made by four governors of Missouri: *only one* of these was to replace a judge *rejected* by the vote of the people! The political parties have respected the plan, and, by and large, have made no effort to influence elections under it. The plan has been strongly defended also by the judges, who find themselves in a position to attend to their court dockets free from worries and pressures about forthcoming political campaigns.

Since 1958 both Kansas and Alaska have adopted variations of the Missouri Plan. The former, which long elected all judges on a partisan ballot, now permits its Governor to appoint the judges of the Kansas State Supreme Court from a list submitted to him by a nominating commission, with the judges subsequently either approved or rejected at the next general election. When Alaska became a state in 1958, its Constitution contained a provision allowing the Governor to appoint the judges of the Supreme Court from a list of nominees submitted by a judicial council. The judges ultimately run for re-election on their record. Iowa and Nevada have evinced considerable interest in the California and Missouri schemes—as has Pennsylvania, whose Pennsylvania Plan has been widely studied of late, but has not been adopted anywhere—least of all in Pennsylvania.

The two leading plans described represent what is probably a happy compromise between the appointive and elective systems

[5] See Laurance M. Hyde, "Choosing Judges in Missouri," 38 *National Municipal Review* 491 (November 1949).

of selection, and they have deservedly engendered considerable support among professionals and laymen. Yet most students of the political scene are inclined to agree that in a representative democracy the appointive system is the more desirable one for the judiciary, provided it is backed up by long tenure—preferably for life—and possesses a genuine degree of independence. The appointing authority is not beyond accountability—and there is no meaningful substitute for effectively lodged governmental responsibility in a free society.

TENURE OF OFFICE

Essential to an independent judiciary is security of tenure, and it is particularly so in the case of appointed judges—our main concern here. Without a lengthy term of office, preferably life tenure, decent remuneration, and stringent safeguards against removal for other than statutorily or constitutionally carefully circumscribed serious breaches of official trust, the concept of judicial independence becomes a mockery. The record of the three major Western democracies in this regard has been a laudatory one generally, and their practices at the level of the national judicial hierarchies are relatively similar.

THE UNITED STATES

At the federal level of the United States of America all judges of the *constitutional* courts—those appointed under the provisions of Article III of the Constitution (the judicial article)—hold their positions during the aforementioned "good behavior," which, in effect, means for life or until they choose to retire. The other federal judges—those of the *legislative* courts, created under the provisions of Article I of the Constitution (the legislative article)— occupy their positions for whatever period Congress may have prescribed at the time of its establishment of the court or in subsequent legislation. In some instances this has meant "good behavior" tenure for them, too, but at least as frequently terms of office ranging between four and fifteen years. The constitutional judges have the additional safeguard, required by the basic document, that their ". . . compensation . . . shall not be diminished

during their continuance in office." [6] Hence, while their salaries
may be increased during their incumbency, they may not be
lowered—short of a constitutional amendment of the section concerned. And were a judge of a constitutional court to be removed
from office other than in the manner expressly permitted by the
Constitution, his salary would indeed be rather drastically "diminished!"

Although far from commensurate with the responsibilities and
prestige of their office, and infinitely lower than comparable positions in private enterprise, judicial salaries are passably adequate.
In 1964-65 their annual range on the federal level—as will be
demonstrated in more detail in Chapters IV and V—was from
$22,500 for judges of the United States Customs Court to $40,000
for the Chief Justice of the United States Supreme Court, his
associates receiving $500 less. But it is hardly for financial gain
that a person would aspire to high judicial office! (Compared to
federal judges, the salaries of state judges are surprisingly good,
ranging from an average of $18,000 for appellate courts down to
$13,000 for all courts.)

Partly to enable aging jurists to step down from the bench in
dignity, and concurrently render their replacement with younger
personnel more palatable, Congress enacted a vastly improved retirement statute in 1937. Under its provisions, federal judges may
retire—a more accurate description is enter inactive status, subject
to temporary calls to duty at the discretion of the Chief Justice
of the United States—on full pay at the age of 70 after having
served ten years on the federal bench, or at 65 after having served
15 years. These requirements are waived in the case of physical
disability, in which case retirement pay is computed in accordance
with length of service. Widows and dependents receive an annual
purse equivalent to 37½ per cent of the judge's average salary.

Despite the liberal provisions of the act, the average federal
judges, in particular members of the Supreme Court, are reluctant
to leave active service. Far more vacancies occur as the result of
death in harness, particularly at the higher levels. Of the 86
Supreme Court vacancies between 1789 and 1961, death in office
was responsible for 48, with 38 representing voluntary retirement
—although since the passage of the 1937 statute of 19 vacancies

[6] Article III, Section 1, Clause 2.

the latter was responsible for 12. It is human to cling to a seat of power and influence, and particularly so to one of such significance and general esteem, which at the same time is removed from the limelight and activities of the normal processes of government and politics.

Removal. The involuntary removal of federal judges is possible only by the process of impeachment and conviction. In accordance with constitutional requirements, impeachment for "Treason, Bribery, or other High Crimes and Misdemeanors" [7] may be voted by a simple majority of the members of the House of Representatives, followed by conviction by a vote of two-thirds of the members of the Senate present and voting, there being a quorum on the floor. To date, the House of Representatives has initiated a total of twelve such impeachment proceedings, of which nine were directed against federal judges; one against United States Senator William Blount of Tennessee in 1789 (charges were dismissed in 1790 for want of jurisdiction, the Senate already having expelled him on grounds of conspiracy to seize Spanish Florida and Louisiana with British and Indian help); one against President Andrew Johnson in 1868 (who was acquitted by the margin of one courageous vote); and one against Secretary of War William Belknap in 1876 (who was subsequently acquitted).

Of the nine impeachment trials involving federal judges, five resulted in acquittals and four in actual removals. The former, briefly sketched below, were headed, chronologically and in importance, by the sole impeachment trial to date involving a justice of the Supreme Court, Associate Justice Samuel Chase.

(1) Samuel Chase. A staunch and partisan Federalist from Maryland, one of President Washington's last two appointments to the Supreme Court, Mr. Justice Chase was impeached by the House in November 1804. He had made himself obnoxious to the Jeffersonians and others by a long series of injudicious and partisan attacks against them, both on and off the bench, by his "tyrannical trials under the Alien and Sedition Law," and by his obvious general favoritism of Federalists. His was indeed not a happy judicial posture, but he had not committed any impeachable offense per se. Accordingly, he was justly acquitted by the Senate in March 1805—a signal victory for the narrow interpre-

[7] Article II, Section 4.

tation of the impeachment process—and he remained on the highest bench until his death in 1811.

(2) James H. Peck, a judge of the U. S. District Court for the District of Missouri, impeached in April 1830, acquitted in January 1831.

(3) Charles Swayne, a judge of the U. S. District Court for the Northern District of Florida, impeached in Demember 1904, acquitted in February 1905.

(4) George W. English, a judge of the U. S. District Court for the Eastern District of Illinois, impeached in November 1926, but proceedings in the Senate were dismissed when the accused resigned his office.

(5) Harold Louderback, a judge of the U. S. District Court for the Northern District of California, impeached and acquitted in May 1933.

Four impeachment trials, however, did result in conviction, with one of these probably unjust, one questionable, and two justified:

(1) John Pickering, a judge of the U. S. District Court for the District of New Hampshire, was impeached for "insanity" by the House in March 1803 and removed from office by the Senate in March 1804, although the language of the impeachment article of the Constitution, as noted above, does not provide for removal for such a reason. John Adams categorized the Pickering removal as "an infamous and certainly an illegal conviction." Indeed, the unfortunate Pickering had been hopelessly insane and an alcoholic for three years.

(2) West H. Humphreys, a judge of the U. S. District Court for the Middle, Eastern, and Western Districts of Tennessee, impeached for "support of secession" and removed in June 1862.

(3) Robert W. Archbald, an associate judge of the now defunct U. S. Commerce Court, impeached in July 1912 for "taking favors from litigants" and removed in January 1913.

(4) Halsted L. Ritter was the last jurist to be both impeached and convicted. A judge of the U. S. District Court for the Southern District of Florida, he was impeached by the House in April 1936 on seven counts of "bringing his court into scandal and disrepute." Shortly thereafter, the Senate acquitted him on six of the seven counts, but found him guilty as charged on the seventh by a vote of 56:28.

The undoubtedly fortunate paucity of success of the impeachment process is not, however, an indication of lack of verbal efforts
by legislators who, partly sincerely and partly for constituent con-
sumption, are eager to "get" federal judges—usually for decisions
repugnant to them for a variety of reasons—in particular the
justices of the Supreme Court. To cite but one recent example:
In June 1953 a special subcommittee of five members was created
by the House of Representatives to consider the impeachment of
Mr. Justice William O. Douglas of the Supreme Court. Introduced
by Congressman W. M. Wheeler (D.-Ga.), the resolution for impeachment charged the jurist with "high crimes and misdemeanors
in office" for having granted a brief stay of the scheduled execution
of the convicted atom spies, Julius and Ethel Rosenberg—a stay
dissolved by the full Court almost at once. Nothing came of Mr.
Wheeler's efforts. Nor are these efforts confined to the people's
representatives. In February 1959, a group of some two dozen men
and women filed with the Clerk of the House of Representatives a
petition to impeach the entire membership of the Supreme Court;
it consisted of foot-long pages, headed "Impeach Warren," a battle
cry taken up with a vengeance by the John Birch Society in subsequent years. And in a colorful brochure, decorated with the flag of
Georgia, that state's General Assembly distributed to the country
its H.R. 174, adopted on February 22, 1957, and entitled "A Resolution Requesting Impeachment of Six Members of the United
States Supreme Court"—namely Justices Warren, Black, Reed,
Frankfurter, Douglas, and Clark (Burton, Harlan, and Brennan
escaping somehow). The main charge: "Unconstitutional . . .
pro-Communist racial integration policies." [8]

The great majority of states follow the federal pattern regarding
removal of appointed judges with lengthy or life tenure, impeachment and conviction being the normal process available in the few
cases where such is indicated—as Tennessee did in 1958 in the
case of Criminal Court Judge Raulston Schoolfield for "corrupt
and injudicious conduct." But other modes of removal exist in
some states. In Massachusetts and New Hampshire judges may
be removed by address of the Governor to both houses of the
legislature; in California, Utah, Washington, and Wisconsin by a
joint resolution of the legislature; in Louisiana, Michigan, and

[8] H.R. No. 174, "A Resolution," pp. 3–12.

New York special courts are provided to hear removal charges; and in several Western states sitting judges may be recalled from office by popular vote.[9] The latter is an intriguingly controversial manifestation of "direct democracy," of which the referendum and the initiative are other illustrations.

BRITAIN

Having come a long way since the days of and before James I (1603–25) and Charles I (1625–49), when the English judges held their office *durante bene placito nostro* ("while our pleasure lasts well"), they today, very much like their cousins in the United States, enjoy what to all intents and purposes is tenure for life. The custom of appointing judges for indefinite terms of office during their "good behaviour," dates back to the Act of Settlement of 1701, which provided that "judges' commissions" be made *quam diu se bene gesserint* ("as long as they will have performed well"). One significant recent change must be noted, however. As a result of the mandate of the Judicial Pensions Act of 1959, a 75-year retirement limit for judges of the superior courts has been adopted for all future appointments at this level, and 72 years, plus a possible three-year extension, for those of the county courts —who had already been recognized by the County Courts Act of 1934, as amended by that of 1959. Retirement pensions are paid on a graduated scale that rises from one-quarter of basic salary after five years of service to a maximum of half of the last annual salary after 15 years.

For practical purposes, the English judges, notably those of the superior courts, are irremovable, the Judicature Act of 1925 providing that all judges, except the Lord Chancellor, hold office "during good behaviour subject to a power of removal by His [now Her] Majesty on an address presented to His [now Her] Majesty by both Houses of Parliament." [10] However, the judges of the county courts are deemed to be removable at the instance of the Lord Chancellor for "inability" and "misbehavior" under various statutes, e.g. the County Courts Act of 1959. The justices of

---

[9] For details see the informative article by Sheldon D. Elliot, "Court-Curbing Proposals in Congress," 33 *Notre Dame Lawyer* 597 (August 1958).
[10] Jackson, loc. cit. p. 233.

the peace are also removable for similar reasons. In effect, the English judges are not protected in any way from a change by statute; Parliament retains, of course, its fundamental power to alter their tenure and emoluments of office—whatever change it might deem appropriate. Suffice it to say that it is highly unlikely to do so in any detrimental sense! In any event, a dismissal of a judge for political reasons is impossible today for all practical purposes. Indeed, the *sole removal* of an English judge since the Act of Settlement of 1701 on what might be viewed as political grounds took place approximately 115 years ago. Even on that one case some uncertainty seems to govern, for Richard M. Jackson, distinguished solicitor and legal scholar, insisted in the most recent revision of his excellent and authoritative *The Machinery of Justice in England* (1960), that "no English judge has been removed since the Act of Settlement."

The salaries of the judges, which range between £4400 (for judges of the County Court) and £14,500 (for the Lord Chancellor, who receives £9500 for being a judge and £5000 for being Speaker of the House of Lords), are voted by Act of Parliament. The executive branch may not move to reduce these while the recipients hold office, and the legislature is similarly enjoined since judicial salaries do not even come up for parliamentary review. A further indication of effective judicial independence is the parliamentary custom that no questions at all may be asked about the conduct of courts in particular cases. Moreover, according to two court rulings now firmly regarded as *res adjudicata*,[11] a judge may not be held for a civil or criminal proceeding because of anything he may have said or done in his judicial capacity, even if it is alleged to have been malicious or in bad faith! Given these cherished safeguards of judicial strength and independence, the English bench has reciprocated in full measure with a record of efficiency and impartiality not likely to be readily matched anywhere in the free world today. Well might Sir Ivor Jennings contend in 1954 that "no allegation" of partiality or corruption or political influence is ever made against judges of the United Kingdom.[12]

[11] *Anderson v. Gorrie*, 91 L.J.K.B. 897 (1922) and *Heddon v. Evans,* 35 T.L.R. 642 (1919).
[12] *The Queen's Government* (London: Penguin Books, 1954), p. 147.

FRANCE

The career judges of the Fifth French Republic who, as we have seen, comprise a branch of the national civil service, also have life tenure. There is no doubt that they are at least as secure in it today as are their English and American counterparts. But it took a considerable while to attain that cherished goal. During the *ancien régime* judicial office went customarily to the favorites of the monarch and especially to those who could afford to pay for it! *La révolution* replaced that interesting system of patronage *cum* purchase with popular election of judges—which was not much of an improvement, if any. Napoleon Bonaparte grandly eliminated that methodology and announced the principle of "irremovability," which, in practice, meant rather complete dependency on him. An ambivalent period of minor changes and improvements was effected by the institutions and individuals that succeeded the colorful Corsican until the days of the Third Republic barely a century ago, when the status of the French judges improved without, however, reaching a truly separate status.

Irremovability as an avowed policy for the career judiciary was resuscitated by a proclamation of the Provisional Government a few days after V-E Day in 1945. It was made a part of the basic document of the de Gaulle Republic by the specific verbiage of the Constitution of 1958, which asserts that these judges are "irremovable." Actually, that is technically incorrect, for they *are* removable—but solely for "misconduct in office," and then only upon the recommendation of the High Council of the Judiciary, which acts as a disciplinary court for judges. When it sits as such, the President of the *Cour de Cassation* is its presiding officer.

The judges of France are not so well paid as are those across the English Channel, but there is no evidence that they are in any sense more susceptible to corruption or injudiciousness than their English counterparts. Strengthened even more by the specific proviso of the de Gaulle Constitution making the President of the Republic the "guarantor of the independence of the judicial authority," and the genuine protective power of the High Council of the Judiciary, they enjoy an extensive degree of both professional freedom and authority.

QUALIFICATIONS
AND MOTIVATIONS: THE UNITED STATES

Although attitudes and practices regarding tenure of office do not differ significantly among the American, British, and French judiciaries, substantial, indeed crucial, distinctions become immediately apparent in any consideration of the qualifications—background, experience, and training—of the judges in these three countries. They represent distinctions that flow rather logically from different traditions and theories regarding the role of government in society, and they are attuned to what, for better or for worse, are deemed the needs and experiences of each land. With these thoughts in mind we turn to a consideration of the interesting problem of judicial qualifications in the United States.

BASIC PREREQUISITES?

In contrast to the specialized requirements that obtain in Britain and France, there is but one standardized prerequisite for qualification as a *federal* judge today—the LL.B. degree of the aspirant. The possession of that degree is not a legal requirement for appointment, but custom would automatically veto anyone without it for judicial service at the federal level. Moreover, the legal profession, which has a very real, if unofficial, voice in today's appointive process, would remonstrate so determinedly that the political powers of the government involved would assuredly acquiesce. Yet at the *state* and local level not even the LL.B. is necessary in many instances! [13]

Theoretically, any graduate of an accredited bona fide school of law with his eye on a federal judgeship may thus look forward to an appointment to the coveted niche—provided that he is politically "available" *and* acceptable to the executive, legislative, and private forces that, in the order enumerated, constitute the powers-that-be which underlie the paths of selection, nomination, and appointment in the judicial process. In the final analysis, of course, it is the President and his immediate advisers concerned—here the Attorney-General and his Deputy—who take the crucial step

[13] Cf. Chapter Four, infra, pp. 129–31 and fn. 2.

of submitting the nominee to the Senate. Thus, excluding President Kennedy, all of the presidents had an opportunity to designate at least one nominee for membership on the highest court of the land—which will be our chief concern in these particular pages—except Presidents William Henry Harrison, Zachary Taylor, and Andrew Johnson. The first two were removed too quickly from the scene by death, the latter was the victim of congressional machinations which successfully prevented him from filling several Supreme Court vacancies. The following table illustrates the number of justices each Chief Executive appointed and who *actually served,* including those not confirmed by the Senate. An example of the latter is the case of John Rutledge's designation as Chief Justice by President Washington in 1795. The Senate refused by a vote of 10:14 to confirm the President's recess appointment of the man whom it had approved as Associate Justice in 1789, but who had resigned two years later without ever sitting in order to accept the post of Chief Justice of the Supreme Court of South Carolina (and hence listed as only one Washington appointment). Counting Mr. Justice Rutledge once, and Justices E. D. White, Hughes, and Stone twice, since the latter three all served both as Associate *and* Chief Justice and were appointed by different presidents in each instance, the 92 individual justices who have served on the Court to date (1961–62 term) provided 30 Presidents with 95 successful appointments.

JUDICIAL EXPERIENCE AND ITS ABSENCE

In view of the minimal, formal basic requirement, it is hardly astonishing to note that many a newly appointed jurist lacks practical judicial experience. Among the appellate courts this has been especially true of United States Supreme Court designees—those of the court level immediately below, that is, the United States (Circuit) Court of Appeals, have often had some lower court experience on the United States District Court. Among the 92 individual justices who had served on the Supreme Court between 1789 and the end of 1961, only 20 had had ten or more years of previous judicial experience on any lower level, federal or state, at the time of their appointment, and 38 had had none, whatsoever. Yet, as may be observed readily by scrutinizing Table II below, the group of the 38 totally "inexperienced" contains many of the greatest and most illustrious names in America's judicial history, among them: Chief Justices Marshall, Taney, Waite, Hughes, and Stone; Associate Justices Story, Miller, Bradley, the elder Harlan and Brandeis—to name but ten.

TABLE I
NUMBER OF SUCCESSFUL PRESIDENTIAL APPOINTMENTS
OF JUSTICES OF THE UNITED STATES SUPREME COURT
WHO ACTUALLY SERVED (arranged chronologically)

President	Number of Successful Appointments
Washington	10
J. Adams	3
Jefferson	3
Madison	2
Monroe	1
J. Q. Adams	1
Jackson	6
Van Buren	2
W. H. Harrison	0
Tyler	1
Polk	2
Taylor	0
Fillmore	1
Pierce	1
Buchanan	1
Lincoln	5
Johnson	0
Grant	4
Hayes	2
Garfield	1
Arthur	2
Cleveland	4
Benjamin Harrison	4
McKinley	1
T. Roosevelt	3
Taft	6
Wilson	3
Harding	4
Coolidge	1
Hoover	3
F. D. Roosevelt	9
Truman	4
Eisenhower	5
Kennedy	2

TABLE II
PRIOR JUDICIAL EXPERIENCE OF U. S. SUPREME
COURT JUSTICES AND THEIR SUBSEQUENT SERVICE

Justice	Year Appointed	Number of Years of Prior Judicial Experience			Years of Service on Supreme Court
		Federal	State	Total	
Jay*	1789	0	2	2	6
J. Rutledge*	1789 and 1795*	0	6	6	½
Cushing	1789	0	29	29	21
Wilson	1789	0	0	0	9
Blair	1789	0	11	11	7
Iredell	1790	0	½	½	9
T. Johnson	1791	0	1½	1½	2
Paterson	1793	0	0	0	13
S. Chase	1796	0	8	8	15
Ellsworth*	1796	0	5	5	4
Washington	1798	0	0	0	31
Moore	1799	0	1	1	5
Marshall*	1801	0	0	0	34
W. Johnson	1804	0	6	6	30
Livingston	1806	0	0	0	17
Todd	1807	0	6	6	19
Story	1811	0	0	0	34
Duval	1811	0	6	6	24
Thompson	1823	0	16	16	20
Trimble	1826	9	2	11	2
McLean	1829	0	6	6	32
Baldwin	1830	0	0	0	14
Wayne	1835	0	5	5	32
Taney*	1836	0	0	0	28
Barbour	1836	6	2	8	5
Catron	1837	0	10	10	28
McKinley	1837	0	0	0	15
Daniel	1841	4	0	0	19
Nelson	1845	0	22	22	27
Woodbury	1845	0	6	6	6
Grier	1846	0	13	13	24
Curtis	1851	0	0	0	6
Campbell	1853	0	0	0	8
Clifford	1858	0	0	0	23
Swayne	1862	0	0	0	19
Miller	1862	0	0	0	28

* Indicates Chief Justice and date of promotion.

TABLE II (*Continued*)

Justice	Year Appointed	Number of Years of Prior Judicial Experience			Years of Service on Supreme Court
		Federal	State	Total	
Davis	1862	0	14	14	15
Field	1863	0	6	6	34½
S. P. Chase*	1864	0	0	0	9
Strong	1870	0	11	11	10
Bradley	1870	0	0	0	22
Hunt	1872	0	8	8	10
Waite*	1874	0	0	0	14
Harlan, Sr.	1877	0	1	1	34
Woods	1880	12	0	12	7
Matthews	1881	0	4	4	8
Gray	1881	0	18	18	21
Blatchford	1882	15	0	15	11
L. Q. C. Lamar	1888	0	0	0	5
Fuller*	1888	0	0	0	22
Brewer	1889	6	22	28	21
Brown	1890	16	0	16	16
Shiras	1892	0	0	0	11
H. E. Jackson	1893	7	0	7	2
White*	1894 and 1910*	0	1½	1½	27
Peckham	1895	0	9	9	14
McKenna	1898	5	0	5	27
Holmes	1902	0	20	20	30
Day	1903	4	3	7	19
Moody	1906	0	0	0	4
Lurton	1909	16	10	26	5
Hughes*	1910 and 1930*	0	0	0	17
Van Devanter	1910	7	1	8	27
J. R. Lamar	1910	0	2	2	6
Pitney	1912	0	11	11	10
McReynolds	1914	0	0	0	27
Brandeis	1916	0	0	0	23
Clarke	1916	4	0	4	6
Taft*	1921	8	5	13	9
Sutherland	1922	0	0	0	16
Butler	1922	0	0	0	17
Sanford	1923	14	0	14	7
Stone*	1923 and 1941*	0	0	0	21
Roberts	1930	0	0	0	15
Cardozo	1932	0	18	18	6
Black	1937	0	1½	1½	

TABLE II (*Continued*)

| Justice | Year Appointed | Number of Years of Prior Judicial Experience | | | Years of Service on Supreme Court |
		Federal	State	Total	
Reed	1937	0	0	0	19
Frankfurter	1939	0	0	0	
Douglas	1939	0	0	0	
Murphy	1940	0	7	7	9
Byrnes	1941	0	0	0	1
R. H. Jackson	1941	0	0	0	13
W. Rutledge	1943	0	0	0	6
Burton	1945	0	0	0	13
Vinson*	1946	0	0	0	7
Clark	1949	0	0	0	
Minton	1949	8	0	8	7
Warren*	1953	0	0	0	
Harlan	1955	1	0	1	
Brennan	1956	0	7	7	
Whittaker	1957	3	0	3	5
Stewart	1958	4	0	4	

In a learned essay, calling for selection of Supreme Court justices "wholly on the basis of functional fitness," Mr. Justice Frankfurter argued keenly that neither judicial experience nor political affiliation nor geographic considerations ought to play a significant role in the appointment of these highest jurists, whose job he viewed as necessarily embodying the qualities of *philosopher*—"but not too philosophical," commented his student Paul A. Freund—*historian, and prophet.* Thus he asserted:

> One is entitled to say without qualification that the *correlation between prior judicial experience and fitness for the Supreme Court is zero.* The significance of the greatest among the Justices who had such experience, Holmes and Cardozo, derived not from that judicial experience but from the fact that they were Holmes and Cardozo. They were thinkers, and more particularly, legal philosophers.[14]

And on this point, Mr. Justice Frankfurter has been fond of quoting the distinguished Judge Learned Hand, who for so many years

[14] Felix Frankfurter, "The Supreme Court in the Mirror of Justices," 105 *University of Pennsylvania Law Review* 781 (1957). (Italics supplied.)

rendered outstanding service on the United States Court of Appeals for the Second Circuit (New York, Connecticut, and Vermont), but who never attained his richly merited promotion to the Supreme Court:

> I venture to believe that it is as important to a judge called upon to pass on a question of constitutional law, to have a bowing acquaintance with Acton and Maitland, with Thucydides, Gibbon and Carlyle, with Homer, Dante, Shakespeare and Milton, with Machiavelli, Montaigne, and Rabelais, with Plato, Bacon, Hume, and Kant as with books which have been specifically written on the subject.[15]

Attitudes Toward Experience. Yet the experience factor for Supreme Court justices, although more or less dormant during some Administrations, such as those of President Franklin D. Roosevelt, is usually revitalized by others, as it was by that of President Eisenhower. Roosevelt paid little, if any, heed to it, whereas Eisenhower, after his initial appointment of Mr. Chief Justice Warren, insisted that his nominees have at least some judicial experience, no matter how slight. Of the nine men who sat on the Court as a result of President Roosevelt's appointments (or promotion to Chief Justice in the case of Mr. Justice Stone), that Chief Justice as well as Associate Justices Reed, Frankfurter, Douglas, Byrnes, Jackson, and Rutledge had no judicial experience, whatsoever, while Mr. Justice Black had exactly one and one half years and Mr. Justice Murphy seven years of service on state tribunals. President Truman followed his predecessor's habit of ignoring judicial background: of his four appointees, Mr. Chief Justice Vinson and Associate Justices Burton and Clark had none at all, Associate Justice Minton eight years of prior service on the lower federal bench. President Eisenhower's four appointees subsequent to that of the Chief Justice, Associate Justices Harlan, Brennan, Whittaker, and Stewart, all had seen some prior service —although the total number of years for the four comprised but fourteen.

Congress, too, is hardly of one mind on the matter of the necessity or even the desirability of judicial experience as a prerequisite for appointment to the highest court in the land. Bills are con-

[15] As quoted in *The New York Times Magazine,* November 28, 1954.

tinually introduced that would require future nominees to the Supreme Court to have upwards of five years of experience on lower court benches. In recent years, such legislation has been sponsored by Senators Long (D.-La.), Smathers (D.-Fla.), Stennis (D.-Miss.), Talmadge (D.-Ga.), Butler (R.-Md.), Bricker (R.-Ohio), and others on both sides of the aisle in both houses of Congress. But all of these bills failed of enactment. Moreover, many other legislators agree with what is clearly a majority of the closest observers of the Supreme Court as well as with the thesis of Mr. Justice Frankfurter just described, that judicial experience, because of the peculiar nature of the Court's work, is not essential. The Supreme Court is not a trial court in the sense of the federal district courts below, nor is it called upon to deal with a particular judicial constituency as are these courts of first instance and, to a considerably lesser extent, the federal courts of appeals that lie immediately above the district courts in the judicial hierarchy. Further, there is very little transition or connection between the experience in the lower and the highest federal constitutional court —the procedural and jurisdictional frameworks are quite different. The type of private litigation at common law, so prevalent below, is practically extinct at the bar of today's Supreme Court, which is almost exclusively occupied with questions of public law, led by cases at constitutional law or with constitutional undertones, review of administrative actions, and other public law questions. Experience on the courts below may well be theoretically desirable —although there are some observers who would not even grant that much—but it should not become a requirement for qualification for the Supreme Court. Again returning to Mr. Justice Frankfurter and Judge Learned Hand, the business of the Supreme Court today is "with the application of rather fundamental aspirations," what Judge Hand calls *moods,* that are embodied in constitutional provisions such as the due process of law clauses of the Fifth and Fourteenth Amendments—clauses and concepts that were quite evidently deliberately designed "not to be precise and positive directions for rules of action." In the well-chosen words of Mr. Justice Frankfurter:

The judicial process in applying them involves a *judgment on the processes of government.* The Court sits in judgment, that is, on the views of the direct representatives of the people in meeting the needs of society, on the views of Presidents and Governors, and by their construction of the will of legislatures *the Court breathes life, feeble or strong, into the inert pages of the Constitution and the statute books.*[16]

No wonder that this function calls for a combination of philosopher, historian, and prophet!

A Case Study. A brief survey of the judicial experience factor in connection with the members of the 1960–61 Supreme Court may aid in demonstrating that even if that specific qualification is largely, or even wholly absent in many instances, experience in other relevant areas of public service is often abundantly present. Of the members of that 1960–61 Court, which adjourned at the end of June 1961, only five had past judicial experience, and in almost all of these cases it was rather negligible. Thus, Mr. Justice Black served 18 months as a police judge in his native Alabama; Mr. Justice Harlan had one year on the U. S. Court of Appeals for the Second Circuit; Mr. Justice Whittaker two on the U. S. District Court for the Western District of Missouri and one on the U. S. Court of Appeals for the Eighth Circuit; and Mr. Justice Stewart had four years of service on the U. S. Court of Appeals for the Sixth Circuit. Only Mr. Justice Brennan, a protégé of long-time New Jersey Chief Justice Arthur T. Vanderbilt, with a record of seven years on State of New Jersey benches, capped by his four-year membership on its Supreme Court, could lay claim to reasonably extensive judicial background. All except Mr. Justice Black, who was appointed by President Franklin D. Roosevelt in 1937 at the age of 51, were elevated to the Supreme Court by President Eisenhower in 1955, 1957, 1958, and 1956, when they were 56, 56, 43, and 50 years old, respectively.

Yet *all* of the members of the 1960–61 Court had a record of considerable experience in public life, frequently of an administrative nature, in addition to or in place of whatever judicial experience they may have had. Thus, upon his designation as Chief Justice at the age of 62 by President Eisenhower in 1953, Earl Warren had practiced law and then devoted 34 years of his full life to public office, eleven of these as Republican Governor of

[16] Frankfurter, loc. cit. at 793.

California—always with strong bipartisan support. Mr. Justice Hugo L. Black had practiced law for 17 years, and had been a Democratic Senator from Alabama for ten when he was appointed to the Court. Mr. Justice Felix Frankfurter, upon his nomination at 57 by President Roosevelt in 1939, had taught law at Harvard University for 25 years, served as an attorney for various federal agencies for seven, and had been in the public limelight as counsel for various civic groups and as a presidential adviser for many years. Mr. Justice William O. Douglas had practiced law, taught it for almost a decade, and had been both a member and Chairman of the U. S. Securities and Exchange Commission for three years, when President Roosevelt appointed him in 1939 at a youthful 41 (only four justices were appointed at a younger age). Mr. Justice Tom C. Clark had been a practicing attorney for 15 years, held public office in his native Texas for five, did a variety of legal work for the federal government for eight, and served as Attorney-General in President Truman's Administrations from 1945 until his appointment in 1949 at the age of 50. Before he entered the federal judicial service in 1954, Mr. Justice John Marshall Harlan, the bearer of his grandfather's proud name, had practiced private law and had served the State of New York in a host of capacities over a period of 30 years. Mr. Justice William J. Brennan, Jr., had practiced law for 15 years, was a decorated army officer during World War II and had served the State of New Jersey when Governor Driscoll appointed him to the state bench in 1949. Mr. Justice Charles Evans Whittaker had also practiced law and served Missouri in a manner similar to his brother Harlan, and over the same span of time, before he went to the federal bench. And Mr. Justice Potter Stewart had practiced law for more than a decade, and had served on the City Council of Cincinnati for five years, when he first entered the federal judiciary in 1954.

If—for the sake of argument—one were to grant the wisdom of judicial experience as a pertinent requirement for Supreme Court nominees, a background rich in nonjudicial experience, such as that just described, does not compensate in and of itself for the lack of actual experience on a lower bench. However, it does indicate that the men—there have been no women on a federal court level higher than the Court of Appeals (Judge Florence

Allen of the Sixth Circuit)—who come to the Supreme Court of the United States, and for that matter to the lower federal courts, have had lengthy legal experience as a bare minimum. Moreover, *all* of the 92 justices who have sat on the highest bench, except Mr. Justice George Shiras (1892–1903), had engaged in at least *some* public service at various levels of government, often elective, or had actively participated in political activity. Nevertheless, unlike the jurists of France, for example, it remains true that a great many among the judges of the major courts in the United States have not been primarily trained as judges per se. England relies on still another system, to be discussed presently. Table III indicates the occupations of the individuals (using the full figure 95 here) as of the time of their appointment to the Supreme Court.

TABLE III
OCCUPATIONS* OF SUPREME COURT
DESIGNEES AT TIME OF APPOINTMENT†

Judge of State Court	20
Judge of Inferior Federal Court	19
Federal Officeholder in Executive Branch	18
Private Practice of Law	14
U. S. Senator	8
U. S. Representative	4
State Governor	3
Associate Justice of U. S. Supreme Court	2
Professor of Law	2
Justice of the Permanent Court of International Justice	1

* Many of the appointees had held a variety of federal or state offices, or even both, prior to their selection.
† In general, the appointments from state office are clustered at the beginning of the Court's existence, those from federal office are more recent.

THE JUSTICES IN COMPOSITE

Whatever individual exceptions may be applicable, and keeping in mind the subjective attitude many an observer brings to bear on the members of the Supreme Court of the United States and their decisions, the calibre of that so select group has been universally high. Indeed, no other unit on the scene of American government could easily match its general record of competence and achievement. An over-all analysis of the background and characteristics of the 94 justices to date (1962—63 term) would produce the following "composite":

> White; generally Protestant (there have been six Catholic and four Jewish justices); 50 to 55 years of age at the time of appointment; Anglo-Saxon ethnic stock (all except five); high social status; reared in an urban environment; member of a civic-minded, politically active, economically comfortable family; legal training; some type of public office; generally well-educated.[17]

MOTIVATIONS UNDERLYING APPOINTMENTS

Regardless of learned commentaries and "inside information" revelations, it is obvious that the only person who knows with certainty why he appointed an individual to the Supreme Court of the United States—and, for that matter, to the lower federal courts, although his involvement is likely to be far less direct here —is the President of the United States who signed the commission. And if the theory of the subconscious mind has any validity, perhaps his conscious motives might not have been his real motives! All the student of constitutional law or the historian can do with honesty and conviction is to hazard a reasonable inference based upon the facts at his disposal. It is always possible that this "educated guess" may be utterly erroneous, but there is an excellent chance that it will contain a considerable amount of truth. If this were not the case, the discipline of history, for one, would be a *non sequitur*. These thoughts as to the uncertainty of a specific analysis govern even when the President may have stated orally or in writing that he nominated X for reason Y, for the assertion may be but an attempt to conceal the rationale for the appointment; in any event, Y may well contain only a portion of the truth.

Even more relevant for present purposes than these thoughts is the patent fact that there is normally more than simply one motive

[17] For two recent studies corroborating this "composite," see John R. Schmidhauser, "The Justices of the Supreme Court: A Collective Portrait," 3 *Midwest Journal of Political Science* 1 (1959) and his *The Supreme Court: Its Politics, Personalities and Procedures* (New York: Holt, Rinehart and Winston, Inc., 1960), Ch. 3, *passim*.

behind any human need. Idealism, altruism, and selfishness are all constituent aspects of the human personality, and a particular action may result from the interplay of a myriad of motivations arising from each or all of these factors. In other words, the reasons for the appointment to the Supreme Court by a particular Chief Executive of a particular individual are usually multiple rather than single, although one motive may, of course, be predominant. Generally speaking, five factors have been taken into account, singly or severally, by the 31 presidents when making selections for the 94 vacancies that have existed during the history of the Court so far. They are the same factors that may be expected to govern lower appointments as well, but they stand out more, and are more "interesting" when applied to the level of the highest bench, where appointments naturally come infrequently. Other factors exist, of course; no claim to exclusiveness is made at all, but the five that follow—not necessarily in order of importance—represent unquestionably those of greatest moment: (1) objective merit; (2) political availability of the designee; (3) his ideological appropriateness; (4) personal factors; and (5) geographical, religious, and other equitable considerations. Something should be said about each of these, coupled with some pertinent examples.

(1) Objective Merit. This factor simply poses the question of whether the candidate possesses the ability and the background essential to an understanding of the complicated questions that come before the Court—Mr. Justice Frankfurter would here require his trinity of philosopher-historian-prophet—and/or is blessed with the creative imagination that a Supreme Court justice ought to have. To determine whether or not the individual under consideration does possess these qualifications, the President could look to the nominee's basic intellectual capacity, his reputation for legal scholarship, his competence in a particular area of law, his experience as a judge, lawyer, or public official, his reputation in and out of his vocational aura, his temperament. Age may well also be relevant here. If the potential nominee is too young, he may be deemed to lack maturity of judgment and wisdom; if he is too old, he may retire or die before he has acquired the experience—one may call it the style—necessary to bring to the fore his full talent as a member of that tribunal. Judge Learned Hand, universally recognized as one of the jewels in America's judicial

crown, was usually deemed "too old" when he was "politically available," and not the latter when the former issue was overlooked!

On the other hand, some critics of President Eisenhower's ultimately successful nomination of Mr. Justice Potter Stewart held him to be "too young"—he was barely 43. Yet in the case of the latter's nomination, practically all of the other factors loomed favorable: although a solid Eisenhower Republican, having campaigned vigorously for the President in both 1952 and 1956, he had actively supported the presidential aspirations of Ohio's Senator Robert A. Taft, "Mr. Republican" himself, in 1948 and 1952; he was a personal friend of Ohio's Senator John Bricker who sponsored him; he had established a fine record during his brief service on the Sixth Circuit Court of Appeals, and his opinions were regarded as examples of superior legal writing by the Department of Justice as well as at least some of his future colleagues; his father was Chief Justice of the Supreme Court of Ohio; he had enjoyed public service; and he was viewed as acceptable to both the liberal and conservative groups who knew his record. His confirmation by the Senate by a vote of 70:17 in 1959 was delayed for four months and received such sizable opposition, all from Southern Democrats, solely in the light of the latter's general antipathy toward the Supreme Court at that time because of the segregation-integration controversy, in general, and because of the nominee's fairly obvious sympathy with the Court's position, in particular. The opposition was not directed against the nominee as such.

Probably the most illustrative example of the objective merit factor and its recognition by the bar, the public, and the political elements alike was that of Mr. Justice Cardozo, whose selection was all but forced upon President Hoover by the country, and who was confirmed unanimously by the Senate at the instant the nomination reached the floor. This despite the facts—conceivably detrimental or even fatal in the case of other nominees, depending upon circumstances—that the nominee came from New York, already "represented" on the bench at that time by Mr. Chief Justice Hughes and Mr. Justice Stone, and that he was Jewish. Hoover raised these considerations during a command-visit by Republican Senator Borah of Idaho, Chairman of the Committee on Foreign Relations, who had been very vocal in urging the Cardozo appointment. The President handed him a list, indicating the names of several prominent individuals he was considering for the vacancy on the Court left by Mr. Justice Holmes's resignation. The last name on the list was that of the Chief Judge of the New York State Court of Appeals, Benjamin N. Cardozo. "Your list is all right," commented Senator Borah, "but you handed it to me upside down!" [18] When President Hoover then strongly urged that his visitor consider the geographical situation involved, and mentioned "possible religious and sectarian repercussions," Senator Borah told him in no uncertain terms that "Cardozo belonged as much to Idaho as to New York," and that geography should no more bar him than the presence of two Virginians on the high bench—John Blair and Bushrod Washington—should have prevented President John Adams from naming John Marshall as Chief Justice.[19] Furthermore, Borah told Hoover, "anyone who raises the question of race [*sic*] is unfit to advise you concerning so important a matter." [20] When the President bowed to what was surely unanimous popular clamor for the Cardozo appointment, he became the recipient of lavish praise, with Senator Clarence Dill of Washington remarking that "when President Hoover appointed Judge Cardozo . . . he performed the finest act of his career as President." [21]

(2) and (3) Political Availability and Ideological Appropriateness. These two criteria often go hand in hand. They include such considerations as whether the choice of an individual will render the President popular, or more popular, among certain groups in the body politic; whether he is indebted to the potential nominee for political services rendered; whether the nominee has been a loyal member of the President's political party; whether he favors the President's policies and programs—his *Weltanschauung*—regardless of his own party membership; and whether he is acceptable, or at least not "personally obnoxious," to the kindred home state politicos, notably those in the Senate. It is a rather firmly adhered to unwritten law of the judicial nominating process at the

---

[18] Claudius O. Johnson, *Borah of Idaho* (New York: Longman's, Green & Co., 1936), p. 452.
[19] *The New York Times*, January 30, 1932.　　[20] Johnson, loc. cit., p. 453.
[21] *The New York Times*, March 2, 1932.

level of the Supreme Court that, as a rule, the President will not normally select a man from the political opposition. To assuage charges of "packing the courts" below, this rule is relaxed purposely at the level of the federal district courts and sometimes even at that of the courts of appeals, but only within "political reason." Nevertheless, it has also happened twelve times on the Supreme Court including two promotions to Chief Justice—with a ready explanation being present in all instances—as follows: Whig President John Tyler appointed one Democrat, Mr. Justice Samuel Nelson. Republican Presidents Abraham Lincoln, Benjamin Harrison, William H. Taft, Warren G. Harding, Herbert Hoover, and Dwight D. Eisenhower appointed eight Democrats—Taft alone three! The eight were Justices Stephen J. Field (Lincoln), Howell E. Jackson (Harrison), Horace H. Lurton (Taft), the Edward D. White promotion (Taft), and Joseph R. Lamar (Taft), Pierce Butler (Harding), Benjamin N. Cardozo (Hoover), and William J. Brennan, Jr. (Eisenhower). And Democratic Presidents Woodrow Wilson, Franklin D. Roosevelt, and Harry S. Truman appointed three Republicans: Justices Louis D. Brandeis (Wilson), the Harlan F. Stone promotion (Roosevelt), and Harold H. Burton (Truman). Some would add a thirteenth case, President Franklin D. Roosevelt's appointment of Mr. Justice Frankfurter, who labeled himself an Independent.

Crossing Party Lines. The *Nelson* designation by President Tyler came after the latter had been defeated by Democrat James K. Polk in the election of 1844. Eager to have history show at least one of his own nominees attain the Supreme Court, the "lame duck" Tyler then named Nelson, who had not been an active political figure, after three of his four first Whig choices had to be withdrawn because of obviously decisive opposition and the fourth one, John Spencer of New York, was rejected by the Senate 26:21.

In 1863 *Field,* who was to serve longer than anyone else to date on the Supreme Court, 34½ years, was chosen by Lincoln, largely for three reasons: First, Field came from California, a part of the country not then represented on the Court, and even though he was a Buchanan Democrat, Lincoln felt his nominee would help to "fuse" the Northern cause by preserving the loyalty of California and strengthening political ties. Second, Field's many influential friends, including Leland Stanford, put considerable pressure on the President. Third, Field's brother, David Dudley Field, a bitter and vocal opponent of slavery, played a considerable role both in the organization of the Republican party and in Lincoln's nomination as its standard-bearer in 1860.

Harrison's choice of *Jackson* was motivated by reasons similar to those that governed the Tyler-Nelson case. Cleveland had already defeated Harrison when the vacancy on the Court occurred, the Democratic Senate was in no mood to confirm the Republican lame duck President's partisan choice, and, happily, Harrison and Jackson, who had served in the Senate together, were close friends —as were their wives.

The Taft appointments of *Lurton* and *Lamar* and his promotion of *White,* all three Southern Democrats appointed by a good Republican, are attributable to a combination of personal friendship or esteem, ideological kinship, and politico-sectional expediency. Taft and Lurton had served together for eight years on the U. S. Circuit Court of Appeals for the Sixth Circuit, where they became fast friends. Taft, who was its Chief Judge, was very much impressed with the legal and judicial ability of the Tennessee Democrat who succeeded him as Chief Judge when the future President went to the Philippine Islands. Conservative kinsmen, they were usually at one in their opinions from the bench and in their general philosophy of government, and Taft called the nomination of his friend Lurton "the chief pleasure of my administration." [22] Although he was not as close to Taft personally as Lurton, Joseph R. Lamar of Georgia readily met the Taft standards of conservatism and general ideological bent. For example, the two men saw eye to eye on the tariff—a matter of the utmost importance to the President. And Taft saw in the appointment of the Confederate Army veteran an additional opportunity for strengthening his position among Southern political leaders who, if they would not vote for him at election time, would at least help him with his legislative program. He promoted White—now in his seventeenth year on the Court—in part because he considered him the ablest administrator among the justices then on the bench; in part because his fellow-justices apparently had petitioned the

[22] Silas Bent, *Justice Oliver Wendell Holmes* (New York: Garden City Publishing Co., 1932), p. 248.

President to designate him rather than Hughes,[23] who had seemed to have the proverbial inside track ("White, Not Hughes, For Chief Justice," read the front-page headline in *The New York Times*[24] when the announcement was made); and in large part because he had voted "right" on the bench in Taft's eyes—among these votes being one to uphold a military tariff in the Philippine Islands, where Taft was then Governor.[25]

Wilson's hotly contested nomination of *Brandeis,* a registered Massachusetts Republican, was confirmed by the Senate only after a lengthy delay and by a margin of 47:22—with 21 of these 22 negative votes coming from the Republican Senators then present! The famed "People's Lawyer," as Wilson was fond of calling him, was a personal friend of the President and a close ideological ally —a political and social liberal who shared his philosophy of life and government. It was primarily the combination of these two factors and his great regard for Brandeis's character and ability that prompted Wilson to ignore the sectional factor (Massachusetts was then already represented by Holmes); possible repercussions because of the nominee's religion (he became the first person of Jewish persuasion to reach the Supreme Court); and to go out on the limb during the 1916 election year to designate such a controversial personage as Brandeis in the face of the violent opposition of the most influential segment of the bar and the business community.

Harding's choice of *Butler* points to three motives. First, the President liked his record of almost four decades of service in the law and in public life; second, and probably most important, Harding found Butler's ideological ultra-conservatism to be entirely sympathetic—he became one of the two leading avowed reactionaries on the bench; and third, the President deemed it politically advantageous to appoint a man who combined the here seemingly desirable factor of being a "safe" Democrat—most Democrats refused to regard Butler as one of their number in roughly the same fashion as the Republicans did Brandeis—with that of being a member of a then "unrepresented" minority re-

---

[23] George Shiras, 3rd, *Justice George Shiras* (Pittsburgh: University of Pittsburgh Press, 1953), p. 130.   [24] December 12, 1910.
[25] Cf. William Howard Taft, *Our Chief Magistrate and His Power* (New York: Columbia University Press, 1916), pp. 99–102.

ligion (Roman Catholic) and a native Minnesotan, only the second nominee born west of the Mississippi to reach the bench. Initially rejected by the Senate, Butler was renominated by Harding on the following day and ultimately won confirmation easily—though veritably scorched by large segments of the public press.

The *Cardozo* appointment by Hoover has already been discussed; he was literally forced upon the President, who eventually came to be proud, indeed, that he had named this model public servant to the "Holmes seat."

President Franklin D. Roosevelt promoted *Stone* largely as a manifestation of unity in the face of the incipient war crisis. When Mr. Chief Justice Hughes announced his intention to retire, speculation as to his successor revolved around Stone and the then Attorney-General Robert H. Jackson. Roosevelt's heart was on the side of Jackson, but he deemed it wiser and more appropriate at this juncture of history to name Stone. In fact, he discussed the matter with Jackson who agreed and later, having become an Associate Justice of the Supreme Court, wrote that the need for judicial leadership and the "desirability for a symbol of stability as well as of progress" were evidently the reasons for Stone's elevation "in the interest of the [fostering of the] judiciary as an institution." [26] Moreover, the retiring Chief Justice himself had strongly urged Stone's elevation on the basis of his record, and suggested that Roosevelt consult Mr. Justice Frankfurter in the matter. The latter told the President:

> . . . when war does come, the country should feel you are a national, the Nation's President, and not a partisan President . . . [to bolster this assessment] you [should] name a Republican, who has the profession's confidence, as Chief Justice.[27]

President Truman's nomination of *Burton*—the first of his four —is often far too readily dismissed merely as a reward to "an old Senate crony." [28] Unquestionably, Truman's personal fondness of the Republican Senator from Ohio and Mayor of Cleveland, who had served so well and so closely with the then Senator Truman on

---

[26] Alpheus T. Mason, *Harlan Fiske Stone: Pillar of the Law* (New York: The Viking Press, 1956), p. 573.   [27] Ibid. p. 567.
[28] For example, see Glendon A. Schubert, *Constitutional Politics* (New York: Holt, Rinehart and Winston, Inc., 1960), p. 38.

the latter's Special Committee to Investigate the National Defense Program, the "Truman Committee," was a factor in the appointment. But there were assuredly others: the advice, given to the President, that he designate a Republican to replace the retiring Mr. Justice Roberts, a Republican; Mr. Chief Justice Stone's advance approval of the nominee because of his valuable legislative experience; Truman's belief in Burton's judicial temperament; the absence of anyone from Ohio on the bench; the fact that the nominee's Senate seat would be filled by a Democrat, as indeed it subsequently was by the incumbent Governor Lausche—a somewhat unpredictable Democrat; and the faithful support Burton had given to the Democratic party on foreign policy, and even on some domestic policy, throughout his tenure in the Senate.

Last is the designation of *Brennan* by Eisenhower, who chose this New Jersey Democrat for a variety of reasons. The President's initial choice had been that state's able Chief Justice, Arthur T. Vanderbilt, who had achieved an outstanding national reputation as head of the then recently reorganized New Jersey court system. Because of his advanced age and his failing health, Vanderbilt declined, but highly recommended the nomination of his colleague and protégé, Associate Justice Brennan of the State Supreme Court. This recommendation was strengthened by the support of Secretary of Labor James Mitchell and that of the two Republican Senators from New Jersey, Clifford S. Case and Alexander H. Smith, and Democratic Governor Robert B. Meyner. Moreover, it was the very eve of the 1956 election, and the choice of a Roman Catholic from the large metropolitan East would hardly hurt the President in the impending campaign. With but Republican Senator Joseph R. McCarthy of Wisconsin voting "no," the Brennan nomination was confirmed by the Senate in March 1957.

The emphasis placed above on the twelve deviations from membership in the political party of the appointing President—some would add as a thirteenth President Franklin D. Roosevelt's appointment of Mr. Justice Frankfurter—is not intended to convey the impression that there is a national trend in that direction. Far from it! There will presumably always be some crossing of party lines, particularly at the district court level, in order to maintain over-all harmony, to placate the opposition, and to establish a measure of bipartisanship, but the practice may be safely predicted to remain the exception rather than the norm. After all, as many a President has been told by his political advisers, Republican or Democratic, as the case may be, "why should we give these plums to the other guys? . . . surely there are just as many good and deserving lawyers on *our side of the fence.*" More often than not this is probably true, and no doubt political patronage will continue to govern as an appointment-maxim in the judicial process. Thus, President F. D. Roosevelt appointed 194 Democratic and eight Republican federal judges; Truman, 128 Democrats and 13 Republicans; and Eisenhower, 178 Republicans and 11 Democrats. Of the first 117 judges President Kennedy had been able to appoint by July 1962, 105 were Democrats and ten Republicans. The trend was evidently being continued! However, in so far as appointees to the Supreme Court are concerned, what is of the greatest importance to the President is what Theodore Roosevelt referred to as the nominee's "real politics"—of which more below.

(4) *Personal Factors.* Although it is perhaps somewhat of an over-simplification, the basic point here is the close personal regard the President may have for an individual—a factor that may well override all other considerations. Although this concept is understandably impossible to measure, there is no doubt that it has played, and will continue to play, a very real role in individual cases. As we have already seen, it figured prominently in President Taft's appointment of Mr. Justice Lurton and, somewhat less so, in those of Mr. Justice Burton by President Truman and Mr. Justice Brandeis by President Wilson. And, to conclude this point with some other obvious examples, the personal friendship factor was of undoubted significance in the Truman nominations of Mr. Chief Justice Vinson and Associate Justices Clark and Minton; it was probably *the* crucial factor in the latter appointment, although Minton was, of course, a good Democrat and had seen eight years of service, however colorless, on the federal appellate bench.

(5) *Geographical, Religious, and Other Equitable Considerations.* We have already observed in the case of several nominees that a President is less likely to look favorably upon a candidate who comes from an area in which reside one or more justices already on the Court—but, again, if he is determined to appoint a certain individual, as in President Wilson's choice of Mr. Justice Brandeis, for one, geography will not be permitted to stand in the

way. And in the case of Mr. Justice Cardozo, the country would not permit President Hoover to allow it to do so. It might well be argued that the consideration of geography is relevant merely to the political propriety of the appointment and should thus be relegated to the second and third categories discussed above. However, the notion that all sections of the country should be "represented" on the Court—to date the justices have come from 29 of the 50 states—has the advantage of being equitable as well as having a political appeal, Mr. Justice Frankfurter's eloquent demurrer notwithstanding. Furthermore, in the earlier days of the Republic when the justices used to ride circuit, it was obviously desirable to appoint for a given circuit a jurist who would be familiar with the area encompassed by it. The last appointees to the Supreme Court literally to ride circuit were the three appointees by President Van Buren, Associate Justices John Catron, John McKinley, and Peter V. Daniel, who came to the Court in 1837, 1837, and 1841, respectively. Geographical considerations, in other words, should not be regarded as the equivalent of political considerations, and should hence be viewed as related to equitable factors generally.

TABLE IV
THE 30 STATES FROM WHICH
THE 97 SUPREME COURT APPOINTMENTS WERE MADE

New York	13	Illinois	3
Ohio	10	North Carolina	2
Massachusetts	8	Iowa	2
Pennsylvania	6	Michigan	2
Tennessee	6	New Hampshire	1
Kentucky	5	Maine	1
Maryland	4	Mississippi	1
New Jersey	4	Kansas	1
Virginia	3	Wyoming	1
South Carolina	3	Utah	1
Connecticut	3	Minnesota	1
Georgia	3	Texas	1
Alabama	3	Indiana	1
California	3	Missouri	1
Louisiana	3	Colorado	1

The same considerations apply; both more and less, to the religious factor. It is at once closely related to the political factor and personifies one of the equitable considerations that have entered the governmental sphere—and it is undoubtedly here to stay, for better or for worse—and surely for worse in this instance. Hence there has arisen the notion of a "Roman Catholic" seat and, somewhat less so, that of a "Jewish seat" on the Supreme Court. Not a healthy development, the religious-group representation concept has become one of *the* facts of American political life, and it was probably a foregone conclusion that it would one day reach the Supreme Court as well. Although less of a problem or consideration there than in the make-up of election slates where, in some instances, such as the City of New York, it has become all but a maxim of politics, religious affiliation is a definite factor regarding Supreme Court nominees. Except for the seven years between Mr. Justice Murphy's death in 1949 and Mr. Justice Brennan's nomination in 1956, when, perhaps oddly in view of the charges of "politics" so frequently voiced against him, President Truman evidently deliberately ignored the practice, members of both the Roman Catholic and the Jewish faith have been on the Court ever since Mr. Justice Brandeis's ascent in 1916. (Roman Catholic: Mr. Chief Justice Taney, Mr. Chief Justice White, Associate Justices McKenna, Butler, Murphy, and Brennan; Jewish: Associate Justices Brandeis, Cardozo, and Frankfurter.) The first Roman Catholic to be appointed was Mr. Chief Justice Taney in 1835 by President Andrew Jackson, and since Mr. Justice McKenna's appointment by President McKinley in 1898 a member of

TABLE V
ACKNOWLEDGED RELIGION OF THE 94 JUSTICES
OF THE SUPREME COURT (at time of appointment)

Unspecified Protestant	25
Episcopalian	23
Presbyterian	16
Unitarian	6
Roman Catholic	6
Baptist	5
Jewish	4
Congregationalist	3
Methodist	3
Disciples of Christ	2
Quaker	1

that faith has always been on the Court save for the seven-year interval of the Truman Administration. Whatever the merit or demerit of the religious factor, it is probably here to stay in the nature of an element of the political aspects of judicial appointments that the nominating authorities, rightly or wrongly, apparently will continue to take into account.

"PACKING THE COURT" AND THE NOMINEES' "REAL POLITICS"

Regardless of the significance and the role each or all of the five factors may play in the presidential selection of justices of the Supreme Court and the lower courts, especially at the highest level, the most important consideration is the nominee's "real politics," i.e. his future voting behavior on the bench. If an appointing President had the power of clairvoyance coupled with that of a check upon the judicial decision-making process, that consideration would present no problem, but in their absence it is entirely normal for the President to endeavor to "pack" the bench to a greater or lesser extent.

The practice of "packing," or of filling vacancies with individuals safely of the President's own views and persuasion, has been associated in the popular mind most prominently with President Franklin D. Roosevelt, who presided over the transition of the "Old" to the "New" Court from 1937 on. Deaths and resignations permitted him to fill nine vacancies—a total exceeded only by President Washington. Moreover, his attempt to have his way at one fell swoop by virtue of his unsuccessful "Court Packing Bill" of 1936—which died in the Senate Judiciary Committee—designed to permit him to appoint an additional justice for each incumbent above 70 years of age up to a total Court membership of 15, has closely linked him with the packing concept. Yet it is an historical fact that Presidents Jefferson, Jackson, and Lincoln, facing similar problems of what they viewed as Court opposition, followed solutions that were basically analogous. And the first President, George Washington himself, who is somehow placed on a pedestal, far removed from what the public usually views as "politics," insisted that his nominees to the Supreme Court—and he nominated ten, even eleven if John Rutledge is counted twice —meet the following five criteria: (1) advocacy of federalism;

(2) a record of active support of the Revolution, preferably as a "fighting participant"; (3) "fitness"; (4) past judicial service; (5) proper geographical apportionment. Every President is necessarily guilty of some packing—it is merely a matter of degree. In short, similarity of views of nominator and nominee is understandably and customarily a controlling factor; membership in the same political party is one as well, and an important one, as are some of the other factors discussed earlier—but far less so than that of the nominee's "real politics." *That* uncertain quantity once caused President Truman to observe with considerable justice that "packing the Supreme Court can't be done, because I've tried it and it won't work. . . . Whenever you put a man on the Supreme Court he ceases to be your friend. I'm sure of that." [29] Most appointing authorities have come to that general conclusion, which is to the credit of the hallowed institution of judicial independence. And they may be well advised to heed the admonition of Professor Chafee that in order to forecast the behavior of a future jurist it is wiser to consider the books in his library than the list of his clients in his law office.

The Nominees' "Real Politics." One of those who endeavored to probe hard for that crucial factor on sundry occasions was President Theodore Roosevelt—and not always successfully. In discussing a potential nominee with his good friend, Republican Senator Henry Cabot Lodge of Massachusetts, the "All-American Boy President" put the matter well:

> . . . the *nominal* politics of the man [Horace H. Lurton, a Democrat] has nothing to do with his actions on the bench. His *real* politics are all important. . . . He is right on the Negro question; he is right on the power of the federal government; he is right on the Insular business; he is right about corporations; and he is right about labor. On every question that would come before the bench, he has so far shown himself to be in much closer touch with the policies in which you and I believe.[30]

[29] Lecture at Columbia University, April 28, 1959. (Reported in *The Philadelphia Bulletin,* April 29, 1959.)

[30] Henry Cabot Lodge, *Selections from the Correspondence of Theodore Roosevelt and Henry Cabot Lodge,* 1884–1918 (New York: Charles Scribner's Sons, 1925), Vol. II, p. 228.

Although concurring in substance, Lodge replied, however, that he could not "see why Republicans cannot be found who hold those opinions as well as Democrats," [31] and he strongly supported the candidacy of another possibility for the position, the Republican Attorney-General, William H. Moody of Massachusetts, whom Roosevelt then nominated. (Lurton, as we have seen, was subsequently sent to the Court, anyway—as the first appointment of another Republican, President Taft.)

Nevertheless, in the words of that eminent student of the Supreme Court, Charles Warren:

> . . . nothing is more striking in the history of the Court than the manner in which the hopes of those who expected a judge to follow the political views of the President appointing him have been disappointed.[32]

Few felt the immediate truth of that statement more keenly than did Theodore Roosevelt with his nomination of the great Mr. Justice Holmes, whose early "anti-Administration" opinions in anti-trust cases, notably in the *Northern Securities* case, were entirely unexpected.[33] So did President Madison with his appointment of Mr. Justice Story in the face of Jefferson's warning that the nominee was a Tory, and, as predicted by Madison's political mentor, Story not only became an immediate supporter of John Marshall, their political and judicial nemesis, but he even "out-Marshalled" the Chief Justice in his nationalism. But perhaps the clearest example of an appointee who proved to be the veritable antithesis of everything his appointor believed in and stood for was the Woodrow Wilson-selected Mr. Justice McReynolds!

Surely, a very considerable element of unpredictability governs the judicial appointing process. To the oft-heard "Does a man become any different when he puts on a gown?" Mr. Justice Frankfurter's pungent reply has always been: "If he is any good, he does!" As for the Chief Executive, he is of necessity a politician and the leader of his party, as well as the leader of the nation. To play the first two roles successfully, he must pay at least some

[31] Ibid. pp. 230–31.

[32] *The Supreme Court of the United States,* rev. ed. (Boston: Little, Brown & Co., 1926), Vol. II, p. 22.

[33] *Northern Securities v. United States,* 193 U. S. 197 (1904).

attention to "politics"—real and nominal—in his choice of judges. But he will probably be a failure in the latter role if he employs that criterion solely in making his selections.

TABLE VI
AVOWED POLITICAL AFFILIATION OF THE 95
APPOINTED SUPREME COURT JUSTICES (at time of selection)

Federalists	13
Whig	1
Democrats	44
Republicans	36
Independent	1

On the Role of the United States Senate

Enough has been said throughout these pages about the general role of the Senate in the judicial appointive process to obviate an extended discussion. But a few additional comments would seem to be called for, especially regarding lengthy delays in confirmation and rejection of presidential nominees to the highest bench.[34] There is no question, of course, that the Senate possesses a veto over a nomination to the Court—and to the lower federal courts— if it chooses to exercise it. Certainly in theory, it may exercise this veto for whatever reason it may choose—and it has done so on occasion. "Senatorial courtesy," described earlier, looms large here, particularly at the level of the federal district courts where the patronage factor is more overt and more prominent than at the higher echelons. Conversely, the Senate will almost inevitably treat as a *cas d'honneur* the presidential designation of one of their own members—witness the unanimous confirmation to the Supreme Court of then-sitting Senators Byrnes of South Carolina and Burton of Ohio. Byrnes was confirmed unanimously without even being submitted to the Committee on the Judiciary, that stern and powerful stumbling block of quite a few nominations! And the Burton appointment was confirmed unanimously on the same day it reached the Senate. A notable exception to this unwritten

[34] These points were discussed in considerable detail in Henry J. Abraham and Edward M. Goldberg, "A Note on the Appointment of Justices of the Supreme Court of the United States," 20 *American Bar Association Journal* 152 (February 1960) and more generally, in Robert B. McKay, "Selection of United States Supreme Court Justices," 9 *Kansas Law Review* 109 (No. 2, 1960).

rule was the controversial appointment of Mr. Justice Black by President Franklin D. Roosevelt, which was referred to the Judiciary Committee for full hearings. The initial reason for that unusual action was Senator Black's strong support of the President's Court Packing bill, which was anathema to a majority of the Senate. But the controversial aspects of the nomination were compounded by the subsequent revelation during the hearings before the committee that Black had once been a member of the Ku Klux Klan in Alabama. Nonetheless, the committee ultimately voted 13:4 in his favor, and the Senate confirmed the appointment by a vote of 66:15.

Two aspects of the Senate's role will mainly be considered here: *unusual delays* and *rejections* encountered by appointees to the Supreme Court. Fifteen nominations were characterized by what were clearly "unusual delays." Nineteen failed to win approval—*not* counting the ultimately confirmed though once rejected Justices Paterson, Taney, Matthews, and Butler—of whom nine were rejected outright by an adverse vote on the motion to confirm, whereas in the instances of ten others the Senate either refused to act or "postponed" action, thus resulting in rejection in all but name.

Unusual Delays in Confirmation. For our purposes an "unusual delay" is one which is markedly longer than that which normally took place during the period in which the appointment was made. Thus, a delay of one month in 1826 was as "unusual" as a delay of six months would be today, when a month's delay would be viewed as a common occurrence. An examination of the 15 nominations at issue indicates not only that the periods of delay have tended to lengthen, but, more significantly, it demonstrates a definite pattern of causes for these unusual delays. In many cases more than one factor appears to have played a role in the delay involved, but three causes seem to be singly or severally present in all:

First, *involvement with a political question or problem,* on which there is a strong feeling on the part of the public, some senators, or organized pressure groups. Thus, to cite a few illustrations, Mr. Justice Robert Trimble's confirmation was delayed for one month in 1826. During his service on the United States Court of Appeals—he was the first justice of the Supreme Court with a background of prior *federal* judicial experience—he had tended to support national powers at the expense of the states. Hence he incurred the wrath of several prominent "state rights" senators, including Senator Rowan from his own State of Kentucky; but despite the latent implications of this early attempt to invoke "senatorial courtesy," Trimble was confirmed, largely due to the stanch support given by Senator Thomas Hart Benton of Missouri and Secretary of State Henry Clay. Mr. Justice Benjamin Curtis's confirmation was delayed for three months in 1851 by senators who believed that he opposed the abolitionist cause and supported the Fugitive Slave Law. It was poetic justice that Curtis turned out to be one of only two members of the Court to oppose the *Dred Scott* decision and, in fact, felt so strongly about it that he resigned from the bench in 1861.[35]

Others whose appointments were delayed because of the political factor were Justices Joseph P. Bradley, by "hard money" Easterners for what was—correctly—believed to be his "soft money" philosophy, for six weeks in 1870; Lucius Q. C. Lamar of Mississippi, by Northern Republicans who disliked and mistrusted the man who had followed his state out of the Union and fought for the Confederacy, for six weeks in 1887; Joseph McKenna, by antitrust and anti-railroad interests (and some anti-Catholics) who feared his close friendship with railroad magnate Leland Stanford, for five weeks in 1897; Mahlon Pitney, by labor because of his record as a New Jersey legislator and jurist, for one month in 1912; Louis D. Brandeis, by a host of elements in the legal and business community (and some anti-Semites) because of his long, outspoken activities as a champion of the social and economic underdog, for over four months in 1916—the longest battle in the history of the Court; John Marshall Harlan, the younger, by ultra-conservative groups and a new breed, the professional "anti-Supreme Court" elements, allegedly because of his supposed sympathy for the cause of world government, for three months in 1955; and Potter Stewart, who was made a whipping boy because of emotional reaction to the Court's decisions in the segregation-integration field, for four months in 1958–59 (during the confirmation battle he served under a recess appointment).

Second, *opposition to the appointing President,* manifesting it-

[35] *Dred Scott v. Sanford,* 19 Howard 393 (1857).

self in opposition to the nominee. Probably the best cases in point here are the appointments of Mr. Chief Justice Roger B. Taney and Associate Justice Philip P. Barbour, whose confirmation in each instance was delayed for two-and-a-half months in 1835. The opposition against the two men was not so much directed against them as nominees as it was against the nominator, President Andrew Jackson. However, the powerful anti-Jackson faction in the Senate—led by the three great names of the time, Clay, Webster, and Calhoun—failed to prevail against Jackson's strong leadership and drive, backed by his immense popularity with the electorate.

Third, *personal senatorial vendettas.* Thus, Mr. Justice Robert H. Jackson's confirmation was delayed over a month in 1941, chiefly because of the vehement opposition of Democratic Senator Millard Tydings of Maryland, who had a long-standing personal feud with the nominee, based on the latter's failure as Attorney-General to prosecute two Washington columnists for what Tydings alleged was a libelous radio broadcast. Mr. Chief Justice Earl Warren was delayed for almost two months in 1954, chiefly due to a fight against his confirmation by Republican Senator William Langer of North Dakota, a senior member of the Senate's Judiciary Committee. Langer and some Southern Democrats went so far as to impugn the nominee's loyalty because of his alleged "left wing" or "liberal" views. It was then and is now widely assumed that the main motivation for the Langer attack was his long-standing wish to secure the appointment for someone—almost anyone—from North Dakota. Mr. Chief Justice Melville W. Fuller's appointment was held up for two-and-a-half months in 1888, chiefly because of a personal filibuster against the nomination by Senator Edmunds of Vermont, the Republican Chairman of the Judiciary Committee, who insisted that President Cleveland had promised him that the position would go to a man from Edmunds's home state, one Edward Phelps. When Cleveland denied this allegation, Edmunds turned the Fuller nomination into a partisan political battle of Republicans against Democrats, with Fuller emerging triumphant solely because of the defection of a few Republicans on the vote to confirm. And while his youth (44) and alleged lack of sufficient public experience may have played a role in the six weeks of delay in the confirmation of John Marshall Harlan, the elder, the real reason was the activity of Senators Timothy Howe of Wisconsin and Isaac Christiancy of Michigan, both of whom had unsuccessfully attempted to gain President Hayes's appointment for themselves.

Rejections. Including under this heading so-called postponements, which were never acted upon and/or were withdrawn, an examination of the reasons for these direct or indirect Senate vetoes points to five major factors. Again, more than one factor was often present, but the five to be discussed comprise the principal ones for the rejection on record:

First, *opposition to the appointing President,* manifesting itself in opposition to the nominee. Five chief executives were affected here. President John Quincy Adams's nomination of John J. Crittenden in 1828 was "postponed" by the Senate by a strictly partisan vote of 17:23 two months after the nomination. The Democrats in the Senate thus foiled a last-minute Whig appointment by the outgoing President and preserved the vacancy for the incoming President-elect, Democrat Andrew Jackson. In the cases of President John Tyler's five nominees, John C. Spencer was rejected without a record vote, and action regarding Ruben H. Walworth, Edward King, and John M. Read was postponed by votes of 21:26, 20:27, 18:29, respectively, in 1844–45, chiefly because of the— mistaken—hope and expectation on the part of the Clay Whigs that their leader would win the election of 1844. (Polk did.) Action on one of President Millard Fillmore's nominees, George E. Badger, was postponed indefinitely in 1852, and no action at all was taken on his two others, Edward A. Bradford and William E. Micou. The purpose of these maneuvers was to enable the incoming Democratic President, Franklin Pierce, to fill these three vacancies—yet he succeeded in filling but one of them, falling victim to related senatorial tactics. President James Buchanan's nomination of Jeremiah S. Black was rejected by a vote of 25:26 in 1861 for several reasons, but chiefly because the Republicans wanted to hold the vacancy for incoming President Abraham Lincoln. And the seat for which President Andrew Johnson named Henry Stanberry was abolished by Congress in 1866 because of its bitter opposition to the long-suffering President.

Assuredly, in many of these cases, the opposition to the appointee also had other important political connotations in that major policy issues were involved, and these issues were naturally connected with the opposition to the President concerned. Hence it was not, of course, simply blind opposition to or dislike of the President which resulted in the rejections.

Second, *involvement with a political question or problem,* on which there is a strong feeling on the part of the public, some senators, or organized pressure groups. Thus, John Rutledge's nomination as Chief Justice in 1795 was rejected by a vote of 10:14. Already serving on a recess appointment, and having been confirmed six years earlier as Associate Justice—a position he resigned without ever sitting—Rutledge's rejection came primarily because of a speech he had made in opposition to the Jay Treaty. Despite the fact that both he and his appointor, President George Washington, were Federalists, the Federalist Senators refused to confirm the appointment of a man who had actively opposed the treaty which they supported so wholeheartedly. President James Madison's selection of Alexander Woolcott in 1811 fell 9:24 largely, although not solely, because the Federalists opposed his vigorous enforcement of the embargo and nonintercourse statutes as U. S. Collector of Customs and his extreme partisanship in office. Similarly, President John K. Polk's designation of George W. Woodward was rejected 20:29 in 1845 because of what was termed gross "nativist American Sentiments"; among those opposing him was Senator Simon Cameron from his home state of Pennsylvania.

The appointment of Ebenezer R. Hoar by President Ulysses S. Grant in 1869 was rejected by an adverse Senate vote of 24:33 after seven weeks. Several senators objected to the recommendations Hoar had made as Grant's Attorney-General regarding the appointment of nine circuit judges. Others did not care for his support of civil service reform. Again others still smoldered because of his opposition to the impeachment of President Johnson; few appreciated his forthright independence. The last nominee to be rejected, U. S. Circuit Court of Appeals Judge John J. Parker, appointed by President Herbert Hoover in 1930, was the victim of the narrow adverse vote of 39:41. Parker was opposed by organized labor because, as a judge, he had handed down an opinion upholding the legality of "yellow dog" contracts; by Negro groups because he had allegedly made anti-Negro remarks in his campaign for Governor of North Carolina ten years earlier; by Progressive Republicans who deemed his economic views too conservative.

Third, *"Senatorial Courtesy."* This custom accounted for several rejections. It appears to have been the *sole* factor involved in the unsuccessful nominations of William B. Hornblower and Wheeler H. Peckham of New York by President Grover Cleveland in 1893–94, by adverse votes of 24:30 and 32:41, respectively. In both instances, the rejection was directly attributable to the outspoken opposition of Senator Hill of New York, who was instrumental initially in Hornblower's defeat on grounds of senatorial courtesy, and who successfully applied the same magic concept when Cleveland substituted another New Yorker, Peckham, four months later. The doctrine was also invoked, although on a secondary basis, in the already described cases of Walworth and Woodward.

Fourth, *the limited ability of the nominee,* considered entirely objectively, has played a definite part in some rejections. Thus, President Grant's nomination of George H. Williams in 1873 was withdrawn by him five weeks later in the face of swelling protests by the legal profession and the public. His talents as a lawyer were mediocre; he had lost several important cases; and the bar simply adjudged him unqualified for this high office. Woolcott's rejection was due, in part, to the lack of support of his fellow Republicans, who considered him to be a man of limited ability.

Fifth, *political unreliability of the nominee.* The best illustration of this factor in rejections of nominees to the highest bench is another among the several unsuccessful Grant appointments—that of Caleb Cushing. Nominated in 1874, after the furor of the Williams designation had subsided somewhat, Cushing's age—seventy-four at the time—was used against him repeatedly in the confirmation debate. But the outstanding reason for the opposition to him was his political instability. A veritable political chameleon, Cushing had been, in turn, a Whig, a Tyler Whig, a Democrat, a Johnson Constitutional Conservative, and a Republican. (Shades of the Vicar of Bray!) No one really knew what his political and ideological positions were, and, with opposition from almost all political factions mounting daily, Grant withdrew the nomination.

Some Concluding Thoughts. Only two individuals both nominated *and* confirmed as Justice of the Supreme Court of the United

States have declined to accept that august office, William Smith in 1837 and Roscoe Conkling in 1882; both men wished to stay in the active political arena. To them, as well as to others who declined to serve during the first half-century of the Court's existence, e.g. John Rutledge, John Jay, Levi Lincoln, John Quincy Adams, such offices as Chief Justice of South Carolina (Rutledge), Governor of New York (Jay), or active political federal office (Adams), seemed infinitely more inviting and important than that of Supreme Court Justice. For the Court did not really come into its own until the long Chief Justiceship of John Marshall raised it to the level of power and esteem it enjoys today.

The appointment procedure was evidently more casual in the early days of the country, for today, if a nomination is made, the President knows that the man will accept if confirmed. This indicates that the office is held in higher esteem, as well as the fact that communications are vastly improved. Of course, we have no way of knowing how many men decline presidential offers of appointment to the Supreme Court or their reasons for doing so, but speculation would indicate that there are not many who would turn down the post if offered to them.

During the first seventy-five years of the country's independence, a substantial number of appointments to the Supreme Court was rejected or delayed on the basis of opposition to the President, rather than opposition to the candidate. Frequently, the Senate decided to wait until after an election or until the inauguration of a new President before it would act. It even went so far as to reject two of Tyler's appointments despite the fact that the Whigs, under Clay, had lost the election of 1844. It might be construed as a sign of increased political maturity to note that no man has been rejected because of opposition to the appointing President since Stanberry in 1866.

Senatorial courtesy or personal senatorial vendettas or both have been major factors in the confirmation procedure. Although some candidates have been rejected on this basis, often the Senator can do no more than delay confirmation for a period of time. While certainly important, these factors are not as potent as is commonly supposed.

Generally speaking, opposition to nominees does not seem to be based on the qualifications or lack thereof of the men appointed.

Perhaps the nominee's personal shortcomings play a bigger role when the appointee is not confirmed, but even here such a generalization is difficult to make because when opposition is personal or political or both, an attempt is made to place the opposition on more "respectable" grounds.

While the name of Charles Evans Hughes (on his appointment as Chief Justice) does not appear on the list of "unusual delays," the struggle in his case was fought with great bitterness—although within a fairly brief period—and almost caused him to withdraw. Brandeis was the man most fiercely opposed for his personal qualities or the deficiencies which his opponents thought they perceived in him. Here too, however, the overt opposition emphasized more "respectable" reasons.

In general, opposition to the confirmation of a Supreme Court Justice seems to reflect the existence of deep-seated concern in the nation. It thus became more frequent and noticeable as the influence of the Court became more apparent. In the early years of the Court's history, relatively little concern was shown about the potentially "unfortunate effects" of justices of uncertain, or certain, convictions. At the present time, when there are so many issues in which large numbers of people are deeply concerned, almost every appointee is made to run the gauntlet; he may even feel slighted if his appointment is unopposed, since this could be interpreted as a sign that he is not regarded as a man who carries very much weight. The appointment and confirmation procedure has become one more battleground on which large issues are fought out before the public eye.

QUALIFICATIONS AND EXPERIENCE:
THE SPECIAL CASES OF ENGLAND AND FRANCE

In endeavoring to explain and analyze the staffing of the courts of England and France and in comparing their respective judiciaries, it is necessary to remain cognizant of the two different types of law that govern the systems concerned—the common or Anglo-Saxon law in England and the civil or Roman law in France. There are fundamental differences between the two countries— and far greater ones become apparent, of course, in contrasting one or both with the prevalent norms and practices in the United

States. But it is above all the very position of the judiciary that provides the key to these differences. Under the Roman law tradition of the Continent, the judiciary is a part of the administrative-executive hierarchy, as will be explained in considerable detail in Chapter VI, and it constitutes a *profession* distinctly separate from that of the practicing lawyer. Where the common law tradition holds, however, the legal profession is practically an autonomous body, the judges being drawn from its ranks—notwithstanding the different mode and mood of selection that governs in England as compared with the common law United States.

Nevertheless, we have already observed that a common ideal, that of impartiality of the appointees, is held by all three lands for both selection and tenure of their judiciaries, and that each is therefore willing, as it must be, to protect their independence and provide a large measure of immunity in order to achieve it. But the techniques of training and selecting judges and ensuring their impartiality differ widely.

ENGLAND

Unlike the United States, England divides its legal profession into two major groups: the *solicitors* and the *barristers*—and it is impossible to be both *concurrently*. The former deal mainly with the general public; they conduct about 95 per cent of the ordinary legal business of the country, leaving the remaining highly important work of advocacy in the courts to the barristers, who see the layman only when so instructed by a solicitor. The best analogy of the difference between the two groups is found in medicine: the general practitioner and the consultant. Barristers are consultants for the solicitors—the latter do all the ordinary work of the law and call in the barristers when they need their services, either for advice or for conducting a case in court. Solicitors *instruct* barristers—that is the key to their relationship.

The Solicitors. The "office lawyers" of the judicial structure, the solicitors are obviously its veritable workhorses. It is they who deal directly with the clients, who do the routine legal office work and who prepare the spadework for cases to be argued at the bar of the higher courts by the barristers. But they also enjoy the right of audience in the magistrates and county courts, and they do a great deal of advocacy in these courts. They handle practically all of the drawing-up of legal documents, such as transfer of property. In short, the approximately 20,000 practicing solicitors do the bulk of England's ordinary legal work. Having determined to become a solicitor on the conclusion of his university career, and having undergone additional legal training, the aspirant then takes a number of special professional examinations. Passing these, he becomes a "Solicitor of the Supreme Court" and commences his career. He will also probably join the Law Society, a voluntary association of solicitors with certain statutory powers. Every practicing solicitor is entitled to become a member of this society, and usually does. Incidentally, university training is not an absolute requirement—over half of the solicitors are not university products.

The Barristers. The approximately 2000 practicing barristers, however, comprise England's best-known legal talent. Their chief function is to render legal advice to solicitors at all times, either generally or in preparation for trial, and, of course, to conduct cases. Thus, they argue all cases in the higher courts—cases which, by custom and tradition, are almost always given to them directly by the solicitors who have processed them in a preliminary manner, rather than by the clients themselves. The barristers are professionally specialized and usually—although not inevitably—highly experienced members of the legal profession. It is from their ranks that the Lord Chancellor normally selects the judges on behalf of the Crown.

The barristers are divided into two groups or ranks: "Junior Barrister" and "Queen's Counsel." The latter are referred to colloquially as "Silks" from the fact that they are entitled to wear a silk gown instead of the "stiff" gown worn by the Junior Barristers. These two gowns are different in style also: those worn by the "Juniors" are like academic gowns with flowing sleeves, those of the "Silks" are along simpler lines. One becomes a "Silk" upon the recommendation of the Lord Chancellor, on reaching the very top status in the profession, seldom until the completion of ten years' successful practice. The "Silks" constitute the elite among the barristers and they receive higher fees than the average barristers. Their main tasks include pleadings in court, where they must be accompanied by a "Junior." It is from the ranks of Queen's Counsel that judges are mainly chosen. Yet sometimes a man may become a judge without being a "Q.C."—e.g. Lord Chief Justice Parker was made a judge as a "Junior." He had been Junior Counsel, the Government vehicle for Crown business in the High Court. Normally those who have "taken silk" for at least seven years, and in the cases of the higher courts for at least ten years, may expect to be called to a judgeship in the event of a vacancy. But the number of superior court judges is low, and when one of the rare promotions does come, it is viewed with great awe and respect by the appointee himself as well as by the legal profession and the public at large. Judges of the High Court are *invited* to become such by the Lord Chancellor—i.e. without soliciting the post—whereas those of the County Court are appointed from the ranks of those who have *applied* to the Lord Chancellor for consideration of appointment.

All barristers are members of one of the four historic *Inns of Court* which, in effect, constitute both a "law school" and a professional organization. They arose as a result of the custom—as old as Magna Charta—of lawyers to live together during terms. Self-governing, historic organizations—dating officially back roughly to the time of Edward I (1272–1307)—the Inns of Court, literally meaning "town houses," used to be residences of noblemen and bishops. There students as well as members of the bar used to study, live, work, eat, and pray. But they are no longer residences in the full sense of the term—although some barristers still do live there. The names of the four are: Lincoln's Inn, Gray's Inn, Inner Temple, and Middle Temple.

Under the tutelage of barristers, England's future lawyers were trained as such in the past in the Inns rather than in a university law school. Today, these students may attend the lectures of the Council of Legal Education, a joint committee for education from the four Inns of Court. They are tested by examiners of the council, and on passing the examination and having kept their "dining terms" for three years, they apply to the "Benchers," the governing body of the Inn, for admission as a barrister. This "dining term" rule is a relic of the days when students of the common law lived in the Inns of Court and had to attend in the hall of their Inn for dinner and for the exercises in "mooting" and other forms of learning before becoming barristers. To this day they thus must dine in the hall on three nights in each dining term if they are also university students; if they are not, they must dine there six nights a term.

Once admitted to the bar, the young barrister remains under the general jurisdiction of his Inn of Court throughout his career, in fact his life, and it is his Inn which constitutes both his professional protector and his disciplinarian. A full measure of *esprit de corps* flows naturally from life and membership in the Inn. Disciplinary problems are further under the supervision of the General Council of the Bar, a special body elected by the members of the Bar to act for it in a wide range of matters. Authority to expel a barrister for misconduct is given to the "Benchers" of the Inn of which he is a member.

The legal education provided by the Law Society for solicitors —nominally the "lower" branch of the profession—differs from that given to the barristers. It is based on intensive courses, practical training, and a year's compulsory attendance at a recognized law school. The future barrister, on the other hand, must pass the bar examinations which involve a background in general legal principles despite the fact that he may not have had specific training in these; that he often does not attend the elaborate series of lectures provided by the Council of Legal Education; and that he is not required to have practical training. However, recently a pledge has been exacted from candidates to spend six months as pupils in chambers. In part as a result of this distinction in preparation, there has been some criticism and clamor, notably in certain segments of the press, e.g. *The Economist*—to effect the following changes: (1) include common basic training for both branches to make possible an easy interchange between them; (2) allow barristers to form partnerships—they are not permitted to do so now, or to deal directly with the clients (even the fees are settled between the solicitor's and the barrister's clerks); (3) alleviate the allegedly strained relationship between the General Council of the Bar and the governing bodies of the Inns of Court.[36] Considerable doubt is thrown on the latter point, however, by the fact that many of the members of the General Council of the Bar are "Benchers" of their respective Inns.

[36] Cf. the analysis in "How to Rescue the Bar?," *The Economist*, January 9, 1960, pp. 86–7.

Moreover, the reason the solicitor is given a thorough practical training in a solicitor's office by being apprenticed to the latter for three years, if a university product, and five years if not, is because solicitors are entitled to practice from the moment they are admitted and can do legal work of practically any kind *at once* for the general public. But a barrister is never employed directly by a member of the public; he is employed, or instructed, by a solicitor—and in practice is a highly trained lawyer before he gets work of any importance from a solicitor.

Even given the possibility of a judicial appointment, his attractive social status, and the "psychic income" he may receive from his membership in the profession, the future of the barrister's branch of that profession is nevertheless undergoing some examination. One of the several significant considerations is his relatively low income, which has undoubtedly been a factor in the gradually declining number of practicing barristers. As of January 1960, fewer than 2000 men—and only 80 women—were active members of the British bar, 75 per cent of these in London. In one recent year, 1957–58, only 91 barristers began practice—the lowest new entry on record, which was more than offset by the 112 members who *left* the bar during that period.[37]

Yet whatever the problems of the parent profession may be—and they have been exaggerated at times—the English judges are very likely the most highly esteemed, the most independent, and, relatively speaking, the most generously paid in the West. There is little doubt that these three factors account in considerable degree for the universally high quality of British justice, properly so often cited and envied by much of the rest of the world.

FRANCE

The Republic of France, together with several other states on the Continent of Europe, goes considerably farther than Britain in distinguishing between judges, public prosecutors, and officials of the powerful Ministry of Justice on the one hand, and privately practicing lawyers on the other. Although there is a clear-cut distinction between the British solicitor and the barrister, both are nonetheless members of the legal profession and may commence

[37] Ibid. p. 86.

their advanced legal training together. In France, however, the bench is a separate career; it is not viewed as a reward for legal excellence or renown as it is in both Britain and the United States.

A future French student of the law must thus decide at the very outset of his schooling whether he wishes to become a private lawyer or a judge or prosecutor or go to the Justice Ministry. If the former, he attends law school and chooses among three specialties open to him: *avocat,* roughly akin to the British barrister; *avouet,* the approximate equivalent of the British solicitor; or a third category, *notaire*—a lawyer especially trained in drafting and registration of legal papers, related in name only to the American notary public who need not be a lawyer. These three groups comprise the French *legal,* not the *judicial,* profession. The French youth desirous of becoming a judge of the lower or appellate courts or one of the other two allied vocations, follows a totally separate path of training, for—as has been explained earlier—the judiciary of France is, in effect, a branch of the government, of the civil service.

Training for a Judgeship. Until the judicial reforms of 1958–59 took place, after finishing law school the prospective member of the judiciary would initially gather some experience, a sort of apprenticeship, in a law office. From there he usually moved on to a minor office in a local court, while awaiting his appointment. In the meantime, when he deemed himself sufficiently qualified, he would take an examination and, if successful, could then look forward to the anticipated placement in the judicial system. It was common practice to assign him first as a public prosecutor and then gradually move him into a jurist's position.

However, as a result of a governmental decree in 1959, designed to broaden and further professionalize their background, experience, and training, all potential applicants for judgeships must now also attended the *Centre National d'Études Judiciaires* (National Center of Judicial Studies) for four years. To become students there, the hopeful are selected on the basis of competitive examinations, both in legal subjects and in the general liberal arts. The students, who are paid by the government for attending the C.N.E.J., must be law school graduates and under 27 years of age. The first year consists of on-the-job training in public departments on all levels of government, the next three of legal studies per se.

The successful graduate is now assigned to one of the courts of first instance, the *tribunaux d'instance,* in accordance with his class standing—assuming he wishes to become a judge. But he is also eligible for the *parquet,* the office of the public prosecutor, or for service in the Ministry of Justice. The National Center of Judicial Studies was evidently designed to do for the judiciary what the National School of Administration (*École Nationale d'Administration*) has done so well for the upper echelons of the general civil service—the creation of a competent, reputable, and esteemed group of public servants.

In the United States and, to a more modified extent, in Britain, the selection of a lawyer as a judge customarily represents the culmination of a long and quite frequently distinguished career in the law—subject to certain obvious political contingencies in the United States. But in France the judge is chosen from the *judicial profession,* for which he prepared by special schooling and examinations—a profession just as medicine, teaching, and the law are. Although he is not particularly well paid, he enjoys considerable prestige and a high social rating. We shall now see him and his *confrères* in action on the bench.

III

COURTS,

COURTROOMS, AND JURIES

TYPES OF COURTS: TRIAL AND APPELLATE

Each of the countries discussed in this book has a system of courts in line with its own needs and choice. Some have similar features, but no two are truly alike. Speaking broadly, however, each of these systems—and in fact practically every known judicial system in the world—has endeavored to separate the jurisdiction of *trial* (first instance) and *appellate* (review) courts. Some courts do fulfill both functions, but in that event—if justice is to have any meaning at all—it will at the very least have separate dockets for each area. This applies, for example, to an English Court of Quarters Sessions and a French *Cour d'Assize*. In a rather limited sense, the Supreme Court of the United States is also constitutionally empowered to exercise jurisdiction in the trial as well as in the appellate area, termed *original* and *appellate* by Article III of the Constitution, where these designations are found. However, that high tribunal's original jurisdiction docket is usually empty; seldom, if ever, has it exceeded more than 1 per cent of the volume of cases handled by the Court. The overwhelming number of cases and controversies that reaches the highest tribunal in the American judicial hierarchy does so under its appellate jurisdiction. In fact, as will be explained in more detail in Chapter V, the Supreme Court may, save in the instance of litigation involving two or more of the 50 states, share its original jurisdiction with courts below—i.e. its original jurisdiction is concurrent with them —which, in effect, means that seldom if ever will the Supreme Court decide such a case in its role of a trial court.

TRIAL COURTS

Trial courts perform the function their title clearly implies: they *try* cases in the first instance, as tribunals of original jurisdiction. Cases commence there because they are statutorily required to do so. More often than not they are also completed upon the pronouncement of the verdict of guilt or acquittal which may or may not, depending upon organizational requirements and—under certain conditions—choice, have come about as a result of a trial by jury. Rather obvious illustrations of trial courts of varied jurisdiction are a United States District Court; a Court of Common Pleas in the Commonwealth of Pennsylvania; a French *Tribunal de Grande Instance;* and the Queen's Bench Division of the High Court of Justice for England and Wales.

Again depending somewhat upon the law of each land and governmental subdivision concerned, both law and fact are taken into account at the bar of a trial court, and both parties to the litigation, plaintiff as well as defendant, are presumably accorded a full opportunity to present their respective sides of the case or controversy. In common law countries, such as most of the English-speaking lands, a single judge customarily—but by no means always—presides over a trial alone; in statutory law systems, such as those found in most continental European states, normally a trio or more judges sit *en banc.* When a jury sits in a case, the judge *charges* (instructs) it at the conclusion of the presentation of pertinent evidence in the law and procedures attendant upon the case. The jury then returns a verdict upon completion of its deliberations, which may last from a few hours to several days.

APPELLATE COURTS

The *raison d'être* of a court of appeals is to provide an appellate forum for decisions rendered in a trial court. Such appeals are presumably limited to questions of law at issue in the litigation below, but in some circumstances they may also deal with questions of fact, either collaterally or on their own merits. In any event, it is often extremely difficult to separate categorically matters of law and fact, and the final word on such a distinction, if it is crucial to the question of the grant of the petition for review, will necessarily lodge in the appellate tribunal itself. In large measure, this decision depends upon the tribunal's statutory authority and the extent and nature of the discretionary review powers given to it. Some appellate courts *must* accept all cases properly presented to them for review—such as the United States (Circuit) Court of Appeals, which has no effective discretionary power to decline to accept appellate petitions. Others, for example the United States Supreme Court, possess all but complete statutory *discretionary* authority as to whether or not to accept a case brought before them for review from below, although in theory there are *some* cases of mandatory review—as will be shown in Chapter V. Again other appellate tribunals, the British House of Lords, for one, have more discretionary power to accept or reject criminal cases than civil cases—or vice versa. Courts of appeals are usually multiple-member bodies; as a rule, three or more judges sit *en banc* to hear the appeal without a jury.

Well-known appellate courts, in addition to those already named above, are two of England and Wales's courts of appeals, the Court of Appeal (for civil cases) and the Court of Criminal Appeal (for criminal cases). The latter court is empowered to *retry* the case, a departure from the normal role of appellate tribunals. The *Cour de Cassation,* at the apex of the regular French judicial system, is a further example of a court of appeals. In the instance of some appellate courts, such as the English Court of Criminal Appeal, appeals may be instituted only by the defendant. In the United States, although the federal government may usually appeal an adverse decision of a trial court on a point of law, it is barred from appealing on a point of fact; this means that, in effect, it cannot appeal an adverse verdict in a criminal proceeding on the basis of the factual evidence presented in court on pain of violating the double jeopardy safeguards of the Fifth Amendment to the United States Constitution. However, since this Bill of Rights provision does not automatically apply to the states—unless it is present in their own constitutions, as it is in many instances—state governments are not necessarily similarly inhibited from appealing a defeat in a court below. A few states expressly permit such appeals by the authorities in these circumstances, among them Connecticut, whose empowering statutory provision was specifically upheld by the U. S.

Supreme Court in the famous case of *Palko v. Connecticut,*[1] against Palko's contention that it deprived him of "due process of law" under the Fourteenth Amendment to the Constitution.

COURTROOM PROCEDURE: GENERAL

There are essentially two methods in which society, through its judicial and legal organs, may approach a member of its body politic accused of an offense—either by presuming his innocence until it has effectively succeeded in proving him guilty under due process of law, or by presuming his guilt unless he successfully disproves that assumption under similar processes.

"INNOCENT-UNTIL-PROVED-GUILTY":
THE ACCUSATORIAL PROCEDURE

It is a cornerstone of Anglo-Saxon justice that an accused is innocent until proved guilty beyond a reasonable doubt. Few, if any, concepts are more deeply rooted in our traditions. There have assuredly been violations of that principle from time to time, especially during periods of war and other emergencies when an occasional departure from it has been justified on the grounds of necessary expediency, however distasteful. Thus, writing painfully for a divided (6:3) bench that ". . . hardships are part of war, and war is an aggregation of hardships. . . ." Mr. Justice Black, one of the outstanding civil libertarians of all time to sit on the Supreme Court of the United States, upheld the compulsory evacuation of 112,000 persons of Japanese ancestry from their homes on the West Coast, among them 70,000 native-born American citizens, none of whom had been *specifically accused* of disloyalty. On the whole, however, the record of the common law countries, such as Britain and the United States, has been good in this regard. The layman may quite naturally be quick to adjudge a person guilty in his own mind—more often than not joined by the press, particularly in America—but the Anglo-Saxon legal profession on both sides of the Atlantic Ocean and throughout the English-speaking world has done its best to adhere to the time-honored principle that a person is innocent until he has been

[1] 302 U. S. 319 (1937). See Mr. Justice Cardozo's opinion for details.

proved guilty beyond a reasonable doubt by due process of law. As Mr. Justice Brennan wrote for the Supreme Court in a decision highly unpopular with Congress and the public at large, in which the Court by a vote of 7:1 reversed the conviction of one Clinton Jencks, a suspected Communist perjurer, who had not been permitted to attempt to impeach testimony given to the Federal Bureau of Investigation, on the basis of which he had been convicted in the trial court: ". . . the interest of the United States in a criminal prosecution is not that it shall win a case, but that justice shall be done." [2] Of course this philosophy applies equally to civil proceedings, whether or not the government is a party to it. In the summary words of one of Mr. Justice Jackson's opinions concerning one attorney's right to compel another to disclose certain papers involved in the litigation concerned, "A *common law* trial is and always should be an adversary proceeding." [3]

Thus, the presumption of the innocence of the accused, until proved otherwise is transformed into courtroom procedure in the Anglo-Saxon countries. Essential to it are the ancient basic safeguards inherent in that philosophy of the law, safeguards which, to a greater or lesser degree, are fundamental to the notions of liberty and justice that pervade the political system of the liberal democratic West. Among these are the privilege against self-incrimination; the right to cross-examine witnesses; the writ of *habeas corpus*—perhaps the most basic right of all; and many others in the same general category, however their interpretation may vary from jurisdiction to jurisdiction (e.g. in the 50 states of the United States, seen as separate entities when dealing with purely state matters in contrast to the specifically enumerated Bill of Rights provisions strictly applicable to the United States as a federal entity).

The Judge's Role. An important feature of the accusatorial type of procedure is that the judge does *not*—except as noted below and in rare instances in order to call forth certain types of evidence, usually of a technical nature—insert himself into the substantive questioning during the trial. Quite naturally, he does, indeed he must, hand down rulings on various motions, points of order, and other problems that may arise during the course of the

---

[2] *Jencks v. United States*, 353 U. S. 657 (1957).
[3] *Hickman v. Taylor*, 329 U. S. 495, at 516 (1946). (*Italics supplied.*)

trial. He is—or certainly he is expected to be—in complete charge of courtroom procedure, and as such possesses a considerable residue of what legal parlance terms *judicial discretion*. In this connection, that intriguing compound noun demands an application:

> . . . enlightened by intelligence and learning, controlled by sound principles of law, of firm courage combined with the calmness of a cool mind, free from partiality, not swayed by sympathy nor warped by prejudice nor moved by any kind of influence save alone the overwhelming passion to do that which is just. . . .[4]

In that discretion, the judge will question a witness only to avert grave injustice, not to advance the case for either side. He is not in any sense an active elicitor of truth regarding the testimony presented. In essence, he is an independent arbiter between the state and the individual or between the litigating parties. This is a concept basic to the common law adversary proceeding mentioned by Mr. Justice Jackson, a system that "sets the parties fighting." According to Professor Max Radin, one of the giants of jurisprudential theory and practice, that system has been in vogue since its adoption in Rome in the fourth or fifth century B.C., when—for better or for worse, and quite conceivably the latter—the judge's task changed from determining the truth to the umpiring of a competition.[5] There is little doubt that many, probably most, of today's lawyers would have great difficulty of conceiving of a trial as anything else.

"GUILTY-UNTIL-PROVED-INNOCENT":
THE INQUISITORIAL PROCEDURE

In France, to use the most obvious example, a different philosophy regarding the legal process in this area obtains. Not independent arbiters, the French judges are part of the machinery of the state, and courtroom procedure in criminal trials is characterized by the *inquisitorial* method, known as the *parquet*. Here, the presumption

[4] *Davis v. Boston Elevated Railway*, 235. Mass. 482, at 496–7. Quoted by Felix Frankfurter, *The Case of Sacco and Vanzetti* (Boston: Little, Brown, & Co., 1927), pp. 90–91.

[5] Max Radin, "The Permanent Problems of the Law," 15 *Cornell Law Quarterly* 10–11 (1929).

may be said to be implicitly one of guilt, although, of course, no civilized land proceeds on such an assumption. (Indeed, Max Radin refers to the notion of presumption of guilt as a "curiously persistent calumny," and views the presumption of innocence as "inherent in the French Declaration of the Rights of Man and the Citizen."[6]) So much painstakingly accumulated preliminary investigation by a professional judge—the *juge d'instruction* (examining magistrate)—has already preceded the courtroom trial that the judge or judges presiding at the trial may presume the defendant to be guilty of the offense charged. Nonetheless, they actively, often vehemently and acidly, participate in the courtroom questioning of witnesses as well as of the accused—who, incidentally, may not invoke the Anglo-Saxon privilege of refusing to take the stand on grounds of possible self-incrimination. But had the investigating judge been unable to find any evidence of apparent guilt, the accused would very likely never have been brought to trial. In a sense, this preliminary "investigation," the *enquête,* is an advanced form of grand jury investigation and indictment—still so prevalent in the American courts—but with the significant distinction that whereas the *enquête* in France is conducted by professional magistrates, the American grand jury is composed entirely of laymen.

The "Juge d'Instruction" and the "Enquête." The office of the *juge d'instruction*—which is not a uniquely French institution—combines the powers of a prosecutor and a magistrate. His function is to determine the truth on behalf of the state, with the aid of the police. But he may commence an investigation only upon notification by the public prosecutor (*procureur*), who had been advised of the crime by the police. The powers of the *juge d'instruction* are awesome, indeed. He may call witnesses and badger them. He may ask suspects to re-enact the alleged crime. He may open mail and tap telephone wires. He may even keep people in jail indefinitely, since the revered Anglo-Saxon institution of the writ of *habeas corpus* is unknown in France. He may commission experts to investigate and report on special aspects. But perhaps the most potent weapon in his considerable arsenal is the famous, or infamous, *confrontation de témoins* (confrontation of witnesses), which is unlike anything in Anglo-American legal procedure. When two or more witnesses tell contradictory stories, the *juge*

[6] *The Law and You* (New York: Mentor M34, 1948), p. 99.

d'instruction calls them into his office together for a *confrontation.* There, under his watchful and experienced eyes and ears, and in the presence of a court official who writes down every uttered syllable, each witness is quoted repeatedly, with the other(s) invited to point out "errors" or "discrepancies" in his testimony. As a result of this *confrontation,* perjured testimony in criminal cases has been almost eradicated.

When the evidence in a case—including that of the police—has been procured, and both the defense and prosecution lawyers, the latter headed by the *procureur,* have had access to the complete *dossier,* the *juge d'instruction,* who will usually consult the *procureur,* can now send the case to trial on his own authority. Since he is highly unlikely to do so unless he has become convinced of the presence of guilt, the resultant trial itself thus turns largely into a public verification of the accumulated record. In the event of a statutorily designated *serious* crime, the entire record of the investigation must be reviewed before it is admitted to trial by a *chambre d'accusation,* a judicial body at the appellate court level.

Although the broad powers accorded to the *juge d'instruction* are sometimes criticized even by French legal scholars as being akin to a "star chamber" proceeding, that charge is grossly exaggerated. The *juge d'instruction* operates in a system which refuses to concede to the contending parties control over the presentation of evidence—either its submission or its impeachment by cross-examination. During the trial, such control becomes the duty of the presiding judge. In the absence of cross-examination, the data procured by the *enquête* are necessary to ensure the accuracy of testimony. That investigation, however "tough" it may have been, is characterized by a patient, painstaking discovery procedure, which has presumably solved mysteries and eliminated discrepancies in testimony. All the evidence is recorded in the *dossier,* enabling the *juge d'instruction* and the *procureur* to build the case against the accused. But it does more: it permits the presiding judge to conduct the trial meaningfully.

In its final impact, the French system of the *enquête* would appear to be at least as effective as the Anglo-American accusational method, where all the evidence is brought out for the first time, almost in the manner of a game, by testimony and cross-examination in open court before trial judge and jury. A grand jury indictment, after all, requires only a *prima facie* case. One may well contend that a criminal trial in a French court is an investigation rather than a battle between two opposing platoons of learned counsel.

"VOX DEI" OR
"VOX POPULI" IN ACTION: THE JURIES

There is no doubt that the institution—if that it be—of the jury is at once one of the most fascinating and interesting and most incredible and exasperating aspects of the judicial process. Many a curse has been uttered against a jury and what it stands for even while the other party to the litigation at hand has voiced a prayer of gratitude in its behalf! Sundry types of juries exist; but essentially a jury is plainly a group of citizens of predetermined number whom a duly constituted public official has called together for the purpose of answering a question. They were evidently first used in Athens as long ago as five or six centuries *before* the birth of Christ, came to Rome some ten centuries later, and then to France in the ninth century. The modern Western world traces their origin to the England of almost 800 years ago, where, in the early stages, they comprised a body of men to aid the monarch in dispensing justice by attesting to certain facts. Whatever their age, they have been praised and attacked ever since. Although many countries, not necessarily excluding dictatorships, still resort to juries, the institution has clearly suffered a steady decline. This is more true of the *grand jury* than it is of the *trial (petit) jury,* but both types have experienced decreased usage, especially in England and Wales, where the grand jury was abolished by the Administration of Justice (Miscellaneous Provisions) Act of 1933, and where the use of the trial jury in civil cases was seriously curtailed by the same law. Today, the jury is used in less than 10 per cent of all cases in the British Isles. In France, the grand jury is, of course, not at all employed in view of the role of the *juge d'instruction.* Juries are still widely used in the United States, particularly on the federal level; in many of the 50 states, however, juries, notably grand juries, have fallen into at least partial disuse. Everywhere, more and more cases are decided by jurists sitting without a jury, sometimes as a result of statutory or constitutional provisions, sometimes by the agreed-upon choice of the parties to the suit. Now it seems almost unbelievable that the courts of Athens in the fifth century B.C. were composed of a jury only—there was no judge at all! Moreover, the more significant the nature of the case, the greater the number of the jurors. Thus Socrates was tried by a panel of 501 in the fourth century B.C., and Alcibiades' trial on charges of treason featured 1501 jurors. These able Attics were drawn from all over the Athenian communities by a complicated but apparently highly effective lot system.[7]

The foundation of the English jury system is traceable to the French empire under the Carolingian kings. As part of their successful attempt to unite their empire, a procedure called the *inquisition* or *inquest* was devised. Carried out by representatives of the monarch, its purpose was to call together various bodies of neighbors in order to ask questions and explain the sovereign's "immemorial" rights. The Norman conquerors subsequently carried the concept of the inquest to England and used it first in the compilation of the 1086 *Domesday Book*. This book, which listed the ownership of all English land, was compiled from data obtained from royal administrators who gathered neighbors together in various parts of the country and used them as their source of information. This served to establish the right of the state to obtain data from its citizenry.

The first true juries were used to discover facts under the various writs of the *Possessory Assizes,* e.g. litigant neighbors decided who was dispossessed and who owned a certain piece of land under the writ of *Novel Disseisin* ("newly dispossessed"). Thus trial by jury was closely linked with the protection of possessions; indeed, Norman dukes and English kings sometimes specifically granted to both private persons and churches the privilege of having their rights ascertained by this method. However, these juries merely filled a particular need at a particular moment in English history; they were permitted to die out and are thus not the bona fide predecessor of the modern English jury. The latter institution was founded under King Henry II in the second half of the twelfth century. Today, it would look strange, indeed, in its initial form, for then it represented what was, in effect, a combination grand

[7] See Charles P. Curtis, *It's Your Law* (Cambridge: Harvard University Press, 1954), p. 102.

and trial jury that enabled the accusing body (the modern grand jury) also to pass judgment on the guilt of the accused (the modern trial jury). Ultimately these two functions were separated, thus heralding the now axiomatic difference between them.[8]

THE GRAND JURY

The chief distinction between a grand jury and a petit (trial) jury is that the former does not pass on a defendant's innocence or guilt. The grand jury merely determines whether, in its hopefully considered judgment, sufficient evidence exists or has been brought to its attention to justify a trial on criminal charges. Grand juries do not ordinarily sit in civil charges. A trial jury, on the other hand, determines whether to convict or acquit. Hence a grand jury does not return a verdict; it listens to a bill of evidence presented to it by the legal representative of the prosecuting authority, who must draw up the formal written accusation, and who almost invariably dominates its deliberations. The grand jury then decides whether or not the evidence warrants an *indictment,* also known as a *true bill.* It does return such an indictment in approximately 95 out of 100 instances. In effect, this charges one or more persons with having committed a felony or misdemeanor. The indicted party thus does not actually have an opportunity to give his side of the story to the grand jury; his day will come in the courtroom in the event of a trial. He is entitled to know the names of witnesses that have appeared before the grand jury, but little else— except, of course, the evidence presented at the preliminary hearing before the committing magistrate. There is no *right* to appear before the grand jury; one is invited or ordered to come before it. When it does not find sufficient evidence the grand jury issues what is known as an *ignoramus,* or a *no bill,* in which case the would-be defendant is not brought to trial.

By most accounts, the institution of the grand jury antedates the Magna Charta of 1215, but its origin is a soure of considerable disagreement. Some have claimed to find its traces among the Athenians. Certainly Athenian history, while mentioning the trial jury repeatedly, is quite silent on any body of citizens whose duty

[8] See Frederick G. Kempin, Jr., *Development of the Common Law* (Philadelphia: Lecture Note Fund, University of Pennsylvania, 1959), I-3-2 and I-3-7.

it was to accuse. The first grand jury, then called *presenting jury,* was apparently established by the Assize of Clarendon in 1166 under King Henry II. Here was enacted:

> . . . that inquiry be made in each county and in each hundred, by twelve lawful men of the hundred and four lawful men of every township—who are sworn to say truly whether in their hundred or township there is a man accused of being or notorious as a robber, or a murderer or a thief, or anybody who is a harborer of robbers, or murderers, or thieves, since the king began to reign. And this let the justices and sheriffs inquire, each before himself.[9]

Interestingly enough, this provision was not intended to protect the liberties of freemen, but rather to protect the monarch's interests. By 1352, in the reign of Edward III, the principle that a man's indictors were not to serve both as grand and trial jurors was firmly established. The modern concept of the grand jury dates from 1368, when Edward III impaneled 24 men to act as county inquisitorial boards. It was not until three centuries later that a grand jury, in two successive cases—*Colledge's Case* and *Earl of Shaftesbury's Case* [10]—for the first time refused to return an indictment, on the grounds of "ignoramus," that it "knew nothing." According to at least one historian, the immediate reason for the ignoramus in one of the cases was that the sheriff and many of the grand jurors were friends of the Earl of Shaftesbury! [11]

Information. In England and Wales, where the grand jury was abolished as a result of the aforementioned statute of 1933, and in parts of the United States, the fast and easy method of *information* has been adopted in its place. It is a simple and efficacious device whereby the public prosecutor merely submits his charges in the form of an affidavit of evidence, supported by sworn statements, to a court of original jurisdiction. Usually a preliminary hearing has here, too, been held before a committing magistrate, and after these brief procedures the accused is ready to stand trial. In France, the already described *enquête* by a professional judge

[9] Ibid. p. 7.
[10] 8 How St. Tr. 550 (1681) and 8 How St. Tr. 759 (1681).
[11] George J. Edwards, Jr., *The Grand Jury* (Philadelphia: George T. Bisel Co., 1906), p. 29.

takes the grand jury's place. Only in the United States is the common law heritage of that body still somewhat popular.

The documented history of the process of information is not nearly so complete as that of the grand and the trial juries. However, Blackstone remarked that "there is no doubt that this process by information . . . is as old as the common law itself." [12] Although its usage lagged until the twentieth century, the process did figure prominently in the now famous case of Peter Zenger, commonly recalled as a milestone in the battle against censorship. In 1735, an attempt was made to indict that courageous editor of a weekly newspaper for libel against the royal government. When the grand jury ignored the bill of charges against him, Zenger was then held on the basis of an information filed by the attorney-general of the province. After a celebrated trial, in which he was so ably defended by Andrew Hamilton, he was acquitted. It was the English settlers who had brought the grand jury with them from their native land, together with all of the other civil rights they had enjoyed there. America's revolutionaries thought of it later as a means to prevent political prosecutions, but it was never tested for that purpose after the founding of the new nation.

Grand Jury Guarantees Today. The opening sentence of the Fifth Amendment to the Constitution of the United States in effect guarantees grand jury action on the *federal* level. Exempting members of the armed forces, it specifies that no person may be held for a "capital, or otherwise infamous crime," unless on a presentment or indictment of a grand jury. At present, there are six capital crimes under federal law (murder, rape, bank robbery, kidnapping with resultant harm, treason, and espionage) for which the ultimate penalty may be imposed—although this is done but rarely today. Under the several state laws some 30 crimes are classified as capital, including aiding a suicide in Arkansas and burning a railroad bridge in Georgia. The grand jury provision of the Fifth Amendment is not automatically applicable to the *states,* the Supreme Court of the United States having held repeatedly that its absence in these constituent parts of the nation does not in and of itself violate those "fundamental principles of liberty and justice which lie at the base of all our civil and political institu-

---

[12] 4 Com. 309.

tions." [13] Indeed, barely one-half of the 50 states still retain the grand jury system; the balance have replaced it with the device of information which may be also employed by the federal government in *noncapital* cases at the district court level.

The standard federal or grand jury consists of a panel of 16 to 23 members, who are presumably chosen at random from the local register of voters. Unlike the trial jury it need not be unanimous even at the federal level, but a minimum of 12 jurors must agree on an indictment or an ignoramus. A grand jury is usually impaneled for a maximum period of 18 months at a time—unless discharged earlier by the judge to whom it reports—and it is called together during that time whenever need for its services arises. Its proceedings are secret and may not be released to the public.

Presentments. In a sense, however, grand juries do considerably more than merely determine the sufficiency or lack of evidence submitted to them; they conduct certain types of public investigations, enabling them to hand up a finding known as a *presentment*. Such an action represents a formal accusation against one or more individuals, made on the grand jury's own motion, calling attention to alleged illegal or improper activities—but not including an indictment. The first presentment on record came in England in 1683, charging certain Whigs, including the Earl of Macclesfield, with disloyal and seditious conduct. The accused brought an action for libel, but the court held for the grand jury, thus establishing the propriety of its report.[14]

Presentments have a habit of stirring up the public as well as the bar and quite frequently give rise to general anguish. Thus, when during the "quiz-show" scandals in 1959 a New York grand jury handed up a presentment on its own initiative, which was highly critical of the television and radio industry, General Sessions Court Judge Mitchell D. Schweitzer impounded and permanently sealed it. He declared that no grand jury had a right to return a report dealing with the activities or morals of a *private* individual or corporation. A bill designed to embody Judge Schweitzer's position in a law subsequently failed to pass the New York State legislature. However, the matter was reopened tangentially two years thereafter when in the *Wood* case the New York

[13] *Palko v. Connecticut,* fn. 1 *supra.* Cf. also *Hurtado v. California,* 110 U. S. 516 (1883).   [14] 10 How St. Tr. 1330 (1684).

State Court of Appeals ruled in a 4:3 decision that a grand jury has the following choices: return an indictment, dismiss the charge, or remain silent.[15] Since this case involved *public* officials only, the ban would now seem to have been extended to all elements of the citizenry. The action in the suit was brought by one James F. Wood, the foreman of a Schenectady county grand jury, to compel Judge Charles M. Hughes of the New York Supreme Court to make public a report the jury had filed on its own motion regarding the county highway department.

The narrowly decided Wood case serves to put the role of the grand jury and its problems into proper focus. The majority decision, written by Judge Stanley H. Fuld—and applauded by most of the lawyers' associations of the State of New York—declared that the jury involved made an inquiry which, by its own admission, failed to find that there was "willful and corrupt conduct" by a public official, the verbiage of the statute under which the jury had been impaneled, and hence simply decided to chart a course of action on its own that was both unauthorized and publicly deprecatory of reputations. The dissenters, on the other hand, urged that such action by the grand jury was a reaffirmation of the basic American principle at common law and of considerations of ethics in government, namely, that an authorized body of citizens may, indeed must, take appropriate action to counter the suppression or burial of evidence of "tyranny and corruption in public office." In April 1961, Judge Schweitzer augmented his earlier action by expressly warning four grand juries he impaneled that "under no circumstances" were they to submit a presentment to his court. And the New Jersey State Supreme Court ruled that presentments must not be used to rebuke individuals in the absence of conclusive proof of wrongdoing.

Whatever the verdict in the above case, there is little doubt that while grand juries have traditionally been vested with broad powers to investigate crimes, such powers are not and cannot be either unlimited or unbridled. They are not powers unto themselves, but are essentially lay bodies whose actions are subject to judicial scrutiny and remedial relief. In that role grand juries have existed for such interesting and significant investigatory and stand-by pur-

---

[15] *Wood v. Hughes,* decided February 23, 1961.

poses as juvenile delinquency, waterfront crime, narcotics traffic, subversive activities, quiz-show manipulation, corruption, and tax evasion, to name but a few of the myriad assignments given to a panel of these jurors who necessarily become fairly well-steeped in their particular area of jurisdiction. And they have often done a good job. The grand jury may well be cumbersome, amateurish, time-consuming, annoying, emotional, and a fifth wheel in the legal process, but on balance it does appear to serve as a potentially powerful arm of direct democracy. This is true if one is willing to accept the philosophy of the institution in the first place and provided one has faith in the competence and intelligence of one's fellow citizens—a not inconsiderable set of assumptions.

THE TRIAL OR PETIT JURY

Normally, when the average person or the public press refers to a jury, he has in mind the trial or petit jury. In some areas, e.g. in parts of Pennsylvania, it is known as the *traverse* jury, a term deriving from medieval days when Norman French was beginning to displace Latin as the official language of the Court of England. As has been indicated, the trial jury has suffered a decline in many parts of the world, but it is still a popular institution. In England and Wales it is employed only sparingly and almost exclusively in criminal cases; the same is true of France, possibly more so. Its last important, and evidently secure, stronghold in the Western world is in the United States, where the concept of a trial by a jury of one's peers still thrives, particularly on the federal level.

In England and Wales, where trial by jury for most cases effectively commenced during the reign of King Henry II (1154–89), the accused is still entitled to such a trial for all serious crimes and for a very limited number of substantial civil infractions. With certain important qualifications, this jury may be demanded in all English and Welsh courts save in the highest and the lowest, but the privilege may be waived if the defendant so wishes. A jury is always impaneled in criminal cases if the accused pleads not guilty to an indictable offense. However, since 1933 the courts in England and Wales have been given considerable discretion as to whether or not to call a jury in a case; it is hence not astonishing that this discretion has been used almost exclusively to prevent a jury impaneling. If a trial jury is employed in a case, it is compiled from local townspeople and customarily consists of ten men and two women, whose verdict of guilt or acquittal must be unanimous. There are a number of reasons for the decline of the trial jury in England and Wales, among which the more important are first, the belief that a judge sitting alone can perform the jury's functions at least as well, and usually better; second, the desire for a speedy trial; and third, the fact that the litigants rather than Her Majesty's government pay the jurors' fees.

The French Republic resorts to jury trials solely at the level of the assizes, the courts of original jurisdiction for serious crimes. Trial by jury has no deep roots in France. Indeed, although it once did exist as part of customary procedure in some parts of the country, it disappeared under Charles VII in the fifteenth century, not to be reimported from England until the Revolution. Today, it consists of 12 local *citoyens;* there is no unanimity requirement, and frequently the verdict is rendered by a simple majority vote. The French have no great fondness for the jury system, and their adherence to the inquisitorial mode in the judicial process leaves little or no genuine purpose for the existence of a trial jury per se. In any event, they generally view the jury as an instrument designed to becloud the issues in a case, prone to confuse everybody concerned.

But the United States, where a total of approximately a million jurors serve in some 100,000 cases annually, has remained broadly faithful to the concept of a trial by jury. This is necessarily true at the level of the federal courts, due to the requirements of the Sixth and Seventh Amendments to the Constitution, so carefully composed by the Founding Fathers. The Sixth ascertains a trial by jury in *all* federal criminal cases; the Seventh does the same for all civil cases where the value of the controversy exceeds the sum of $20—which today to all intents and purposes means in practically every instance. Although all 50 states also provide for at least *some* type of trial by jury, the specific guarantees of the Bill of Rights, as noted in several instances above again do not automatically apply to them—the Supreme Court never having viewed this procedural right as being "implicit in the concept of ordered liberty." [16] But the highest tribunal does insist that a

[16] *Palko v. Connecticut,* fns. 1 and 13, *supra.*

defendant in a state proceeding be given a *fair trial,* on pain of a violation of the Fourteenth Amendment's due process of law and equal protection of the laws clauses. Among the several state practices affecting juries that have *inter alia* been held to constitute an *unfair* trial, were the systematic exclusion of Negroes from juries [17] and the labeling of Negro jurors with brown, and white jurors with white, selection tickets.[18] Moreover, if a state law or the state constitution expressly calls for a trial by jury, that state must grant it.

However, since each of the states may prescribe its own brand of jury system, a variety of practices exists—and many, if not all, of these would be unconstitutional if practiced by the federal authorities. Thus, some states grant a jury trial only in criminal cases, others in just a few civil cases, again others in a few of each. At the federal level, it is generally possible to *waive* a trial by jury, provided common consent of the parties to the suit and of the judge assigned to the case is obtainable; but many states will not permit such a waiver, especially not in capital cases. Another significant procedural difference between federal and state practices of judicial procedure is that the common law mandated unanimity requirement for the 12 federal jurors is not necessarily present on state juries. Using the calendar year of 1961, exactly one-half of the states authorized a jury verdict by 75 per cent of the jurors in civil cases, with eight states extending this form of split verdict also to noncapital criminal cases. Some 20 states authorized civil trials with juries of less than 12 members, usually merely six—the Central District Court of Worcester, Massachusetts, for example. The governing question concerning these state practices at the bar of the United States Supreme Court is not a matter of comparison or method, but the essential one of whether or not the defendant received a fair trial under due process of law.

SELECTION AND IMPANELING OF JURIES

As a rule, American juries are drawn by the jury clerk from the voting lists of area citizens; in England and Wales, by the sheriff

[17] *Norris v. Alabama,* 294 U. S. 587 (1935).
[18] *Avery v. Georgia,* 345 U. S. 559 (1953).

from a list of householders compiled by local authorities; in France, from departmental lists of male citizens of 30 years of age and over who possess all civic and political rights. In Switzerland, juries sitting with the Criminal Chamber of the Federal Tribunal to try certain criminal cases are *elected* by the people for six-year terms on the basis of one juror for each 3000 inhabitants. Happily, in more and more jurisdictions, notably in the United States, automation has entered, with I.B.M. machines increasingly taking over the task of clerks and mahogany drums in choosing the jurors to be called for service. In two tests in New York and New Jersey, these electronic jury pickers put on a fine show by selecting eight jury panels of 275 names, each in 20 minutes—a process that formerly averaged two days! Theoretically, every adult of voting age is eligible for jury duty and may expect a call, unless he has served for more than a year in prison on a criminal charge and has not been pardoned for that offense. This limiting proviso is statutorily applicable only to the federal government, but most of the 50 states now have the same, or at least a similar, requirement. While everyone else of voting age might thus expect to get a jury call at one time or another, it is not only relatively easy to avoid jury duty—incidentally one of the chief criticisms leveled against the jury system—but entire segments of the body politic are exempt either by law or by custom. Among the occupational groups exempt almost automatically in the vast majority of jurisdictions, especially in the United States, are professionals such as lawyers (a jury composed of arguing and battling lawyers would, indeed, be an interesting experience!); physicians (too busy to serve); pharmacists (likewise more or less indispensable professionally); clergymen (a jury must deliberate, not pray); teachers (essential occupation); and others in similar capacities. Other busy employed people can normally avoid jury service by submitting affidavits of indispensability from employers. Again others, such as nursing mothers and those with a large family of young children, will normally have to do little more than to write a letter to the court concerned in order to be excused by the judge. But a failure to do at least that much may conceivably result in a citation for contempt of court, which occurred in the case of one young Iowa mother who repeatedly flouted requests for an explanation by the court and finally found herself incarcerated for criminal contempt. Generally, however, in most states women need not serve at all, if they so choose, and in a good many others they are automatically exempt.

If none of the reasons cited is acceptable to the court as a bona fide excuse, an irresponsible citizen can, of course, still evade his presumed civic duty by confessing to one of the many otherwise validly disqualifying factors present in jury impaneling. Among these are: confession of prejudice for or against one of the litigants, acquaintance with either party to the suit, however slight; predisposition against capital punishment in a crime for which it may be imposed; allegation of sympathy with or opposition to certain pertinent philosophies of life involved in the case, no matter how tangentially; and so forth. In fine, only those who are really willing and able to serve will normally do so in the long run. On the other hand, jurors may naturally be removed from a panel for any one of the above or a myriad of other reasons by the procedure of appropriate *challenges* that are granted both to the defense and the prosecution as a matter of regular courtroom procedure in Britain and France as well as in the United States. In the United States, challenges are essentially of two types, *peremptory* and *for cause*. A peremptory challenge entitles either side of the parties to the suit to request the removal of a would-be juror by *fiat*—no reason need be given; the mere request, whatever the motivation, will be honored. A limited number of these challenges are granted to both sides, the defense customarily being permitted more than the prosecution. But when a panelist is challenged for cause, the challenger must be in a position to advance a bona fide reason for his demand for the disqualification, and it will have to be one sufficiently related to the substantive or procedural aspects of the litigation involved in order to be acceptable in the eyes of the court.

These challenges not infrequently delay the impaneling of the trial jury for days, occasionally even for weeks. For instance, the arduous and delicate task of selecting a jury to sit in the trial of the eleven top-echelon members of the Communist Party-U.S.A. in Judge Harold Medina's U. S. District Court for the Southern District of New York in 1949, consumed a total of six weeks! In view of the nature of the charges of the case, which ultimately resulted in the conviction of all eleven (although with varying sentences),[19] both defense and prosecution were painstaking in their questioning of each prospective juror, many of whom managed to extricate themselves from serving by simply acknowledging that they could not possibly have an open mind regarding the guilt of the accused. In a completely different vein, it has proved so difficult at times to impanel a jury that clerks of courts literally have had to stoop to "grabbing" people off the streets in search of a trial panel—as occurred near City Hall in Philadelphia in 1955 and 1956 and to a U. N. delegate taking a walk in Paterson, New Jersey, in 1958.

"Blue Ribbon" Juries. Among the charges voiced frequently against juries, both grand and petit, are that they merely give vent to the established community prejudices; that they are utterly unqualified to render judgment; and that, worse still, they are composed quite consistently of people who are not only uninformed in civic affairs but are actually not interested. In Illinois, at least for a while, the names of those persons who consistently failed to vote were placed at the top of prospective jury lists. This intriguing practice was apparently based on the assumption that nonvoters make excellent jurymen! In large part to meet the general criticism of unsatisfactory juries, some states in America have statutorily adopted either a special jury-test or, more commonly, the *blue ribbon jury.* This device is used in various jurisdictions of California and Utah, for example, with judges of certain courts giving potential veniremen a series of test questions involving legal terminology that the jurors would almost certainly encounter. If an otherwise eligible juror misses more than one or two of these chiefly multiple-choice and matching questions, his chances of disqualification in these courts are excellent.

Blue ribbon juries made their first appearance in England in 1730 (then called *struck juries*) and were employed solely at the level of the King's Bench and only for "trials of great consequence" or when the subject matter of the case was beyond "discussion of the ordinary freeholder." Court officials would choose 48 men "competent, intelligent, and less prejudiced than the ordinary juror." Somewhat later, the privilege to impanel such a blue ribbon

[19] *United States v. Dennis,* 72 F. Supp. 417 (1949).

jury was extended to all courts, who could authorize it for either of the above two reasons or, generally, when an ordinary jury "could not be impaneled."

In New York County (Manhattan), where the controversial device of the blue ribbon jury was adopted at the turn of the current century, some 3000 among the regular jury panel of 60,000 veniremen are designated for that special jury duty. According to the New York State statute, which permits resort to the blue ribbon jury in all counties of more than one million population in those cases in which the court of jurisdiction believes "the public interest would be served," it may "in its sound discretion" order a trial by a panel of these blue ribbon jurors on application of either party in a civil action and by either the prosecution or defense in criminal cases. However, as the law specifies, the motion may be granted only on a showing that "by reason of the importance or intricacy of the case, a special jury is required"; or "the issue to be tried has been so widely commented upon . . . that an ordinary jury cannot without delay or difficulty be obtained"; or that for any other reason "the due, efficient and impartial administration" of justice in the particular case would be advanced by the trial of such an issue by a blue ribbon jury. On the whole, the veniremen on these juries are professional people and white collar workers—but expressly exempted are clergymen, physicians, dentists, pharmacists, embalmers, optometrists, attorneys, as well as servicemen, firemen, ship's officers, pilots, editors, reporters, and copy readers. Women are equally qualified with men, but since they also are granted exemption, a woman may serve or not at her discretion; in general, this has meant that blue ribbon juries are practically always all male panels.

New York County blue ribbon jurors—or *special jurors,* as the law refers to them—are selected from those accepted for the general panel of 60,000 by the county clerk, but only after each has been *subpoenaed* for a personal appearance and has testified under oath as to his qualifications and fitness. The statute carefully prescribes standards for selection by declaring ineligible and directing elimination of sundry categories which necessarily go far beyond the ordinary panel disqualification tests. The special jury panel is not one brought into existence for any particular case under New York State's practice or for any special class of offenses or type of accused. It is part of the regular machinery of trial in those counties that meet the above-mentioned required minimum population figure, which New York County, with its approximately two million inhabitants, does more than amply.

It is hardly surprising that the institution of the blue ribbon jury, which today is in general use in approximately one-quarter of the states,[20] would ultimately face a test at the bar of the highest court of the land. It came in 1947, not surprisingly involving the New York County special jury, and it was closely followed by a similar test barely one year later.[21] By the narrowest of margins of 5:4, the Supreme Court of the United States upheld the statute and the practice against the dual challenge that it violated both the due process of law and the equal protection of the law clauses of the Fourteenth Amendment to the Constitution. The majority of the Court contended that the professionals and white collar workers on the jury could well come from widely varying salary groups, and that neither clause cited requires that a jury must represent all components of society. As Mr. Justice Jackson wrote for the majority in the first case: "Society also has a right to a fair trial. The defendant's right is a neutral jury. He has no constitutional right to friends on a jury." [22] Furthermore, the majority felt that a state might reasonably use blue ribbon juries as a means of rendering the administration of justice more efficient. But four justices dissented vigorously, led by Mr. Justice Murphy, who insisted that an accused person was entitled to be tried by a jury fairly drawn from a true cross section of the population, and that a blue ribbon jury simply could not be representative of that basic concept. "One is constitutionally entitled to be judged by a fair sampling of all one's neighbors," wrote President Franklin D. Roosevelt's ex-Attorney-General in his dissenting opinion, joined by Justices Black, Douglas, and Rutledge,

> not merely those with superior intelligence or learning . . . The vice lies in the very concept of "blue ribbon" panels—the systematic exclusion of all but the "best" or most learned or most intelligent of the general jurors. Such panels are com-

[20] E.g. Ala., Del., Ind., Mich., N.J., N.Y., Tenn., Vt., Va., W.Va.
[21] *Fay v. New York,* 332 U. S. 261 (1947) and *Moore v. New York,* 333 U. S. 565 (1948).   [22] *Fay v. New York,* loc. cit. at 288.

pletely at war with the democratic theory of our jury system, a theory formulated out of the experience of generations.[23]

However, the majority decision has never been overruled and thus stands as *res adjudicata*. A blue ribbon jury may be both unfair and undemocratic, but these qualifications do not render it *ipso facto* unconstitutional. Furthermore, it may be well to reiterate that the notion that juries should be composed of men and women from all walks of life is a relatively recent one. At its English origins, the jury was composed of favorites of the Crown, men of position, or men who were indebted to the Crown. In the early history of the jury in the United States, it comprised a handful of propertied men. Several decades passed before sex and property qualifications, to name but the two more obvious restrictions, were no longer prerequisites to participation in jury duty.

THE TRIAL JURY AT WORK

The typical trial jury of twelve men and/or women, augmented by one or more alternates to guard against a case of sudden indisposition of a juror, sits *en banc* throughout the course of the trial. It does so no matter how long the trial may take, generally compensated inadequately on a daily fee basis. Each of its members is presumed to listen impartially and with an open mind to both sides of the case; may not discuss the trial with anyone, no matter how near or dear; and, at least in theory, is not permitted to read, view, or hear any media of communication whatsoever during the trial. The latter requirement may well be an illusory one: there is every reason to believe that, regardless of a juror's conscientiousness and dedication, few public-spirited individuals would in fact literally deny themselves the news of the day. However, if either side in the litigation succeeds in presenting incontrovertible proof of such an aberration, it may move for a mistrial or even a directed verdict of acquittal. The jurors are not permitted to take notes; they are to "register the evidence as it is given, on the tablets of [their] memory and not otherwise." [24] When the presiding judge

---

[23] *Moore v. New York,* loc. cit. at 570.

[24] Indiana Supreme Court, as quoted by L. L. Bromberger, "Jurors Should Be Allowed to Take Notes," 32 *Journal of the American Judicature Society* 57–8 (1948).

has delivered his charge—to be discussed below—to the jury at the end of the trial, the jury retires for its deliberation until it reaches a verdict. If this proceeding stretches into the night, the jury is "locked up" in a nearby hotel and will subsequently continue its work on the following day or days. If, after a reasonable period of time and repeatedly unsuccessful balloting, a trial jury is unable to arrive at a verdict of guilt or acquittal, the judge will declare it to be a *hung jury,* dismiss it, and remit the case to the docket for a trial *de novo* before an entirely different judge and jury.

"Hung" Juries. A famous example of a hung jury was that of the first Alger Hiss case,[25] when the jury deadlocked 8:4 for conviction after countless ballots, and Federal District Judge Samuel Kauffman declared it hung. Not long thereafter, Hiss was convicted of perjury in a new trial and with a new jury before Federal Judge Henry W. Goddard.[26] A sensationalized illustration of not just one but two hung juries in succession was the highly publicized Finch-Tregoff murder-conspiracy case in California. The first trial ended in a hung jury in March 1960, after 13 weeks of courtroom action, with the jury hopelessly deadlocked upon 37 hours of deliberation. At that time it stood 10:2 for convicting Dr. R. Bernard Finch, but 8:4 for his mistress Carole Tregoff's acquittal. The retrial was completed in November 1960, and again ended in a hung jury, this time having lasted 17 weeks, with the jury taking 59 ballots during 70 full hours of active deliberation. Mr. Edwin Fry, foreman and the only male on the standard size jury, reported that the 12 jurors had unanimously found Dr. Finch guilty of the murder of his wife, but were divided 9:3 on the degree of murder to be charged—three jurors stubbornly insisting on a second-degree finding. On Miss Tregoff the jury had split 9:3 on the degree as well as the guilt—and that same count held against both regarding the conspiracy charge! Another seemingly interminable trial finally resulted, ending the fiasco in March 1961 in a clear-cut verdict against the two defendants: both were found guilty of conspiracy, Dr. Finch being convicted of first-degree murder, Miss Tregoff of second degree. (Reference is sometimes made to a *hanging jury,*

[25] *United States v Hiss.* Jury hung in August 1949.
[26] *United States v. Hiss,* 88 F. Supp. 559 (1950). See also *United States v. Hiss,* 107 F. Supp. 128 (1952).

which is a *grand jury* that has earned a reputation for almost certain indictments.)

INSTRUCTING THE JURY: THE JUDGE'S CHARGE

One of the highlights of a trial in the pertinent federal and state courts of the United States, and a crucial point in its evolvement, is the presiding judge's *charge* to the trial jury upon completion of testimony, arguments, and motions by all concerned. It comes after the summations by the prosecution and the defense, the latter customarily speaking last. Much thought goes—or should go—into this charge, which is intended as an exposition of the law, and is rarely, if ever, given in writing. The judge must take great care to ascertain that its contents are clear, to the point, comprehensive, illuminating, and that they pose readily discernible alternatives to the jury panelists, who *now* may take notes and sometimes ask for further instructions on details. It is a highly complicated business for them. Thus, in the words of an appellate tribunal:

> The trial judge should not as a rule limit himself to stating good set terms of law culled from the codes and the reports. Jurors need not legal definitions merely. They require proper instructions as to the method of applying such definitions after reaching their conclusions on the facts.[27]

Moreover, the judge must see to it that his charge is scrupulously fair to both sides in the dispute. But it is of supreme importance to the accused. It should be "the safeguard of fairness and impartiality and the guarantee of judicial indifference to individuals." [28] Many a charge has ultimately ended in a mistrial; many another has been found to be defective on points of law by appellate courts. In brief, the judge's charge to the jurors, which is almost always necessarily complicated, sums up the case, pinpoints the chief issues involved, and concludes with the admonition that the jury must bring in a verdict of "guilty" or "not guilty"—addressing itself to each of the charges and/or counts at issue and, if a choice is permissible under law in homicide cases, determining the degree of punishment. Any verdict of "guilty" must have taken into ac-

[27] *People v. Odell*, 230 N.Y. 481 at 487–8 (1921).   [28] Ibid.

count the absence of *reasonable doubt,* often a very difficult problem. There are no in-between stages of a verdict, although in certain cases in some of the 50 states juries are empowered to mitigate their judgment of guilt in homicide cases by a recommendation for mercy, which is normally binding upon the judge. It was just such a binding recommendation by the third jury in the Finch-Tregoff murder case that saved Finch from the electric chair.

Under certain limited circumstances, a judge may express a value judgment on the evidence in charging his jury, but this is valid only in isolated instances. Superior Judge Leroy Dawson in the second Finch-Tregoff case startled courtroom observers by telling the deadlocked jury that the evidence showed "a willful and deliberate taking of human life." When one of the defense attorneys repeatedly attempted to stop the judge from reading his comments, he found himself twice cited for contempt. Judge Dawson cited a 1934 amendment to the California Constitution as his authority and a San Diego case in 1958 as his precedent.[29] Since his own case resulted in a hung jury, Dawson's action was not challenged further. On the other hand, judges everywhere are free to comment upon a jury's verdict once that has been announced, although many jurists believe that practice, too, to be at least unwise if not unethical; but it is not illegal, unless expressly interdicted by statutory or constitutional mandate.

Setting a Verdict Aside. In *civil* cases, but generally not in *criminal* cases save for a few states that permit it, a judge may *reverse* the jury's verdict. This frequently occurs in so-called *negligence* cases, in which jury lawlessness, in the form of excessive verdict, is not uncommon. A federal case of this nature, which was widely featured in the public press in 1959 because of an open clash between Justices Whitaker and Douglas, was *Inman v. Baltimore and Ohio Railroad.*[30] A District of Columbia jury had held the railroad negligent in stationing a man where he could be knocked down by a drunken driver, and it awarded the former $25,000. However, the judge who presided over the trial in his United States District Court set the verdict aside as being "irrational." When the United States Court of Appeals upheld the district judge, Inman appealed to the United States Supreme Court which, in a 5:4 opinion, af-

[29] *The Sunday Bulletin* (Philadelphia), November 6, 1960.   [30] 361 U. S. 138.

firmed the judgment below. What provoked the headlined outburst by Mr. Justice Douglas, and his insistence that the Supreme
Court has a duty to enforce the guarantee of a jury trial and to
prevent the lower courts from setting too strict a standard, was
Mr. Justice Whitaker's concurring opinion. In it, the latter had
scoffed at the idea that the railroad had been negligent and suggested that the only way that it could have prevented the accident
was to have the employee encased in an army tank. This, in the full
glare of an "Opinion Monday"—to be described in detail in Chapter V—Mr. Justice Douglas denounced, in person and from the
bench, as "smart-alecky." Barely one year later, however, with
Justices Black and Douglas dissenting vehemently, the Supreme
Court itself, for the first time in 24 years, reversed a jury's verdict
awarding damages to an injured railroad worker.[31] Judge Charles
E. Wyzanski, Jr., of the federal trial court below had upheld the
jury's verdict, but denounced it in no uncertain terms, asserting the
case was devoid of "any evidence of negligence"—and had re-
frained from setting it aside solely because he felt bound by what
until then had been Supreme Court doctrine in these cases.[32]

The judges may also set aside a jury verdict if it is clearly based
upon an obviously mistaken notion of the law involved in a case.
Yet all these practices in American courts are a far cry from the
English and Continental systems, where the trial judge is permitted, if not expected, to comment upon the weight of the evidence and the credibility of witnesses throughout the course of the
trial, and to allow the jury to know his opinion on the merits of
the case. On the other hand, the average judge in the United States,
too, has the power in all cases to order a verdict of *directed
acquittal* before a case goes to the jury—a motion made often by
defense counsel almost as a routine matter, but granted rarely.
Moreover, the judge may take a case out of the jury's hands if it
becomes evident that there are only questions of law involved, no
facts being in dispute at all. And among the myriad of reasons why
a judge may order a *retrial* is, a clear case of basic confusion
among the jurors—one that obviously affected the verdict in such
a fashion that there is grave doubt in the mind of the presiding

[31] *New York, New Haven, and Hartford y. Hennagan,* 364 U. S. 441 (1960).
[32] Ibid. As reported in 272 F. 2d 153, at 155–6 (1959), and in *The New York
Times,* November 22, 1960.

judge that the jury has fulfilled its part in seeing that justice is done. Thus, in a New Jersey automobile accident case the jury had returned from its deliberations and its foreman upon being asked by the judge, "Have you agreed upon a verdict, Mr. Foreman?" answered, "My name isn't Foreman. My name is Admerman." When the trial judge refused to recognize this interesting reply as sufficient reason to declare a mistrial, defendant Naomi Haberli appealed to the Appellate Division of the New Jersey State Superior Court, which unanimously ordered a retrial, citing Mr. Admerman's response, as well as the grossly excessive award granted by his fellow-jurors, as a *prima facie* example of the type of "basic confusion" necessitating a new trial.[33] But it should be understood that no trial or appellate judge will readily tamper with a jury's verdict, no matter what his private opinion may be.

"General" and "Special Verdicts." On the basis of the somewhat questionable assumption that the jury fully comprehends the judge's instructions concerning the applicable substantive legal rules, it is usually required to return a *general* or *over-all* verdict in favor of one party or another. Theoretically, as already indicated, this jury verdict is based on the *facts* of the case, the judge himself having determined the rules of *law*—although it is not always possible to separate facts and law. In practice, however, the general verdict permits the jury to do what it pleases: it gives no details, simply reports its decision, and no one either really knows or may safely predict just what facts a jury found from the evidence. Judge Jerome Frank, a life-long and severe critic of the jury system as a fact-finding institution, viewed the judge's charge as little more than an elaborate ceremonial routine, and he argued that of all the possible ways that could be devised to arrive at the falsity or truth of testimony, "none could be conceived that would be more ineffective than trial by jury." [34] He and many other legal authorities have long contended that *special* verdicts, in which the jury is asked to answer a *specific* question of fact, are a far preferable method of arriving at a verdict that is just to all concerned. In a special verdict procedure the trial judge charges the jury to report its findings—presumably even if these are simply beliefs—

---

[33] *The New York Times,* December 15, 1960.
[34] Jerome Frank, *Courts on Trial* (Princeton: Princeton University Press, 1949), p. 20. (Italics supplied.)

about certain particular issues of fact raised during the course of the trial, facts which, at least in theory, a jury should be able to weigh and determine with a modicum of accuracy and reliability. Whatever the type of jury verdict advocated, the degree of perfection one may expect from the human institutions that comprise the judicial process is necessarily a limited one.

The British judges employ a charge rather similar to that found in the tribunals of the United States, but they provide more guidance to the jury during the trial. No charge is used in the courts of France. Instead, the French presiding judge, who actively directs the proceedings in the courtroom by interrogating the accused and witnesses, submits to the jury—in the infrequent instances of its presence in a case—a list of questions which the twelve panelists are required to answer with a simple "yes" or "no." Standard examples of these queries would be, "Did the accused prove his alibi?"; "Was the accused present at the scene of the crime when it was committed?"; "Was the act of homicide one of self-defense?"; and always, "If you find the defendant guilty, were there any extenuating circumstances?" Clearly, by his interrogation the judge tries to give to the jury the most lucid picture possible as a matter of guidance. The jury, its members voting individually and in secret, answers these questions specifically and thereby reaches its verdict—if necessary by a *majority* vote, in contrast to the unanimity requirements of the American federal judicial system. However, should the division among the jurors prove to be uncomfortably close, such as 7:5 or even 6:6, the presiding judge may assume the power of determining the verdict with the aid of the two associate judges (there are always three judges at the assize-trial level). But in that event the verdict is almost certain to be one of acquittal.

In West Germany today the entire courtroom examination in criminal trials is conducted by the judges, while the prosecuting attorney and counsel for the defense sit mute and take notes. Counsel is privileged to put a question only when the judges have completed an examination calculated to bring out fully and fairly all that a witness might tell. Jurors are taken from a local list of "outstanding" citizens and impaneled for a term of one year. Judge and jury sit on the bench together and participate jointly and equally in deliberation on a case.

JURIES: BLESSING OR EVIL?

It is not easy to be objective about juries—and few observers are. Certainly there is but little doubt that juries throughout the Western world have declined considerably both in significance and esteem during the past century. Often, when they are not held in utter contempt by their professional critics, they are merely tolerated as a necessary, and at times admittedly convenient, evil. In large measure, the juries have brought this opprobrium on themselves—no matter how innocent and perhaps even understandable their response to the demands of the legal process may be. But it is difficult, indeed, to defend the institution in the face of some of the seemingly inexhaustible fiascos in which they seem perpetually to find themselves. Examples are legion, and a few will suffice as illustrative of the patent fact that it is not easy to be a defender of the system.

Thus, we again turn to the aforementioned Finch-Tregoff case, this time the first 1960 trial, to find the jury at its worst. According to an interview (!) granted to United Press International by one of the members of the panel of five men and seven women that had just been declared a hung jury:

> . . . at one point a near fight broke out. At the height of one heated debate, a male juror threatened to throw another [a female] out of a window and turned over the jury table—he used to be boxer—before she ran to the door. She was hysterical and pounded on the door for the bailiff.[35]

Another woman juror, who also readily and beamingly gave an interview to U.P.I., reported that at least three "propositioning" notes had been passed to one of the women on the panel. An extra bailiff was then brought in to stand guard at another woman's hotel room door after the former notes came to light.[36] Another illustration is the young mother from Bedford, Indiana, who confessed that as a member of a jury panel in the 1950's she voted to convict the accused of rape—despite the fact that she believed him to be innocent. She did so against her own judgment, she readily

[35] *The New York Times,* March 13, 1960.   [36] Ibid.

admitted, because "I knew I had those children at home and we would never get out of there if we tried to argue it out with the others." [37] And to conclude the unfortunately almost inexhaustible instances of the kind of antics that have served to bring opprobrium to the institution: In March 1961, under the guise of registering a *coup* in what it called "public service," the Hearst Corporation-owned station WBAL-TV in Baltimore induced, evidently without any difficulty, nine of twelve jurors to appear before the studio camera and re-enact their deliberations that resulted in the conviction of one Melvin Davis Rees, Jr., for murder and kidnapping. This intriguing performance, which featured in great detail the thoughts and reasoning that culminated in the verdict, came on the evening *prior* to the scheduled sentencing of the convicted man! As a result, defense counsel succeeded in obtaining at least a temporary postponement of sentencing and raised a series of legal questions based upon this jury TV debut—which the *Baltimore News Post,* also a Hearst-owned medium, termed "a reportorial breakthrough of the traditional silence of the jury room." [38] Considerations of law, ethics, morals, and taste were evidently deemed insignificant.

Evil? Continuing naturally at this juncture of the analysis with the indictment of the institution of the jury—which Balzac once defined as "twelve men to decide who has the better lawyer"— there is considerable, indeed fairly conclusive, evidence that the average jury reaches its verdict in most instances by a kind of "happy" compromise. Not being able to agree on a financial award in a civil case, for example, the various panelists will write down separate figures, add the total, divide it by the number of jurors, and thus attain peace of mind! In homicide cases a host of revelations again and again points to jury compromises. Thus, unless they are expressly forbidden to do so by statute or by the judge's charge, jurors will frequently decide a case of murder by "compromising" between first degree murder and acquittal by settling for a second degree conviction—usually totally unjustified by the facts in the case. Or the flip-of-the-coin or lot method is employed in order to get the nasty business over with. Our legal periodicals

[37] As quoted by John F. X. Irving, "The Jury May Be Out Permanently," 6 *National Review* 177 (September 1958).
[38] See Jack Gould's article in *The New York Times,* March 25, 1961.

and other literature are replete with data corroborating what has been said above.[39]

Moreover, it is almost impossible for the wandering mind of the ordinary juror to overcome conclusively the histrionics that so often characterize presentation by counsel. Both prosecution and defense generally conduct what is to all intents and purposes a legal sporting combat, with each side following evidence by counter-evidence, examination by cross-examination, witnesses by counter-witnesses, each one sworn to tell the truth and nothing but the truth. Not infrequently, this touching search for the truth results in statements in open court that are clearly out of order. But even if the judge so holds, as he often does, and asks the jury to disregard the statement at issue, it has been uttered, of course, and it is conjectural at best whether it can be wiped from the jurors' minds. To arrive at the veritable truth behind what one long-time observer of juries styled "the curtain of flimflam and obfuscation," [40] may well boil down to a jury verdict on the basis of which side, in its judgment, seemed to tell fewer lies. Hence, in the words of Judge Frank, based on his many years of active experience in the legal and judicial processes:

> . . . the jury is the worst possible enemy of the "supremacy of the law." For "jury-made law" is, par excellence, capricious and arbitrary, yielding the maximum in the way of lack of uniformity, of unknowability.[41]

Accordingly, he and others would prefer the trial judges to hear and decide cases alone, the assumption being that judges are presumably trained in the law, which jurors are not, and that they function in a setting which is open to considerably more scrutiny than juries.

Blessing? A natural and main source of endorsement of the jury system is the trial lawyer, who has a vested interest in influencing it—even if this is done by persuading the generally bewildered jurors that black is really white. Few, if any, defense

[39] Cf. Frank, op. cit. p. 122, and the University of Chicago jury studies, conducted by Prof. Harry Kalven.
[40] David A. Dressler, "Trial by Combat in American Courts," 222 *Harper's Magazine* 32 (April 1960).   [41] Frank, op. cit., p. 132.

lawyers in a criminal case would argue against it! But the venerable institution's defense does not need to rest its case on such
pragmatic grounds. Many a legal scholar, far from decrying the
factors of emotion, prejudice, and sympathy that are undeniably
major determinants in jury verdicts, holds that these very factors
advance the cause of justice because they represent the "socially
adapted intuitive law" of the various communities to which we
belong. Thus, Charles P. Curtis and Harold J. Berman have contended repeatedly that the jury reflects "the intuitive part of us,"
which they view as a necessary counterbalance to the equally
essential "intellectual part of us" in the judge.[42] This is particularly appropriate if one keeps in mind that, in the final analysis,
the first and foremost function of a jury is to choose between conflicting testimony, testimony so frequently beclouded by histrionics and legalistics as to render an "intuitive" judgment all but
inevitable—at least up to a point. Something can certainly be said
for the time-honored principle of being judged by a group of one's
peers. Moreover, much of the adverse criticism would appear to
depend on which side of the case one's interests lie, and whether
the jury sits in a civil or criminal case.

One of the most articulate and influential champions of the jury
system was the distinguished John Henry Wigmore, who advanced
four main arguments in favor of the principle: First, that it prevents popular distrust of official justice since it gives the average
member of the body politic a share in the political process. Second,
that it provides for some necessary flexibility in legal rules and
regulations in that it enables an adjustment of the "general rule
of law to the justice of a particular case," whereas the judge is
rightly expected to be consistent and consequential in his rulings
for all. Third, that the jury system educates the ordinary citizen in
the administration of justice by cultivating the judicial habit in
him and by creating in him a respect for law and order, thus
making him conscious of his duty to society and his share in the
governmental process. Fourth, that the jury system ameliorates the
verdict because it is based on the amalgam of a host of tempera-
ments and viewpoints.[43] In essence, this is a plea on behalf of the

[42] See Curtis, op. cit. pp. 101–4.
[43] As discussed and quoted by William Wirt Blume, "The Place of Trial in
Criminal Cases," 43 *Michigan Law Review* 64–5.

institution based on the recognition of the role of common sense in the judicial process.

Unquestionably, the Wigmore roster of exhortation is subject to serious exception—especially since it is based, at least in part, on a rather optimistic, happy, and sanguine view of human nature and the willingness as well as the ability of the average citizen to accept and adapt himself to these laudatory notions of participation in the responsibilities of society and state. Some of the negative illustrations presented in connection with the adverse criticism of the institution would appear to raise some crucial doubts regarding Professor Wigmore's analysis. Be that as it may, despite its shortcomings the jury system has been generally regarded by the public at large as a laudable instrument in the quest for justice. "It is so justly regarded," once applauded Joseph H. Choate:

> as the best and perhaps the only known means of admitting the people to a share in maintaining their wholesome interest in the administration of justice. . . ." [44]

The ultimate question remains, however: is it and does it? It is difficult to discount the haunting doubts.

FROM OFFENSE
TO TRIAL: A PROCEDURAL NOTE

The practices and customs that characterize the legal process differ widely in the various jurisdictions discussed herein; this also applies to the procedures followed in the lengthy and often difficult path that leads from the commission of the offense to its ultimate adjudication in or out of the courtroom—for the vast majority of cases are in fact settled by mutual agreement before they reach the trial stage. Indeed, on the whole it is only the so-called "trouble cases" that actually traverse the tedious process through the entire courtroom sequence. The purpose of this procedural note is to illustrate in necessarily brief and generalized fashion the various stages that confront participants in a full-length legal proceeding. The model employed, which will distinguish between

[44] As quoted by Justice Barnard Botein, *Trial Judge* (New York: Simon and Schuster, 1952), p. 195.

civil and criminal cases, is an average jurisdiction in the United States of America.

PROCEDURE IN CIVIL CASES

Step 1 is the *commencement of the action* by the *plaintiff,* the party bringing the suit, against the *defendant.* If it is a matter of an *appeal* rather than the bringing of an initial suit, the party who appeals is known as the *appellant,* the other side as the *respondent* or *appellee.* The plaintiff or appellant may also be termed *petitioner.* A word of caution: while it is easily possible to determine who the two sides to a respective suit are at the initial stage of a new suit, once that proceeding has reached the various appellate stages it is considerably more difficult to do so, and the only safe manner is to read the few opening paragraphs of the case. In order to bring his suit, a plaintiff will have to do at least three things: (1) select the correct and proper tribunal; (2) have the defendant or his possessions brought before it; and (3) present his charges and ask for appropriate remedies.

In order to achieve the second requirement, the plaintiff must ask the proper authorities to serve a *summons,* which is issued after the petitioner has "sworn it out" and is presumably obeyed. Failure to respond to the summons will normally result in a judgment against the respondent by default. A more compelling order to appear is a *subpoena duces tecum,* a writ that, unlike the summons, must be served on the respondent in person; it directs appearance on pain of being held in contempt of court (or of whatever other judicial or quasi-judicial authority may be empowered to issue the writ). If the respondent resides outside of the court's jurisdiction, but owns property therein, the latter may be *attached* in order to commence a suit.

Closely related to the three tasks of the plaintiff in order to commence the action, is an attempt by the two impending parties to the suit to narrow the factual and legal issues involved by virtue of an exchange of one or a series of formal written statements stating the claim at issue, known as *pleadings.* These follow logically as a result of the plaintiff's initiation of his *complaint. Step 2* is designed solely to formulate the issues in the case and consists of the formal pleadings, now presumably involving the legal battery for both sides. This stage of the pleadings features the formal exchange of documents between the two sides, with the respondent required to file an *answer*. Often the lawyers are able to settle matters at this stage, but since we are here concerned with a sketch of the entire procedure, we assume that instead of acquiescence or agreement the future defendant will file a *motion to dismiss* the complaint, sometimes also known as a *demurrer*. If the plaintiff rejects these formal counterclaims, the stage will now have been set for the docketing of the case on the calendars of the court of proper jurisdiction. A *pretrial conference with the judge* may conceivably settle matters at this juncture and avoid an actual trial— it will very likely serve to narrow further some of the problems involved. The next formal stage is the trial itself.

The nature and character of *step 3,* the *trial,* depend largely on whether the issue between the litigants is one of law or of fact. If the issue is solely one of *law,* the court receives the case via a legal *argument* presented by the attorneys for both sides. Since there are no facts to be determined, jury and witnesses are not called; the judge decides the dispute strictly on the basis of the law, as he sees it. But if the dispute is either "mixed" or one strictly of *facts* the case will be tried before judge and jury, depending somewhat upon its nature and, as has been described earlier in the chapter, whether or not a jury trial is waived by mutual consent where that is possible and desirable. The next four steps, *verdict, judgment, appellate review* (if any), and *enforcement,* if not self-explanatory, have already been delineated above or will be discussed in subsequent chapters.

PROCEDURE IN CRIMINAL CASES

Because of the very nature of the offense, the procedure in a criminal case is *ipso facto* both more formal and more elaborate, and it involves the machinery of the state to a much more important degree. Above all, the state, as was demonstrated in Chapter I, necessarily is a party to the suit—at least in the sense that it is responsible for the prosecution of the offense. Step 1, therefore, is very simply the *apprehension* of the prospective defendant within the territorial limitations of the governmental jurisdiction concerned—i.e. unless he voluntarily surrenders to the authorities, he is literally caught and arrested, either in the act of commission, while fleeing, or as a result of an arrest warrant, which the arresting officer must obtain in advance from properly constituted authority. Step 2, closely related to the first, sees the arrested person brought before a magistrate for the *preliminary examination* in order to determine whether he shall be released or shall be *held to answer*. If the latter, the accused will be held either in *custody* or released on *bail* to await the decision of the public prosecutor or the grand jury on the question of whether or not an *information* or an *indictment* shall be filed against him (practices that have already been explained). The preliminary examination is a crucial and highly significant stage in criminal procedure: more than 50 per cent of the individuals arrested are freed as a result of it, which, in effect, customarily closes the books on the matter.

Step 3 represents the formal *accusation* by the grand jury, the public prosecutor, or the *juge d'instruction,* in accordance with statutory requirements or practices in the several jurisdictions concerned, as we have seen. This is logically followed by the *arraignment,* constituting *step 4.* An arraignment consists simply of the official, formal reading of the terms of the indictment or the information to the accused by the court of jurisdiction. The arraignment concludes with the significant question, "How do you plead?" —giving the accused the choice of "guilty" or "not guilty." (Under some circumstances, but rarely in criminal proceedings, the accused may also plead *nolo contendere* or "no contest," by which he throws himself upon the mercy of the court without admitting guilt per se.)

Step 5 is the *trial* itself, if there is one at all—if not, the judge's verdict takes its place, as is true in many, but not all, pleadings of guilty. A host of proceedings, with which we need not concern ourselves here, antedates the trial—including various motions for dismissal of the case, change of pleadings, placing of depositions, request for change of *venue,* possible dismissal or change of charges. The trial is conducted by the judge, either with or without the jury as the case may be, under the legal posture and the government concerned, and terminates with the next four steps: *verdict, judgment and sentencing, appellate review* (if any), and *execution of the sentence imposed* (if any).

This bare procedural sketch does not take into account the sundry aspects and ramifications of the manifold practices, procedures, and safeguards that surround this fascinating aspect of the judicial process.

Despite the relatively drastic distinctions in judicial theory and practice between the common law and statutory law lands of the free West, the justice meted out under both legal systems is similar in its ultimate degree of fairness, if not in its efficiency. Each system is characterized by obvious advantages and disadvantages, and each features methods that are peculiar to the needs or predispositions of the particular governmental jurisdiction concerned. As is so pre-eminently true of most practices in the realm of free government, they, too, are specifically adapted to the needs of the people directly involved. They are steeped in their own culture and tradition, and it is sheer folly for outsiders to endeavor to impose their own systems—even in theory. Sir Stafford Cripps once remarked wisely that methods and institutions of government are not simply commodities of international commerce, thus echoing the timeless statement made by the sage Alexis de Tocqueville in his *Democracy in America* in 1831:

> The more I see of this country [the United States] the more I admit myself penetrated with this truth: that there is nothing absolute in the theoretical value of institutions, and that their efficiency depends almost always on the original circumstances and the social conditions of the people to whom they are applied.

IV

COURTS AT HOME:

I THE LESSER TRIBUNALS

A DUAL SYSTEM OF COURTS

As a result of the federal system that prevails in the United States, the national government and now fifty state governments all make and enforce law. In effect, this means that there exist side by side, two major court systems that are wholly distinct bodies in the sense that they are created under different basic authorities—the respective national and state constitutions. The jurisdiction of these two systems may, and in some highly significant instances does, regularly "merge" at the bar of the final interpretative authority of the Supreme Court of the United States. However, such a "merger" can come about only if a *substantial* federal question has been validly raised in the proper state court below and, all remedies at the state level having been duly exhausted, that question has been successfully brought to what is in all but a handful of cases the *discretionary* attention of the Supreme Court. It is axiomatic that the path to the highest court in the land is long, expensive, arduous, difficult, and thus not traveled frequently. Other than in this appellate process, and possibly in the vexatious and procedurally intricate realm of injunctive relief, the national and state courts in the United States are separate entities. Nonetheless, it should be noted that through its constitutional power to establish *"inferior* courts," [1] Congress possesses the power to draw a rigid line between the *jurisdiction* of these federal and state courts. But it has not seen fit to do so except in a number of fields of relatively narrow jurisdiction, such as matters involving admiralty, bankruptcy, copyright, patent, and a few other specific subjects.

[1] U. S. Constitution, Art. III, Sec. 1, Par. 1. (Italics supplied.)

THE STATE COURTS

It would require a book, or certainly a lengthy monograph, in order adequately to describe the courts in the fifty states, where the great majority of the legal business of the American public begins and ends. The character, jurisdiction, quality, and complexity of these courts vary considerably from state to state in accordance with the myriad considerations of public policy, need, size, and constitutional practice that characterize the heterogeneous component parts of the nation. Every state constitution either establishes a judicial branch for its invariably tripartite government or, either in whole or in part—as is true under Article III of the Constitution of the United States—authorizes the legislature to provide for a judicial system. Although the terminology and structure among the state courts differ significantly, a discernible structural pattern does exist. The base consists of a system of justices of the peace and trial courts, with the pyramid gradually winding its way upward through a more or less elaborate appellate system, culminating in a supreme court (not invariably termed "Supreme Court").

THE JUSTICE OF THE PEACE

With rare exception, the lowest court at the state level—and there are those who would put the noun "court" into quotation marks in this particular connection—is the *Justice of the Peace,* often, and sometimes irreverently, referred to as the "J. P." He is also occasionally styled *squire* and, in many cities, e.g. New York. *magistrate*. By no means necessarily a lawyer, this official is usually elected for a two- to six-year term in counties, townships, and towns, but sometimes he is appointed by the executive in the cities. The office he fills boasts of an honorable and indeed ancient tradition that came to the colonies from England, initially designed to aid in the administration of justice in minor matters at the local level. Today, the Justice of the Peace, who is usually also a notary public, still performs a modicum of court work, but most of his duties are quasi-legislative, quasi-judicial, and quasi-administrative, including the characteristic performance of civil marriages. Most of these tasks are performed on a fee basis—probably a regrettable practice in view of its close link to meting out justice. He does, however, retain at least the appearance of a court of first instance in minor civil and criminal matters. In the former, his jurisdiction extends only to cases involving less than $100 to $200; in the latter, it is confined almost exclusively to misdemeanors.

With some notable exceptions, again usually confined to some urban areas—e.g. New York City, where the magistrates have legal background, are appointed for ten-year terms of office, and receive close to $20,000 annually—the Justice of the Peace's lack of training and qualifications is exceeded only by his sure-fire penchant for convictions, which have averaged 96 per cent in civil and 80 per cent in criminal cases. A study made in 1956 of the minor judiciary of North Carolina, for one, pointed out that not a single J. P. in that state then had a law degree; that 75 per cent had never gone to college; and that 40 per cent had never even attended high school! [2] Even in a cosmopolitan city such as Philadelphia, and despite the salary of $12,500 ($15,000 for the Chief Magistrate), only one of its 28 elected magistrates held a law degree in 1961–62. All this represents an unfortunate state of affairs, for, given the suitable climate of integrity and proper qualification, the Justice of the Peace might well still provide able and inexpensive adjudication and settlement of minor legal problems in the judicial process. On the other hand, Philadelphia's Chief Magistrate, Joseph J. Hersch, insisted in an interview in December 1961 that the job of a magistrate is "more social than legal," and decried the need for a law degree, stating:

> A law degree doesn't make a magistrate more qualified. Living with people is more essential than going to a law library to find out what it's all about . . . If you take Purdon's law books away from them [the lawyers], they're out of business.

THE MUNICIPAL COURT

Again because of varying needs, different nomenclature attends the *Municipal Court,* the next higher level of court ordinarily found

[2] Isham Newton, *The Minor Judiciary in North Carolina* (Unpublished Ph.D. Thesis, University of Pennsylvania, 1956).

in the several states. Some of the more common designations are *Court of Small Claims, Traffic Court, City Court, Night Court,* and *Police Court.* The Municipal Court, whatever it may be called, is almost always a court of original jurisdiction and normally also the first court of record in the judicial hierarchy of the state. By the same token it is normally the first properly to deserve the title of "court." Its jurisdiction is customarily limited to circa $500 to $1000 in civil cases, and to misdemeanors where it does have criminal jurisdiction. The Pennsylvania Court of Small Claims, for example, handles civil cases only. These courts provide the parties before them with a fast and inexpensive procedure, and they are generally staffed by judges who possess legal training.

THE COUNTY COURT

Next in line is what is by all odds the work-horse court of the average state judiciary, the *County Court.* It is a court of general civil and criminal jurisdiction, as a rule covering three major types of cases and controversies: ordinary civil beyond the limit of the court of jurisdiction just below; criminal other than routine misdemeanors; plus probate and inheritance. As its name implies, the County Court's geographical jurisdiction is limited to that subdivision of the state. If juries are used on any level of the state judiciary at all—and, of course, they usually are, although there is no *state* obligation to provide juries under the terms of the Bill of Rights in the *federal* Constitution—they will be found at the County Court. A whole coterie of allied or subsidiary courts is usually present at this level or takes the place of the County Court. Among these may well be all or some of the following, often self-explanatory, judicial county helpmates: *Common Pleas* (the County Court in Philadelphia); *Oyer and Terminer* (a criminal court with jurisdiction over capital crimes and other felonies); *Quarter Sessions* (a criminal court with jurisdiction in less than felony cases that usually meets four times annually, and sometimes consists of the same personnel as Oyer and Terminer); *Orphans; Probate* (for wills, estates, and deeds); *Juvenile* (for youthful offenders); *Domestic Relations; Surrogate* (similar to Probate in some counties); *Chancery* (specializing in equity matters); *Equity;* and still other designations.

The Intermediate Court of Appeals

Beyond the County Court lies the intermediate court, or courts, of appeals, usually termed *Appellate Division, State Appellate Court, Superior Court,* or *Intermediate Court of Appeals.* The jurisdiction of this tribunal is almost wholly appellate—certain writs being the exception in some states. It receives and adjudges appeals from decisions of the County Court and the Municipal Court, in rare cases from others. More often than not its decisions are final, although it is possible to go up from here to the final level, since it is an *intermediate* appellate court. Not all states resort to such an intermediate stage, but all of the larger ones do. Some of these have an elaborate appellate structure; The State of New York has an intricate system of more than 150 appellate courts at this level; and the appellate structure of the State of California enabled Caryl Chessman to file 14 appeals in its system (which he augmented with 28 appeals to the federal courts)!

The Final Court of Appeals

At the apex of any state system lies its *Final Court of Appeals,* which receives and adjudicates appeals in major questions emanating from the courts below, normally from the intermediate appellate level. It has the last word in the state on all constitutional questions. It will not lightly accept cases that are merely concerned with questions of fact; its main purpose is to find the law. Usually this highest state court is known as the Supreme Court, but in New York, for instance, where the Supreme Court is a trial court at the lower rung of the state judiciary, it is called the *Court of Appeals,* and in Connecticut it is termed the *Supreme Court of Errors.* Its decisions are thus final and authoritative as to state and, by virtue of the unitary structure involved, local law. The United States Supreme Court insists that "all remedies below" must have been exhausted before it will consider a request for review from a party that "lost" in the final court of appeals of a state. Nevertheless, if a federal question of a substantial nature is allegedly involved, and if that question has been properly raised below, a chance, however slim, does exist that the highest court in the land will accept the case for review. In rare instances, the Supreme Court of the United States theoretically *must* accept a case appealed from the highest court—but, as will be described in the next chapter, this presumed duty is not without significant loopholes.

THE FEDERAL COURTS

When we look at the other prong of the "dual system of courts" at issue, we are confronted with the federal system, which is in many ways considerably less varied and confusing than the understandably heterogeneous state systems. Certainly the federal courts are infinitely less numerous and, indeed, the hierachical and jurisdictional arrangements of the three major constitutional courts—as demonstrated in Chart A—are readily comprehensible and clearcut. Nevertheless, there is more to the structure and organization of the federal system of courts than is immediately apparent. Above all, there are two major *types* of federal courts from the point of view of their creation and functions: the *constitutional* courts and the *legislative* courts. Briefly, the former are created under Article III, the judiciary article of the Constitution, whereas the latter are created under Article I, its legislative article. Consequently, the safeguards of tenure, salary, and independence that accrue to judges of the constitutional courts by virtue of the explicit and inherent safeguards of Article III, are not necessarily present for the judges of the legislative courts. However, since they are created by Congress, nothing prevents that body from clothing the judges of the legislative courts by statute with the same or similar prerogatives as are constitutionally guaranteed to those of the constitutional courts. Indeed, even before Congress changed the status of three legislative courts—the United States Court of Claims,* the United States Customs Court, and the United States Court of Customs and Patent Appeals—to that of constitutional courts in 1953, 1956, and 1958, respectively, it had already granted them the same "good behavior" tenure provisions enjoyed by the judges of the constitutional courts. A more significant difference between the two types of courts is that the legislative courts are endowed with functions that are nonjudicial, i.e. legislative and administrative, as well as judicial. Moreover, while they

---

* *Zdanok v. Glidden*, 288 F. 2d 99 (1961), challenged the constitutionality of the change; the Supreme Court granted certiorari.

are tied into the constitutional appellate structure for certain purposes, they are primarily created to aid in the administration of specified congressional statutes. Nonethèless, their judgments are as much *res adjudicata*, authoritative settled law, as are those of the constitutional courts.

THE FEDERAL LEGISLATIVE COURTS

As its basic power for the establishment of *legislative* courts, Congress utilizes Article I, Section 8, Clause 9, which extends to it "the power to create tribunals inferior to the Supreme Court." The lawmakers (or their aids in the Legislative Reference Service) then expressly or impliedly join that fundamental power via the "necessary and proper" clause—the famous "implied powers" clause (I-8-18) of the Constitution—with that congressional authority in the particular field in which the court is to perform its main functions. For example, the taxing power (I-8-1) for the United States Customs Court (now a constitutional court) or the power to "make rules for the government and regulation of the land and naval forces" (I-8-14) for the United States Court of Military Appeals. Other legislative courts have existed in the past, of which the now defunct *United States Commerce Court* created under congressional power over interstate and foreign commerce (I-8-3) is an example. But today, if we exempt the now officially transformed United States Court of Claims, United States Court of Customs, and United States Court of Customs and Patent Appeals, there are merely two bona fide legislative courts: the United States Court of Military Appeals and the several Territorial Courts. Some observers would contend that the United States Tax Court, known as the *United States Board of Tax Appeals* until 1954, ought to be classified as a legislative court. Its 16 members, who are appointed by the President with the advice and consent of the Senate for 12-year terms at $15,000 annually, and who are removable in the same manner as members of the independent regulatory commissions, do have the official designation of judges. Yet in a very real sense the United States Tax Court is actually more of an adjunct of the executive branch, a quasi-administrative agency independent of the Internal Revenue Service, than a court per se. The Tax Court and its subdivisions have jurisdiction to review proposed deficiency assessments of income, gift, self-employment, and prior excess profits taxes that have been challenged by the taxpayer concerned. The United States Commissioner of Internal Revenue is thus necessarily always the defendant party. This court, which may hold hearings anywhere in the United States, is a busy agency! Its removal from the executive branch was strongly recommended by the Hoover Commission, but no action to that effect has been taken to date.

The United States Court of Military Appeals. This "G. I.'s Supreme Court" was created in 1950 as part of the revised Uniform Code of Military Justice, which, in turn, had largely resulted as a consequence of the severe criticism heaped upon the military's concept and practice of justice before, and especially during and after, World War II. That system of justice, steeped in the court-martial tradition, had been predominantly concerned with notions of military efficiency and chain of command, and had lodged all but dictatorial powers in the persons of the various commanding officers. Other than the unlikely "court of last resort" in the person of the President of the United States, all appeals—if indeed they could be accorded that judicial terminology—went to higher military commanders. The new code altered this arrangement drastically and dramatically by granting accused military personnel new rights before a court-martial and by creating the civilian *Court of Military Appeals.* This does not mean that members of the armed forces are now under the full protection of the Bill of Rights, for they are not—congressionally enacted *military* law still governs them. It does mean, however, that they now have a genuine appellate tribunal to apply and interpret that military law. In effect, the door has been opened for civilian observance and a modicum of civilian control.

The United States Court of Military Appeals is staffed by three civilian judges who receive $25,500 annually. They are appointed for staggered 15-year terms of office by the President, subject to confirmation by the Senate—the first three were sworn in on June 20, 1951—and they are eligible for reappointment. The President has the power to designate the Chief Judge. He may remove a member of the court only for neglect of duty or a mental or physical disability. No more than two of the judges may be from the same political party. Those who had been appointed through 1961 had all had judicial and/or other public service, not necessarily excluding past military duty. For example, at the time of his appointment in 1956 by President Eisenhower, Judge Homer Ferguson had been an attorney-at-law, a judge, a United States Senator, and Ambassador to the Philippine Islands; he had seen no military service.

This court, which determines its own rules of procedure, is authorized to review *at its discretion* decisions of courts-martial involving bad-conduct discharges and prison sentences of more than one year, on being petitioned by the accused serviceman, provided that the petition had already been passed upon by a Board of Review appointed by the Judge Advocate General. It *must* review all courts-martial decisions, as affirmed by a Board of Review, involving general or flag officers—i.e. generals and admirals; all those cases in which the death penalty has been decreed below, regardless of the rank of the accused; and all cases certified for its review by the Judge Advocate General. However, the court's powers of review extend solely to matters of law, not of fact—although that line, as we shall have occasion to note repeatedly, is sometimes a very fine one.

An illustration of one type of decision the Court of Military Appeals may render is the case of one Russo, a member of the Air Force, whom a duly convened court-martial had found guilty of premeditated murder and sentenced to death. On reviewing the record of the case, the staff judge advocate recommended approval of the sentence by the convening authority, but concurrently recommended that it be commuted to a dishonorable discharge from the Air Force, coupled with life imprisonment. When the Board of Review concerned received the case, it indicated its belief that the suggested commutation was appropriate. However, it held that it was "powerless to effect the change in penalty . . . [because] Congress has not granted that power to Boards of Review." Hence, it affirmed both the findings of guilt and the originally imposed sentence. Since this judgment involved a death penalty, and had been approved by the Board of Review below, review by the Court of Military Appeals was mandatory. In a decision written by Judge Homer Ferguson, the court denied various other points of appeal advanced by Russo, but held that both a court-martial convening authority and a Board of Review have the authority to lessen the severity of a death penalty. The court then reversed the judgments below and returned the record of the Russo trial to the Judge Advocate General of the Air Force for action consistent with its decision.[3] Half of all cases to date won reversals.

To all intents and purposes, there is no appeal from the final judgments of the Court of Military Appeals. However, the United States Supreme Court, as well as the other federal constitutional courts, could quite conceivably exercise jurisdiction to "pick up" or review a case in a *habeas corpus* proceeding—such as claims of illegal detention, illegal procedure, or deprivation of basic constitutional rights (if applicable). In 1953, the Supreme Court did indicate that it had that power in a much-discussed case, but a 6:2 majority went on to point out that under the law federal constitutional court review would probably be limited to determinations of military court jurisdiction and considerations of "fair claims of justice."[4] Justices Black and Douglas dissented, contending that the Fifth Amendment should be held to apply to military as well as civilian trials.

The Territorial Courts. Perhaps the several Territorial Courts are in a slightly different category than the standard legislative courts, but they are established by Congress under its power to ". . . make all needful rules and regulations respecting the territory or other property belonging to the United States. . . ." (IV-3-2). Created for and located in such diverse areas as the Canal Zone (1912), Guam (1900), Puerto Rico (1900), and the Virgin Islands (1917), the jurisdiction of these courts is necessarily extremely varied.[5] Generally, but specifically excluding Puerto Rico where they have federal jurisdiction only—Puerto Rico having a set of separate local courts—it includes matters analogous to those in the jurisdiction of state and local courts as well as the federal District Courts. The judges of the Territorial Courts are appointed in the usual manner by the President and confirmed by the Senate; but their term of office, which varies from four to eight years, represents an uncommonly brief period for members of the federal judiciary. In creating the various Territorial Courts,

---

[3] *United States v. Russo,* 11 USCMA 252, 29 CMR 168 (1960).

[4] *Burns v. Wilson,* 346 U. S. 147.

[5] For statistical purposes *only,* these courts and their judges have been counted throughout this work as "U. S. District Courts."

Congress has generally followed the wise policy of tailoring them to specific local needs, while retaining the *fundamental,* as distinguished from the *formal,* safeguards of the Constitution of the United States.

EX-LEGISLATIVE "SPECIAL" CONSTITUTIONAL COURTS

Until their already indicated conversion by Congress from their status as legislative to that of constitutional courts in the 1950's, the three most important and best known of these federal legislative courts were the Court of Claims, the Court of Customs, and the Court of Customs and Patent Appeals. Although they are now constitutional courts, they nevertheless still occupy a special niche in the federal court system; they may be regarded as special constitutional courts with quasi-legislative court duties. Despite their new station, they still perform certain quasi-legislative and quasi-administrative functions—or at the least they may be viewed as performing them. However, there is no doubt that public laws of Congress specifically changed their erstwhile status, and it must be assumed theoretically that Congress will henceforth not bestow upon these three the kind of nonjudicial powers that have always been considered inappropriate for members of the bench of the constitutional courts.

The United States Court of Claims. Created in 1855, after four earlier bills seeking to establishing it had failed, the Court of Claims consists of five judges, who receive $25,500 annually, and 11 "commissioners" who report findings for citizens to sue the Government of the United States for damages. Most, but certainly not all, of these suits represent claims arising out of public contracts. Others involve just compensation for the taking of private property for public use. Some represent suits for injuries caused by negligent or wrongful behavior of a government employee. The court is, in fact, an institutionally arranged denial of the age-old theory that the sovereign cannot be sued. Through the Court of Claims, sometimes referred to as "the keeper of the nation's conscience," the federal government does in fact permit itself to be sued by affected persons—and thus becomes the only proper defendant—but only within rather narrow limits, such as the already mentioned contractual disputes. Because of the volume of these complaints and the time consumed in their adjudication, the existence of the Court of Claims—with its jurisdiction extending to territories and possessions as well as the United States proper—represents a genuine blessing to the general courts, whose dockets might otherwise be clogged considerably more than they already are. Moreover, the Court of Claims as well as the other specialty-area courts are a welcome time-and-trouble-saving device for Congress itself; for there is no question that a good many of the matters now handled and adjudicated by these courts would otherwise have come to the halls of the federal legislature in the form of requests for special or local bills or as amendments to general statutes.[6]

Essentially, the jurisdiction of the Court of Claims is thus limited to *original* jurisdiction in all contractual, tax, injury, and other *non-tort* claims against the Government of the United States. (A tort is any wrongful act, *other than* a breach of contract, for which an injured party may bring a civil action against the alleged wrongdoer.) It does, however, possess a very limited power of *concurrent appellate review* with the United States Circuit Courts of Appeals in certain tort actions against the federal government decided in the United States District Courts. Decisions of the Court of Claims are subject to Supreme Court review in appropriate instances, and some of the latter's more famous cases did in fact "come up" from the Court of Claims, among them *Humphrey's Executor (Rathbun) v. United States,*[7] which arose out of suit in the Court of Claims against the United States to recover a sum of money allegedly due the deceased Humphrey. In 1933, President Franklin D. Roosevelt had removed him from his job as a member of the Federal Trade Commission, to which he had been reappointed by President Hoover for a second seven-year term in 1931. Contending that he had been illegally removed, Humphrey—and upon his death his executor, one Rathbun—sued to recover his salary. The Court of Claims, evidently somewhat uncertain of its grounds, certified some questions regarding the President's removal power to the Supreme Court. That tribunal subsequently held unanimously that the Chief Executive had no authority to remove summarily members of independent regula-

[6] James Willard Hurst, *The Growth of American Law: The Law Makers* (Boston: Little, Brown and Co., 1950), p. 67.   [7] 295 U. S. 602 (1935).

tory commissions clothed with quasi-legislative, quasi-judicial, quasi-executive powers, thereby decisively restricting his power of removal. This decision stands today, reaffirmed and reinforced in a case in 1958, involving President Eisenhower's dismissal of War Claims Commissioner Wiener.[8]

The United States Court of Customs and Patent Appeals. Utilizing the severally delegated powers to regulate commerce with foreign nations and among the states (I-8-3), to levy taxes (I-8-1), and "to promote the progress of science and useful arts" (I-8-8), Congress established the Court of Customs and Patent Appeals in 1910. Its five members, appointed in the customary manner, receive $25,500 per annum, and now serve "during good behavior." The functions of the court are primarily threefold: (1) to review decisions of the *Customs Court* regarding duties levied on goods imported into the United States and the classification of such goods; (2) those of the *Patent Office* regarding decisions on patents and trademarks; and (3), on a more legally restricted scale, those of the *Tariff Commission* relating to import practices.

For example, in one case on record the Tariff Commission, on reviewing an appeal by an importer, held that the attempted importation and sale of certain synthetic sapphires and rubies described in an established United States patent represented not only "unfair methods of competition," but also "unfair acts in importation," which tended substantially to injure the industry of the patent's owner. The commission consequently recommended proceedings against the importer involved, and the latter appealed to the Court of Customs and Patent Appeals. The court held that the evidence at hand amply supported the findings below that the patent owner's industry was operated efficiently and economically within the United States; that the imported stones fell within the description of the patented articles; that the patent had been properly secured; that the importer's actions had a tendency substantially to injure the aforesaid owner within the meaning of the statute; and that where no holding of invalidity of patent was alleged, it would be regarded as valid.[9]

A rather different instance of the work of the court concerned an action in August 1955 by President Eisenhower, who, pursu-

[8] *Wiener v. United States,* 357 U. S. 349 (1958).
[9] *re Von Clemm,* 229 F. 2d 441 (1955).

ant to a recommendation of the Tariff Commission, set certain new import duty rates on bicycles manufactured abroad. However, in so doing he had neither acted within the time limit prescribed by law nor had he really followed the Tariff Commission's advice—instead his announced rates represented a *compromise* with it. The importers filed a suit in the Customs Court which held against the United States Government. The latter appealed on the legal issue involved to the Court of Customs and Patent Appeals. The court ruled that, by following the course of action described, the President had violated the basic statute, which provides that Tariff Commission recommendations must either be accepted or rejected outright.[10] All parties concerned acquiesced in that 1960 decision. It was not until the late winter of 1961 that President Kennedy, acting on a new Tariff Commission advisory, restored the level set by his predecessor. The Court of Customs and Patent Appeals, unlike the Court of Claims, possesses only *appellate* jurisdiction and it is confined to matters of law. Appeals from its decisions may go to the Supreme Court.

The United States Customs Court. The largest of the three courts at issue, the Customs Court has nine members—of whom no more than five may be members of the same political party—who receive a somewhat lower salary than the other two courts, $22,500 annually. A successor of the United States Board of General Appraisers, and with roots extending back to pre-independence colonial days, the modern version of the court was created by Congress in 1926 under its commerce and taxing powers. Sitting in sections of three judges each, this special court, which meets in its New York headquarters and all other ports of entry in both the continental United States and the territories and insular possessions, has jurisdiction to review the rulings and appraisals on imported goods by the ubiquitous collectors of customs. As we have seen, appeals from its decisions go to the Court of Customs and Patent Appeals, although, in rare instances, it is possible to go directly to the Supreme Court.

An illustration of the work of the Customs Court is a case involving International Packers, Ltd., in 1959. Involved was the firm's contention that it should be permitted to deduct from the appraised value of goods imported from Argentina a certain per-

[10] *United States v. Schmidt Pritchard & Co.,* 47 CCPA 152, C.A.D. 750 (1960).

centage of the purchase price it had to pay to the Argentine authorities on their export. The United States Government's customs officials rejected this claim. On bringing action for adjudication in the Customs Court, the plaintiff convinced that body that the 15 per cent levy exacted by the Argentine Government was a "necessary expense from the place of shipment to the place of delivery." Accordingly, the court ruled that the percentage involved was properly allowable as a deduction in computing the United States value of the merchandise under the Tariff Act." [11]

Review of tariff controversies by the Court of Customs is not limited to the statutory provisions of the various congressional enactments. The right to sue before it applies to practically every legal controversy between an importer-taxpayer and the federal government. The fact that the Secretary of the Treasury or some other public official might have handed down an administrative ruling thus does not preclude an appeal to this interesting watchdog-court.

The Federal Constitutional Courts

We now turn to the three chief *constitutional* courts, the United States District Courts, the United States (Circuit) Courts of Appeals, and the United States Supreme Court—but the most important of these, the Supreme Court, will deservedly be the sole subject of the next chapter. All three were created under Article III of the United States Constitution. In its key Section 1, that article mentions only "one supreme court," but it goes on to point to "such inferior Courts as the Congress may from time to time ordain and establish." The two lower of these three constitutional courts hence owe their origin to one of the very first acts passed by the First United States Congress, the Judiciary Act of 1789,[12] of which Senator Oliver Ellsworth, soon to be the second Chief Justice of the United States, was chief author. The act established and fairly well spelled out the national system of constitutional courts, which, as has been demonstrated, received no hierarchical additions until the Court of Claims was designated a constitutional

---

[11] *International Packers, Ltd. v. United States*, 171 F. Supp. 854.
[12] Act of September 24, 1789, 1 Sta. 73.

court in 1953, followed by the Customs Court in 1956 and the Court of Customs and Patent Appeals in 1958. These six courts and their judges are clothed with the significant and essential benefits of tenure, irreducible salary, prestige, and independence. In the opinion of many an observer of the American scene, including the author of this book, there are no positions of greater desirability available in the entire structure of American government than those occupied by the members of the three leading constitutional courts.

General Jurisdiction. Omitting the already discussed jurisdiction of the several "special" federal courts, constitutional as well as legislative, the general jurisdiction of these three chief federal constitutional courts is amazingly well spelled out by the verbiage of Article III, Section 2, of the Constitution. In what is surely one of the most succinctly worded paragraphs of the entire basic document, the first sentence of the first paragraph of that section makes clear at once that the judicial power of the United States ". . . shall extend to all Cases, in Law and Equity, arising under this Constitution, the Laws of the United States, and Treaties made, or which shall be made under their Authority. . . ." Thus, in addition to announcing the sweeping realm of over-all jurisdiction, that verbiage comes to grips with one of the crucial aspects of the jurisdictional process, namely that it is limited to "Cases" (and "controversies," by implication). This signifies the necessity of the presence of a bona fide case or controversy involving litigants of opposing points of view who bring to the federal courts a genuine conflict of interest. In the absence of these basic elements, the three constitutional courts have no jurisdiction— which pinpoints the important truth that they neither can nor will accept manufactured or trumped-up cases or controversies, devoid of the essential elements described, nor can or will they render *advisory* opinions per se. This collective ban is as applicable to official as it is to private personages, and even extends to the influential government official who might feel the urge of convenience to run to the chambers of the Supreme Court with a fervent plea for an opinion on the legality of an issue, be it pending or dormant. Thus, as early as 1792, the Supreme Court declined to advise the government because it deemed the advisory function to be one more properly belonging to the Cabinet—a precedent that has not been violated.[13]

After having disposed of that crucial aspect, the constitutional paragraph at issue goes on to outline the particular types of jurisdiction available to these courts. Generally speaking, they fall into two groups: (a) because of the character or nature of the *subject matter* of the *case;* and (b) because of the character or nature of the *parties* to the suit. Under group (a) the courts may hear and dispose of cases and controversies in law and equity arising under:

(1) the Constitution, a federal law, or a treaty;
(2) admiralty and maritime laws.

Under the necessarily larger and more complex group (b) the courts may hear and dispose of cases and controversies in law and equity if:

(1) the United States is a party to the suit;
(2) one of the 50 states is a party to the suit (but, in accordance with the provisions of the Eleventh Amendment, *not* if the suit was commenced or prosecuted *against* a state by either an individual—*any* individual—or by a *foreign* country);
(3) they are between citizens of different states;
(4) they affect ambassadors and other bona fide representatives, duly accredited, of a *foreign* country;
(5) they arise between citizens of the *same* state because of a dispute involving land grants claimed under titles of two or more states.

However, despite this very specific and extensive jurisdiction it does not necessarily follow that the federal courts will inevitably exercise it. There is no barrier in the language of the Constitution against congressional assignment of certain aspects of it (theoretically probably even all!) to the 50 states, either on a concurrent or even exclusive basis—for example, the requirement that the value of a controversy in civil suits between citizens of different states must exceed $10,000 in order to qualify for original federal jurisdiction. Moreover, Congress may distribute the seven areas of federal jurisdiction among the various federal courts. It has always done so and continues to do so in accordance with need,

[13] *Hayburn's Case*, 2 Dallas 409 (1792).

more often than not as a result of suggestions by the members of the judicial branch itself.

Overlapping Federal and State Jurisdiction. Whether or not Congress assigns concurrent or even exclusive jurisdiction in *federal* matters to *state* courts, it is axiomatic, of course, that in some areas the *state* courts have *exclusive* jurisdiction. It may be possible to raise a *federal issue* in a matter arising under state law or the state constitution, but the *original* jurisdiction of state courts over their own affairs is complete as is that of the federal courts in their own sphere. But there are also some areas in which *both* court systems have jurisdiction, as in the case of bank embezzlement involving a federally insured bank or in that of the theft of an automobile that subsequently crosses state lines. In the two instances cited both systems have jurisdiction, depending somewhat upon the specific circumstances involved, and the guilty party or parties are subject to prosecution and punishment by *both*. The United States Supreme Court has held repeatedly that such dual prosecution and even dual punishment violates neither the Bill-of-Rights ban against double jeopardy nor the "due process of law" clause under the Fourteenth Amendment.[14]

As indicated above, Congress has purposely granted *exclusive* jurisdiction over certain federal matters to the states. It has done so largely on behalf of the federal courts from the point of view of their work load in such areas as the particularly voluminous one of diversity of citizenship disputes—suits between citizens of different states. Hence it has enacted the requirement of a minimum value of $10,000 as the admission ticket to the federal courts in these cases—here the United States District Courts. Going beyond that proviso, however, Congress has seen fit to grant *concurrent* jurisdiction in diversity of citizenship cases and controversies to the states even when the value meets or exceeds $10,000—provided the parties to the suit are willing to go there. As a further aid to the over-docketed federal courts, especially the work-horse District Courts, Congress in the late 1950's enacted a long overdue statute dealing with the citizenship status of corporations for purposes of legal actions. As a result, corporations are now viewed as "citizens" not only of the states in which they have been incorpo-

[14] Cf. *Bartkus v. Illinois,* 359 U. S. 121 (1959) and *Abbate v. United States,* 359 U. S. 187 (1959).

rated—which had been the case heretofore—but also as "citizens" of those states in which they have their principal place of business, regardless of their status of incorporation in the latter.

On the other hand, Congress has seen fit to vest *exclusive* original jurisdiction in the federal courts in a number of areas: suits between two or more of the fifty states (Supreme Court only); cases involving *foreign* ambassadors and other accredited *foreign* representatives; all bankruptcy proceedings; and all prosecutions for violations of federal criminal laws. Chart A demonstrates the over-all jurisdiction of the three major federal constitutional courts.

CHART A
THE JURISDICTION OF THE THREE MAJOR FEDERAL CONSTITUTIONAL COURTS OF THE UNITED STATES

COURTS CREATED UNDER ARTICLE III OF THE FEDERAL CONSTITUTION †

1 *Supreme Court of the United States,* 9 judges, has:

Original jurisdiction in actions or controversies:
- *1. Between the United States and a state.
- 2. Between two or more states.
- *3. Involving *foreign* ambassadors, other *foreign* public ministers, and *foreign* consuls or their "domestics or domestic servants, not inconsistent with the law of nations."
- *4. *Commenced by a state against* citizens of another state or aliens, or *against* a foreign country. (N.B.: if these actions are *commenced by the citizen or alien against a state,* or by a foreign country *against* a state, the suit must *begin in state court,* according to the provisions of Amendment XI.)

Appellate Jurisdiction from:
- 1. All lower federal *constitutional* courts, most, but not all, federal *legislative* courts, and the *territorial* courts.
- 2. The highest state courts having jurisdiction, when a "substantial federal question" is involved.

† For the purposes of this chart, the three "special" courts (U. S. Court of Claims, U. S. Court of Customs, and U. S. Court of Customs and Patent Appeals) are omitted.

* *Jurisdiction not exclusive*—i.e. while cases, according to Article III of the Constitution, are to originate here, legal arrangements may be made to have them handled by a different level court. For example, Congress has the power to give the federal District Courts *concurrent original jurisdiction* over cases affecting foreign ambassadors and *some* cases in which a state is a party to the suit. Cf. *United States v. Ravara,* 2 Dallas 297 (1793); *Bors v. Preston,* 111 U. S. 252 (1884); and *Ames v. Kansas,* 111 U. S. 449 (1884).

11 *United States (Circuit) Courts of Appeals,* 78 judges, have:

Appellate Jurisdiction *only* from:
  1. U. S. District Courts.
  2. U. S. Territorial Courts, the U. S. Tax Court, and some District of Columbia Courts.
  3. The U. S. Independent Regulatory Commissions.
  4. Certain federal administrative agencies and departments (for review, but also for *enforcement* of certain of their actions and orders).

92 *United States District Courts,* approximately 311 judges, have:

Original Jurisdiction *only*** over:
  1. All crimes against the United States.
  2. All civil actions arising under the Constitution, laws, or treaties of the United States, wherein the matter in controversy exceeds $10,000 (unless the U. S. Supreme Court has jurisdiction as outlined above).
 *3. Cases involving citizens of different states or citizens and aliens provided the value of the controversy is in excess of $10,000.
  4. Admiralty, maritime, and prize cases.
 *5. Review and *enforcement* of orders and actions of certain federal administrative agencies and departments.
  6. All such other cases as Congress may validly prescribe by law.

**A case can be made for the contention that it also has a measure of *appellate* jurisdiction, involving certain actions tried before specially designated U.S. Commissioners.

The United States District Courts. By all odds the work horses of the federal judiciary, the 92 District Courts, with their some 311 judges—perpetually an insufficient total—comprise the trial courts of the federal system. Established under the Judiciary Act of 1789, their jurisdiction extends to the initial trial of almost all civil and criminal cases arising under the vast realm of federal jurisdiction. It is here that the United States Government commences, and usually ends, its prosecutions—e.g. the government's victorious anti-trust suit against the electrical appliance concerns, which began and terminated in the United States District Court for Eastern Pennsylvania in Philadelphia in February 1961, Judge J. Cullen Ganey rendering the famous decision.[15] It is here also that most suits arising under the federal statutes begin and end—viz., one Abrikossoff's action to recover certain property that had been

[15] Case not reported in F. Supp. See Reporter's Transcript in Office of the Clerk, U. S. District Court, Eastern District of Pennsylvania. Also see Clerk Gilbert W. Ludwig's letter to author, dated June 8, 1961.

disposed of by the Alien Property Custodian under the Trading with the Enemy Act.[16] And it is here that the trial (petit) juries sit in the federal system; they do so in roughly half of all cases commenced at that level. The District Courts have *original* jurisdiction only. However, when necessary, they do have the duty to *enforce* as well as review actions and orders of certain federal administrative agencies and departments; certain actions tried before United States Commissioners (see below) may be reviewed by them; and certain other classes of cases may be *removed* to them under specific statutory authorization from the state courts. Hence in the vast majority of instances, the decisions of the District Courts are, in effect, final. And there is a veritable flood of business: they now decide upwards of 200,000 cases annually. In 1959, to cite one busy year, a total of 187,201 proceedings were *commenced* in the District Courts. No wonder that delays are common here—as well as elsewhere in the American judicial system! At the level of the *federal* courts the time interval between the point when a case was "at issue" and the trial itself ranged in 1959 from 4.1 months to 39.1 months. In the *state* courts, during the same year, it varied from 1.0 months to 52.9 months.[17]

Each of the 50 states of the Union, the District of Columbia, Puerto Rico, Guam, the Canal Zone, and the Virgin Islands contains at least one federal district with a District Court and a District Judge. There is no cutting across state lines, but in many instances the large number of cases to be adjudicated compels a subdivision of labor within a particular district. Thus while many of the districts have only one judge, others have two or more. Indeed, one— the Southern District of New York (Manhattan, the Bronx, and the adjacent suburban counties to the North) with its high proportion of complex commercial litigation—had the 1961–62 maximum of 24. Almost half of all litigation occurs in the 12 District Courts that are located in the larger metropolitan areas.[18] The Chief Justice of the United States (who is the same individual as the Chief Justice of the Supreme Court of the United States) has the authority to transfer district judges temporarily from their

[16] *Abrikossoff v. Brownell,* 145 F. Supp. 18 (1956).
[17] See the symposium, "Lagging Justice," 328 *The Annals of the American Academy of Political and Social Science* (March 1960).
[18] Cf. the *Annual Reports* of the U. S. District Courts.

home circuit to a more congested one, but only with the former's consent. These judges are then known as "visiting judges." It was as Visiting Judge for the Eastern District of Arkansas that United States District Judge Ronald N. Davies, whose home district was North Dakota, issued the new famous injunction [19] against Governor Orval E. Faubus and other state officials of Arkansas in September 1957 when they had actively interfered with an earlier court order upholding the Little Rock School Board's desegregation plan.[20] Judge Davies had been temporarily transferred because of a mounting backlog of cases. To cite one other procedural example: in order to remedy a staggering congestion on the civil calendars of the District Court for the Eastern District of New York (Kings, Queens, Nassau, Suffolk, and Richmond counties), Mr. Chief Justice Warren, acting on the invitation of Chief Judge M. W. Byers of that court in 1959–60, assigned 15 district judges from other circuits to help in clearing the accumulation. They did, and in short order!

But no matter how many judges may be permanently or temporarily assigned to a district, it is customary for a lone District Court judge, sitting with a jury—unless that institution has been validly waived—to preside over a trial in the roughly 350 localities where they now are held in the United States. However, in some instances of particular importance, Congress has statutorily provided for adjudication by *Three-Judge District Courts*. They customarily consist of two district judges and one circuit judge; in any event, the Judicial Code provides that at least one judge must be from the circuit—the next higher echelon in the judicial system. As a matter of practice, the Chief Judge of the Circuit Court involved rarely, if ever, assigns more than that absolute minimum. Suits required to be heard by these Three-Judge District Courts are usually those seeking to restrain *by an injunction* the enforcement, operation, or execution of both federal and state statutes and orders of state administrative agencies on grounds of *unconstitutionality,* or orders of the Interstate Commerce Commission. A few other instances are also provided by statute, some of these with injunctions to cover certain violations of the federal anti-trust laws.

[19] *United States v. Faubus,* 156 F. Supp. 220 (1957).
[20] *Aaron v. Cooper,* 143 F. Supp. 855 (1956).

The busy judges of the District Courts are provided with relatively ample assistants to carry on their tasks, all of whom are appointed by the judges themselves (some were mentioned in an earlier chapter). Among them are the *United States Commissioners, Law Clerks, Bailiffs, Court Reporters, Stenographers, Clerks,* and *Probation Officers.* These positions are more or less self-explanatory, except for that of United States Commissioner, who, as has been pointed out, is in charge of some of the preliminary steps involved in the pretrial process, such as to issue arrest warrants and, often, to hear evidence in order to determine whether to hold the arrested person for grand jury action—in which case the Commissioner may set the bail. His judge appoints him for a four-year term of office, and he is paid from court fees. The two most important officers present in a district, but not appointed by the judge directly, are the *United States Marshal* and the *United States Attorney.* The latter, appointed for each of the districts by the President with the advice and consent of the Senate, functions under the authority of the Attorney-General rather than that of his District Judge. He, in turn, appoints a number of Assistant United States Attorneys, often in conjunction with the patronage wishes of influential members of his political party. The U. S. Marshal, appointed in the same manner as the U. S. Attorney, makes arrests; executes routine court orders, such as the summoning of witnesses; guards prisoners; and generally maintains the decorum of the courtroom of the District Court of the United States.

The United States (Circuit) Courts of Appeals. Standing immediately above the United States District Courts in the federal constitutional court hierarchy, the 11 United States (Circuit) Courts of Appeals—sometimes simply called "Circuit Courts" or "Courts of Appeals"—are essentially what their name implies: *appellate* courts only. They do, however, have a statutory obligation to *enforce,* when necessary, as well as review actions of a host of federal executive agencies that are clothed with quasi-judicial functions. Among these, to cite but a few, are certain rulings of the National Labor Relations Board, wage orders of the Administration of Wage and Hour Division of the Department of Labor, and orders under anti-trust or unfair practice laws of the Interstate Commerce Commission, the Federal Communications Commission, the Civil Aeronautics Board, and the Board of Governors of the Federal Reserve System. But even if we are to classify aspects of the review and enforcement of the activities of these quasi-judicial units of the federal government as original jurisdiction—and they are that only by stretching the concept considerably—the vast majority of the work of the United States Courts of Appeals is clearly appellate. In effect, it is at once the first and last stop for appeals from below in all instances save those that go on up to the United States Supreme Court and those few that are permitted to bypass it from below en route to the Supreme Court. Other than the appeals from the highest state courts of record, which go directly to the Supreme Court without touching the other federal courts, the Circuit Courts of Appeals may be validly bypassed only in the following instances: (1) in decisions by the Three-Judge District Courts, as explained above; (2) where a direct appeal is statutorily authorized to the Supreme Court from a limited number of ordinary District Court cases, such as when a federal statute has been held unconstitutional by a District Court and the United States is a party to the suit; and (3) upon a showing that a case is "of such imperative public importance . . . as to require immediate settlement."

But in all other instances, both civil and criminal, the Circuit Court of Appeals is the natural appellate tribunal for the approximately 5500 cases that come up annually from the United States District Courts in the 50 states, the District of Columbia, and the territories, and from the many independent regulatory commissions, agencies, and cabinet departments that are endowed with quasi-judicial powers and functions. In 1955, for example, the Court of Appeals for the District of Columbia, sometimes referred to as the Eleventh Circuit, held, on reviewing the denial of one Schachtman's passport application by the Department of State, that the latter had violated the due process of law clause of the Fifth Amendment in the circumstances at issue.[21] The Department of State subsequently complied with the court's mandate. An illustration of a case arising from a decision of a District Court rather than that of an administrative agency or department is the unsuccessful appeal to the United States Court of Appeals for the Second Circuit by Alger

[21] *Schachtman v. Dulles,* 225 F. 2d 938.

Hiss for reversal of his conviction on perjury charges in connection with the theft of United States Government documents.[22]

Although officially stripped of the term "circuit" in 1948, this important court level in the federal judicial process is still generally referred to as Circuit Courts. There are ten such numbered circuits in the United States and the nonnumbered eleventh one, known as the *Court of Appeals for the District of Columbia*, which are as follows:

First Circuit:	Maine, Massachusetts, New Hampshire, Rhode Island, Puerto Rico.
Second Circuit:	Connecticut, New York, Vermont.
Third Circuit:	Delaware, New Jersey, Pennsylvania, Virgin Islands.
Fourth Circuit:	Maryland, North Carolina, South Carolina, Virginia, West Virginia.
Fifth Circuit:	Alabama, Florida, Georgia, Louisiana, Mississippi, Texas, Canal Zone.
Sixth Circuit:	Kentucky, Michigan, Ohio, Tennessee.
Seventh Circuit:	Illinois, Indiana, Wisconsin.
Eighth Circuit:	Arkansas, Iowa, Minnesota, Missouri, Nebraska, North Dakota, South Dakota.
Ninth Circuit:	Arizona, California, Idaho, Montana, Nevada, Oregon, Washington, Hawaii, Alaska, Guam.
Tenth Circuit:	Colorado, Kansas, New Mexico, Utah, Oklahoma, Wyoming.

Each of these circuits is theoretically headed by one of the nine justices of the United States Supreme Court who are historically said to be "riding circuit"—the junior justices usually being assigned the two "extra" circuits. Indeed, this is what they used to do, more or less literally, at the beginning of America's nationhood, but the practice necessarily soon fell into disuse. Today, lack of time prevents them from more than token or nominal participation, although they continue to be faithfully and formally "assigned" at the beginning of each term.

The eleven Circuit Courts of Appeals comprise a total of 78 judges who, except for the judges of the District of Columbia,

[22] *United States v. Hiss*, 185 F. 2d 822 (1950).

must be residents of the assigned circuit during the time they serve and even thereafter—because, though they may have retired, they are nevertheless still subject to assignments by the Chief Justice of the United States. There is a Chief Judge for each of the Circuit Courts who, upon reaching the voluntary retirement age of 70, retains his powers as a full-fledged member of his court— assuming he neither chooses to retire nor has accumulated sufficient time to do so on full salary—but ceases to be head of the court involved. This arrangement also applies in the District Courts, but not in the Supreme Court. From three to nine judges may sit *en banc* to hear cases, although there are usually only three in view of the work load; a quorum is two. Proceedings before the Courts of Appeals are conducted on the basis of the record made below—i.e. before the United States District Courts or one of the administrative agencies. New evidence may thus not be presented at the bar of this appellate tribunal, just as it may not be introduced in the appellate cases reaching the highest ranking court in the American judicial hierarchy, the Supreme Court of the United States.

Administering the Federal Judiciary

Before turning to the latter tribunal in the following chapter, something should be said about the administration of the federal judicial system. Considerable thought may well have been given for many years to the establishment of a centralized administrative structure for these courts, but it was actually not until shortly prior to the second quarter of this century that the judicial and legislative branches, particularly the former, had recognized the urgency of the problem to the extent of doing something about it other than to declaim and exhort on what had become an increasingly deplorable state of administrative anarchy. Fortunately, Congress yielded to mounting pressure by bar, bench, and interested laymen, and the establishment of the Judicial Conference of the United States and the Administrative Office of the United States Courts in 1922 and 1939, respectively, effected considerable improvement.

The Judicial Conference of the United States. The 1922 statute requires "the Chief Justice . . . to submit to Congress an annual report of the proceedings of the Judicial Conference and its recommendation for legislation." This is done faithfully and to considerable advantage by the "Chief" in his position as head of that body, which consists, in addition to him, of the chief judge of each of the eleven federal judicial circuits, a district court judge from each of these circuits, and the Chief Judge of the United States Court of Claims. The Judicial Conference meets at least once annually for the legislatively established purpose of making a "comprehensive survey of the conditions of business in the courts of the United States and [of preparing] plans for assignment of judges to or from circuits or districts where necessary." It is also required to submit suggestions to the various courts "in the interest of uniformity and expedition of business." This vital body of prestigious and influential experts has done an excellent job in keeping abreast of the needs of an efficient judiciary and has done its utmost—in conjunction with the Administrative Office of the United States Courts, for which it establishes policy—to realize these needs. Although not all of its recommendations have either been adopted by Congress or adopted speedily—this applies especially to those involving the creation of new judgeships—the legislative branch has displayed considerable regard for the wisdom of the Judicial Conference and its committees. Confirmation of that benign approach is, for instance, the fact that in 1958 Congress passed a law authorizing the Judicial Conference to set up committees of judges, lawyers, and law professors to study the rules of procedure in the federal courts. On receiving the committees' recommendations, the Judicial Conference may pass judgment on them and then send them on to the Supreme Court for similar action. Adopted changes become effective in 90 days unless they are specifically disapproved by Congress during that time.

The Administrative Office of the United States Courts. This judicial housekeeping agency and veritable gold mine of statistics is headed by the director, who is appointed by the Supreme Court. He possesses no administrative jurisdiction vis-à-vis the Supreme Court, but he and his subordinates are crucially involved in the administrative business of the subordinate federal courts. (Indeed, an increasing number among the 50 states have begun to establish similar bodies—e.g. California, Iowa, New York, and Pennsylvania.) Among these tasks are the compilation of the suggested budgets; determination of personnel needs; examination of the dockets; auditing of accounts; procurement and allocation of supplies; preparation of all vital statistics in connection with the business of the courts (its *Annual Report* has become essential for all those interested in the judicial process); and all such other duties as may be assigned to the director and his staff by either the Supreme Court or the Judicial Conference—both headed by the Chief Justice of the United States. The Administrative Office of the United States Court has become an essential arm of the judicial system; it has been widely and just acclaimed; it has, in effect, become indispensable to the orderly and successful operation of the courts. The distinguished federal jurist, who characterized its creation in 1939 as "probably the greatest piece of legislation affecting the judiciary since the Judiciary Act of 1789," [23] was eminently correct in his analysis. Nonetheless, constant vigilance to bring about further improvement in the operation and function of the courts, high as well as low, is essential throughout the United States in the interest of justice.

[23] As quoted by Hurst, loc. cit. p. 114.

V

COURTS AT HOME:
II THE SUPREME COURT

AT THE ZENITH:
THE UNITED STATES SUPREME COURT

The most dazzling jewel in the judicial crown of the United States is the revered and often controversial United States Supreme Court. It is the sole court—federal or state—mentioned in Article III of the Constitution. All other federal courts were created by statute under the provisions of that article. The Supreme Court, the national symbol of justice, stands at the very pinnacle of the judiciary: there is no higher court, and all others bow before it— or, at least, are expected to do so. At times having had as few as five and as many as ten justices in the first 80 years of its venerable history, the Court has stood at nine ever since the first term of President Grant in 1869. Prior thereto, as dictated by various policy considerations, its congressionally fixed membership comprised: six in 1789; five in 1801; six in 1802; seven in 1811; nine in 1837; ten in 1863; and eight in 1866.

The Supreme Court consists of the Chief Justice and eight Associate Justices, the former being rewarded since 1955 with an annual salary of \$35,500, the latter with \$35,000 each—this is less than judges of some states, e.g. New York, receive. But the nonsalary compensations, frequently called "psychic income" by college professors, are undoubtedly considerable. Their retirement prerogatives have been discussed in Chapter II.

ORIGINAL JURISDICTION

The United States Supreme Court has both *original* and *appellate* jurisdiction, but it exercises the· former in only rare instances.

156

Moreover, the Eleventh Amendment to the Constitution, ratified in 1798, has seriously abridged that phase of its work by removing from its jurisdiction as spelled out in the original body of the Constitution, all those cases in which one of its own citizens or one of another state or of a foreign country, or even a sovereign foreign country itself, wishes to sue one of the states of the United States. In effect, the Eleventh Amendment enacted the necessity of obtaining *a state's permission to sue it* in all litigation involving the above-mentioned categories.

The Eleventh Amendment was adopted as a direct result of a Supreme Court decision in 1793 in the case of *Chisholm v. Georgia*.[1] There the Court, in a broad decision, but in accordance with the terminology of Article III of the Constitution, held 4:1 that one Chisholm, a citizen of one state (South Carolina) could sue another state (Georgia) in the federal courts—an outrageous and shocking pronouncement in the eyes of the citizens with confirmed "state-rights" views. It was especially galling since the matter involved concerned debts owed to British creditors for whom Chisholm acted as an executor. The Supreme Court's judgment triggered instantaneous and profound opposition. For example, the lower house of the legislature of the State of Georgia passed a bill to punish by hanging "without benefit of clergy" any person endeavoring to aid in the enforcement of the decision! Merely two days had passed after the announcement in *Chisholm v. Georgia* when the future Eleventh Amendment was introduced into both houses of Congress.

Thus, the *original* jurisdiction docket of the Supreme Court has become a very minor factor in its work. Not counting *memorandum orders,* to be explained later, at the outset of its 1960–61 term the Court had rendered decisions under the original jurisdiction clause of the Constitution—Article III, Section 2, Paragraph 2, as amended—in only 123 cases since its first term in 1789.[2] The cases that now still commence under it do so as a *matter of right* under its provisions. Theoretically, these comprise the following four categories of cases or controversies: (1) between the

[1] 2 Dallas 419.

[2] For a detailed analysis, including a list of these 123 cases, see "The Original Jurisdiction of the United States Supreme Court," 11 *Stanford Law Review* 665–719 (July 1959).

United States and one of the 50 states; (2) between two or more states; (3) those involving *foreign* ambassadors, other *foreign* public ministers, and *foreign* consuls, or their "domestics or domestic servants not inconsistent with the law of nations"; and (4) those *commenced by a state* against citizens of another state or aliens, or *against* a foreign country. (But note that if these actions are *commenced by the citizen or alien or foreign country* against a state, that litigation *must begin in state court,* in accordance with the provisions of the Eleventh Amendment.)

However, the Supreme Court does not exercise *exclusive* original jurisdiction even in the four categories cited, with the sole exception of cases or controversies involving two or more of the several states. There it, and it alone, exercises original jurisdiction. But, accompanied by the Court's plaudits, Congress has extended *concurrent original* jurisdiction to the federal District Courts in litigation affecting category (3) and in *some,* but not all, cases in which a state is party to the suit at issue. Hence, most of the cases the Supreme Court has heard on its original jurisdiction docket have indeed involved two or more states. For example, the nine successive actions the State of Virginia filed against West Virginia in the lengthy and trying history of their debt controversy were all heard at the bar of the Supreme Court.[3] More recent controversies have involved Maryland and Virginia in their eternal oyster disputes and California and Arizona in their evidently equally persistent water squabbles. All of these cases must, and do, commence in the Supreme Court. Yet if a determination of *facts* is required, the Court here often utilizes the device of referring these disputes to a special *master*—frequently an ex-jurist—for a hearing and report to it, as it did in the Western water litigation.

APPELLATE JURISDICTION

The primary task of the Court is *appellate.* In that capacity it serves as the final arbiter in the construction of the Constitution of the United States, *and* it thus provides a uniform interpretation of the law—although its very power to do so presumably also enables it to change its mind from case to case. However, at least to a considerable degree, it attempts to adhere to precedent, the doc-

[3] For example, see *Virginia v. West Virginia,* 246 U. S. 565 (1918).

trine known as *stare decisis,* i.e. let the decision stand—giving to precedents the authority of established law. We shall examine this philosophy of law and the extent of its success in Chapter VIII.

Appellate cases come to the Supreme Court from the subordinate federal courts and the state courts of last resort (which are usually, but not always, the state supreme courts). Actually, there are five different sources of appellate cases that reach the Court: (1) from the state court of last resort having jurisdiction in a particular action, provided that a federal question has been raised validly and further provided that all remedies have been duly exhausted below; (2) from the United States Circuit Courts of Appeals; (3) from the United States District Courts; (4·) from the United States Court of Claims and the United States Court of Customs and Patent Appeals in *judicial* rather than *administrative* matters; and (5) from one of the legislative or territorial courts, if permissible under the laws that establish them.[4]

WRITS OF REVIEW GENERALLY

Cases or controversies normally reach the Supreme Court for purposes of review under its appellate jurisdiction in one of three principal ways—each member of the Court considering every application for review: (1) on a writ of appeal, as a matter of right (usually simply called *appeal*); (2) on a writ of certiorari, as a matter of Court discretion (usually simply called certiorari or cert.); and (3) by certification. The old writ of *error,* a common law process roughly akin to today's writ of appeal, was statutorily discontinued in the federal courts in 1928. It brought the entire record of a proceeding in a lower court before the Supreme Court for its consideration of "errors of law," allegedly committed below. We may also quickly dispose of *certification.* Rarely employed, it presents the Court with even less cases than those on its original jurisdiction docket. It covers "any question of law in any civil or criminal case in which instructions are desired" by the lower court, usually a Court of Appeals or the Court of Claims.

Appeal. In the instance of a writ of *appeal,* the aggrieved party has an absolute, *statutorily granted right* to carry a case to the United States Supreme Court, which in theory must review it.

[4] Ch. 81, Title 28, U. S. Code.

However, the high tribunal retains the very considerable loophole of being empowered to reject such an appeal on the grounds that the federal question, otherwise validly raised, is "insubstantial." This highly significant discretionary element in the area of the Court's so-called compulsory appellate jurisdiction caused it to dismiss 70 appeals in the 1955–56 term, for example. Of these 40 were rejected "for want of a substantial federal question," the balance on other jurisdictional grounds. In the 1959-60 term, 63 of a total of 113 appeals were dismissed on the insubstantiality ground! As a rule, fully 50 to 60 per cent of the writs of appeal are thus dismissed or the judgment below affirmed without printing the record or oral argument.

In effect, the appeal is hence used but sparingly—to date in approximately 9 per cent of all cases or controversies presented to the Court. But whatever the practice, there are a total of five instances in which an aggrieved party may resort to it: (1) if a state court of last resort has declared a federal law or treaty, or parts thereof, unconstitutional; or, (2) if it *upholds a state law against a substantial challenge that it conflicts* with a provision of a federal law or treaty, or the United States Constitution; (3) if any federal court declares a federal law or treaty, or parts thereof, unconstitutional, provided the United States is a party to the suit; (4) if a federal Court of Appeals *strikes down a state law as being contrary* to a federal law, treaty, or the Constitution; and (5) in certain statutorily specified cases from the federal District Courts and all other "courts of the United States" (e.g. if a case, required to be heard by any three-judge federal District Court, has resulted in an order granting or denying an injunction). By far the largest number of cases on appeal come to the Supreme Court either from a state court of last resort—usually its highest court—or from one of the special three-judge courts at the federal District Court level (which must include at least one federal Circuit Court of Appeals judge). Many of the segregation-integration cases have reached the Supreme Court via the latter route.

Certiorari. In all other cases involving a "federal question of substance" the disappointed litigant in a suit has *no right* to appeal to the Supreme Court the adverse decision he sustained, but he does have the *privilege* of petitioning the highest bench in the land to grant him a writ of *certiorari.* Generally, each such petition comprises the two sides' arguments both for and against its grant, plus a record of the proceedings below. Ninety per cent of the cases decided by the Supreme Court reach it by that method, and practically all of these come to it from the Circuit Courts of Appeals.

The grant of certiorari signifies the willingness of the Supreme Court to review the case. It directs the lower court to send up the record in the case for review so that the decision may be made more certain. Needless to say that Court is quite chary with its writs of certiorari, and unless it detects an issue of substantial significance in the case or controversy, or it happens to be especially interested in it, chances are that the application for the writ will be denied with a terse "certiorari denied"—a designation commonly found at the top of a published listing of a large number of petitions thus disposed of. The Court's own Rule 19 states that certiorari will be granted only "where there are special and important reasons therefor." Among these, according to the language of Rule 19, are the following: where two federal Circuit Courts of Appeals or two three-judge federal District Courts have rendered conflicting decisions (e.g. two diametrically opposed judgments involving the constitutionality of so-called "Blue Laws" by two three-judge federal District Courts sitting in Boston and Philadelphia, striking down and upholding such Massachusetts and Pennsylvania laws, respectively); [5] where a state court or a federal appellate court has passed on an important question of federal law on which the Supreme Court has never passed, or if these lower courts have done so in a manner conflicting with applicable precedent established by the United States Supreme Court; or where a federal court has so far departed from the accepted canons of judicial proceedings as to call for exercise of the Supreme Court's power of supervision. In any case, as Mr. Justice Frankfurter has viewed the Court's power to control its docket, ". . . [it] carries with it the responsibility of granting review only in cases that demand adjudication on the basis of importance to the operation of our federal system; importance of the outcome merely to the parties is not enough." [6] In an address

[5] *Crown Kosher Super Market v. Gallagher,* 176 F. Supp. 466 (1959); *Two Guys from Harrison-Allentown v. McGinley,* 179 F. Supp. 944 (1959).
[6] *Wilkerson v. McCarthy,* 336 U. S. 53 (1949).

to a group of Illinois lawyers he illustrated what the Chief Justice, who plays an important role in certiorari grants, might say:

> This is a very interesting and important question . . . , but we can't do any better than Judge Julian Mack [late judge of the United States Court of Appeal] did with it below. He really knows more about this field of law than the rest of us. I suggest we deny this petition for certiorari.[7]

Still, to be a case of substance does not necessarily mean "big" or "major" case. In its 1959–60 term, for example, the Supreme Court reached down to the Police Court of Louisville, Kentucky, to set aside, as a violation of the due process of law clause of the Fourteenth Amendment to the Constitution, two $10 fines for loitering and disorderly conduct.[8] The case symbolized the willingness of the highest court in the land to look at the smallest matters if necessary to ensure justice. Here, in a criminal conviction, one Sam Thompson took his claim of lack of evidence successfully to the Supreme Court on certiorari because, under Kentucky law, the fines involved were too small to be reviewed by any state appellate court. Speaking for the unanimous Court, Mr. Justice Black noted that "Our examination of the record presented in the petition for *certiorari* convinced us that *although the fines here are small, the due process questions presented are substantial and we* therefore granted *certiorari* to review the police court's judgment."[9]

Since the Court has complete discretionary power over grants of certiorari—a power bestowed upon it in the necessary and desirable "Judges Bill" of 1925, which was largely the creation of Mr. Chief Justice Taft—it denies in excess of 90 per cent of all applications, and does not usually explain its reason for the denial. Gone are the days when the Court was expected to devote an all-too-large portion of its valuable time and energy merely to correct errors of lower courts which primarily affected the rights of parties to a particular case or controversy. In the words of Mr. Chief Justice Vinson:

---

[7] As quoted by Anthony Lewis, "How the Supreme Court Reaches Decisions," *The New York Times Magazine*, December 1, 1957, pp. 51–4.
[8] *Thompson v. City of Louisville et al.*, 362 U. S. 199 (1960).
[9] Ibid. at 203. (Italics supplied.)

To remain effective, the Supreme Court must continue to decide only those cases which present questions whose resolution will have immediate importance far beyond the particular facts and parties involved.[10]

In order to grant certiorari, at least *four* of the justices must vote to do so. A working rule devised by the Court itself, this Rule of Four also applies to noting probable jurisdiction on writs of appeal —an interesting development in view of the important distinction presumably governing the two writs. Of course, the Court can also change its mind on a grant for review; there is nothing to prevent it, on thinking the matter over, from ultimately dismissing a writ as having been "improvidently granted." According to a statute of 1863, however, *six* justices constitute a quorum to hand down a decision. This means that a plurality of four justices can *decide* a case. In the event of a tie vote, the decision of the lower court stands as the final word in the controversy at issue. But a single justice may—unless or until overruled by action of his brothers on the bench—grant a stay of execution or a writ of *habeas corpus*. Pertinent illustrations of this significant prerogative are the grants of requests for stays of execution, although denying requests for writs of *habeas corpus,* by Mr. Justice Douglas, in the sensational case of the convicted atom spies, Ethel and Julius Rosenberg, in June 1953. Although vacating the stays of execution just twenty-four hours after they had been granted, Mr. Chief Justice Vinson took note inferentially of the intemperate reaction in the public press, and especially in Congress (where bills of impeachment were at once introduced in the House of Representatives), by writing that "Mr. Justice Douglas had power to issue the stay. No one has disputed this, and we think the proposition is indisputable." [11]

Considerable disagreement exists among not only the many observers of the Court but among the justices themselves as to the true meaning of a denial of an application for a writ of certiorari. Mr. Justice Jackson viewed it as a tacit agreement by a quorum of the justices that the decision below is good enough to stand. "The

[10] From an address to the Assembly of the *American Bar Association* in St. Louis, September 9, 1944, entitled "Work of the Federal Courts."

[11] *Rosenberg v. United States,* 346 U. S. 273 (1953), at 285.

fatal sentence," wrote he in his beautiful prose, "that in real life writes finis to many causes cannot in legal theory be a complete blank." [12] Mr. Justice Frankfurter, however, insisted on several occasions (again, for instance, fairly recently in a denied request for review of the sensational murder-conviction case of "Dr. Sam" Sheppard of Cleveland [13]) that no significance attaches to the denial of certiorari, that it "in no wise" implies Court approval of the decision below. All it means, he pointed out once more in that case, is that for reasons seldom, if ever, disclosed, four justices evidently do not think that the case ought to be reviewed. On another occasion he had spelled his reasoning out more precisely:

> . . . [it] seemed . . . to at least six members [of the Court] . . . that the issue was either not ripe enough or too moribund for adjudication; that the question had better wait for the perspective of time or that time would bury the question or, for one reason or another, it was desirable to wait and see; or that the constitutional issue was entangled with nonconstitutional issues that raised doubt whether the constitutional issue could be effectively isolated; or for various other reasons not related to the merits.[14]

No matter which of these two contrasting views may be "correct," the effect in the eyes of the disappointed petitioner is necessarily the same—at least for the present he has lost.

WORK LOAD

All cases to be disposed of are placed on one of the Court's three dockets: the *Original,* the *Appellate,* and the *Miscellaneous.* In the 1959–60 term the Court had more cases (2178) on these dockets and disposed of more (1787) with finality than ever before. It granted certiorari in 177, a considerable number, but falling well short of the record number of 208 established in the 1957–58 term. The previous records of the Court's total work load were set in the 1958–59 term when it docketed 2063 and disposed of 1783. The increase in the work load over previous years came

---

[12] Concurring opinion in *Brown v. Allen,* 344 U. S. 443 (1953), at 543.

[13] *Sheppard v. Ohio,* 352 U. S. 910 (1956).

[14] Dissenting opinion in *Darr v. Burford,* 339 U. S. 200 (1950), at 227.

CHART B
UNITED STATES SUPREME COURT REVIEW

CASES NORMALLY REACH THE U. S. SUPREME COURT FOR PUR-
POSES OF *REVIEW* (as distinct from original jurisdiction) IN ONE OF
TWO PRINCIPAL WAYS:

(1) on APPEAL, i.e. as a matter of right;
(2) on a writ of CERTIORARI, as a matter of Court discretion.

(A third way, by CERTIFICATION, will be omitted for present purposes.
It is rarely used—presenting the Court with even less cases than those on
its original docket. It covers "any question of law in any civil or criminal
case as to which instructions are desired" by the lower court, usually a Court
of Appeals or the Court of Claims. The old writ of ERROR, a common
law process strongly akin to (1) above, was statutorily discountinued in the
federal courts in 1928. It brought the entire record of a case proceeding in
a lower court before the Supreme Court for its consideration for alleged
"errors of law" committed below.)

N.B. Title 28 of the United States Code, formulated as a result of congressional legislation, governs the types of review available to an appellant.

I. *Cases reaching the U. S. Supreme Court on APPEAL* (i.e. the Court
   reviews because it *must*).
   A. *From the State Court of Last Resort* having statutory jurisdiction in
      any particular case (usually, but not always, the *Highest State Court,*
      which normally, but not always, is the State Supreme Court).
      1. When a state court has declared a federal law or a federal treaty,
         or provisions thereof, unconstitutional.
      2. When a state court has *upheld* a state law or a provision of the
         state constitution *against* the challenge that it *conflicts* with the
         federal constitution, a federal law, a federal treaty, or any provi-
         sion thereof.

   B. *From the U. S. (Circuit) Courts of Appeals:*
      1. When a state law or a provision of a state constitution has been
         invalidated because of a conflict with a federal law, a federal
         treaty, or a provision of the federal constitution.
      2. When a federal law has been held *unconstitutional, provided* the
         United States, or one of its agencies, officers, or employees is a
         party to the suit.

   C. *From the U. S. District Courts:*
      1. When a federal statute has been held *unconstitutional, provided*
         the United States, or one of its agencies, officers, or employees is
         a party to the suit.
      2. When the United States is a party to a *civil* suit under the fed-
         eral interstate-commerce, communication, or anti-trust laws.

3. When a *special three-judge District Court* (which must include at least one circuit judge) has granted or denied an interlocutory or permanent injunction in any proceeding required to be heard by such a court. (These three-judge courts usually sit in suits brought to *restrain enforcement, operation, or execution of federal or of state statutes or orders of state administrative agencies* on the grounds of unconstitutionality; *or* because of an order of the Interstate Commerce Commission.)

D. *From "Any Court of the United States"* (comprising the *constitutional, legislative,* and *territorial* courts)—and specifically including, a.o., the *Court of Claims,* the *Court of Customs and Patent Appeals,* etc.:

1. When a federal statute has been held *unconstitutional* in any *civil* action, suit, or proceeding, *provided* the United States, or one of its agencies, officers, or employees is a party to it.

II. *Cases reaching the U. S. Supreme Court on a writ of CERTIORARI* (i.e. because a minimum of four Supreme Court Justices has agreed to a review.) Writs of certiorari are granted or denied at the *discretion* of the Court—subject always to the latent power of Congress to define and limit the *appellate* power of the Court.

A. *From the State Court of the Last Resort having statutory jurisdiction* in any particular case (usually, but not always, the *Highest State Court,* which normally, but not always, is the State Supreme Court).

1. In all cases, *other than* those for which the remedy is APPEAL (see I, A, 1 & 2 above), in which a *"substantial federal question"* has been properly raised. (The Court itself determines just what constitutes such a question.)

B. *From U. S. (Circuit) Courts of Appeals* (and, in all pertinent cases, from the *U. S. Court of Claims,* and the *Court of Customs and Patent Appeals*):

1. When a decision involves the *application or interpretation* of a federal law, a federal treaty, the federal Constitution, or provisions thereof.

2. Where the U. S. Court of Appeals has *upheld* a state law or a provision of a state constitution *against* the challenge that it conflicts with a federal law, a federal treaty, the federal Constitution, or provisions thereof.

almost entirely in the so-called *miscellaneous* cases, which are handwritten or typewritten papers filed by indigent persons, often prison inmates. This category of cases rose sharply to a record of 1119. Indigents obtain authority to file from the federal *in forma pauperis* statute, which gives to a citizen of the United States the right to enter proceedings in any federal court, provided he issues such an oath. Of course, this does not guarantee a Supreme Court review—although in its 1959–60 term the Court agreed to hear 35 of these cases, an unusually generous number. Moreover, it summarily vacated or reversed 21 other lower court decisions challenged by indigent persons. The purpose of this interesting statute clearly was to protect indigent persons—a large proportion of whom, according to a bitter remark by Mr. Justice Jackson, represent "our convict population." And Mr. Justice Douglas, certainly a sympathetic friend of the underdog, commented that the claims made in these pauper cases "are often fantastic, surpassing credulity . . . [and] are for the most part frivolous." [15] Of the 2178 cases filed during the 1959–60 term, 356 were not disposed of and thus went over to the 1960–61 docket. That residue represented the largest number of cases carried forward to a new term since the Clerk of the Supreme Court commenced to keep these statistics in 1930. But it rose to 385 for 1961–62!

Although there is some disagreement among the justices themselves on the point, most observers of the work of the Court believe firmly that it is overburdened with cases. In large measure, this is due to the flood of petitions that reach it; but to some degree it may also well be due to the fact that the Court has persisted in taking cases which are at best trivial, sometimes dealing simply with matters of fact, without presenting any truly imperative constitutional questions. This, of course, is a matter of judgment. Yet it would seem that at least in the areas of tax and railroad or maritime injury-negligence cases, particularly the latter group which usually involve a question of fact as to who was at fault in the accident, the Court has at times unnecessarily overextended itself in granting petitions for review. That a good many of the justices feel quite strongly about the matter is indicated by a veritable stream of comments by Mr. Justice Frankfurter, who, in case after case in this field, would pen a comment to the extent that "the case . . . is so trivial that the Court should dismiss its grant of review as improvident." And in a dispute, early in the 1960–61 term, involving the question whether a jury should hear the case of a wrench falling on a seaman's "left great toe," Mr. Justice Harlan, speaking for a minority of four justices, delivered a three-page dissent that began with the comment:

[15] Address to the Cornell University Law School, April 8, 1960.

At the opening of a term which finds the court's docket crowded with more important and difficult litigation than in many years, it is not without irony that we should be witnessing among the first matters to be heard a routine negligence . . . case involving only issues of facts. I continue to believe that such cases, distressing and important as they are for unsuccessful plaintiffs, do not belong in this court.[16]

Mr. Justice Frankfurter went even further here and opined that the Court should not even have agreed to consider such a case in the first place, and he once again voiced his long-standing lament against consideration of minor negligence cases.

An intriguing and possibly highly significant decision by the Court, during the 1960–61 term, gave Mr. Justice Frankfurter additional reasons for expounding on the theme of unwise, non-jurisdictional, unnecessary case work. Over his lone 58-page dissenting opinion, the eight-man majority held that policemen and other local officials who violated a citizen's constitutional rights under the Civil Rights Act of 1871 could be sued for damages in *federal* courts *even if these officials acted without state authority*. The Frankfurter dissent not only charged the majority with violating federal-state relationships, relying heavily on the legislative history of the act as he saw it to prove his point, but he also decried what he viewed as rank court interference. Envisaging a veritable flood of petitions, he insisted that the broad construction here adopted by the Supreme Court made the federal Constitution

a law to regulate the quotidian business of every traffic policeman, every registrar of elections, every city inspector or investigator, every clerk in every municipal license bureau in this country.[17]

Whatever the number of cases docketed, it ought to be fairly obvious that the lawyer who grandiosely and proudly informs both his client and the public press that "we'll fight this case all the way to the Supreme Court," really means that *if* the funds are present he will *attempt* to do so—unless a pauper's oath is involved the

[16] *Michalic v. Cleveland Tankers, Inc.*, 364 U. S. 325 (1960).
[17] *Monroe v. Pape*, 365 U. S. 167 (1961).

standard case will consume a solid outlay of $10,000—and *if* the Court will grant review he will *endeavor* to convince it of the righteousness of his client's case. The average case takes from two to five years to reach the highest bench. Alone the preparation and printing of the record and the writing of briefs normally consumes five months. Seldom does the Court actually *hear oral arguments* on more than 100 to 150 of the cases it disposes of annually; the balance is dismissed on procedural or some other jurisdictional ground. Of those actually heard, formal *written opinions* by the Court are usually handed down in 75 to 85 per cent of the cases, the others being decided *per curiam*—an anonymous opinion that expresses the summary judgment by the Court as a whole and not by a single justice with whom the others concur. In other words, a *per curiam* is an *unsigned,* normally very brief, opinion for the Court, its authorship unknown to the outside world, applying *res adjudicata*—settled law—usually for a unanimous Court. It was employed in the final disposition of the famous *Girard College Case* [18] in Philadelphia in 1958. There has ensued considerable criticism about the increasing resort to *per curiam* decisions. However, it may very well be that this simply represents an attempt by the Court to resolve the conflict between rendering fully reasoned opinions and affording the finality of Supreme Court adjudication to as large a number of litigants as possible.

Typical of the Court's average work load was the 1956–57 term. There it granted certiorari in 142 cases and decided 121 on appeal—then an unusually generous number in both instances. In all, the Court *disposed* of 1670 cases during that term, leaving 351 on the docket for future disposition. Cases decided on the *merits* were 263, of which 130 were with *full written opinion,* the remainder by *memorandum order.* Of these 263 cases, the Court *affirmed* only 67 and *reversed* 101, *dismissing* the balance. Of the 130 full written opinion cases, 115 represented "opinions of the Court," of which 115 were *per curiam.* The discrepancy between the figures 115 and 130 is due to the fact that, as is the Court's common practice, several opinions covered more than one case—for instance, in two "obscenity" cases, one federal and one state,

[18] *Pennsylvania v. Board of Directors of City Trusts of the City of Philadelphia,* 357 U. S. 570 (1958).

which the Court decided jointly as 354 U. S. 476 on one of the last days of that term.[19]

Reconsideration. A petitioner whose request for review has been denied by the Court for one or more of the reasons discussed above is not, of course, barred from trying again. Accordingly, some sanguine souls are rather persistent in these efforts—although they rarely if ever succeed unless their new petition serves to convince four justices of the merits of the renewed appeal. Among well-known illustrations of such unsuccessful attempts are the cases of Morton Sobell, convicted of complicity in the atomic espionage case of Ethel and Julius Rosenberg and the doomed-to-die-in-the-gas-chamber Caryl Chessman. Sobell filed nine petitions for review of his conviction between 1953 and 1958; all were denied by the Court without comment. Chessman filed fully 16 petitions for review with the Court between his conviction in 1948 for 17 crimes (including kidnapping, attempted rape, sex perversion, robbery, and car theft) and his execution in 1960, prompting even Mr. Justice Douglas to comment ". . . the conclusion is inevitable that Chessman is playing a game with the courts." The latter's battle ended in failure only after having filed a total of 42 appeals with various federal and state courts. This procedure covered 12 years, caused extensive debates on the merit of capital punishment, and made Chessman's name a household word throughout the world.

Rehearing. On the other hand, it is also possible for a defeated litigant to ask the Supreme Court for a *rehearing* after the announcement of the unfavorable decision, in the dim hope that the Court in the person of one or more of the justices, may undergo a change of mind on rehearing the case; this is especially true when the erstwhile decision was a very close one and featured a sharply divided Court. But under the rules of the Supreme Court a rehearing may not be granted unless a member of the *majority* in the original decision votes for one. Nevertheless, the rules clearly give every litigant the right to seek reconsideration of a decision.

A notable illustration of one of the infrequent successes gained by a petitioner on rehearing, was the group of "military justice" cases, involving Mesdames Clarice Covert and Dorothy Smith-

[19] *Roth v. United States* and *Alberts v. California,* decided on June 24, 1957.

Krueger, both civilians, who killed their respective spouses while stationed with them at overseas bases. The cases were argued together at the bar of the Supreme Court initially in 1956, the constitutional issue being the validity of the section of the United States Uniform Military Code of Justice that authorized the military trial of civilians accompanying the armed forces abroad.[20] The Court upheld the disputed section in a 5:3 decision, delivered by Mr. Justice Clark, while the three dissenters—Warren, Black, and Douglas—protested they were being rushed at term's end; and Mr. Justice Frankfurter refused to participate other than to file a "reservation," because of "lack of adequate time to consider" the issues involved and "their complexity." Clearly, this was the type of decision in which able counsel for defendants might well see a distinct ray of hope for a rehearing. A motion for a rehearing was duly filed; it was accepted by a 5:3 vote, the three original dissenters and Mr. Justice Frankfurter being joined in approving the petition for rehearing by Mr. Justice Harlan, a member of the original majority.[21] Matters certainly seemed to look up for the grieving widows! The case was duly reargued early in 1957, and during the waning days of that term the Court handed down its decision, reversing itself and declaring the section in question to be unconstitutional by a 6:2 vote.[22] Only Justices Clark and Burton remained of the erstwhile majority, Justices Minton and Reed having retired from the Court, Mr. Justice Harlan having changed his mind, and a new member, Mr. Justice Brennan, joining the majority. The ninth member, Mr. Justice Whittaker, just appointed to replace Mr. Justice Reed, did not participate in the decision. It should be re-emphasized, however, that a grant of a petition for rehearing is the exception to the rule.

A related, but distinct, practice is an order for *reargument,* when the Court—for reasons best known to itself—orders a case back on the docket for reargument rather than hand down a decision. At the end of 1956–57 term it did this in ten cases that had already been briefed and argued before it. The famed *Segregation*

[20] *Kinsella v. Krueger,* 351 U. S. 470 and *Reid v. Covert,* 351 U. S. 487 (June 11, 1956).

[21] *Reid v. Covert* and *Kinsella v. Krueger,* 352 U. S. 901 (November 5, 1956). On petition for rehearing.

[22] *Reid v. Covert* and *Kinsella v. Krueger,* 354 U. S. 1 (June 10, 1957). On rehearing.

Cases[23] represent a pertinent earlier example. Initially argued in December 1952, they were ordered reargued in December 1953, and were decided in May 1954.

THE UNITED STATES SUPREME COURT AT WORK

The concluding sections above illustrated a marginal function of the Court. But how does this most impressive and most dignified of all governmental bodies in the United States generally conduct its work? Annually, since 1873, it sits for 36 weeks customarily, from the first or second Monday in October until the end of June, sometimes longer. On rare occasions, such as in connection with the Little Rock, Arkansas, school desegregation crisis in August-September 1958,[24] and the case of the seven German saboteurs in 1942,[25] a Special Session may be convoked. But there have been only four such sessions in this century. Yet be it stated at once that the business of judging, at least at the level of the federal government, is a year-round occupation, regardless of formal sessions. All of the Court's sessions are now held in its magnificent Corinthian white marble structure near Capitol Hill in Washington, D. C., constructed in 1935—patterned after the Temple

FIGURE 1

THE 1961–62 COURT

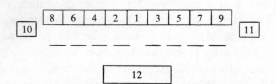

1. Chief Justice Warren

2. Mr. Justice Black	3. Mr. Justice Frankfurter
4. Mr. Justice Douglas	5. Mr. Justice Clark
6. Mr. Justice Harlan	7. Mr. Justice Brennan
8. Mr. Justice Whittaker	9. Mr. Justice Stewart

10. The Clerk's Desk   11. The Marshal's Desk

12. Counsel's Desk

[23] *Brown v. Board of Education of Topeka*, 347 U. S. 483 (1954).
[24] *Cooper v. Aaron*, 358 U. S. 1.   [25] *Ex parte Quirin*, 317 U. S. 1.

of Diana at Ephesus (one of the seven wonders of the ancient world), the words "Equal Justice Under Law" carved above the majestic entrance, enhanced by great bronze doors. Here convenes the Supreme Court of the United States, its nine justices clad in black robes and seated behind the raised bench in high-backed swivel chairs of varying size against a background of full red draperies. The justices are arranged according to length of continuous service on the bench; the Chief Justice sits in the center, flanked by the senior Associate Justice on his immediate right, the second-ranking on his immediate left, then alternating in that manner in declining order of seniority.

ORAL ARGUMENT

In this impressive setting the Court listens to oral arguments—in the cases it has agreed to hear—for the first four days in two weeks out of each month. Its justices spend the other two weeks behind closed doors in consideration of cases and writing of opinions. For the oral arguments 40 copies of the printed briefs must have been filed with the Clerk of the Court well in advance. As already explained, those bona fide paupers whose cases are treated on the special miscellaneous docket may, however, file handwritten or typewritten briefs. Oral argument, heard on designated days from 10:00 a.m. to noon and from 12:30 p.m. until 2:30 p.m., is at once the most significant and the most fascinating aspect of the *public* portion of the Court's work. There is at least a chance that it may sway members on the spot, although this is far less likely in the great than in the small cases; still, first impressions count. The pressure on the arguing lawyers, who must speak from the floor level, is naturally enormous. They are frequently questioned sharply by the justices—questions that may conceivably forecast the ultimate decision of the Court, although in few, if any, is it possible to give an accurate prognosis. Some justices ask very few questions (Mr. Justice Douglas, for one); others have a habit of asking a great many (Mr. Justice Frankfurter, for example). John P. Frank reported that in one particular case he witnessed—perhaps a somewhat extreme illustration—the justices interrupted counsel 84 times during 120 minutes of oral argument, with 93 questions and interpolations chargeable to Mr. Justice Frankfurter alone! [26] Woe unto counsel who is ill-prepared or uncertain of himself—and the justices frown on reading from the prepared text. In fact, Rule 44 of the Court states that it looks "with disfavor" on such a practice. But the justices may also well prove to be helpful to counsel. Thus, during one oral argument heard in the 1960–61 term, Mr. Justice Frankfurter sharply questioned an obviously flustered arguing lawyer several times, only to see Mr. Justice Douglas intervene each time with a helpful answer! "I thought *you* were arguing this case," shot Mr. Justice Frankfurter to grateful counsel, who responded, "I am, but I can use all the help I can get." [27]

Unlike the days of old, especially during Mr. Chief Justice John Marshall's reign when a Daniel Webster would sometimes address the Court with mounting eloquence for days, the present-day lawyers are severely limited in the time granted to them for argument. Normally, the limit is one hour for each side, sometimes merely a half-hour. One of the rare suspensions of the time limit rule took place in the case of *United Steel Workers of America v. United States*,[28] involving the legality of the injunctive provisions of the Taft-Hartley Act. In the 1958–59 term only 220 hours of argument were allotted to counsel severally. They use a lectern to which two lights are attached; five minutes before time is up a white light flashes; when the second light, appropriately a red one, flashes, the lawyer must stop instantly—unless he is granted permission by the Chief Justice to continue. According to one of Mr. Chief Justice Hughes's law clerks, that "Chief" was so strict on the score of time that he once stopped a leader of the New York Bar in the middle of the word "if"; and that, on another occasion, upon being asked by the same attorney how much time remained, Hughes replied icily, "Fourteen seconds, Mr. Counsel." [29]

To argue cases at the bar of the Supreme Court a lawyer must be admitted to practice before it. This is a relatively routine matter, although not without its ceremonial by-products. It is cus-

[26] *The Marble Palace* (New York: Alfred A. Knopf, 1958), pp. 104–5.
[27] As reported by Anthony Lewis in "The Justices' Supreme Job," *The New York Times Magazine*, June 11, 1961. (Italics supplied.)
[28] 361 U. S. 49 (1959). Another was *Arizona v. California*, 16 hours (!), in Jan. 1962.
[29] Edwin McElwain, "The Business of the Supreme Court as Conducted by Chief Justice Hughes," 63 *Harvard Law Review* 6 (1949).

tomary for the Solicitor-General of the United States to "introduce" to the Court all bona fide applicants at its first session in October; this being done their admission is automatic. Thereafter, admission to the bar is an almost daily routine occurrence during the court term available to all lawyers who have been members of the bar of their state's highest court for three years. There is a $25 "admission fee," which the Court uses to cover expenses of indigent parties that come before it.

The Solicitor-General. The *Solicitor-General* is the third-ranking official in the U. S. Department of Justice, following the Attorney-General and the Deputy Attorney-General. Because of its special relationship to the Supreme Court, the post of Solicitor-General has always enjoyed a high reputation in legal circles, has been eagerly sought by members of the legal profession, and has not infrequently been filled by legal scholars—viz., President Kennedy's appointment of Professor Archibald Cox of the Law School of Harvard University as his first Solicitor-General.

The Solicitor-General is in charge of all of the government's litigation in the Supreme Court, which comprises in excess of 50 per cent of the Court's total work load. He and his staff argue all of the government's cases before it. His office supervises all government briefs filed in the Court, and he must personally approve, or disapprove, any case before the government takes it to the Court. Moreover, the Solicitor-General has supervisory authority over other government appeals. Only if he gives his approval may the government appeal from an adverse decision in a trial court. (In a federal criminal case, if either a judge or a jury has heard *evidence* and has found the defendant innocent on that evidence, the government cannot appeal at all. However, the Supreme Court has *upheld* appeals by some *states,* where state law— as in Connecticut—permits government appeals even in criminal cases.) Sometimes much to the chagrin of certain members of both the executive and legislative branches, the Solicitor-General's office has developed a commendable tradition of alertness toward any unfairness in government cases. When he detects such a situation, the Solicitor-General will usually file a "Confession of Error" in the Supreme Court, in which he asks that it set aside a victory won by the government in the lower court. Although this practice is of the very essence of the meaning of justice—which, after all, should be the aim of all litigation—it may be doubted that a large number of private counsel would be similarly willing to forego a victory. All too frequently litigation is viewed as a courtroom battle between two opposing teams of high-powered trial lawyers bent upon "victory" rather than upon the triumph of justice.

BEHIND CLOSED DOORS

Each Friday during the Court's term is *Conference Day*. (Until changed by Mr. Chief Justice Warren, Saturday used to be that important day.) On Conference Day the justices meet in secret, usually from 10:00 a.m. until 5:30 or 6:00 p.m. with less than one hour for lunch, in the oak-paneled, book-case-lined conference chamber, adjacent to the office of the Chief Justice, under his chairmanship. The role of the "Chief" is that of *primus inter pares,* although some have tended to be more *pares* than *primus,* as we shall presently see. Here the justices discuss the cases they have heard, as well as all pending motions and applications for certiorari. They are expected to be ready to indicate their tentative stand, having been previously advised which cases would be up for discussion—generally those just heard by them on the four "argument days" during that week or those recently heard in the case of conferences meeting during the two recess weeks in which no oral arguments are presented. The conference "list" may run from 25 to 150 items; 75 is about normal. The importance of this traditional conference, for that matter any conference of appellate judges at which they review law cases and controversies, was thus well stated by Mr. Justice Jesse W. Carter of the California Supreme Court:

> [The conference] is not a prayer meeting where everyone is expected to nod "amen"; it is more like a battleground where opposing philosophies meet in hand-to-hand combat.[30]

The justices are seated around a large rectangular conference table, each chair bearing a nameplate. All shake hands with one another on entering the room. The Chief Justice sits at the south end and the Senior Associate Justice on the north end. On the

[30] As quoted in *The New York Times,* March 16, 1959.

sides, in the usual order of seniority, sit the remaining seven associate justices. Looking down on this scene is the sole portrait in the room—that of Mr. Chief Justice John Marshall. The incumbent Chief Justice, whose personality and administrative talent loom large in these meetings, customarily gives his own view first in the case up for discussion, followed by that of the other justices in order of seniority. Each justice must be prepared to recite and do so persuasively—if he feels strongly about an issue involved. Upon completion of this phase of their deliberations, the nine members of the Court take a tentative vote on the particular case, the justice with the lowest seniority voting first this time, presumably so that he will not be influenced by the votes of his more experienced brothers. Each justice has a hinged, lockable docket book, in which all votes are duly recorded.

The Role of the Chief Justice. Although he is theoretically merely *primus inter pares,* the "Chief," as already indicated, has a potential influence that may well outweigh that of the ordinary presiding officer. Two of his functions—probably the only two—lend themselves ideally to the exercise of that influence. One is the aforementioned chairmanship of the Court's own conference, including his highly important role in the sifting of writs of certiorari, the other his assignment of opinions (to be more fully described later in this section). When the "Chief" opens discussion of a case by giving his own views first, he has an excellent opportunity to state the case as he sees it, to indicate the questions to be decided, and to give his opinions on the issue or issues involved. This is a far from inconsiderable power, for there is a good chance that his initial analysis of a problem will have at least some influence on that of others in the room. It is, of course, by no means inevitable that the man who selects the issues to be discussed will dominate or determine the ultimate results—to which the lasting and profound differences in reading the meaning of the Constitution among justices on a host of issues bear witness. Still, there is a chance that he may do so, and often a good chance.

But there are other tasks, implied or actual, that confront a Chief Justice and play a role in history's regard of him as an effective or ineffective leader. Among them is his ability to keep peace among the several justices, who are often deeply divided along intellectual as well as personal lines. Justices Jackson and

Black, for example, became increasingly hostile during the waning days of Mr. Chief Justice Stone's tenure, resulting, or so it is believed, in President Truman's compromise "peacemaker appointment" of Fred Vinson as Stone's successor on the latter's death. Vinson, a person of far less judicial and intellectual stature than Stone, had a reputation as a conciliator and, apparently, succeeded at least in keeping the feud among the two justices *en famille.* Mr. Justice McReynolds, a confirmed anti-semite, refused even to speak to his newly appointed colleague, Mr. Justice Brandeis, from 1916 to 1919—with Mr. Chief Justice White unable to alter the situation, but the amiable and popular Mr. Chief Justice Taft apparently succeeded in mitigating it somewhat. While by no means able to stop entirely the public barbs exchanged on the bench on occasion between, for example, Justices Frankfurter and Whittaker, on the one hand, and Justices Black and Douglas, on the other, Mr. Chief Justice Warren apparently smoothed over many a ruffled feeling, despite being personally involved in an outburst or two, as some of the illustrations to follow will indicate.

Another significant facet of the "Chief's" work is to keep an eye on the clock during the conference, with a view of getting its tasks accomplished. Although there has been some disagreement as to the extent of the Court's burden—Mr. Justice Douglas, evidently a minority of one on that issue, does not view the Court as overworked [31]—there is little doubt that the pressure of case work is enormous. Unless a firm hand rules the conference, time will flee—especially as the justices are quite naturally given to extensive speaking, Mr. Justice Oliver Wendell Holmes, Jr., interestingly enough, being a notable exception. No Chief Justice controlled his flock so firmly as did Hughes, whom most students and observers of the Court, as well as those who served with him, have generally regarded as the most effective—even if on occasion somewhat arbitrary—organizer, leader, and disciplinarian along these lines since Mr. Chief Justice Marshall's regime.

For example, Hughes would accord an average of three and one-half minutes of conference time to a petition for certiorari and no more, having himself gone through and thoroughly analyzed

[31] See his address to the Cornell University Law School, fn. 15, loc. cit.

all of them *before* the conference and being fully prepared to make recommendations on each to his colleagues. Mr. Justice Stone, whose philosophy of his role as "Chief" was drastically different, declined to put any time limit on either certiorari discussions or on a particular series of cases. Stone simply refused to engage in what he viewed as "high pressure tactics." Thus, more than once, Hughes would finish a conference docket in four hours, whereas Stone would require four days for a similar docket. This did not make Stone a less qualified jurist, but it probably made him a far less effective "Chief" than Hughes or another effective Chief Justice, Taft—who, however, was certainly considerably below the calibre of Stone as a justice. Some observers, although distinctly in a small minority, believe that the virtues of Hughes as Chief Justice were overstated and those of Stone underrated. One of these, John P. Frank, a law clerk of Mr. Justice Black, complained that Hughes's tactics of "business efficiency" meant that ". . . discussion in conference was perforce a statement of conclusions more than an exchange of mutually stimulating ideas . . ." and he charged the Chief Justice with "intellectual flexibility for the sake of the appearance of unanimity." [32] Be that as it may, Mr. Chief Justice Hughes was immensely popular as a leader of his bench, and he was the only member of the Court to whom Mr. Justice McReynolds would defer. We have Mr. Justice Frankfurter's word that "if he made others feel his moral superiority, they merely felt a fact . . . all who served with him recognized [his] extraordinary qualities." [33] Mr. Justice Black attested to his own "more than impersonal and detached admiration [for Hughes's] extraordinary intellectual gifts." [34] And Mr. Justice Roberts wrote that "Men whose views were as sharply opposed as those of Van Devanter and Brandeis, or those of Sutherland and Cardozo, were at one in their admiration and affectionate regard for their presiding officer." [35] There is little, if any, doubt that Charles Evans Hughes was the epitome of a great Chief Justice.

[32] John B. Frank, "Harlan Fiske Stone: An Estimate," 9 *Stanford Law Review* 629n (1957).

[33] *Of Law and Men* (New York: Harcourt, Brace, & Co., 1956), p. 148. (Edited by Philip Elman.)   [34] Black to Hughes, June 3, 1941. Hughes Papers.

[35] Address to the Association of the Bar of the City of New York and the New York County Lawyers' Association, December 12, 1948.

ASSIGNING AND WRITING OPINIONS

The practice of writing the Opinion of the Court stems from the days of Mr. Chief Justice John Marshall, prior to whose adoption of this time-saving procedure the justices delivered their opinions *seriatim*—a practice still prevalent with the Law Lords of the British House of Lords. Today, following Marshall, full opinions are written for the Court—some of these *per curiam,* as we have seen—in all cases heard on the merits, other than those decided by memorandum order. However, no opinion is written in the event of a tie vote, nor does the Court announce on which side of the tie the justices stood. The effect of a tie vote is to sustain the decision below, e.g. the Court's 4:4 vote in the case of *Bailey v. Richardson,*[36] in which it thereby affirmed the 2:1 upholding of the loyalty dismissal of Dorothy Bailey by the federal government by the Court of Appeals for the District of Columbia. The even division of the Court in this instance came about as a result of Mr. Justice Clark's failure to participate in the case; since he was still Attorney-General at the time of Miss Bailey's travail and dismissal, he deemed it unethical to take part in her appeal. The members of today's Supreme Court are extremely cautious about even the faintest of taints of conflict of interest, be this of a social, economic, personal, or political nature. "When in doubt, do not sit" is a firmly established custom among the justices—although no statute governs this matter. This was not always so in the early days of the Court—as Mr. Chief Justice Marshall's refusal to disqualify himself in *Marbury v. Madison,*[37] in which he was directly involved, clearly demonstrated.

The work load of preparing opinions of the Court is usually very well distributed. If the Court is unanimous or if the Chief Justice is in the majority, he may, and often does, write the opinion of the Court himself. In the latter instance, provided he speaks for at least four other justices, it would be known as the *majority opinion.*

But, of course, nothing prevents him from asking another member of the Court, when it is unanimous, or of the majority when he himself is on that side, to write the opinion. The only exception to

[36] 341 U. S. 918 (1951).   [37] 1 Cranch 137 (1803).

this practice is the long-standing tradition of permitting every newcomer to the Court to select his first opinion. Gone long ago are the days of Mr. Chief Justice Marshall who, especially during his early years on the bench, would himself write practically every opinion. In fact, during his first four full years (1801–1805) he personally authored all but two of the opinions of the Court! But when the Chief Justice is on the minority side of a decision, the Senior Associate Justice on the side of the majority either writes the opinion of the Court himself or assigns it to one of the other members among the majority. For an illustration of an equitable distribution of the work load of preparing *opinions of the Court,* the 1958–59 term may be cited: Four justices wrote ten opinions each; two wrote 11; and three wrote 12. In the realm of the 30 concurring opinions filed, Mr. Justice Harlan led his brothers with seven, with the Chief Justice writing none at all. Mr. Justice Frankfurter headed the Court in the 72 *dissenting opinions* filed with 13; followed by Justices Brennan (12), Douglas (11), Black and Harlan (9 each), Clark (6), Mr. Chief Justice Warren and Justices Harlan, Whittaker, and Stewart (4 each). In all cases disposed of, whether by full opinion or memorandum order, the justices cast 230 dissenting *votes,* led by Mr. Justice Douglas's 46; the latter had also been that category's champion in the 1957–58 term with 42. Although, as a rule, *unanimous opinions* are rendered in a minority of full opinion cases—they have averaged 25 per cent through the years—the Court was unanimous in fully 40 per cent of its full opinions in its 1958–59 term. (The percentage dropped to 23 again in the 1959–60 term.) Memorandum orders, which, quite naturally, enjoy a far higher degree of unanimity, were up to 84 per cent during that term of "sweet agreeability." [38]

Dissenting Opinions. As these statistics demonstrate, dissenting and concurring opinions as well as simple dissents and concurrences are quite common. Yet only when the former method of registering disagreement with the decision and/or the opinion of the majority is employed does the practice become meaningful for the governmental process. A simple *dissent,* without explanation, for example, such as "Mr. Justice Butler dissents" in *Palko v.*

---

[38] Several good sources for these statistics exist; a.o., in the *Annual Report of the Director of the Administrative Office of the U. S. Courts;* in law reviews; and in the annual March issue of the *American Political Science Review.*

Connecticut,[39] ranks as a vote-on-the-other-side; but it says little to the expert and layman alike save that a justice, for reasons known only to himself, chose to dissent—no matter how understandable and even predictable that dissent might have been to the close student of the Court and its personnel. Be that aspect of disagreement as it may, it is entirely possible, of course, for honest, competent men to arrive at sharply divided opinions in a case; hence, *dissenting opinions,* both short and long, are quite common. In fact, the first *reported* decision of the Supreme Court was rendered by a divided Court, Justices William Cushing and Thomas Johnson dissenting to the Court majority's grant of an injunction to Georgia.[40] As one of the best-known dissenters, Mr. Justice Holmes, said, "General propositions do not decide particular cases." One of the classic statements on the subject was made by the then ex-Associate Justice and future Chief Justice Hughes:

> A dissent in a court of last resort is an appeal to the brooding spirit of the law, to the intelligence of a future day, when a later decision may possibly correct the error into which the dissenting judge believes the court to have been betrayed.[41]

And this from the pen of a jurist who rarely wrote dissenting opinions himself, who rarely dissented, and who exerted a greater dominance over the Court than any other Chief Justice save Marshall! Mr. Justice Carter, the colorful State of California jurist mentioned earlier in these pages, was fond of observing: "I welcome dissents, for they test the soundness of my own opinions." [42] (Both men meant dissenting *opinions,* of course.) Or, as Roscoe Pound once remarked, ". . . dissenting opinions may be the symptom of life in the law of time." [43] To Thomas Reed Powell they were ". . . most valuable equilibrators in the undulating course of the law." [44]

Many among the most memorable opinions of the Court initially on the dissenting side, have eventually become majority opinions

[39] 302 U. S. 319 (1937).   [40] *Georgia v. Braisford,* 2 Dallas 402 (1792).
[41] C. Evans Hughes, *The Supreme Court of the United States* (New York: Columbia University Press, 1928), p. 68.   [42] Cf. fn. 30, loc. cit.
[43] "Preface," in *Justice Musmanno Dissents* (Indianapolis: Bobbs-Merrill, 1956).
[44] "The Logic and Rhetoric of Constitutional Law," 15 *Journal of Philosophy, Psychology, and Scientific Method* 654 (1918).

—especially some by such eloquent spokesmen of the then minority viewpoints as Justices William Johnson, Harlan Sr., Holmes, Bandeis, and Stone. One obvious example is the lone Harlan dissenting opinion in 1896, his eloquent remonstrance against the "separate but equal" doctrine in *Plessy v. Ferguson,*[45] which became the unanimous opinion of the Court in 1954 in *Brown v. Board of Education of Topeka.*[46] Another is the lone dissenting opinion of Stone in 1940 in the *Gobitis* case,[47] arguing forcefully, but unsuccessfully, against the compulsory flag salute required by the Minersville, Pa., school district even of those who found it to be religiously objectionable. Scarcely three years later this became the opinion of the Court when a majority of six held a similar West Virginia Board of Education requirement to be an unconstitutional attachment of freedom of religion in the *Barnette* case.[48] Mr. Justice Cardozo, also a not infrequent dissenter, viewed the dissenting opinion as an entirely proper place for recording "the best inspiration of the time," for instruction in moral values still battling for general acceptance in the political process.[49] "It's grand to fight," once remarked Mr. Justice Black. "The Supreme Court does disagree. I hope it always will. It does have men who express their differences. I hope it always will have. Because I subscribe to the theory that there is no progress when differences are stifled." [50]

There is thus little doubt that a dissenting opinion is pre-eminently the result of a profoundly held conviction; consequently, it may well be regarded as strengthening rather than weakening a particular case as an authority. However, it may also serve to muddy the waters, to force extremist positions, and to confuse the public. For example, there are those students of the *Dred Scott* case—and not necessarily only the apologists for Mr. Chief Justice Taney—who contend that the latter's extremist position for the majority was forced upon him by the extremist position of Mr. Justice McLean's dissenting opinion.

Concurring Opinions. On the other hand, at times the reasoning

[45] 163 U. S. 537.   [46] 347 U. S. 483.

[47] *Minersville School District v. Gobitis,* 310 U. S. 586.

[48] *West Virginia State Board of Education v. Barnette,* 319 U. S. 624.

[49] Benjamin M. Cardozo, *Selected Writings* (New York: Fallon Publishers, 1947), p. 274. (Edited by Margaret E. Hall.)

[50] Quoted in *The New York Times,* June 5, 1961.

of the justice assigned to write the opinion of the Court may not be palatable to all of the component members of the majority side. In that event, one or more *concurring opinions* may be written—an increasingly frequent practice during the past few decades. Broadly speaking, it usually signifies the concurrence of its author in the *decision,* but not in the opinion, reasoning, or judgment of the Court. One illustration would be the two separate concurring opinions of Justices Black and Douglas in the 8:0 decision of the Supreme Court in *Rochin v. California.*[51] While agreeing with the Court that the State of California had engaged in grossly brutal, and hence obviously illegal, conduct in its apprehension and conviction of Rochin, a narcotics peddler, the two justices strongly disagreed with the grounds on which the Court based its reversal of Rochin's conviction: a violation of the due process of law clause of the Fourteenth Amendment of the U. S. Constitution. But in the firmly held judgment of Black and Douglas, the State of California had actually violated individual liberty safeguards specifically enumerated in the Bill of Rights—in fact thus contending, as they had done ever since their appointment to the Court in 1937 and 1939, respectively, that the specific provisions are per se applicable to the states (via the Fourteenth Amendment) as well as to the federal government. Another example of the use of the concurring opinion is that by Mr. Justice Frankfurter—a frequent "concurrer"—in *Cooper v. Aaron (The Little Rock Case),*[52] which was decided in the Special Session in the summer of 1958. There, not only in order to show its continuous unanimity in cases basically following *Brown v. Board of Education,*[53] but also to make clear that those justices (Brennan and Whittaker) who had not participated in *Brown* were at one with the remaining seven members of that historic opinion, the Supreme Court issued its opinion in the form of a joint authorship, with the names of each of its nine unanimous members specifically listed *seriatim* at the head of the "Opinion of the Court." However, obviously deeply grieved and disturbed by the clear flouting of the law as well as the high echelons of the federal judiciary by the officials of the State of Arkansas, led by Governor Orval E. Faubus, Mr. Justice Frankfurter was moved to write a separate concurring opinion,

[51] 342 U. S. 165 (1952).   [52] 358 U. S. 1 (1958).
[53] 347 U. S. 483 (1954).

which was issued and published some time thereafter. In it, he gave what in effect was a profound and moving lecture to the country in general, and the South in particular, on the meaning of "the supreme Law of the Land" and the federal system. Written with scholarship and feeling, this independent statement nevertheless probably diminished somewhat the effect of the joint opinion of the Court.

Techniques of Assignment. The preceding discussion raises the interesting problem of the selection of the opinion writers by the Chief Justice, or by the Senior Associate Justice when the duty of designation devolves upon him. Giving due attention to the need of distributing the work load relatively evenly (and permitting a Court newcomer to select his own first opinion), the average Chief Justice's assignments—approximately 85–90 per cent of the cases —may well be said to follow a fairly common pattern. It is a pattern, based upon the considerable influence that governs the actions of the "Chief" in making his selections, that will take account of all of the following considerations: First, the so-called "great," "big," or "important constitutional" cases—although these are necessarily somewhat subjective concepts—should be authored by the "Chief" himself, e.g. Mr. Chief Justice Warren speaking for the unanimous Court in *Brown*. Or Mr. Chief Justice Hughes's majority opinion for the narrowly divided Court (5:4) in the immensely significant case of *West Coast Hotel Co. v. Parrish*,[54] upholding the State of Washington minimum wage law for women—sometimes, perhaps flippantly but probably not altogether unjustly, called "the-switch-in-time-that-saved-nine" case. Here, the Court not only departed from its erstwhile stubborn adherence to the narrow construction of the concept of "freedom of contract" under the Fifth and Fourteenth Amendments to the Constitution by overruling the specific precedent of *Adkins v. Children's Hospital*[55] (where it had struck down [5:3] a similar, though federal, law for the District of Columbia); but that departure also clearly indicated a change of position by the Chief Justice *and* Mr. Justice Roberts. The latter's switch was especially significant because he then normally represented the swing vote between the so-called pro- and anti-New Deal factions on the Court. His new stance heralded more or less clear sailing, at least

[54] 300 U. S. 379 (1937).　　[55] 261 U. S. 525 (1923).

on constitutional grounds, for the legislative programs enacted by the then still high-riding New Deal Roosevelt Administration.

Second, no matter what the importance of a case, the selection must take into account the possible importance of the decision as a precedent. Justices may well differ in their views on whether the decision should be lodged on a broad or a narrow construction of the issue and on the ground on which it is to be based. For instance, the movie, *Lady Chatterley's Lover,* had been banned by the New York State Board of Regents on grounds of a statutory provision that forbade showing of films that present "acts of sexual immorality, perversion or lewdness" as being "desirable, acceptable, or proper patterns of behavior." Speaking for a majority of five, Mr. Justice Stewart held that particular provision of the New York licensing-statute unconstitutional as a violation of the Fourteenth Amendment; but there were four separate concurring opinions which, while agreeing that the New York statute could not be validly applied in this case, held that the Court should have reversed New York on *statutory construction* grounds and not reached the *constitutional* issue. Justices Black and Douglas, although members of the majority of five, joined in another opinion in which they contended that this statute, like all other prior censorship of movies, should be thrown out lock-stock-and-barrel as being unconstitutional "on its face" as a prior restraint on freedom of speech and press.[56] Obviously, here the Chief Justice's assignment had to take into account that prospective authorship which would be sufficiently acceptable, or least offensive, to five justices—evidently Stewart's.

Third, although some observers would disagree, there is considerable evidence that the "Chief" is conscious of an element of "public relations" in designating his opinion writer. This is particularly true in cases undoubtedly unpopular to a sizable segment of the population. In other words, he is not unmindful of the importance of making a decision acceptable to the public, or, when applicable, of coating the bitter pill about to be swallowed. A fascinating illustration of this point was brought to light by Professor Alpheus T. Mason in his fine biography, *Harlan Fiske Stone: Pillar of the Law.*[57] In 1944, the Court conference on the

[56] *Kingsley International Pictures Corporation v. Regents,* 360 U. S. 684 (1959).
[57] (New York: The Viking Press, 1956), pp. 614–15.

Texas "White Primary" case, *Smith v. Allwright*,[58] had clearly evidenced that all of the justices save Roberts were agreed that this constitutionally challenged Texas statute was unconstitutional as a violation of the Fifteenth Amendment—the South was bound to react with great vehemence. Mr. Chief Justice Stone assigned the opinion to Mr. Justice Frankfurter, an eloquent stylist and profoundly serious and scholarly jurist, not given to pamphleteering. One day after the conference, having discussed his misgivings with some of the justices, Mr. Justice Jackson, a good friend of the principals involved, wrote a highly unusual and probably quite unprecedented letter to the Chief Justice, candidly and fervently suggesting that the nature and importance of the issue in the case were so far-reaching and made of such emotional matter that the Frankfurter selection was bound to "grate on Southern sensibilities." He continued:

> Mr. Justice Frankfurter unites in a rare degree factors which unhappily excite prejudice. In the first place, he is a Jew. In the second place, he is from New England, the seat of the abolition movement. In the third place, he has not been thought of as a person particularly sympathetic with the Democratic party in the past.[59]

Jackson went on to point out that he realized that a consideration of every one of the listed factors was utterly distasteful, and that he mentioned them only with the greatest reluctance and "frank fear of being misunderstood." He had discussed the matter with Frankfurter and had advised him of his intention to write to the Chief Justice. Evidently persuaded by the Jackson argument, Stone, with Frankfurter's knowledge and agreement, substituted Mr. Justice Stanley Reed, who was: (a) an old-line Kentuckian; (b) a Protestant; (c) a native-born, in contrast to Mr. Justice Frankfurter who was born in Vienna; and (d) a Democrat of long standing. This did not make the wounds of the South any less severe, but at least they were administered, in a manner of speaking, by a kinsman, however removed now.

In the same general vein, the Chief Justice will normally make it a practice to assign so-called "liberal" opinions of the Court to

---

[58] 321 U. S. 649 (1944).   [59] Mason, loc. cit. p. 615.

"conservative" justices and so-called "conservative" opinions to "liberal" justices—again in the hope of making them more palatable. Thus, Mr. Chief Justice Stone assigned to one of the Court's leading liberals, Mr. Justice Black, the majority opinion in what has been widely labeled as the worst racist decision in the recent history of the tribunal, *Korematsu v. United States*.[60] There, the Court upheld 6:3 the forcible removal of 112,000 persons of Japanese ancestry, including 77,000 native-born American citizens, from their West Coast homes to inland war relocation centers. Although none of these evacuees had been specifically accused of disloyalty, the Black opinion upheld the removal as an emergency measure necessitated by the facts-of-life of wartime, as an "exercise of power of the government to take steps necessary to prevent espionage and sabotage in an area threatened by Japanese attack." And when the Court, in a 7:1 opinion in 1957, severely limited the application of the Smith Act in the prosecution of Communist party leaders and members, Mr. Chief Justice Warren assigned the case to a member usually found on the "conservative" side, Mr. Justice Harlan.[61] This strategy, if that it be, is not always employed, but it is resorted to with sufficient regularity to make a distinct pattern detectable, mild and unpredictable though it may be.

Fourth, when the conference has indicated a split decision, no matter how many may be in the latent minority, the Chief Justice will endeavor to assign the opinion to a justice whose views come closest to the would-be dissenters without, however, being one of them. The theory here is that the justice would, in this case—and probably in others—be a "center justice," whose "middle" approach would be acceptable, more or less, to both majority and minority.[62] For example, in *United States v. Butler*,[63] a majority of six declared the Agricultural Adjustment Act of 1933 unconstitutional as an illegal use by Congress of its powers over taxation and commerce at the expense of the principle of "dual federalism." This was one of thirteen New Deal laws or provisions thereof that

[60] 323 U. S. 214 (1944).   [61] *Yates v. United States*, 354 U. S. 298.
[62] For an able and extensive discussion of this, and related points, see the interesting paper by David J. Danelski, "The Influence of the Chief Justice in the Decisional Process of the Supreme Court," presented at the 1960 American Political Science Association Meeting, New York City, September 9, 1960.
[63] 297 U. S. 1 (1936).

the Court would invalidate on constitutional grounds in little more than one year's time during 1935–36. Reasoning that an opinion by one of the four "ultra-conservative" justices—Butler, McReynolds, Van Devanter, and Sutherland—would only serve to increase the fury of both the executive and legislative branches, Mr. Chief Justice Hughes assigned Mr. Justice Roberts to speak for the Court. The latter wrote an opinion that adopted the broad Hamilton-Story interpretation of the "general welfare" clause of the Constitution (I-8-1), but struck down the particular tax at issue as substantially an illegal regulation of local affairs. There is evidence that the Chief Justice went along with the majority only because Roberts wrote the opinion—and there was enough in that opinion to permit the minority of three, and their allies on both ends of Pennsylvania Avenue, to nourish hopes for a better day! It came scarcely a year later.

The critical role of the Chief Justice in assigning opinions is thus axiomatic. Much depends on his skill, diplomacy, tact, and sheer powers of persuasion. No other "Chief," in the opinion of Mr. Justice Frankfurter, a long-time member of the bench who served under four Chief Justices and knew three others, "equaled Chief Justice Hughes in the skill and wisdom and disinterestedness with which he made his assignments." Pointing out that Hughes's governing consideration was always "what was best for the Court as to the particular situation," he closed his observations with this wise admonition:

> The grounds for the assignment may not always be obvious to the outsider. Indeed, they are not always so to the members of the Court; the reasons normally remain within the breast of the chief justice. But these involve, if the duty is wisely discharged, perhaps the most delicate judgment demanded of the chief justice.[64]

Yet no matter how hard he may try, or how skillful he may be, a Chief cannot compel unanimity. As we have already seen, separate opinions are the rule rather than the exception. It is thus not at all uncommon to find five, six, seven, or even nine opinions in a single case. The *Dred Scott* case [65] and the *License*

[64] *Of Law and Men, op. cit.,* pp. 137 and 142.   [65] 19 Howard 393 (1857).

cases [66] featured nine such opinions! The *Steel Seizure* case [67] brought seven, and the *Douds* [68] and *Dennis* [69] cases five separate opinions. This may be a valuable and intriguing practice, but it hardly lends itself to certainty. However, certainty is not inevitably an end in itself. Indeed, certainty and unanimity in the law are generally possessed only under a dictatorial system of government—to which, in fact, they are indispensable.

Drafting and Circulating Opinions. Following the assignment of opinions, the laborious task of drafting commences. Here the power of persuasion by an author—presumably actively supported by the Chief Justice, whenever feasible—looms large in this phase of the judicial decision-making process. Again, we know but little of what takes place during these backstage activities, but from those few sources that are available—papers, biographies, law clerks, various memoirs—we do acquire an outline of this terminal phase of the preparation of a Supreme Court opinion, collective as an end product but with the distinct imprint of the minds and labor of nine individuals. As opinions are drafted, and on whatever side of the tentative decision they may be, printed "proof" copies are circulated by their authors among the members of the Court. These copies, indeed all of the Court's publications, are composed by a special unit of printers who labor in secrecy, to the extent of locking themselves in during working hours, and utilize the basement of the Court building rather than the Government Printing Office.

Depending upon comments by his brothers, an author of an opinion may draw additional drafts in an attempt to gain adherence, if possible; a concurrence rather than a dissent; or any one of the other devices that may soften disagreement where disagreement exists or make more forceful an opinion where unanimity seems attainable. This labor of persuasion is undertaken irrespective of how the several justices may have voted in conference, the theory being that "there is always hope." The process is frequently a difficult and laborious task, sometimes running into months or even years. *Brown v. Board of Education* [70] was in various stages of writing from 1952 to 1954, probably largely due to Mr. Chief

---

[66] 7 Howard 283 (1849).
[67] *Youngstown Sheet & Tube Co. v. Sawyer,* 343 U. S. 579 (1952).
[68] *American Communications Association v. Douds,* 339 U. S. 94 (1950).
[69] *Dennis v. United States,* 341 U. S. 494 (1951).   [70] 347 U. S. 483 (1954).

Justice Warren's herculean efforts to obtain a unanimous Court, undoubtedly a delicate and difficult matter on the subject at issue —the declaration of unconstitutionality of compulsory racial segregation in the public schools. Although still very much a case of conjecture, apparently the last holdout on the Court was Mr. Justice Reed. It is certain that this decision was the collective product of common and deliberate labor.

We do know of some specific cases of persuasion, thanks to the papers left by the justices. In one instance, Mr. Justice Butler, who had voted in conference to reverse the decision of the lower court, evidently succumbed to the persuasive powers of his colleague Stone. Sending a copy of his "surrender" to Mr. Chief Justice Taft, who ever tried to turn a dissenting opinion into silent acquiescence, he wrote to case-author Stone as follows:

> I voted to reverse. While this sustains your conclusion to affirm, I still think reversal would be better. But I shall in silence acquiesce. Dissents seldom aid in the right development or statement of the law. They often do harm. For myself I say: "lead us not into temptation." [71]

In another and later Stone opinion, Mr. Chief Justice Hughes wrote to him: "I choke a little at swallowing your analysis, still I do not think it would serve any useful purpose to expose my views." [72] Although as Chief Justice, Stone exercised far less persuasive pressure than Hughes, he did work for unanimity whenever possible. At times, this would involve—as it does quite frequently—a switch from a decisional ground initially agreed upon to another. For example, in one of the cases brought during Stone's tenure, *Edwards v. California*,[73] he successfully persuaded Mr. Justice Byrnes to change his conference vote. Now delivering the opinion of the Court, Byrnes's switch resulted in adopting a *ground* for the decision on which five members of the Court could agree—the interstate commerce, rather than the "privileges and immunities" clause of the Constitution. Four justices concurred in the decision, thus rendering it unanimous, but indicated their preference for the latter ground. An extreme example of the drive for agreement was provided in a difficult double jeopardy case

[71] As quoted by Danelski, op. cit. pp. 19–20.   [72] Ibid. p. 2.
[73] 314 U. S. 160 (1941).

in 1959, when Mr. Justice Brennan wrote the opinion of the Court *and also a separate opinion* in which he expressed views he had evidently been unable to persuade his colleagues to accept.[74]

Much of what has been said of the backstage give-and-take is corroborated by what is probably the only full-scale study of that phase of the Court's work, an excellent book by Professor Alexander M. Bickel of Yale University Law School, who was one of Mr. Justice Frankfurter's law clerks, *The Unpublished Opinions of Mr. Justice Brandeis*.[75] Based on the private papers of Louis Dembitz Brandeis, as they relate to his career as Justice of the Supreme Court of the United States from 1916 to 1939, the book is rich in illustrations of the persuasive processes that accompany the drafting of opinions for ultimate delivery. One or two examples will suffice to illustrate the point further: A photograph of a note from his brother Holmes to Brandeis indicates that Holmes had revised his opinion in *Bullock v. Florida*,[76] now adopting the result Brandeis had urged upon him. Having been persuaded by Brandeis's point of view, Holmes did so willingly enough, but his note showed much concern lest his changed opinion now cause dissatisfaction among the former majority and perhaps result in a reassignment of the case to someone else—which did not happen, however.[77]

In another instance, it was Brandeis's turn to give in. He had felt quite strongly about the construction of a statute at issue in a 1924 railroad case opinion, which had been assigned to Mr. Justice McReynolds.[78] In discussing the case some years later with the then Professor of Law Felix Frankfurter, he said that he had told the Chief Justice (Taft) that "he couldn't stand for" McReynolds's opinion, that it contained too much that would "bother us in the future." Mr. Justice Van Devanter, continued Brandeis,

> worked with McReynolds and made changes, and the Chief asked me whether that will remove my sting. The corrections weren't adequate, and finally the Chief took over the opinion

[74] *Abbate v. United States,* 359 U. S. 187 (1959), at 196.
[75] (Cambridge, Harvard University Press, 1957.) Subtitled, *The Supreme Court at Work.*   [76] 254 U. S. 513 (1921).
[77] Bickel, loc cit. insert between pp. 118–19, last photographic plate.
[78] *Railroad Commission of California· v. Southern Pacific Railway Co.,* 264 U. S. 331.

and put out what is now the Court's opinion and I suppressed my dissent, because, after all, it's merely a question of statutory construction and the worst things were removed by the Chief.[79]

But by far the most important fact revealed by this glimpse into the Supreme Court's inner sanctum is that many, if not all, of the Court's opinions, though ostensibly the work of one man, are really the product of many minds in the sense that the justice who writes the opinion often has to add to, delete, or modify his original draft in order to be able to retain the support of his colleagues, many of whom are far from agreeing with him or with each other. Indeed, it is essential to recognize that each member of the Court participates in each and every stage of the consideration of a case. Once we grasp this crucial notion, we can readily understand why a considerable number of the Court's decisions are vague or contain several apparently contradictory statements. Since the views reflected in a given opinion are rarely identical, that opinion may well turn out to be either ambiguous or maintain several varying postures, in order that each man who supports it will be able to reconcile it with his own particular position. A pertinent example is the laborious forging of Mr. Chief Justice Stone's majority opinion in *In Re Yamashita*,[80] in which the Court upheld the conviction by a United States military commission of the Japanese general who was accused of violating the laws of war in failing to prevent his troops from committing atrocities against American and Philippine citizens. This case is quite unclear on the question of whether the due process clause of the Fifth Amendment is binding on such a military commission. The opinion, on the whole, tends to give the impression that the answer to this question is in the negative, but some slight support can be found for the contrary view. According to Professor Mason, Stone's biographer, the latter's original draft contained the assertion that Yamashita's trial would have to adhere to the requirement of this clause. However, to meet at least in part the objections of Justices Black and Reed, who apparently were of the opinion that these commissions were not bound by the provisions of the due process clause, Stone deleted the assertion and added some confusing language which

[79] As quoted and described by Bickel, loc. cit. pp. 209–10.
[80] 327 U. S. 1 (1946).

Black and Reed could more or less reconcile with their own views on this matter.[81] The end product, though it did not entirely satisfy either its readers or the bench as a whole, at least had the virtue—if that it be—of receiving the support of the majority of the Court.

No matter how intriguing and important to an understanding of the Supreme Court these various data undoubtedly are, the absolute secrecy that attends the backstage work and deliberations of the Supreme Court—the "Purple Curtain," as Professor Fowler Harper once called it—is essential. No one save the nine justices is present in the conference; no record of the discussions is kept. When clerks bring messages, the justice who is junior in seniority —no matter what his age—goes to the door to get them. There simply are no leaks. This is not to say, however, that no leaks have ever occurred. The most serious of these on record came in connection with the *Dred Scott* case,[82] when Mr. Justice John Catron evidently told President-elect James Buchanan the "line-up" of the justices in the pending momentous decision one month prior to its announcement! The incoming President, troubled and weak, used this information in his inaugural address on March 4, 1857, and told the country that the Court would soon settle the much disputed territorial question. Two days later Mr. Chief Justice Taney delivered the 7:2 opinion of the Court—which, as history proved all-too-soon, did anything but settle the problem and, indeed, acted as a catalyst in bringing on the Civil War.

However, that instance was a rare and crass exception. Complete secrecy does, and must, exist. The Court can neither open its backstage deliberations to the public nor hold news conferences. To do either would fatally affect its position as well as its effectiveness. For a description of what goes on behind the doors we depend almost entirely on the kind of papers and biographies of the justices discussed above, and, on occasion, on revelations, usually appearing after the death of the justice involved, by their law clerks. Yet even these revelations are more often than not confined to matters of procedure. This is emphatically as it should be. We know enough of the operation and functions of the highest court in the land to enable us to appreciate, study, and, hopefully, understand them in the context of its so significant role in the

[81]Mason, loc. cit. pp. 667–9.
[82] *Dred Scott v. Sanford*, 19 Howard 393 (1857).

process of free government. To repeat, the secrecy of the Court's proceedings behind that "Purple Curtain" is a necessary by-product of its work. In a widely read article endeavoring to explain Mr. Justice Roberts's famous so-called "switch-in-time" to the side of the "liberals" on the Court in 1937, Mr. Justice Frankfurter viewed it in these terms:

> Disclosure of Court happenings not made public by the Court itself, in its opinions and orders, presents a ticklish problem. The *secrecy that envelops the Court's work is not due to love of secrecy or want of responsible regard for the claims of a democratic society to know how it is governed.* That the Supreme Court should not be amenable to the forces of publicity to which the Executive and the Congress are subjected is essential to the effective functioning of the Court. But the passage of time may enervate the reasons for this restriction, particularly if disclosure rests not on tittle-tattle or self-serving declarations. . . .[83]

OPINION DAY

The final stage in the Supreme Court's decision-making process is Opinion Day. On that important occasion, usually alternate Mondays, sometimes three Mondays in each month, the entire Court meets in solemn public session and announces, or "hands down," the decisions it has reached. Other than those disposed of *per curiam* or decided by memorandum order, the cases now thus made public cover the full reasoning of the Court and set forth all viewpoints expressed by the justices. The various opinions are either read verbatim, paraphrased, or summarized by their authors, as the spirit and the occasion may dictate; sometimes simply the decision is given. The opinions may run from fifteen minutes to several hours—although the Chief Justice would almost certainly try to discourage the latter. Nevertheless, a visitor to the Supreme Court Chamber on an Opinion Monday ought to be prepared for an average session of two hours' duration. This interesting practice of announcing opinions orally is not generally practiced in the lower courts, where a case is "announced" simply by

[83] "Mr. Justice Roberts," 104 *University of Pennsylvania Law Review* 313 (1955). (Italics supplied.)

filing its disposition with the clerk. Prior to the Chief Justiceship of Charles Evans Hughes, the Court's announcements were even lengthier, for the justices generally persisted in reading opinions word for word, not infrequently in an unrelieved monotone. Hughes, however, sensing a golden opportunity to make, in the words of Edwin McElwain, one of his law clerks, "a public demonstration of the dignity and responsibility of the Court to the bar and to the thousands of visitors who came to the new Supreme Court Building during his regime," [84] not only encouraged paraphrasing and summarizing of opinions but also impressed upon his brothers of the bench the need to deliver them forcefully and convincingly. The Chief Justice himself was such an impressive figure—with his magnificent head, white beard, and sonorous voice, that more than once visitors to an Opinion Day, hearing him deliver one of his opinions with dramatic impact, likened him to a latter-day Moses—a concept not entirely displeasing to Hughes, not so much for himself but for Court and Law.

Even after the justices have assembled for the announcement of their opinions, should any one of their number have some last-minute qualms regarding one about to be handed down, all he has to do is to ask the Chief Justice to "let it go over"—such is the concern with each justice's sensibilities. The now public opinions presumably confine themselves to the issue involved in the various cases, but the voicing of profoundly held beliefs, and at times even a swipe at a colleague, is quite common. Thus cleavages among the justices, those of an intellectual, policy, and at times even personal nature, become apparent in the written opinions—no matter how skilled an arbiter the Chief Justice may be. Fortunately less frequent are *ad hoc* outbursts from the bench on Opinion Day; these are not found in the written record, but they do occur—justices are human. Perhaps the most famous one is Mr. Justice McReynolds's explosion in 1935, while reading his dissent in the *Gold Clause Cases*,[85] when he veritably screamed from the bench: "This is Nero at his worst. The Constitution is gone."

Judicial Tempers. But, to give some brief recent illustrations of this aspect of Opinion Day, in November 1960, Mr. Justice

[84] "The Business of the Supreme Court as Conducted by Chief Justice Hughes," 63 *Harvard Law Review* 20 (1949).
[85] *Norman v. Baltimore & Ohio Railroad Co.* 294 U. S. 240.

Douglas, having just heard Mr. Justice Whittaker read the 6:3 opinion for the Court in a tax case, commented acidly from the bench that the issue decided this day was "narrow and technical"; that he would not have filed a dissent had not the "majority's error been so egregious"; and he closed with the observation: "But six make the law, and sometimes very bad law." Earlier that year, Mr. Justice Frankfurter had characterized as "judicial somersault" an opinion for the Court by Mr. Justice Stewart in a criminal law case.[86] On Opinion Monday, March 30, 1959, Mr. Justice Frankfurter, while reading the majority opinion upholding the successive federal and state trials of one Bartkus for the same criminal act, against the charge of double jeopardy, made a passing reference to "the so-called Bill of Rights." When Mr. Justice Black's turn came to read his dissent in the case, he declared passionately: "This case concerns the Bill of Rights, not the 'so-called Bill of Rights!' "[87] And within little more than a month, during the waning days of the 1960–61 term, the public and the Court were treated to two serious *ad hoc* outbursts from the bench on two Opinion Mondays, involving Mr. Chief Justice Warren and, again, Mr. Justice Frankfurter. In the first instance, a sharp dissent by the latter provoked an oral rebuttal by the former, which was even more unusual because the Chief Justice, on the side of the 5:4 majority, had written no opinion in the case. But in stating his dissent, Mr. Justice Frankfurter—in an extemporaneous summary, as are all of his opinions—took nearly fifteen minutes to sharpen the written language and heighten his criticism of the majority position in the criminal case at issue. Evidently hurt and annoyed by Frankfurter's tone of voice and the contents of his summation, the Chief Justice told the courtroom that "since so much has been said here that was not in any written opinion," he wanted to add a word as to why he joined the majority.[88]

Yet an even more serious manifestation of judicial temper-flaring occurred several Opinion Mondays later, again featuring the same two justices. The Court, once again by a 5:4 vote, as is so frequently the case in criminal cases involving Bill-of-Rights interpretations, had reversed the murder conviction of one Stewart in

---

[86] *Elkins and Clark v. United States,* 364 U. S. 206 (1960).

[87] As reported by Anthony Lewis, "Justice Black at 75: Still the Dissenter," *The New York Times Magazine,* February 26, 1961, p. 74.

[88] As reported in *The New York Times,* March 21, 1961.

the District of Columbia. In a ringing dissent, Mr. Justice Frank-furter, going far beyond anything he had written, accused the majority of "plucking out" of the lengthy trial record an isolated episode, and suggested that judges find in the record "what the mind is looking for." He went on to categorize the majority opinion as an "indefensible example of finicky appellate review of criminal cases," and warned against "turning a criminal appeal into a quest for error." When he had finished, Mr. Chief Justice Warren leaned forward and with evident emotion stated that the dissent just heard was not a proper statement of an opinion, but rather a

> lecture . . . a closing argument by a prosecutor to a jury. It is properly made, perhaps, in the conference room [of the Court], but not in the court room . . . The purpose of reporting an opinion [there] is to inform the public and is not for the purpose of degrading this court.[89]

But at the end of the session the two adversaries were engaged in friendly and cordial conversation!

Ratio Decidendi and Obiter Dictum. It is important to distinguish—although this is sometimes far more easily said than done—between the *ratio decidendi* of an opinion and the frequently present *obiter dictum* or *obiter dicta. Ratio decidendi* refers to the essence, the vitals, the necessary core of the decision; *obiter dictum* is a more or less extraneous, presumably unnecessary, point made by the author of an opinion. In other words, the former constitutes the legal rule to be followed and adhered to below; the latter is an expression of a belief, viewpoint, or sentiment which, at least in theory, has no binding effect. It is not surprising, however, that, on occasion, an *obiter dictum* lives long after the *ratio decidendi* has been forgotten! Moreover, as U. S. District Court Judge P. M. Hall of California once put the matter: "I am not unmindful of the fact that in the last analysis the Judges of the Supreme Court are the final arbiters as to what is or is not dicta in a previous opinion." [90] Nonetheless, it is the *ratio deci-dendi* that makes the decided case one of record and renders the matter at issue *res adjudicata,* i.e. a matter upon which a com-

[89] As reported in *The (Philadelphia) Evening Bulletin* and *The New York Times,* April 25, 1961.

[90] *Odikubo v. Bonesteel,* 60 F. Supp. 916, at 930, fn. 28 (1945).

petent court of law has passed judgment and which it will therefore not examine (all other things remaining equal, which of course they do not always).

One of the most famous expounders of the *obiter dictum* was Mr. Chief Justice John Marshall, who delighted in employing that technique as a medium for the constitutional education of the people of his time. His famous opinions in *Marbury v. Madison,*[91] *McCulloch v. Maryland,*[92] and *Gibbons v. Ogden,*[93] for example, are full of *dicta* which history has so merged with the *ratio decidendi* in these cases as to make the two concepts almost indistinguishable. Nor has that approach become extinct in our own days, to which illustrations on two levels of the judiciary bear witness: In the case of *Shachtman v. Dulles,*[94] three judges of the U. S. Circuit Court of Appeals for the District of Columbia held unanimously that the grounds for the Secretary of State's denial of a passport to the petitioner constituted an arbitrary, and hence unconstitutional, denial of due process of law under the Fifth Amendment. That was the *ratio decidendi* of the case, but the author of the opinion of the tribunal, Circuit Judge Fahy, in an interesting *obiter dictum,* based the privilege of a passport upon the "natural right" to travel, "to go from place to place as the means of transportation permit." At the level of the Supreme Court, *Watkins v. United States* [95] dealt with the refusal of a former labor organizer, John T. Watkins, to answer certain questions put to him by a subcommittee of the House Committee on Un-American Activities, which was investigating "Communist activities in the Chicago area." In a 6:1 decision, speaking through Mr. Chief Justice Warren, the Court set aside Watkins's conviction for contempt of Congress in the District Court below because neither Congress nor the Committee had ever satisfactorily apprised him whether the questions he had refused to answer were "pertinent to the subject under inquiry." This failure on the part of the legislature was thus held to render the conviction void on grounds of vagueness under the due process of law clause of the Fifth Amendment. Here we have the *ratio decidendi* of the *Watkins* case. But resorting to the device of the *orbiter dictum,* Mr.

---

[91] 1 Cranch 137 (1803). [92] 4 Wheaton 316 (1819).
[93] 9 Wheaton 1 (1824). [94] 225 F. 2d 938 (1955).
[95] 354 U. S. 178 (1957).

Chief Justice Warren also discussed matters, however related, which had not really been specifically raised by the petitioner Watkins in his allegations. Warren's long and fervent *dictum* clearly represented a lecture to Congress—and, hopefully, the public at large—on the rights of individuals and congressional abuse of its power to investigate, featured by the admonition: "We have no doubt that there is no congressional power to expose for the sake of exposure." [96]

COMPLIANCE

When officially announced as decided, the case becomes binding on all lower federal courts and on all state courts where applicable. It is now *the* controlling opinion, *res adjudicata,* the law of the land, as enunciated and/or interpreted by its highest tribunal. Then it is duly recorded and published by the federal government in an invaluable, precise series of volumes, known as the *United States Reports,* which constitutes the sole *official* record of the actions of the Supreme Court of the United States—there are also several unofficial publications available.[97] (The *Reports* and their fore-runners, kept by official court reporters, are on file back to 1790.) However, although compliance with the Court's decisions may be expected to be a foregone conclusion insofar as the lower *federal* courts are concerned—Chapter Eight will discuss some of the problems of compliance and enforcement by nonjudicial govern-mental bodies generally—it is not always necessarily simple and automatic.

For example, in September 1960, Judge Ashton Williams of the U. S. District Court for South Carolina disqualified himself from a segregation suit on the ground that *he* considered the Su-preme Court's decision and subsequent order in *Brown v. Board of Education* [98] to be unconstitutional! He announced that another judge would have to hear the case, brought by four Charleston Negroes, which involved compulsory segregation of the Charles-ton municipal golf course. Contending that the Supreme Court's decision barring separate facilities for Whites and Negroes in such

[96] Ibid.

[97] For example, the *Supreme Court Reporter* and the *Lawyers' Edition of the Opinions of the United States Supreme Court.*

[98] 347 U. S. 483 (1954) and 349 U. S. 294 (1955).

public recreational facilities was based "on unconstitutional grounds," he nonetheless stepped aside rather than disobey, and declared: "Since as a Federal judge I have to follow that decision I will disqualify myself because I have taken an oath to sustain the Constitution." [99]

Another U. S. District Court jurist, the then 87-year-old Judge William H. Atwell of Texas, went considerably further in 1956; he simply *refused* to carry out the desegregation ruling of the Court, and resorted to every conceivable judicial roadblock to prevent it. Although he had been reversed by the Fifth U. S. Circuit Court of Appeals,[100] after his initial rejection of the plaintiffs' petition,[101] he again refused to set a date of desegregation of the Dallas school district because such a step would cause "civil wrongs." In order to make quite clear where he stood on the issue, Atwell announced:

> I believe that it will be seen that the [Supreme] Court based its decision on no law but rather on what the Court regarded as more authoritative, more psychological knowledge. . . . It will be recalled that in 1952, Mr. Justice Frankfurter said it [the Supreme Court] was not competent to take judicial notice of "claims of social scientists." [102]

The Court of Appeals naturally again reversed the second Atwell decision in short order.[103] But far from acquiescing, Judge Atwell now embarked upon a course of action in the opposite extreme by ordering all Dallas schools integrated in the middle of the academic year! [104] This decision was also reversed by the higher court.[105] Three or four years later, Atwell retired permanently—he had been recalled for temporary duty—and another federal District Court judge, ultimately ordered a "mild" form of desegregation. This was broadened and amended by the Fifth Circuit Court of Appeals in accordance with the Supreme Court's 1954

[99] As reported in *The New York Times,* September 8, 1960.
[100] *Brown v. Rippy,* 233 F. 2d 796 (1956).
[101] *Bell v. Rippy,* 133 F. Supp. 811 (1955).
[102] *Bell v. Rippy,* 146 F. Supp. 485, at 486 (1956).
[103] *Borders v. Rippy,* 247 F. 2d 268 (1957).
[104] 2 *Race Relations Law Reporter* 985 (1957).
[105] *Rippy v. Borders,* 250 F. 2d 690 (1957).

and 1955 mandates,[106] with desegregation scheduled to begin on a one-grade-a-year basis in September of 1961 [107]—which indeed it did without incident. It should be pointed out, however, that the nature of the implementation order, as handed down by the Court in the second *Brown* case,[108] was tailor-made for dilatory tactics by federal District Court judges. It vested in them inherent authority to use their discretion in ordering desegregation by suggesting that they take due notice of the peculiarities of the local situation. In effect, they were guided solely by the Court's mandate that the judges require a "prompt and reasonable start toward full compliance" and that they take such action as may be necessary to bring about the end of racial segregation in the public schools "with all deliberate speed." [109]

But lest the impression arise that all defiance and deviation from the law as stated by the Court are confined to the segregation-integration controversy, we have another, and quite different, example, involving an eminent jurist, Chief Judge John J. Parker of the Fourth U. S. Circuit Court of Appeals. In 1940 the Supreme Court had held 8:1 in the first of the *Flag Salute Cases* [110] that Pennsylvania could validly require children of Jehovah's Witnesses attending public schools to salute the flag, against the claims of violation of the concept of freedom of religion. Only Mr. Justice Stone had dissented. But two years later, and no Supreme Court reversal having taken place, Judge Parker held an identical West Virginia statute unconstitutional.[111] He went to some length to point out that this really was not defiance, since three members of the 1940 majority had publicly confessed error on the occasion of a different case involving another constitutional claim by Jehovah's Witnesses,[112] and that two others had retired from the bench in the two-year interim, thus leaving the supporters of the compulsory flag salute in a minority of three. His analysis and implied prediction proved to be correct, because the Court did specifically overrule itself 6:3 when that very same West Virginia case [113] reached

---

[106] *Brown v. Board of Education,* 347 U. S. 483 (1954) and ibid. 349 U. S. 294 (1955).   [107] *Boston v. Rippy,* 275 F. 2d 850 (1960).

[108] Loc. cit. 349 U. S. 294 (1955).   [109] Ibid.

[110] *Minersville School District v. Gobitis,* 310 U. S. 586 (1940).

[111] *Barnette v. West Virginia,* 47 F. Supp. 251, at 253 (1942).

[112] *Jones v. Opelika,* 316 U. S. 584, at 623–4 (1942).

[113] *West Virginia State Board of Education v. Barnette,* 319 U. S. 624 (1943).

it—but, of course, Judge Parker could neither safely predict that event nor did it lessen the fact of his deviation.[114]

However, these illustrations of deviations by lower court federal judges are exceptions to the general rule of compliance with the orders emanating from the highest tribunal above. There may be disagreement with such an order, but one must, and may, expect that it be followed. The comments below by U. S. District Court Judge Charles E. Wyzanski, Jr., of Boston are in the best tradition of compliance, no matter how extensive the substantive disagreement. At issue was one of the ever time-consuming negligence cases, involving a trial jury's grant of $30,000 in damages to an injured New Haven Railroad worker, one Mrs. Henagan. The New Haven, upon receiving the jury's verdict in Judge Wyzanski's court, asked him to set it aside. He replied that he would if he could, but that he was not free to do so because the Supreme Court had consistently held in favor of railroad employees in similar cases, and that the Court's precedent commanded his obedience. But he went on to indicate his feelings in no uncertain terms:

> I cannot read the record as a whole in a way to find any evidence of negligence [by the New Haven]. But I know that my method of reading the record is different from that of a majority of the Supreme Court of the United States as exhibited in past cases, and I hope *I am a lawful judge,* and I recognize the limits of my authority whether appellate judges do or not.[115]

Ironically, as matters developed, the Supreme Court, for the first time in a quarter of a century, a short time thereafter reversed a jury verdict by a 6:2 majority because it found insufficient negligence on the part of the railroad—and the case was Mrs. Henagan's! [116]

By State Courts. When it comes to compliance with Supreme Court decisions by state courts an entirely different element enters.

---

[114] For an enlightening article on compliance, see Walter Murphy "Lower Court Checks on Supreme Court Power," 53 *American Political Science Review* 1017–31 (December 1959).

[115] *New York, New Haven, & Hartford v. Henagan,* as reported in 272 F. 2d 153, at 155–6 (1959). *Do. The New York Times,* November 22, 1960. (Italics supplied.)

[116] *New York, New Haven, & Hartford v. Henagan,* 364 U. S. 441 (1960).

In effect, the Supreme Court has no power to make a *final determination* of any case in which it reviews *state* court judgments. All it can do in these instances is to *decide the federal issue and remand* it to the state court below for final judgment. Because the state courts possess the power to raise new issues after they receive the case back from above, they are provided with an opportunity to evade the substantive effects of the reversal by the Supreme Court in a number of ways. And once a new issue is raised, the ultimate disposition of the case may, of course, go either way. That this is not an illusory conclusion is demonstrated by certain statistics gathered and published by the *Harvard Law Review* some years ago.[117] For example, from 1941 to 1951, the Supreme Court remanded 175 cases to the various state courts for further proceedings "not inconsistent with this judgment." In 46 of these (almost 27 per cent of the total), further litigation ensued, with 22 of the parties who *won* in the Supreme Court now *losing* in the state courts as a result of the final judgment below. In the decade immediately preceding, the Court had reviewed 187 state court cases and remanded them. In 34 of these (somewhat above 18 per cent), new issues were raised below, and in a mere nine (!) of these did the ultimate state court decision favor the party who had "won" in the Supreme Court of the United States.[118]

Whatever the difference in the degree of compliance with the decisions of the highest court in the land, it is fair to conclude that their nationwide impact is often uneven. The many diverse local conditions that characterize the federal system are all but tailor-made for considerable latitude in compliance.

OUTSIDE INFLUENCES ON COURT PERSONNEL

Much has been written and pronounced on various outside sources that allegedly prey upon and lobby with the Court and endeavor to influence its decision-making process. A good deal of this commentary has been exaggerated; much has been spurious; some has been made with nothing less than evil intent and ill will; and some

[117] See the two *Notes*, "Final Disposition of State Court Decisions Reversed and Remanded by the Supreme Court, October Term 1931 to October Term 1940," 55 *Harvard Law Review* 1357 (1942), and "Evasion of Supreme Court Mandates in Cases Remanded to State Courts since 1941," 67 *Harvard Law Review* 1251 (1954).   [118] Ibid.

has been sheer nonsense. Of course, the justices are subject to "influence," but it is an entirely different type of "influence" than that normally associated with "lobbying." Let it be stated at once and unequivocally, that the sort of lobbying and the button-holing and back-slapping approaches utilized by one and sundry to influence (a) legislators and (b) executives, not only would not work with the members of the federal judiciary, in general, and the justices of the Supreme Court, in particular, but would meet with withering disdain. As the British would say, "this simply is not cricket!" Moreover, the so welcome and necessary independence of the federal judiciary and the almost Olympian position of regard and esteem the justices rightfully enjoy by and large in the popular mind, would militate against any of the myriad approaches, ingenuous or ingenious, to which the average official or unofficial lobbyist resorts in Washington and the various other seats of federal and state power in the United States of America. If, however, we mean by "influence" a well-reasoned and ably written brief, be it by one of the litigants or a brief *amicus curiae* (see below); a persuasive oral argument on behalf of an issue at bar; a timely, thoughtful, and convincing book, monograph, speech, or law review article on the general or specific issue; a strategically timed use of a bona fide test case—*that* type of influence, as well as the intriguing concept of the "climate of public opinion" (to be discussed in Chapter Seven), falls into a different category. In the final analysis, here the justices remain the complete masters of their own house.

In elaborating somewhat on the several sources of influence that may bear upon the Court, we may omit the more obvious and self-explanatory, such as the well-written brief, the persuasive oral argument, and most literature. Some others do deserve separate treatment, including the alleged gray eminences behind the justices, the law clerks.

LEGAL PERIODICALS

Articles that appear in law reviews and other legal periodicals undoubtedly have exerted a formative influence on the law for some time. This is only natural since the best legal thinking finds expression in these periodicals (only the top law students "work on" law reviews while in law school). The jurists are part of the legal process and are quite naturally generally familiar with the thinking that presents itself in their pages; indeed, they must be familiar with it if they wish to keep their finger on the pulse of the profession and, as Mr. Justice Holmes put it so cogently, "the felt necessities of the times." In an interesting article, based on work leading to his doctorate, Chester A. Newland presented the results of a close study of the use made by the Supreme Court of legal periodicals during the period between 1924 and 1956.[119] In most cases the law review and other articles cited by the justices constituted minor references in the opinions concerned although a few seemed to be close to the *ratio decidendi*. In any event, there were numerous references in each term after 1937, with an average of 25 opinions (or about one-quarter of the number handed down by the Court in a typical term) citing a total of between 40 and 70 periodicals.[120] Not surprisingly, the justices varied in the frequency of use they made of these references, evidently depending, more or less, upon their scholarly bent and interest. Among the justices appointed after 1937 who cited legal periodicals in at least 20 opinions thereafter, the most frequent citer of legal periodicals was Mr. Justice Rutledge, whose per-term average was 7.4 opinions; next came Mr. Justice Frankfurter with 5.5; third was Mr. Justice Jackson with 4.1; low man was Mr. Justice Burton with a per-term average of 2.0.[121] For whatever significance it may have, the statistics indicate also that the four most frequently cited journals during the 32-year period covered by Professor Newland's study [122] and the number of times referred to, were the: *Harvard Law Review* (399); *Yale Law Journal* (194); *Columbia Law Review* (176); and *Michigan Law Review* (165).

There is little doubt that reliance on the legal periodicals by both bar and courts during the past generation or so has increased. Although difficult to determine objectively, this particular genre of the written word exerts a formative influence, and it does, of course, represent an outside influence. Yet it may well be asked how "outside" this particular type of influence is? Moreover, commentators as well as students of the legal process are hardly agreed

[119] "Legal Periodicals and the United States Supreme Court," 3 *Midwest Journal of Political Science* 58–74 (February 1959). [120] Ibid., compiled from p. 60. [121] Ibid., compiled from p. 61. [122] Ibid. p. 62.

upon its extent. To cite one of the more extreme points of view on the matter, in a speech in the House of Representatives, Congressman Wright Patman (D.-Tex.) viewed any reliance upon legal periodicals as all but evil and sinister, and contended that it was subversive of traditional judicial processes:

> In adopting and relying upon such pseudo-legalistic papers disseminated by the lobbyist-authors thereof the result is that the theories advanced by these pretended authorities were presented and received by the Court in an ex parte fashion.[123]

Replying to Patman in his article, Professor Newland, on the other hand, charged the veteran Congressman with "some measure of naïveté," and pointed out that if law reviews and other legal journals were not to limit their interests solely to the past, they were bound to be vehicles for the expression of views on current policy issues.[124] He concluded his observations by putting the problem into its proper focus:

> Critics may properly object that some views expressed in legal periodicals and adopted by the courts are contrary to policies which they deem desirable. But no greater unanimity of opinion usually exists among law faculties and reviews than exists on the Supreme Court. Legal periodicals appear to be "political" in somewhat the same way that the Courts are.[125]

TEST CASES

Since the American federal judicial system is based on the concept of litigation by virtue of an actual case or controversy brought before the courts by parties directly concerned, who must have standing to sue either as individuals or as personally and directly involved members of a class, the solution of an issue in the judicial process depends upon the decision handed down by the tribunal having jurisdiction. Consequently, neither the United States Supreme Court nor any of the lower constitutional courts can decide an issue unless it is before it. Here the employment of "test cases" becomes a fortiorari crucial, and both the timing and the presenta-

---

[123] *Congressional Record,* 85th Congress. 1st Session, Vol. 103, Part 12, p. 16160.
[124] Newland, loc. cit. pp. 73–4.   [125] Ibid. p. 74.

tion of the case are of the utmost importance. So long as the plaintiff or petitioner is a bona fide litigant it does not matter whether or not he pays for the almost always considerable expenses involved; nor does it matter to the outcome whether he personally is vitally interested in the decision. Provided that he is directly involved and is willing to go to court, it is of no legal significance that, in effect, he may thus well act as a front or a foil. Some states do have laws against barratry, a form of induced litigation, but this practice is extremely difficult to prove, unless the litigant so acknowledges. This is particularly unlikely in those "class action" cases personified by the segregation-integration controversy. The first really important case in that area came before the Supreme Court through the auspices of a Missouri Negro, Lloyd Gaines, to whom that state had statutorily denied admission to its public law school,[126] but who mysteriously disappeared just a few days prior to his significant 7:2 victory in the Court. Ever since that time, test cases have been brought with increasing frequency by discriminated-against Negroes avowedly with the active encouragement, backing, and financing of the National Association for the Advancement of Colored People (NAACP). It is neither surprising nor subject to doubt that the latter organization, dedicated to the aim inherent in its title, has acted and will assuredly continue to act very much like a strategy board of a field command, with due regard to the manifold tactical and strategic problems that beset such a command. In that sense, it resorts to the device of the test case to get its day in court, as do a host of other organizations for their own purposes.

Another illustration of the practice is the concerted drive by the Jehovah's Witnesses to obtain a maximum of religious freedom, as the Witnesses conceive of it, through the device of testing in the courts alleged restrictions and attacks upon their members. During the second quarter of this century, individual members of that sect, actively supported by the parent body, brought in excess of fifty *bona fide* test cases to the Supreme Court. Of these they won all but five! Nor is this practice confined to so-called minority groups. Almost every segment of the body politic has resorted to the device of the test case to gain—or lose—a point. The question arises just how much pressure or influence-peddling on the Court

[126] *Missouri ex rel Gaines v. Canada*, 305 U. S. 337 (1938).

is involved here? Those who suspect a burglar under every judicial bed would quite naturally view test cases as an all but subversive scheme. Yet test case or regular case, a case is a case, provided it meets the jurisdictional requirements of the Court. And the line between a "plotted" or "instigated" case and a "real" or "natural" one is so thin that it almost defies detection except in the most obvious cases. Moreover, the Court is the master of its own calendar and will not accept frivolous litigation, much less hand down a decision. Finally, if an issue of constitutional magnitude is duly and properly brought before the Court, all legal remedies below having been exhausted, all the requirements of the judicial process having been met, and the Court has agreed to review it, does it *really* matter whether the issue was instigated or just happened in the natural course of events?

THE BRIEF AMICUS CURIAE

Closely related, indeed often essential, to the technique of test cases encouraged and supported by interest groups is the resort to the brief *amicus curiae*. It is a brief filed by an outside individual or group—it is almost always a formal organization in the latter category—who is not a litigant in the suit but who is vitally interested in a decision favorable to the side it espouses. The device of the brief *amicus curiae,* i.e. "friend of the court"—which may well be a misnomer in a given situation—enables the interested party filing these briefs to enter the case, however tangentially. But there are obstacles as well as limitations to the filing of an *amicus curiae.* If all parties to a suit consent to the filing of such a brief, the Supreme Court's rules require its acquiescence. However, such mutual consent by the litigants is by no means always readily forthcoming. In that event, a party may petition the Court itself for permission to file an *amicus curiae,* a request which may or may not be granted, depending entirely on the judgment of the justices. Moreover, in all cases in which the United States Government is a party to a suit, which is true of approximately one-half of the total number of all cases before the Supreme Court, consent for leave to file briefs *amici curiae* must be given by the Solicitor-General ere the Court will admit them. In general, that high government official has been quite liberal in this connection, but on some occasions the Court has granted organizational requests for briefs *amici curiae* over the former's refusal to consent.

Who files these briefs? Theoretically any interested party may do so; in practice, however, most briefs *amici curiae* have come from active civic organizations and other pressure groups and, not surprisingly, from the federal government itself via the Solicitor-General. According to an authoritative study of applicants for leave to file during relatively recent times,[127] most requests have been filed—often, but by no means always, granted—by the following organizations: the American Civil Liberties Union (a tireless and effective battler for civil liberties); the NAACP (a militant and broadly successful spokesman for the Negro); the American Jewish Congress (in roughly the same category as the ACLU, but with emphasis on cases concerning matters involving its own particular interests); and the chief interest group for the vast labor movement, the AFL-CIO. Also very active have been the American Bar Association and the National Lawyers Guild (the splinter lawyers' group); various veterans pressure groups, led by the American Legion; and, quite often of late in matters involving the segregation-integration field, the United States Government.

To cite a specific case example of the successful use of an *amicus curiae* by the latter, the government filed such a brief in the 1960 case of *Boynton v. Virginia* [128] through the auspices of Solicitor-General J. Lee Rankin. Here a bus terminal restaurant in Richmond, Virginia, segregated passengers according to color, regardless of their destination. The plaintiff rested his brief on the equal protection of the laws clause of the Fourteenth Amendment, under which so many cases in the area of racial segregation had been won by Negro petitioners. However, the Solicitor-General's brief *amicus curiae* used an entirely different approach and contended that since the restaurant involved was "an integral part" of a bus line's interstate passenger service, the Interstate Commerce Act of 1887—a federal statute—forbade such segregation. More or less ignoring the litigants' arguments and briefs, the Supreme Court fastened upon the contents of Mr. Rankin's *amicus curiae* and decided 7:2 in the plaintiff's favor. In a dis-

---

[127] Clement E. Vose, "Litigation as a Form of Pressure Group Activity," 319 *Annals of the American Academy of Political and Social Science* 20–31 (September 1958).   [128] 364 U. S. 454 (1960).

senting opinion joined by Mr. Justice Clark, Mr. Justice Whittaker, however, chided the Court majority for deciding the case on the commerce clause which had been raised *solely* by the Government as *amicus curiae.*

Unless the evidence is as clear-cut as in the aforementioned instance, it is very difficult to determine how far, if at all, the Court's decision and/or opinion make use of briefs *amici curiae.* What some commentators in this field report as the gospel's truth is not infrequently laced with conjecture and sheer guesswork, some of it with prejudiced motivation. On the other hand, it would be fair to state that the flood of briefs *amici curiae* filed by the NAACP in the area of its own special interest had at least some persuasive influence in the outcome of the many cases handed down by the Court in the 15 years between the end of World War II and 1960, for example—in which the cause espoused by the NAACP gained 50 victories! A specific illustration of one of these is the momentous decision by the Court in *Shelley v. Kraemer,*[129] the most important of the *Restrictive Covenant Cases.*[130] That case apparently still holds the record for the number of main briefs and briefs *amici curiae* filed and accepted: nineteen by the NAACP and others favorably disposed to its point of view here; five by opposing groups, chiefly real-estate interests; and one by Solicitor-General Philip B. Perlman on behalf of the U. S. Department of Justice, siding with the Negro plaintiff.[131] Speaking for the unanimous six-man Court—Justices Reed, Jackson, and Rutledge having disqualified themselves from participation—Mr. Chief Justice Vinson ruled that although racially restrictive *private* covenants did not in themselves violate the Fourteenth Amendment of the Constitution, *court enforcement* of such contracts would constitute state action and thereby violate the equal protection of the laws clause of that amendment—a signal victory for the cause of the NAACP.

Surely, briefs *amici curiae* may, and sometimes do, influence members of the Court. To acknowledge that entirely plausible, and

[129] 334 U. S. 1 (1948).
[130] Ibid. plus *Hurd v. Hodge,* 334 U. S. 24 (1948); and *Barrows v. Jackson,* 346 U. S. 249 (1953).
[131] Clement E. Vose, *Caucasians Only: The Supreme Court, the NAACP, and the Restrictive Covenant Cases* (Berkeley and Los Angeles, University of California Press, 1959), Ch. 8.

in many cases quite conceivably salutary, phenomenon is one thing; to lower it to the level of a sinister or subversive cops-and-robbers plot is quite another. In this realm of alleged outside influence, as well as in those discussed earlier, the fact remains that the justices, when all is said and done, have the final word on whether or how far, if at all, they permit themselves to be influenced within the accepted framework of the judicial process.

THE LAW CLERKS

In a somewhat different category among the "outside pressures" on the Court are its law clerks. Depending upon the point of view advanced, these able and intelligent young aides to the justices, all recent law-school graduates, are either in the category of a private secretary aide-de-camp to their justices or in that of a gray eminence, a sort of judicial Rasputin, indeed the veritable power behind the throne! Thus, in an angry speech on the floor of the United States Senate, Senator John Stennis (D.–Miss.), a vigorous critic of the Court's attitude on segregation and subversion cases, called for an investigation of the activities of the clerks; the establishment of statutory minimum qualifications for them; and their confirmation by the Senate just like the justices themselves— all this because of what the Senator termed "their ever-increasing importance and influence." The law clerks, he said, might be occupying roles in government far more important than those occupied by undersecretaries and assistant secretaries of the executive branch, and that:

> To the extent that they participate in shaping the work of the court, they are deciding vital questions of national effect. Within the Judicial branch, these are equivalent to policy-level decisions in the executive branch.[132]

Yet we have the word of ex-law clerk after ex-law clerk that their influence on the justices to whom they were assigned was nil in so far as the judicial decision-making process is concerned. Thus, John P. Frank, once clerk to Mr. Justice Black, wrote that in his year with the latter, "my Justice made approximately one thou-

[132] As reported in *The New York Times*, May 7, 1958.

sand decisions, and I had precisely no influence on any of them." [133] Dean Acheson, one of several of Mr. Justice Brandeis's law clerks who later rose to national prominence, reported that his Justice would sometimes let him work on a draft opinion, largely for the sake of criticism, but:

> When I finished my work on a draft which had been assigned to me or got as far as I could, I gave it to him. [As is evident from the Brandeis files], he tore it to pieces, sometimes using a little, sometimes none.[134]

And of all the law clerks who have written or otherwise reported on their experiences behind the "Purple Curtain," only a rather recent one, William H. Rehnquist, suggested the possibility of some *"unconscious* slanting of material by clerks." [135] But even he readily admitted of his experiences as Mr. Justice Jackson's clerk in the 1952–53 term that the notion of the law clerk "exerting an important influence on the cases actually decided by the Court, may be discarded at once . . . I certainly learned of none." [136]

Just who are these law clerks and how are they selected? As indicated above, they are recent law-school graduates of the highest caliber. Each is chosen by an individual justice to work for him for a year, sometimes for two. The practice was initiated by Mr. Justice Horace Gray late in the nineteenth century. Today, each associate justice selects two, the Chief Justice three, although Mr. Justice Douglas has usually contented himself with just one clerk. Some justices do their own selecting, either as a result of a personal interview or written data, almost always the former; others rely chiefly on experts' recommendations—viz., Justices Frankfurter and Brennan, whose clerks are chosen for them by Professors Sachs and Freund at the Harvard Law School. From there Professor of Law Felix Frankfurter sent a number of his own outstanding students, sometimes referred to as "Felix's Happy Hot Dogs," to the Court as clerks. In short, the clerks are really the purely personal patronage of the justices, who are free to base their selections on whatever criteria they desire. John P. Frank avowed that his Justice,

---

[133] *The Marble Palace* (New York: Alfred A Knopf, 1958), p. 119.
[134] As quoted by Bickel, op. cit. p. 92.
[135] "Who Writes Decisions of the Supreme Court?" *U. S. News and World Report,* December 13, 1957.   [136] Ibid.

Mr. Justice Black, "tries to get Southern boys—and tennis-players where possible." [137] To use one year as an example, the 1957–58 term of the Court saw eighteen law clerks chosen by the nine members of the Court, Mr. Chief Justice Warren selecting three, Mr. Justice Douglas one, all others two. The young men came from ten different law schools; seven from Harvard University; three from the University of Chicago; one each from the University of Pennsylvania, Yale University, New York University, the University of California (Berkeley and Los Angeles one each), Washington University, the University of North Dakota, and Southern Methodist University.

Exactly what work a justice assigns or delegates to his clerk depends upon the former's inclination—or, as Mr. Justice Jackson once stated, "on the justice's temperament and experience." Apparently, most of the justices—Mr. Justice Frankfurter evidently being an exception to the practice—use their clerks to wade through the manifold petitions for certiorari that are filed annually. Typically, a law clerk may read such a petition and the opposing party's response, and then type or pen a brief memorandum to his justice stating the issues involved and setting forth arguments for and against a grant of the desired writ. Suffice it to note that the justice concerned will, of course, make up his own mind. Some of the justices may go somewhat further in employing their clerks by asking for a so-called "bench memorandum" on a particular case now and then; such a memorandum may propound certain approaches and point to precedents and thereby suggest questions to be asked by the justices of counsel during oral argument. The most intensive tasks performed by the law clerks is probably that of the necessary drudgery of research once an opinion has been assigned to a particular justice. Here commences the time-consuming task of investigating, of sorting and checking precedents, citations, historical data, congressional records—the host of materials so vital to the decision-making process. Beyond that, the chief role of the law clerk is to serve as a type of foil, friend, critic, sounding board. In the final analysis, however, quoting one former clerk:

> In the course of my year, we never changed the justice's mind on the result of any case. Our influence was close to nil.

[137] *The Marble Palace*, loc. cit. pp. 115–16.

There was the fullest discussion, but he made the decisions
. . . The judge will listen if you say that some statement in
his draft opinion is too broad or that a case is cited incorrectly.
But if you tell him that such-and-such a constitutional amendment doesn't mean what he believes, you might as well stay in
bed.[138]

The clerks are important tools for the justices in the judicial process,
perhaps indispensable ones, yet they are hardly classifiable as
powers behind the throne. Essentially, they are law *clerks*—able,
intelligent, and undoubtedly often, if not always, of considerable
procedural aid to their justices. But they are not members of the
Court in any sense of the term. And, as has been contended repeatedly in connection with the entire matter of influence upon it,
in fine the Supreme Court of the United States is master of its
own house—which does not, however, mean that it is not aware of
the existence of other houses both in and out of the governmental
compound.

[138] As quoted anonymously in *The New York Times,* October 14, 1957.

VI

COURTS ABROAD

Constant reference has been made, especially in the earlier chapters, to the practices and theories of jurists and judicial systems of other lands—indeed, wherever appropriate, since the comparative element is one of the essential characteristics of this work. The newly emergent states of the world adapt their needs to the legal and social patterns of other states. The United States has both profited from and contributed to other systems. Basically English in origin and design, features of its judicial system and process nevertheless both resemble and differ drastically from that of others. The legal systems of England and Wales, France, and the Soviet Union—the last in a totally different vein—are most useful in an analysis in this connection. In the following pages a relatively brief view of the courts of these three countries will be presented, with a diagram for each system.

THE COURTS OF ENGLAND AND WALES

It is in fact incorrect to think of the courts of "Great Britain" or of the "United Kingdom" as a unified judicial system. For there exist actually *three different systems* in the United Kingdom of Great Britain and Northern Ireland: one for England and Wales; one for Scotland; and one for Northern Ireland. Only at the ultimate appellate level of the House of Lords is it possible to speak with accuracy of a unified system for the United Kingdom; because that body in its judicial aspect represents the final court of appeals —in those very few cases that manage to reach it—from the judgments of the highest courts of Scotland and Northern Ireland as well as from those of England and Wales. The following description is of the judicial system of England and Wales—for convenience referred to as "England"—unless specified otherwise.

216

In the United States the same tribunals ordinarily have both civil and criminal jurisdiction—with some minor exceptions for certain low level state courts, such as the Court of Small Claims in Pennsylvania. But in the England of today justice is meted out in two separated judicial hierarchies, one for civil cases and one for criminal cases—although the judges are often the same. This separation is based upon the Supreme Court of Judicature (Consolidation) Act of 1925, as amended, the progeny of a series of Judicature Acts commencing with that of 1873. The latter statute brought order into what was a truly bewildering array of distinct tribunals—e.g. some seven or eight leading courts had original jurisdiction in civil cases! However, unlike France, neither England nor the United States has a bona fide system of administrative courts—although some of the English administrative courts, e.g. Railway Rate Tribunals, existed long before World War II and others have begun to make their appearance since; and some of the special and/or legislative tribunals in the United States are at least quasi-administrative.[1]

THE CRIMINAL COURTS HIERARCHY

It is perhaps somewhat unorthodox to disuss the criminal courts hierarchy before that of the civil courts, but the English structure lends itself peculiarly well to such a procedure—in part because of a considerable amount of interchange of judges between the two hierarchies, despite the rigid structural segregation inherent in the system. Jurisdiction over criminal offenses has been exercised as a separate entity for almost 700 years.

The Justice of the Peace and the Stipendiary Magistrate. At the base of the criminal courts hierarchy in England is the unpaid *Justice of the Peace,* who must live within 15 miles of his judicial area of jurisdiction. There are approximately 4000 "J.P.s" at work today. In the larger cities there is instead the *Stipendiary Magistrate* —London alone, where he is called Metropolitan Magistrate, has roughly 35 of these officials—who, unlike his cousin, the Justice of the Peace, must be a full-time professional lawyer, usually a barrister, and is paid. With the exception of the Duchy of Lancaster, where they are designated by its own Chancellor, the judges at

---

[1] See Chapter Four, *supra,* for details.

this lowest level of the criminal hierarchy are appointed on behalf of the Crown by the Lord Chancellor after careful screening and recommendation by local advisory committees in each county. That politically designated officer, who was discussed earlier,[2] is not only the highest judicial officer in the British system, but he is also a member of the Cabinet and its foremost legal adviser, and a member as well as *ex officio* the presiding officer of the House of Lords.

Sitting *en banc* without a jury, the Justice of the Peace or Stipendiary Magistrate, in his role as a tribunal of first instance, is exclusively a court of summary jurisdiction for criminal offenses. But he may also double as a committing judicial officer by holding an accused for action by a higher court in the event of "indictable" offenses. These would normally require grand jury action at the federal level in the United States; but in England, since the statutory abolition of the grand jury in 1933, the process of "information" has replaced it. Except for minor matters, trials at this lowest level of original jurisdiction are conducted by one, two, or three justices of the peace but by only one stipendiary magistrate—a vital distinction between the two types of similar officials. The chief function of these officials is to try relatively minor criminal offenses, although they do have jurisdiction in certain domestic relations—matrimonial, bastardy, and rate cases, and a few administrative functions—and, as indicated, determine whether there is sufficient evidence to commit the offender for trial before a jury in a higher court.

Many of the offenses handled by the J.P. or the Stipendiary Magistrate concern traffic violators, and the maximum fine he may impose here is £5. Generally speaking, his jurisdiction is restricted to cases involving a maximum fine of £100 or a six months' jail sentence or both. In many instances the accused is permitted the option of a trial before the Justice of the Peace or the Stipendiary Magistrate or before a higher judge (and jury, when appropriate). Experience has demonstrated that the accused will almost invariably choose the former because of considerations of expeditiousness.

Still at the same level of the judiciary, when two or more justices of the peace, or one stipendiary magistrate, sit, a *Court of Petty*

2 See Chapter Two, *supra.*

Sessions is said to exist. As will be explained subsequently, appeals from this level are possible either to the Court of Quarter Sessions or to a three-judge Divisional Court of the Queen's Bench Division of the High Court of Justice, depending upon the nature of the appeal, and provided that the defendant did not plead guilty— although in London he is free to appeal even in the latter event if the sentence is more than one month in prison or a fine of more than £3. Appeals in matrimonial cases go to the Divisional Court of the Probate, Divorce, and Admiralty Division of the High Court of Justice.

The Court of Quarter Sessions. Immediately above the J.P. level is the *Court of Quarter Sessions,* still called by that ancient name because it meets four times annually in its proper area of jurisdiction. Clothed with appellate as well as original jurisdiction, it is the first court in which an accused, given the proper circumstances, is entitled to a trial by jury. The Court of Quarter Sessions consists of all the justices of the peace in a given county, presided over by a legally qualified chairman. But since the enactment of the Justices of the Peace Act of 1949, no more than nine members of the Court may sit *en banc* in any given case. In some boroughs it consists merely of the paid *Recorder,* selected from barristers of at least five years' experience. He sits only occasionally as such, however, and continues in practice as a barrister.

In theory, the Court of Quarter Sessions may try any cases other than those permitting the death penalty or a sentence of life imprisonment on first offense; in practice, however, it rarely handles those cases that call for more than five years' imprisonment. The Court has an Appeal Committee, numbering from three to twelve justices, which constitutes an appellate tribunal for the defendant —without a jury, of course—for convictions and sentences by justices of the peace and stipendiary magistrates below, both on points of law and fact. But normally it is the court of last resort on questions of fact. The number of appeals coming to it is relatively small. In 1957, to cite a typical year, of 786,330 persons convicted below, only 2046 filed appeals.[3]

[3] Richard M. Jackson, *The Machinery of Justice in England,* 3d ed. (Cambridge: Cambridge University Press, 1960), p. 110. This is an excellent book, and one of the very few up-to-date ones available on the British judiciary. It presents a superb explanation and analysis of its subject matter.

Appeals from the Court of Quarter Sessions do not go to the Court of Assize immediately above, but to the next higher level, the Court of Criminal Appeal. On a point of law any convicted defendant may appeal to the latter, and he may do so on a point of fact with leave of the trial judge or the Court of Criminal Appeal. The latter's permission is necessary for an appeal against the sentence itself.

The Assize Court. At the next level above lies the most important tribunal in the criminal hierarchy of England, the *Assize Court.* Its jurisdiction covers all major felonies, such as homicide, robbery, larceny, rape, and so forth. Justices commit cases either to it or to the Court of Quarter Sessions below, depending on the nature of the offense. The Assize Court meets three times annually in an important town in each county of the seven judicial circuits into which England is divided, but assizes sit throughout the year in most big cities. An Assize Court is ordinarily presided over either by a professional judge "on circuit" from the Queen's Bench Division of the High Court of Justice (a civil court) in London or by a *Commissioner*—an experienced Queen's Counsel, who is thus tried out for future judicial office. It was Lord Parker, the Lord Chief Justice, who, in his capacity as a judge of the Queen's Bench Division, presided over the spy trial that took place in the spring of 1961 in England's capital. (The Lord Chief Justice is the head of the Queen's Bench Division.)

Because of the nature of the offenses tried before them, the assizes always sit with a jury. Much traditional pageantry and fanfare attend their sessions, the proper judicial manner being very much in evidence. The Assize Court for Metropolitan London is the *Central Criminal Court,* widely known as the "Old Bailey" because of the name of the interesting building where it meets for its 12 sessions annually, one each month.

Appeals from judgments of the Assize Court are possible to the next higher level court, the Court of Criminal Appeal, broadly in accordance with the terms and qualifications of appeals from the Court of Quarter Sessions to that tribunal, just described above. Again, an acquittal is not appealable.

The Court of Criminal Appeal. Appeals from the two lower levels in the hierarchy, to which only defendants are entitled, may be taken directly to the *Court of Criminal Appeal,* created in 1907, assuming the necessary conditions are present and leave to file has been obtained. It is the most important tribunal of appellate jurisdiction in the criminal hierarchy of England. Sitting without a jury, it hears appeals on the transcripts of the evidence taken at the trial. But the hearing is not a retrial in the sense that the witnesses are heard over again by the Court of Criminal Appeal. It is composed of the legally qualified and salaried judges of the Queen's Bench Division of the High Court of Justice. Usually there are three members—the quorum—but whatever the number, it must be uneven.

Because of the stipulated assumption that any appeal involves a retrial, the Court of Criminal Appeal has the power to revise the erstwhile sentence in three situations: (1) if it is not legally justified; (2) if it was based on improper evidence; and (3) if the length or severity of the sentence points to an error in "some matter of principle" by the trial court. The Court of Criminal Appeal may even substitute conviction of another offense for the initial one if it appears that the defendant should have been convicted for it rather than for the one for which he was below. But it has no power to order a trial *de novo*.

The House of Lords. In rare instances, the accused—never the prosecutor—has one last and very much restricted path of appeal from the Court of Criminal Appeal to the *House of Lords* (an institution to be more fully described in connection with the civil hierarchy). Yet such an appeal is possible only when a point of law of "general public importance" is involved, and leave to file for appeal to that august body must be given by the Court of Criminal Appeal or the Divisional Court of the Queen's Bench Division of the High Court of Justice—or by the House of Lords itself if refused by the aforementioned tribunals. Such appeals have averaged but one a year.[4] Moreover, since the House of Lords habitually confines its rulings on the specific, often narrow, point of law involved—here very much like the Supreme Court of the United States—broad legal pronouncements are unlikely indeed.

Until a statutory change was effected in 1960, permission to appeal to the House of Lords was even more circumscribed than the present procedure. Leave to appeal could be granted only by the Attorney-General, the senior law officer of the Crown, and

4 Ibid. p. 112.

then only if the point of law involved was deemed of *"exceptional public importance."* Thus, in the famous Guenther Padola loss-of-memory murder case of 1959, for example, the Attorney-General, Sir Reginald Manningham-Buller, refused to grant such permission. All other channels of appeal had previously been exhausted, and the Old Bailey jury had decided in the trial court that the alleged amnesia was faked. The accused consequently paid the ultimate penalty.

The Civil Courts Hierarchy

Although some of the terminology will be similar and some of the judicial personnel, in fact, the same, the existing hierarchical distinctions between the criminal and civil courts are highly significant to a proper understanding of the judicial process in England. Again, we commence at the lowest level of the courts.

The County Court. The court of first instance in civil matters is the *County Court*—so called by virtue of the adoption of the ancient name of the local courts of the county in early Anglo-Norman times, despite the fact that the jurisdiction of these tribunals today does not necessarily coincide with county boundaries; in fact, it has nothing to do with them. The districts they serve are arranged so that a County Court is within ready reach everywhere; they are subject to geographic alteration by the Lord Chancellor. The between 400 and 450 county courts are presided over by some 80 judges who have been appointed by the Crown on the advice of the Lord Chancellor—again with the exception of the Duchy of Lancaster, as in the case of the justices of the peace. To qualify, they must be barristers in good standing with at least seven years of experience. They retire at 72 or exceptionally at 75.

County court judges—who are well paid, as is generally true of Britain's jurists—live in their districts and hold court once or twice a month in the pertinent towns, referred to as their circuit, depending upon the work load docketed. Each County Court is assigned a *Registrar,* a solicitor appointed by and subject to removal by the Lord Chancellor, who is not only in charge of the court's office staff, but who may also act as a lesser judge. By leave of his judge and in the absence of objections by any of the parties, he deals mainly with matters not involving more than

£30. With the consent of the litigants, he may exercise even wider jurisdiction.

The jurisdiction of the County Court, although strictly limited statutorily, is extensive, and the number of cases commenced at this level is vast. In 1957, for instance, a total of 1,078,097 proceedings were entered here,[5] and this astonishing total has not declined over the years since that time. Broadly speaking, the large majority of cases fall into the area of actions based on contract and many, but not all, types of tort claims up to a maximum of £400 (under certain conditions increasable by high authority to £500). Yet more than 95 per cent of these cases do not exceed £100 in value. Other areas of County Court jurisdiction include equity matters up to £500; real-estate actions up to £100; a limited range of admiralty and bankruptcy matters. And a highly significant field of its jurisdiction arises under so-called "social" or "collectivist" statutes, a by-product of today's welfare state. Since 1934, appeals from the county courts must be taken directly to the Court of Appeal, thus by-passing the next higher court level.

The High Court of Justice. Immediately above the County Court in the hierarchy of the civil courts stands the *High Court of Justice*—an ancient institution deriving from the Norman *curia regis,* which was the monarch's personal instrument for the dispensing of justice. It has chiefly original but also some—divisionally restricted—appellate jurisdiction. As we now know the famous tribunal, established in 1873, it is staffed by three presiding officers and 45 distinguished *puisne* judges who have had a minimum of ten years—many have had 20 and 25—of experience as barristers. The three divisions of the "High Court," as it is commonly called, comprise: the 28-member *Queen's Bench Division,* including its presiding officer, the Lord Chief Justice, who ranks immediately after the Lord Chancellor in the judicial hierarchy; the seven-member *Chancery Division,* including its nonsitting presiding officer, the Lord Chancellor; and the President and nine judges of the *Probate, Divorce, and Admiralty Division.*

Of the three, the Queen's Bench Division is by far the largest and busiest, partly because its judges must—as was explained above—participate also in the work of the higher criminal courts

[5] Ibid. p. 28.

as a matter of exercising original jurisdiction, and partly because with three or five of its judges sitting as the *Divisional Court* of the Queen's Bench Division, it hears certain appeals in criminal cases from the courts of summary jurisdiction, i.e. the Justice of the Peace and Stipendiary Magistrate Court and the Court of Quarter Sessions. Coupled with its jurisdiction over the general field of the common law, its work range thus extends to: (1) ordinary civil actions; (2) its appellate and supervisory jurisdiction *en banc* in its mantle of Divisional Court of the Queen's Bench Division; (3) appellate functions exercised by a single judge; and (4) its extensive, original criminal jurisdiction.

As the presiding officer of the Queen's Bench Division, the Lord Chief Justice enjoys a considerable degree of authority and prestige. In his capacity he is the directing figure of the criminal courts of England. Members of the British legal circles are fond of stating that the Lord Chief Justice is in somewhat the same position as the Pope in that what he says on any given occasion may influence not only the other judges but also the lawyers, the magistrates, and even the police.[6] He is indeed a towering figure on the scene of government, and he is regarded with much awe, confidence, and respect.

The Chancery Division has exclusive jurisdiction in some cases, and concurrent jurisdiction with the Queen's Bench Division in others. In the extensive former category are equity matters of bankruptcy, companies, execution of trusts, wardships, foreclosures of mortgages, etc. Its *Divisional Court* hears appeals on bankruptcy matters from the County Court.

The Probate, Divorce, and Admiralty Division has jurisdiction in the areas indicated by its name—giving valid title to the estate of deceased persons; matrimonial decrees as to divorce, nullity, restitution of conjugal rights, judicial separation, presumption of death and dissolution of marriage, declaration of legitimacy; various matters affecting ships under maritime law. Its *Divisional Court* hears appeals from the Magistrates' Courts level in matrimonial cases. In popular lingo, the Probate, Divorce, and Admiralty Division is often referred to as the "Wrecks" Division because it is said to deal with "wills, wives, and wrecks." Lord Goddard, who was Lord Chief Justice for 12 years, amended

[6] Cf. *The New York Times*, March 23, 1961.

this ancient jest recently as dealing with "wrecks of wills . . .
marriages . . . and ships." [7]

In addition to its specialized jurisdiction just explained, the
High Court of Justice has over-all jurisdiction in all cases that are
eligible for hearings in the County Court as well as those that lie
outside that tribunal's jurisdiction. But it will not normally entertain cases under its original jurisdiction if these can be handled by
the County Court—e.g. routine controversies with a value of less
than £400. Together with the Court of Appeal, the High Court
of Justice forms the *Supreme Court of Judicature*—a body that is
actually neither supreme nor a court, but serves as a type of cover-
all for these two entirely separate branches of the civil courts
system.

The Court of Appeal. Appeals from any of the Divisions of the
High Court of Justice go to the *Court of Appeal,* consisting of the
Lord Chancellor, any former Lord Chancellor, the Lords of Appeal
in Ordinary, the Lord Chief Justice, the Master of the Rolls, and
the President of the Probate, Divorce, and Admiralty Division of
the High Court as members *ex officio,* and eight Lords Justices of
Appeal, the regular sitting members, who must have 15 years of
experience as barristers or have been High Court judges. But of
the *ex officio* members only the Master of the Rolls, who has always
practiced in the Chancery Division, actually sits with three of the
regular sitting judges of the Court of Appeal. Its appellate jurisdiction extends to points of law arising out of civil cases from the
County Court or the High Court of Justice.

Appeals on points of law coming from the County Court reach
the Court of Appeal as a matter of right if the amount of the
claim involved exceeds £20 or when the remedy is an injunction.
In other appeals the judge below must give permission. In the
cases coming from the High Court, appeal is automatic on points
of law but not on points of fact. If the Court of Appeal grants
an appeal, retrial of the case will normally take place below; however, it may also reconsider the evidence itself, but without taking
new testimony from witnesses.

The House of Lords. From the Court of Appeal, if the matter of

[7] Lord Goddard, "Organization and Jurisdiction of the Courts of England." 44
Journal of The American Judicature Society 62 (August, 1960). (See his entire
article for a fine description, pp. 60–65.)

law involved is deemed to be of sufficient importance, there remains the final path of appeal to the *House of Lords*—an expensive (£1000 for printing costs alone is an average expenditure) and uncommon one—provided that the appeal has been certified by the Court of Appeal or granted by the House of Lords itself, a historic right dating back to the practices of the Norman institution of the *magnum concilium,* the Great Council. The Lords do not, of course, sit in a mass body for that purpose—there are over 850 members! Instead, the legal section of the House of Lords comprises a small, highly skilled, distinguished group of judicial experts, the nine *Law Lords,* also known as the *Lords of Appeal in Ordinary,* plus the Lord Chancellor, the presiding officer of the House of Lords, and augmented by any other peer who may have held or now holds high judicial office under the Crown.

This small group of appellate experts was created originally by the Appellate Jurisdiction Act of 1876 to supplement the judicial strength of the House of Lords. It remains the sole United Kingdom-wide judicial body, and as such always has some members from Scotland and, on occasion, one from Northern Ireland. These few dignitaries with a background of at least fifteen years as barristers or of high judicial office for two years, who are all professional, paid judges with life peerages, and who ordinarily take no part, whatever, in the political business of the Lords, thus constitute the Supreme Court of the United Kingdom of Great Britain and Northern Ireland. But unlike the Supreme Court of the United States and the other United States federal and state courts, neither the House of Lords nor any other English or Welsh court, no matter how high, possesses the power of judicial review (which will be fully documented in the following chapter).

The Judicial Committee of the Privy Council. One other major appellate tribunal, sitting somewhat astride the regular court system just described, exists in the British Isles. It is the important *Judicial Committee of the Privy Council,* which constitutes the final court of appeal for cases from the ecclesiastical courts of the Church of England, colonies, protectorates, trust territories, the Isle of Man, and the Channel Islands. It is also available as the ultimate appellate body for all those members of the Commonwealth that might wish to avail themselves of its services. But in recent years with the rare exception of isolated cases from Ceylon, New Zealand,

Australia, Ghana, and Malaya, Commonwealth members have normally preferred to adjudicate their problems in their own judicial structure. However, until 1949 it did constitute the final court of appeal from Canada on constitutional matters.

Only privy councillors are eligible for membership on the Judicial Committee. In practice, most of the work has been done by the Law Lords of the House of Lords, but other high judicial officers from the United Kingdom as well as from the Commonwealth and the other areas the Judicial Committee serves have participated in its functions.

FIGURE 2

THE CRIMINAL AND CIVIL COURTS OF ENGLAND AND WALES

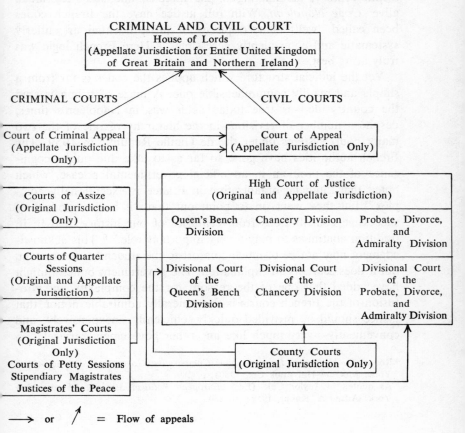

THE COURTS OF FRANCE

If imitation may be regarded as indication of approval, the popularity and acceptance of the French judicial system among the older as well as the newer states of the world represent such approval in the highest degree. Far more than the Anglo-American has the French administration of justice become a model abroad. To a large extent this is attributable to its base—those marvelous civil, criminal, penal, commercial, and procedural codes, drafted under the often personal direction of Napoleon Bonaparte at the end of the eighteenth and especially at the beginning of the nineteenth century, culminating in the famous, and still very much alive, *Code Napoleon*. With full justice have the French codes been called "well-balanced pieces of jurisprudential art, utterly systematic and conveniently accessible." [8] Here French logic was truly at its best.

Yet the judicial structure which applies the codes is far from a simple and readily comprehensible one. A maze of tribunals stud the countryside—as true today as it was in Napoleon's times, despite a number of revisions in the hierarchy of one of the two major court systems under the de Gaulle Republic in 1959. The French authorities have gone so far as to take due public cognizance of the problem in an official governmental release, which noted that "judicial organization in France is exceptionally complex," but they went on to point out that "it is the product of successive contributions from centuries of our history, and in it, tradition continues to play a very important role." [9] This acknowledgment may not be of much comfort to the student of the system, but it does serve as an explanation. The government bulletin might have added that one of the reasons for the complexity and profusion of the French courts is the generally admirable notion that justice should be provided quickly, efficiently, inexpensively, and conveniently—very much like any other government service!

[8] Robert G. Neumann, *European and Comparative Government,* 3d ed. (New York: McGraw-Hill Book Co., 1960), p. 289.
[9] As quoted in Taylor Cole (Ed.), *European Political Systems,* 3d ed. (New York: Alfred A. Knopf, 1959), p. 234.

Two Major Divisions

The courts of France are characterized by two quite separate and distant hierarchies: first, the *ordinary* or *regular* courts; second, the *administrative courts*. (A substructure of commercial and certain other special courts need not concern us at this juncture; they may be viewed as falling generally under the ordinary courts.) In case of doubt as to proper jurisdiction, the *Tribunal des Conflits* (Tribunal of Conflicts), created especially for that umpire-role, determines to which of the two major court systems a case goes.

Again, the chief reason for this interesting division of responsibility between the hierarchies is an historic one. Fearful that the ordinary courts might interfere with the administrative or executive branch of the government, the legislative bodies of France, dating all the way back to the days of the Revolution, wrote into laws and constitutions specific provisions that expressly forbade judicial bodies to intervene. For example, the Law of December 22, 1789, provided: ". . . Judicial power should not trouble local administrative agencies in the exercise of their functions." And that of August 16–24, 1790, spelled the matter out more clearly:

> The judicial functions are and will remain forever separate from the administrative functions. The judges will not be allowed, under penalty of forfeiture, to disturb in any manner whatsoever, the activities of the administrative corps, nor to summon before them the administrators, concerning their functions.[10]

This was all very well in theory, but it soon became clear that someone or something would be needed to check certain administrative excesses of power. Hence the adoption of the system of administrative courts, designed to check administrative abuses and at the same time retain the cherished principle of separation of powers in so far as the judicial and executive-administrative functions are concerned. The separated hierarchies have flourished and

[10] Stephan Riesengeld, "The French System of Administrative Justice: A Model for American Law," 18 *Boston University Law Review* 48 (1938).

survive, essentially unchanged in design and principle, although not in certain organizational details and nomenclature.

THE ORDINARY OR REGULAR COURTS HIERARCHY

On March 1, 1959, the de Gaulle government effected several judicial reforms, chiefly designed to give the courts a corps of more specialized judges and to distribute these more equitably geographically in a rearranged system of ordinary courts, geared more closely to modern demands and realistic population distribution. The effect of these changes is reflected in the following description.

The Court of Instance (TRIBUNAL D'INSTANCE). The de Gaulle Reorganization Bill abolished the time-honored, but outdated, lowest of the ordinary courts, the local *Juge de Paix*—again our friend, the Justice of the Peace—and replaced that popular institution with a new local court of first instance, the *Tribunal d'Instance*. Heretofore 740 *juges de paix*—with law diplomas, unlike most of their British and American counterparts—had brought justice, more or less, to the 3040 *cantons* of France by way of a completely informal, inexpensive, and often inconsequential procedure in the usual type of petty, chiefly civil, infractions, which obliged them to "ride circuit." Now 455 of the new *tribunaux d'instance* exist in the capitals of the various *arrondissements*—the administrative geographical level above the *canton*. Each of these new courts may have several judges—who are required to live in the area of jurisdiction of the tribunal—but decisions are rendered by a single judge. The *tribunaux d'instance* and their judges have been given considerably more effective adjudicatory power in civil and criminal cases than that possessed by the old *juges de paix*. Indeed, they are fully intended to become the most important unit in the revised judicial system.

The Court of Major Instance (TRIBUNAL DE GRANDE INSTANCE). Replacing the old civil *Court of First Instance* (*Tribunal de Première Instance*), of which one was located in every *arrondissement,* is the newly created *Tribunal de Grande Instance*. The old criminal section of this level, the *Correctional Court* (*Tribunal Correctionnel*), has been retained, however. In place of the erstwhile 359 courts, the new 172 *tribunaux de grande instance* will have jurisdiction throughout the *département*—the highest administrative subdivision in France—not merely in a single *arrondissement*. According to the number of inhabitants and the "degree of economic activity," [11] the larger *départements* will be entitled to two or more of the tribunals. Each case is tried by several judges sitting *en banc,* usually three, but always comprising an uneven number, with the decision reached by majority vote.

In civil cases the *tribunaux de grande instance* have unlimited original jurisdiction; they also have appellate jurisdiction from the *tribunaux d'instance.* In criminal cases the correctional courts sit in the less severe felony cases and in misdemeanors such as assault, embezzlement, and theft. They are also empowered to hear certain limited appeals, primarily those dealing with infractions of police regulations.

The Court of Appeal (COUR D'APPEL). The 1959 reforms did not make any substantial changes in the structure of the *Court of Appeal* (*Cour d'Appel*), the appellate tribunal for *civil* cases from below, and none at all in the number of the 27 judicial districts, each including several *départements,* in which one of these tribunals operates. However, the jurisdiction of the *Cour d'Appel* has been extended materially to include some of the special courts, alluded to earlier, particularly in the field of social and economic legislation. Thus, appeals to a *Cour d'Appel* may come from any one of the following, in addition to the considerable number of appeals that come up from the *tribunaux de grande instance* in the regular hierarchy below: the *Labor Conciliation Board* (*Conseil de Prud'hommes*), composed of an equal number of employers and employees who, chosen by their own groups, hear disputes arising out of industrial contracts; the *Commercial Court* (*Tribunal de Commerce*), consisting of businessmen elected by their peers to act in certain statutorily designated commercial cases; the *Juvenile Court* (*Tribunal pour Enfants*); the *Farm Lease Court;* and the *Social Security Commission*—all of which have several court units. Each of the 27 courts of appeal, with from five to seven judges sitting, hears a case before it entirely *de novo;* their decisions on points of fact are final.

The Assize Court (COUR D'ASSISE). Whereas the Court of Appeal hears appeals in civil cases, the appellate tribunal for *criminal*

[11] *Ambassade de France.* French Affairs Bulletin—No. 84 (May 1959), p. 32.

cases, functioning on the same level and collateral with the latter, is the *Assize Court* (*Cour d'Assise*). But in addition to being the appellate body for the Correctional Tribunal—the criminal section of the Court of Major Instance below—the *Cour d'Assise* has original jurisdiction in all major criminal cases, such as homicide. It does not sit with a jury when acting as an appellate tribunal, but a jury is normally present when it tries cases in its original jurisdiction. There are 90 assizes, one in each *département,* each being usually staffed with three judges from the 27 units of the courts of appeal. However, depending upon the work load and the availability of personnel, two of the three judges may be drafted from the local *tribunal de grande instance,* but the presiding judge is invariably a member of the *Cour d'Appel.*

The Court of Cassation (COUR DE CASSATION). At the pinnacle of the regular courts of France stands its *Court of Cassation* (*Cour de Cassation*). Largely unaffected by the Judicial Reorganization Act of 1959, it may be regarded as the Supreme Court of Appeal of the Republic. Appropriately sitting in Paris—as ever the heart and pulse of *la patrie*—the 110-member-body consists of 83 judges or, more precisely, 77 counselors (*conseillers*), the Chief Justice (*Premier Président*), three presidents of sections and two other senior judges, plus the Chief Prosecutor (*Procureur-Général*) who, together with his staff of 17 and nine clerks of court, is attached to it. Its jurisdiction extends throughout the French Republic, and it enjoys great prestige and respect.

The *Cour de Cassation* is divided into three sections (*chambres*), each headed by a *président*—one of the favorite French titles—with the entire tribunal presided over by the First President or Chief Justice. One *chambre,* known as the Screening Section, receives and evaluates all petitions and requests for review, conducts a preliminary inquiry into their merits, dockets those it deems to be worthy of review by the court, and rejects all others. A second *chambre* handles all civil cases; the third all criminal cases. Like the House of Lords, but unlike the Supreme Court of the United States, the *Cour de Cassation* has no original jurisdiction; all cases that come to it in the hierarchy of the ordinary courts do so by way of appeal from the assizes and the courts of appeal immediately below.

Casser, the French verb for "break" or "smash," indicates the actual role of this respected and dignified tribunal. It is distinctly a limited role, for the *Cour de Cassation* rules only on the legal appropriateness of the decision rendered—i.e. it merely passes judgment on *the point of law involved in the decision,* emphatically not on the substance of the case. It neither "decides" nor "retries" a case. It possesses simply the power to quash, *elle casse,* the legal point of a case, and *then remand it below for retrial* by a court of the same rank as the one from which it came, but not the same court.

In no sense of the term does the *Cour de Cassation* possess the power of judicial review. Indeed, it ruled itself in the case of the newspaper *Le National* that a law which had been "deliberately promulgated according to constitutional forms" was beyond attacks on grounds of unconstitutionality under the French system of separation of powers.[12] The absence of judicial review is a deficiency of power that the French courts have shared with their friends

FIGURE 3
THE REGULAR (ORDINARY)
COURTS OF THE FIFTH FRENCH REPUBLIC

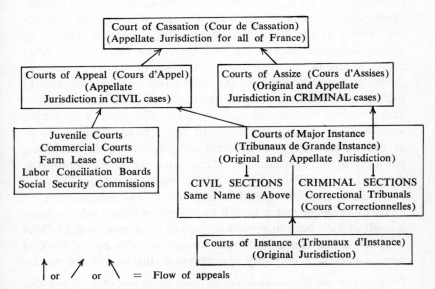

↑ or ╱ or ╲ = Flow of appeals

[12] See VII *Political Studies* 51–3 and 60–61 (February 1959).

across the British Channel. However, a system of what might be called quasi-judicial review, lodged in an extra-judicial body lying outside the judicial hierarchy, the *Constitutional Council (Conseil Constitutionnel)*—to be fully described in the following chapter—was adopted by the Constitution of the Fifth Republic as a successor to its rather anemic relative of the Fourth Republic, the *Constitutional Committee (Comité Constitutionnel)*. But, as will be readily perceived, the French system of quasi-judicial review is a far cry from the bona fide power and authority vested in the United States judiciary.

ADMINISTRATIVE TRIBUNALS GENERALLY

We now turn to what is unquestionably the more intriguing, because more novel, second judicial hierarchy in France, the popular and entirely separate *administrative courts* that are more or less foreign to the Anglo-Saxon world. Despite some modifications initiated in 1947 and 1946, respectively, the United Kingdom and the United States still hold, by and large, to the ancient Anglo-Saxon principle that "the king can do no wrong"—which, in effect, signifies that the sovereign, the state, cannot be sued without its expressed consent. Accordingly, the acts of government officials are viewed as the acts of ordinary citizens and are judged by exactly the same rules of law and before the same courts. After all, it is one of the underlying principles of the philosophy of democratic government that any citizen is presumably capable of participating in it (a notion dear to the heart of President Andrew Jackson—and popularized well by him—who used it to justify, some erroneously contend to invent, the "spoils system"). Thus, as one of Britain's great students of government, A. V. Dicey, put it often, every government official, from the Prime Minister on down to the lowliest clerk, is "under the same responsibility for every act done without legal justification as any other citizen." [13]

This has meant that a British or American citizen who believes himself to have been aggrieved or injured by a government official in either of the two lands would *have to sue that official* who, in turn, would have to justify his actions at the bar of the regular

---

[13] For example, see his *Introduction to the Study of the Law of the Constitution,* 9th ed. (New York: The Macmillan Co., 1939).

courts. Thus, if Citizen John Smith believes that he has been wronged or maltreated by Sheriff James Doe, in the latter's capacity as an officer of the law, he may bring suit. But such a suit must be brought against Sheriff James Doe in a regular court of jurisdiction, *not* against Doe's State of Virginia, whose laws he was presumably enforcing (or against the United States, if the arresting officer had been a federal official), and the suit will read *Smith v. Doe*. Moreover, to collect damages, which would presumably come out of Doe's pocket, Citizen Smith must demonstrate successfully that Sheriff Doe has exceeded his discretionary authority under the law—an extremely difficult task in most instances.

Whatever the underlying philosophical justifications for personal liability of government officials, its practical implications are often unsatisfactory, to say the least, and may well be fraught with danger both to the individuals involved and the system which they serve and under which they live. Among these implications and the lessons of experience are: the possibility that an official may perform his duties timidly or haphazardly; that he may not perform them in accordance with his most considered judgment but according to expediency; the difficulty, already alluded to, of collecting from an individual government servant; the question why, in performing a duty for his government, he should be personally responsible in the first place. Moreover, there are the inevitable delays in getting a case docketed in the courts; the slowly grinding judicial process, especially in as large a country as the United States; the inconvenience and expense of bringing a case to court. All these represent factors that may well, and often do, outweigh any monetary recompense that might eventually accrue to the plaintiff.

In recognition of these very real problems, Britain and the United States have gradually begun to provide tribunals in which the state may be sued directly. No abandonment of the old philosophy of a single, unified judiciary has taken place, nor is it likely to take place in the near future—although Britain has shown considerable interest in the institution of the Danish *ombudsman,* a sort of "people's watchdog" over administrative abuses with a great deal of influence and esteem, though little direct power, who disposes of some thousand cases annually with dispatch and expertise.[14] The two nations, however, have taken at least two steps in the direction of rendering matters a bit more palatable to government employees and citizens alike. Thus, Britain adopted the Crown Proceedings Act of 1947 which, under certain circumstances, makes the government responsible for the actions of its servants. Purposely provided with many loop-holes and exceptions, the act nevertheless now enables ordinary citizens to sue the government in the same manner and before the same tribunals "as if the Crown were a fellow-citizen." Hence, the injured or aggrieved party sues the state as a matter of right. Furthermore, the act makes government departments responsible for common law as well as statutory duties. However, it should be noted that the act confines itself, more or less, to the *non-law-enforcing* agencies of government, thus leaving unchanged the path of claims that might arise under the law-enforcing units, such as police, military services, foreign affairs. Nevertheless, the statute does represent a wholesome and welcome change.[15]

What the above statute did for Britain, the Tort Claims Act of 1946 had done, broadly speaking, for the United States one year earlier insofar as the federal government is concerned. Under it, a citizen allegedly injured or aggrieved by an employee of the federal government, or the government itself, may bring suit in any civil action, other than a breach of contract—which is not a tort—against the United States for negligence or wrongful acts, no maximum monetary ceiling existing on the claim. It is also possible to make claims of less than $1000 directly to the head of any federal agency allegedly responsible for a loss caused by "negligent or wrongful act of omission of an employee," but the agency is *not required* to sanction such claims. Appeals under the provisions of the Tort Claims Act are possible to the Court of Claims and, under certain conditions, to the regular constitutional court hierarchy.

The Court of Claims, established in 1855, as was demonstrated in some detail in Chapter Four, is itself a vehicle for citizens to sue the federal government for damages, and as such represents a

---

[14] See, for example, my article, *Denmark's Folketingets Ombudsmand: A People's Watchdog*, 20 *Public Administration Review* 152 (Summer 1960).

[15] For a brief evaluation of the Act, see Harry Street, *Government Liability: A Comparative Study* (Cambridge: Cambridge University Press, 1953).

modification of the "sovereign-can-do-no-wrong" principle. But its limited jurisdiction is confined to contractual, tax, and other non-tort claims against the Government of the United States. The Tort Claims Act contains, as does its British counterpart, many deliberate exceptions and ambiguities—such as excluding

> any claim based upon an act or omission of an employee of the Government exercising due care, in the exercise of a statute or regulation, whether or not such statute or regulation be valid, or based upon the exercise or performance or the failure to exercise or perform a discretionary function or duty on the part of a federal agency or an employee of the Government, whether or not the discretion involved be abused.*

but, hopefully, it personifies a salutary trend in adjudication.

THE FRENCH ADMINISTRATIVE COURTS

The hierarchy of courts that administers the *droit administratif* in France is very much part and parcel of the governmental system, however separated it is from the ordinary courts. To the French—and to many careful observers in the Anglo-Saxon world as well—theirs is the only logical system of supervising the administrative branch of the government, not only because of its rapid, convenient, and efficient adjudicatory process but also because of the expertise inherent in its judicial personnel staffing the administrative courts. This is even more remarkable in view of the fact that these administrative courts are actually more closely linked to the executive than to the judicial branch. Evolving gradually since revolutionary days, the *droit administratif* has a long and honorable history, beginning with the creation of the first *Council of State* (*Conseil d'État*) under Napoleon Bonaparte.

The structure of the French administrative court system is infinitely less complicated than the regular court system with fewer

---

* It should not be forgotten, of course, that in both countries exist numerous *quasi-judicial* agencies and/or tribunals that, among other duties, *adjudicate administratively* claims upon the government. These are, for example, the independent regulatory commissions and agencies in the United States, and the 35-odd, ministerially appointed "special administrative tribunals" in the United Kingdom, established to deal with cases arising out of the application of social policy, e.g. the Licensing Authority for Public Service Vehicles.

subdivisions. It consists of but two levels: first, the old *Interde-partmental Prefectural Councils* (*Conseils de Préfecture Interde-partmentaux*), now known simply as *Regional Councils* or *Ad-ministrative Tribunals* (*Tribunaux Administratifs*), since they are no longer arranged in *départements* but according to twenty-three national regions plus Paris; second, the famous multi-purpose, and powerful, *Council of State* (*Conseil d'État*) at the apex. (There is also a number of special collateral administrative tribunals, some-times known as "inferior councils"—such as the *Council of Public Instruction* (*Conseil d'Instruction Publique*) and the *Draft Review Board* (*Conseil Militaire de Revision*), which may be omitted for present purposes.)

The Regional Councils (TRIBUNAUX ADMINISTRATIFS). It is to the *Tribunal Administratif* of his region that a French citizen with a complaint against the administrative branch of *La République* turns initially. In almost all instances involving the *droit adminis-tratif*, the *Tribunal Administratif* thus acts as the administrative court of first instance. It is staffed with able, experienced civil servants who have been recruited either from the administrative branch itself, provided they have law degrees, or they are merit appointees who have passed competitive examinations. The caliber of the five members of each *tribunal administratif*—one *président,* of course, and four *conseillers*—is thus almost always outstanding even at this first instance level.

In line with the simplicity and inexpensiveness that so fortu-nately characterize the administrative court system of France, all a plaintiff at the bar of his *Tribunal Administratif* has to do is to execute and file the official complaint form which costs practically nothing. Normally, the tribunal will conduct the investigation of the complaint by way of written statements to both sides of the complaint. Sometimes an oral hearing is held, at which the liti-gants may either present arguments personally or through legal counsel. When the tribunal is ready to render a decision it will do so publicly; usually that settles the matter. Far more often than not, the complaining *citoyen* wins his suit, and can then look for-ward to speedy compensation from the public treasury for any damages. So prevalent have been these citizen victories that con-siderable criticism has ensued among both legal scholars and prac-titioners, who believe that the administrative court system has caused the French Government to be "too tough on itself," that there exists what might be viewed as a distinct bias *against* it.

The Council of State (LE CONSEIL D'ÉTAT). With its appellate jurisdiction from the *tribunaux administratifs* as well as original jurisdiction in certain stipulated "important" and/or "delicate" cases, the *Conseil d'État* justly enjoys enormous prestige. Actually, it is far more than a merely administrative tribunal; only one of its five sections—a most renowned and most important one, the *Litigation Section* (*Section du Contentieux*)—deals with the *droit administratif*. The other four are concerned with drafting of legislation for the cabinet; advisory opinions on legislative and executive matters; supervision over rules of public administration; and other significant functions in the governmental process. Roughly one-half of the council's membership of 179, nominally headed by the Minister of Justice, but actually by its Vice-President, works in the administrative court section, and its personnel is uniquely trained and qualified.

The 80-plus members of that Litigation Section—as are those of the other branches of the council—are recruited in two ways: The "second class auditors"—those who enter the council at the bottom of the ladder—are drawn from graduates of the three-year course at the justly celebrated *École Nationale d'Administration,* which provides expert personnel destined for the highest levels of the corps of civil servants in France. Admission to the *École* is by stiff competitive examination, most of the applicants having had some training in the law or in political science. The school graduates fewer than 150 students annually, and those who do obtain their diplomas are indeed highly trained and qualified. The personnel of the higher echelons of the council either come from the upper levels of the ministries and the prefects, from the legal ranks, or are promoted from lower echelons. France is justly proud of her corps of *conseillers* in the Council of State; it is truly an elite body and richly merits its great prestige and acclaim.

Eleven subsections, numbered chronologically, constitute the section of the council which handles the *droit administratif*. Each of these subsections consists of a *président* and a number of *conseillers*. Although roughly half of the subsections operate independently in readying cases for decision, two must meet jointly to render final judgment. Important cases are considered by the full "judicial section," consisting of the presiding officers of the 11 subsections plus two members of the subsection(s) where the report of the case was prepared. The highest organ of the *Conseil d'État* is its Plenary Assembly, for which are reserved cases of "extreme importance." It is composed of the 17 highest officers of the council, in this instance including four *conseillers* from its administrative sections. Decisions by all of these organs are of equal weight, and they are final and binding.

Review Procedure. As already illustrated briefly, the procedure for obtaining review in the French administrative court hierarchy is as simple as it is inexpensive. In large measure, the latter is due to the fact that the French state assumes responsibility for investigating both the facts and the law involved in a plaintiff's petition. Moreover, since under the French inquisitorial procedure the judiciary plays an active role throughout the judicial process, the role of the petitioner is reduced to a summary statement as to the alleged facts and the relief prayed. He may request either of two types of review actions: (1) proceedings for the annulment of an *ultra vires*—beyond powers—administrative act (*recours pour excès de pouvoir*); or (2) proceedings to order some type of affirmative administrative action, such as payment of monetary damages (*recours de pleine juridiction*). Most petitions for review fall into the first category. Having received the petition, the administrative tribunal takes over; petitioner need not even retain legal counsel in the first type of case unless he chooses to do so. In any event, he need not worry, his interests will be amply guarded by the mills of the *droit administratif*. Moreover, the Council of State, *on its own cognizance,* has added a third ground for review going beyond the concept inherent in *ultra vires*—i.e. an official action beyond the scope of legal authority—namely, the famous French administrative law concept of *détournement de pouvoir,* most equitably translated as rank *abuse* of power. In its eyes, *abuse* of power is a different concept from that of an illegal *application* of power, which is governed by the first review category under *ultra vires*.

Once the Council of State has granted the availability of review, it must define the extent or scope of its reviewing power on the merits. This is especially true in the first category cases, under which the legality of an administrative action may be challenged on three grounds, all of which fall under the *ultra vires* concept:

(1) lack of jurisdiction; (2) failure to observe procedures defined by law; (3) error of law. To these three the special category of abuse of power is then added.

Evaluation. It is hardly surprising that the Council of State is literally swamped with petitions for action and review! The same applies to the lower rung of the administrative court system. The French people look up to it as a reliable and virile guardian of individual rights against administrative encroachment. Moreover, as well they might, they have great faith in the ability of these high-class civil servants to dispose of the thousands upon thousands of cases that reach them year by year. Small wonder, as has been indicated, that Anglo-Saxon states have given considerable thought to the adoption of a similar system. The Task Force of the Second Hoover Commission in the United States, for one, urgently suggested some form of administrative court system for its federal government.

Not only does the French system provide for fuller review of administrative action than the average Anglo-Saxon one, but the cost of litigation is smaller; accessibility to the courts is greater; review is more easily available; scope of review is larger; state liability for damages is less circumscribed; and settlement is far more prompt and efficient. The French state, whatever the wisdom of its philosophy of government here may be, simply considers itself totally liable for service-connected faults of public officers and state agencies. That liability has even been extended to cover most cases in which the damage is caused by personal fault of public officials, for the administrative courts have held that such faults are often inseparably connected with the administrative service of which the official is an agent. In such cases, the state indemnifies the damages to the injured citizen, and the officer at fault becomes personally liable to the state.

Yet not only does the French state accept liability for fault under the *droit administratif,* but, as outlined earlier, also for risk. In other words, if proper administrative action results in an unequal burden on, or a social injustice to, a citizen, the state bears the cost of equalizing the burden—without the need to introduce a private bill in the legislature. In effect, the *droit administratif* is developing in the direction of absolute liability to ensure equitable sharing among all citizens of the burden of government action. This may well be far from an unmixed blessing; but the French administrative court system, with the *Conseil d'État* standing at its apex,[16] has operated so successfully and has proved to be such a bulwark against arbitrary actions by the centralized state, that it richly merits the careful attention that it has begun to enjoy increasingly by students and practitioners of government alike.

A NOTE ON
THE JUDICIARY OF THE SOVIET UNION

Because of the oligarchical nature of the effective instrumentalities of government in the Union of Soviet Socialist Republics, law and judiciary—the entire judicial process—are in a category of their own. Despite a series of mild reforms that were adopted in the mid and late 1930's and some more significant ones as recently as 1957-59, law in the Russia of today is employed principally as a tool of the state; it is utilized for purposes of strict conformity; it is an organ of state power *par excellence*. The rights of the citizen under such a system are largely illusory, and they are granted only in so far as such a grant is in accordance with the wishes of the government of the day. Moreover, certain rights, specifically enumerated under the Constitution of the USSR, are qualified by such tellingly realistic phrases as ". . . unless otherwise provided by law . . . ," such as the articles of the Constitution of 1936 dealing with the rights to counsel, public trial, independent judges, inviolability of the person, and so forth,[17] although the reforms of 1957 have, at least in theory, rendered these concepts somewhat more meaningful—in a limited manner.

The arbitrary characteristic of Soviet law is a logical by-product of the traditional concept of Marxism, where law is viewed as an instrument of domination, as a coercive tool of the state in its transition from socialism to communism, where the duties of a citizen prevail over his rights. This coercive interpretation has been embraced quite naturally by the Soviet jurists, who follow

[16] For a superb, up-to-date, and the sole available complete study of the *Conseil d'État*, see Charles E. Freedman, *The Conseil d'État in Modern France* (New York: Columbia University Press, 1961).

[17] *Constitution of the Union of Soviet Socialist Republics* (London: Soviet News, 1955).

Lenin's dictum that law is "nothing if there is no apparatus adapted to coerce people into observing its provisions." [18] Hence the absence of meaningful guarantees to freedom under Soviet rule. It should be noted, however, that the machinery of justice in the Soviet Union grinds in an entirely different manner when it concerns an ordinary transgression—one not involving the state as a politico-economic institution. In the former case, adjudication will be effected by the tribunals involved in roughly the same manner known throughout the world; but in the latter, law becomes the political organ of state power, the instrument of the class that constitutes the regime of the land, a mere adjunct of state power in pursuit of conformity within Soviet society.

THE ABSENCE OF AN INDEPENDENT JUDICIARY

There is not, indeed there cannot be, a truly independent judiciary under Soviet rule. Any meaningful power to check and balance the other branches of the government—assuming there are purposeful distinctions at all—is necessarily illusory. On the contrary, the judiciary of the Soviet Union is effectively subjugated to the legislative bodies or to those governmental bodies that provide legislative functions—even if these are really nothing or little more than Communist Party-sanctioned decrees.

The judiciary does not, of course, possess the power of judicial review. If that power exists anywhere at all in the USSR—really an academic question—it resides in the Presidium of the Supreme Soviet, which is specifically charged under the Constitution with the "interpretation of the laws."

Moreover, throughout the judicial hierarchy, both the professional and the lay judges, known as *assessors,* are *elected* for short terms of office—not exceeding five years—by legislative bodies, soviets, or residents of the districts in which they serve, *and* they are all subject to recall at any time. Either faithful party members or acceptable "non-party Bolsheviks," these judges represent the political power of the state, and the eyes of the dominant elements of Soviet society are constantly fixed upon them.

[18] From V. I. Lenin, *Sochineniia,* as quoted by George C. Guins, *Soviet Law and Soviet Society* (The Hague: Martinus Nijhoff, 1954), p. 45.

THE COURT HIERARCHY

One of the most salient features of the judicial hierarchy of the USSR is its high degree of centralization, despite the federal structure of the government and despite the myriad number of courts in the various and manifold geographic subdivisions below. The sole truly "federal" court is the Supreme Court of the USSR, which enjoys corrective power over the lower courts. But more important is the overriding supervisory power of the "boss" of the entire judicial system, the Procurator-General, the "supreme overseer of Soviet legality," who will be described more fully below.

The Comradely Court. At the lowest level of the Soviet judiciary is the *Comradely Court,* a rather unique institution that actually falls outside the regular hierarchy. More appropriately, these units, which may be found at local levels everywhere in the land, have been called "honour courts." [19] Staffed by local citizens for the adjudication of disputes between individuals, comradely courts are organized as *ad hoc* bodies in villages, farm co-operatives, apartment houses, factories, or any other place of work or dwelling where they might be needed to deal with the sundry petty offenses that invariably take place among people everywhere, whatever their political philosophy may be. The "judges" of the Comradely Court in a particular unit or locality are normally elected for each case that arises by the membership of the geographical or occupational unit concerned, or they may comprise all those present at a meeting of that unit. They may levy reprimands and small fines.

But since these comradely courts are really not recognized as courts per se, their decisions are subject to annulment by the level immediately above, the People's Court. This is true for all judgments *except* a new classification, devised in 1959, concerning decisions of special comradely courts in connection with "speculators, hooligans, unemployed elements, etc." Those found guilty of one of these offenses at a meeting of "friends and neighbors," constituted as the Comradely Court of jurisdiction, may be punished to a maximum of banishment from their place of residence.[20] The People's Court above may not review that type of decision, although the local *soviets* (legislatures) do have that power.

[19] Robert G. Newmann, op. cit. p. 616.   [20] Ibid.

The People's Court. If we omit the level of the quasi-tribunal just discussed, the base of the Soviet judiciary is actually occupied by the *People's Court.* Organized on a district basis throughout the Soviet Union, the people's courts are strictly courts of original jurisdiction in both criminal and civil cases—except for their tangential supervisory power over the comradely courts. As the work horse courts of the entire system, they handle the bulk of the minor criminal and civil cases in the USSR. The Council of Ministers of the pertinent Union or Autonomous Republic concerned determines the number of people's courts to be established in each district (*raion*). They are locally staffed by one judge, as chairman, and two assessors; the former is elected by the inhabitants of the district for five years and the latter for two. The judge is not statutorily required to be a professional, although he usually is; the assessors, being "lay judges," have no formal judicial or legal background.

Assessors, who come from all walks of life and who usually serve only for a brief period—perhaps up to two weeks annually— are emphatically not to be regarded as jurors in the Western sense. No juries as the West knows them exist in the Soviet Union. When the assessors hear and decide a case, they act as judges and have a full voice and vote on the various aspects of the facts and law of a case as well as in the decision itself. Although the experience of the professional judge on the People's Court normally carries more weight and more often than not prevails, it would be erroneous to view the assessors as mere adjuncts or a fifth wheel. They are part and parcel of the judicial process here.

The Courts of the Region, Autonomous Region, and Autonomous Republic. Now matters become somewhat more complicated. At the next level, or really at the next three levels, lie the intermediate courts, arranged according to territorial division that bridge the hierarchical gap between the level of the People's Court and that of the *Supreme Court of the Union Republic.* Not all multiple rungs of these intermediate courts will inevitably be present in all union republics, certainly not in the smaller ones—yet sometimes there will even be a fourth (the Area)—but they are sufficiently standardized to represent a definite pattern. Their jurisdiction is both original and appellate. In the exercise of the appellate function, they review decisions coming to them from the sundry people's courts of their respective territories, and when an appeal has been decided by a minimum of three regular judges sitting *en banc* it is final.

The courts of the regions, autonomous regions, and autonomous republics have original jurisdiction in the more serious criminal and civil cases. Among the former, according to the criminal code, are "counterrevolutionary activities, crimes against administrative orders when they involve particular danger to the state, the pillaging of socialist property, and other important economic crimes." In the realm of civil jurisdiction lie cases involving the state and social institutions, public enterprises, and organizations. The work of these courts is usually performed by panels of five professional judges and assessors, holding the titles of chairman, deputy chairman, members, and people's assessors, all of whom are elected for five-year terms by the soviets of the areas or regions concerned.

The Supreme Court of the Union Republic. In each Union Republic—the largest constituent part of the federal structure of the Soviet Union—lies a *Supreme Court of the Union Republic,* constituting the highest judicial body of that division. Its members, headed by five professional judges, are elected for five-year terms by the Supreme Soviet of the Union Republic. These high courts have both original and appellate jurisdiction. In the latter sphere of their work, they are empowered to set aside the decisions of any inferior court in the Republic; and appellate decision rendered here becomes final and binding. Related to that jurisdiction is their power to supervise all inferior courts by receiving and acting on "protests" against verdicts rendered below, coming to them from the Procurator-General or the Chairman of the Supreme Court of the USSR or by the corresponding officials of the lower echelons —one of the more intriguing practices in the Soviet Union! The Supreme Court of the Union Republic has original jurisdiction in the more serious criminal and civil cases, including those involving infractions committed in office by the higher officials of government in the Republic. Its decisions are final.

The Supreme Court of the USSR. At the pinnacle of the judicial hierarchy in the Soviet Union stands the *Supreme Court of the USSR,* classified by Article 104 of the Constitution of 1936 as its "highest judicial organ." Elected by the Supreme Soviet of the

USSR for five-year terms of office, its membership consists of a Chairman, two vice-chairmen, nine professional judges, and 20 people's assessors. Moreover, attached to it as members *ex officio* are the 15 chairmen of the supreme courts of the union republics, but these do not necessarily sit on a steady basis. The regular members of the Supreme Court are divided into three specialized *collegia* (panels), one each for civil, criminal, and military matters, but the entire Court is charged to meet at least once every three months in plenary session (the *plenum*). The Chairman may preside over any case before the Court and he has the power to relieve or discharge any inferior court in the Soviet Union of a case in order to "protest" it in plenary session—sessions that are invariably attended by the Procurator-General.

Despite the implications of the Supreme Court's division of labor and jurisdiction, it is basically a court of review and appeals, a supervisory court. As such it even has the authority to initiate legislation dealing with the judicial system, although that power is not very meaningful. Yet, as already explained, it emphatically lacks the power of judicial review; nor does it possess the authority to interpret laws, a function theoretically reserved, as is the former, to the Presidium of the Supreme Soviet of the USSR. But it may give advice to the Presidium in cases of interpretation. Nevertheless, the civil and criminal *collegia* do serve as tribunals of original jurisdiction in cases of exceptional nation-wide significance. When it exercises original jurisdiction, a *collegium* consists of one professional judge as chairman and two assessors; in its appellate or review jurisdiction all its members are regular judges. The remaining *collegium,* the military, has jurisdiction in a small number of particularly significant cases of treason, espionage, and other high crimes against the state. It may also review appeals from and protests against the judgments of lower military tribunals. Except in the sense that there is always the possibility of an appeal to the Presidium of the Supreme Soviet, decisions of the Supreme Court of the USSR are final and binding. But far more significant on the scales of power and authority in the judicial system of the Soviet Union than any court is the Procurator-General and his own extensive hierarchy of procurators throughout the land.

THE PROCURATOR-GENERAL

The best indication of the subordination, centralization, and lack of independence of the judicial hierarchy in the Soviet Union is the existence of the *Procurator-General,* sometimes known as Public Prosecutor or Public Procurator. No official associated with the legal or judicial process of comparable authority exists anywhere—certainly not in the free world. An institution conceived by Lenin in 1922, he combines the position of supreme overlord of the entire judiciary with that of watchdog of the application and interpretation of criminal law on all levels of government, either directly or indirectly, as well as all civil law. Chosen by the Supreme Soviet of the USSR for a term of seven years, the Procurator-General, in turn, appoints or causes to be appointed, the various procurators on the lower levels throughout the USSR (see chart below) for five years. His is truly a centralized and centralizing posture, and although he is technically responsible for his actions to the Supreme Soviet, in effect he is responsible solely to the Communist Party's top echelon, the Presidium and the Secretariat. His subordinate procurators, too, are independent of all local organs of government; as guardians of local conformity they are responsible solely to their chief, the Procurator-General in Moscow.

Powers and Functions. Always held by a high-ranking, trusted member of the Communist Party, and not infrequently a jumping-off spot for advancement on the ladder of power in the Soviet Union, the position of Procurator-General is eagerly sought and influential. Andrei Vyshinsky, who occupied the office during the famous purge trial years in the late 1930's, whence he steadily advanced, ultimately to become Foreign Minister and Russia's Representative to the United Nations, described the Procurator-General as the "watchman of socialist legality, the leader of the policy of the Communist Party and of Soviet authority, the champion of socialism." [21] Even if this appraisal be somewhat embellished, it comes close to the verities of a system of law in which the Procurator-General personifies an omnipotent force.

In addition to his basic authority, outlined in Article 113 of the Constitution, to ensure the strict observance of the law by all min-

---

[21] *The Law of the Soviet State* (New York: The Macmillan Co., 1948), p. 537.

FIGURE 4
THE JUDICIARY AND PROCURACY OF THE USSR

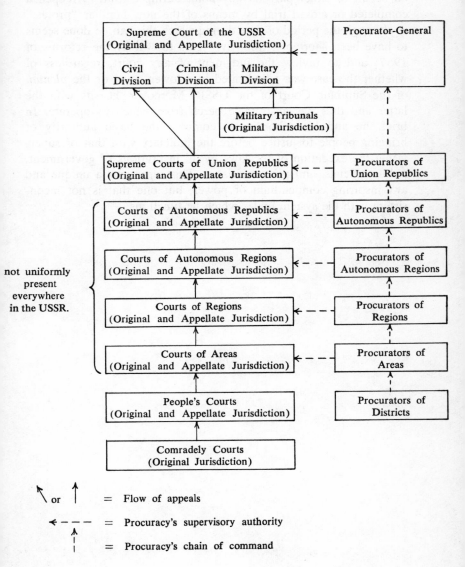

or ↑ = Flow of appeals

←--- = Procuracy's supervisory authority

↑ = Procuracy's chain of command

istries and institutions as well as by all officials and citizens of the Soviet Union at large, he has the right to appear in any civil case on behalf of either party at any point during a trial; to reopen a completed or closed trial by means of the now familiar "protest" —although the period of time during which this can be done seems to have been shortened from five years to two by the reforms of 1957; and to review the judgment of any court, regardless of whether the case was adjudicated in a lower court or the *plenum* of the Supreme Court of the USSR. Moreover, he sits with the latter and thus has a strategic perch from which to operate. In brief, he and his subordinates combine the basic authority of bringing people to justice before the judiciary with that of supervising the execution of the laws by all institutions of government, public officials, and private citizens. This represents a unique and awe-inspiring compendium of power, but one that is not inconsistent with the system under which he functions.

VII

JUDICIAL REVIEW:
I THE SUPREME POWER

DEFINING JUDICIAL REVIEW

Certainly the most controversial and at the same time the most
fascinating role of the courts of the United States in general, and
of the Supreme Court in particular, is the exercise of the power of
judicial review. It is commonly viewed with almost equal amounts
of reverence and suspicion. In its full majesty and range it is a
power that the *ordinary* courts—i.e. those that are part of the
formal judicial hierarchy—of merely a handful of other countries
in the world possess with varying degrees of effectiveness; among
these are Australia, Brazil, Burma, Canada, India, Pakistan, and
Japan, of whom most have federal systems of government. It is all
but axiomatic that the practice would be found more readily in
federal than in unitary states. Briefly stated, judicial review is the
power of any court to *hold unconstitutional and hence unenforce-
able any law, any official action based upon it, and any illegal action
by a public official that it deems*—upon careful, normally painstaking, reflection and in line with the canons of the taught tradition of
the law as well as judicial self-restraint—*to be in conflict with the
Basic Law, in the United States its Constitution*. In other words,
in invoking the power of judicial review, a court applies the *superior* of two laws, which at the level of the federal judiciary of
the United States signifies the Constitution instead of the legislative statute or some action by a public official allegedly or actually
based upon it.

In the United States, which will serve as the chief subject in
this treatment of judicial review, this highly significant instrument
of power is theoretically possessed by every court, no matter how

251

high or low on the judicial ladder. Although admittedly unlikely, it is thus not at all impossible for a judge in a low-level court of one of the 50 states to declare a federal law unconstitutional! Such a decision would quite naturally at once be appealed to higher echelons for review and almost certain reversal, but the possibility does exist. Conscious of the nature and purpose of federalism and the need to permit legislative bodies to act in accordance with their best judgment, no matter how unwise that may well be at times, courts are understandably loathe to invoke the judicial veto. Yet their power to do so, and especially that of the Supreme Court of the United States, serves as an omnipresent and potentially omnipotent check upon the legislative branches of government. While that highest tribunal, in a total of 82 or 83 cases (depending upon the count), has to date (winter 1961–62) declared but 89 provisions of *federal* laws unconstitutional out of a total of over 65,000 public and private laws passed, some 700 *state* laws and provisions of *state* constitutions have run wholly or partly afoul of that judicial checkmate since 1789. A recent example of the latter action is the Court's unanimous ruling in *Torcaso v. Watkins:* [1] in it it struck down a provision of the Maryland Constitution on the ground that to compel officeholders to declare belief in God constituted a "religious test for public office" that invaded the individual's right to religious freedom. In many ways, the Court's power over state actions is of more significance to the federal system than the much more publicized and more well-known power over federal actions.

Tables VII and VIII illustrate in some detail the power of judicial review over legislative enactments as exercised by the Supreme Court at the *federal level only*. But it is interesting to note that more statutes of the State of Louisiana have been declared unconstitutional than those of any other state—Louisiana being the sole *state* with civil law at the base of its judicial system. Regarding the sparse number of federal statutes held unconstitutional by the post-"anti New Deal" Supreme Court in recent times, the six provisions of congressional enactments that have fallen since 1937—actually since 1943—all did so because they infringed personal liberties safeguarded under the Constitution, with three

[1] 367 U. S. 488 (1961).

involving actions by military authorities who proceeded under congressional statutes. The six Court decisions were as follows:

(1) *Tot v. United States* (1943).[2] A statutory presumption that a known criminal in possession of firearms or ammunition must have carried them in violation of the Federal Firearms Act, Section 2(f), was invalidated 8:0 as a violation of the due process of law clause of the Fifth Amendment.

(2) *United States v. Lovett* (1946).[3] Section 304 of the Defense Appropriation Act of 1943, which barred the salaries of certain specifically named federal employees, was struck down 8:0 as violative of the constitutional prohibition against a Bill of Attainder.

(3) *United States v. Cardiff* (1952).[4] A section of the Food and Drug Act, dealing with factory inspection, fell 8:1 as unconstitutionally vague under the due process clause of the Fifth Amendment.

(4) *United States ex rel Toth v. Quarles* (1955).[5] The court held unconstitutional 6:3 Section 3A of the Uniform Code of Military Justice when applied to a *former* member of the United States Air Force, as violative of the guarantees of the civilian judicial process inherent in Article III of the Constitution.

(5) *Reid v. Covert* (1957) coupled with *Kinsella v. Singleton, et al.* (1960).[6] These two cases concerned a series of related decisions in which the Court dealt with several aspects of the Uniform Code of Military Justice, and found some of these unconstitutional as applied to various civilians accompanying the armed forces by votes ranging from a high of 7:2 to a low of 5:4. The application of certain sections of the Code in the five cases here at issue thus fell as violative of the individuals' rights under Article III and Amendments V and VI of the Constitution, including the right to a trial by jury, indictment by grand jury, and public trial in a civilian court before an impartial jury of one's peers.

(6) *Trop v. Dulles* (1958).[7] Here the narrowly divided Court struck down section 401(G) of the Nationality Act of

[2] 319 U. S. 463.   [3] 328 U. S. 303.   [4] 344 U. S. 174.
[5] 350 U. S. 11.   [6] 354 U. S. 1 and 361 U. S. 234.   [7] 356 U. S. 86.

1940, holding that Congress had exceeded its military and expatriation powers in making desertion in time of war punishable by expatriation. The Court ruled 5:4 that to expatriate for such a reason constituted "cruel and unusual punishment," forbidden by the verbiage of Amendment VIII.

State legislation, too, has—with generally minor exceptions [8] —been held unconstitutional largely because of infringement of civil liberties, although a number of instances involved cases of state interference with national interests, especially in the realm of interstate commerce.

TABLE VII

U. S. SUPREME COURT DECLARATIONS
OF UNCONSTITUTIONALITY OF FEDERAL LAWS, I (Arranged chronologically in accordance with tenure of the Chief Justices.)

Time Span	Chief Justice(s)	Number of Declarations of Unconstitutionality	Commentary
1789–1801	Jay J. Rutledge Ellsworth	0	Weak, placid Court
1801–1835	Marshall	1	1803: *Marbury v. Madison*
1836–1857	Taney	0	
1857–1864	Taney	1	1857: *Dred Scott v. Sanford*
1864–1873	Chase	10	1870: *Legal Tender Cases*
1874–1888	Waite Fuller	8	1883: *Civil Rights Cases*
1888–1910	Fuller	14 (15)	1895 *Income Tax Cases*
1910–1921	White Taft	13	1918: *Child Labor Case*
1921–1930	Taft	13	1923: *Minimum Wage Case*
1930–1936	Hughes	16	Of these 13 came in 1934–36!
1936–1943	Hughes Stone	0	
1943–Present	Stone	2	See explanation p. 253, *supra.*
	Vinson	1	
	Warren	3	
		82 (83)	

[8] cf. *Wood v. Lovett,* 313 U. S. 362 (1941) and *Morey v. Doud,* 354 U. S. 451 (1957).

Thus, after the famous decision in *Marbury v. Madison* [9] in 1803, to be described presently, in which Mr. Chief Justice Marshall enunciated the doctrine of judicial review—although it was not really the first instance of its application—[10] no other federal legislation was declared unconstitutional by his Court during the remaining 32 years of his long tenure of 34 years. The Circuit Court for the District of Columbia did strike down 2:1 a congressional statute in *U.S. v. Benjamin More* only six months after *Marbury v. Madison*. Nevertheless, the Marshall Court wielded immense power and, guided by the dominant figure of the great Chief Justice, did more than either of the other two branches of the national government to make the young United States a strong, vigorous, powerful nation, and its Constitution a living, effective, elastic Basic Law. Not until Mr. Chief Justice Taney's crucial decision in *Dred Scott v. Sanford* [11] in 1857 was another federal statute struck down by the Court; and the greatest crisis evoked by that power of the Supreme Court did not arrive until, dominated by the doctrinaire conservatives among the so-called "Nine Old Men," the Court declared unconstitutional no less than 13 New Deal laws in 1934–36.

TABLE VIII
U. S. SUPREME COURT DECLARATIONS
OF UNCONSTITUTIONALITY OF FEDERAL LAWS, II

Under Chief Justice	Recorded Declaration Number	Citation of Case and Year Decided	Vote
Marshall	1	*Marbury v. Madison,* 1 Cranch 137 (1803)	6:0
Taney	2	*Dred Scott v. Sanford,* 19 Howard 393 (1857)	7:2
Chase	3	*Gordon v. United States,* 2 Wallace 561 (1865)	8:2
Chase	4	*Ex parte Garland,* 4 Wallace 33 (1867)	5:4
Chase	5	*Reichert v. Felps,* 6 Wallace 160 (1868)	8:0

[9] 1 Cranch 137.   [10] cf. this text, p. 271 and fns. 33–7, *infra*.
[11] 19 Howard 393.

Under Chief Justice	Recorded Declaration Number	Citation of Case and Year Decided	Vote
Chase	6	*The Alicia,* 7 Wallace 571 (1869)	8:0
Chase	7	*Hepburn v. Griswold,* 8 Wallace 603 (1870)	4:3
Chase	8	*United States v. DeWitt,* 9 Wallace 41 (1870)	9:0
Chase	9	*The Justices v. Murray,* 9 Wallace 274 (1870)	9:0
Chase	10	*The Collector v. Day,* 11 Wallace 113 (1871)	8:1
Chase	11	*United States v. Klein,* 13 Wallace 128 (1872)	7:2
Chase	12	*United States v. Baltimore & Ohio Railway,* 17 Wallace 322 (1873)	7:2
Waite	13	*United States v. Reese,* 92 U. S. 214 (1876)	7:2
Waite	14	*United States v. Fox,* 95 U. S. 670 (1878)	9:0
Waite	15	*Trade Mark Cases,* 100 U. S. 82 (1879)	9:0
Waite	16	*United States v. Harris,* 106 U. S. 629 (1883)	8:1
Waite	17	*Civil Rights Cases,* 109 U. S. 3 (1883)	8:1
Waite	18	*Boyd v. United States,* 116 U. S. 616 (1886)	7:2
Waite	19	*Baldwin v. Franks,* 120 U. S. 678 (1887)	7:1
None*	20	*Callan v. Wilson,* 127 U. S. 540 (1888)	8:0
Fuller	21	*Monongahela Nav. Co. v. U. S.,* 148 U. S. 312 (1893)	8:0
Fuller	22	*Pollock v. Farmers' L. & T. Co.,* 157 U. S. 429 (1895)	6:2
Fuller	23	*Wong Wing v. United States,* 163 U. S. 228 (1896)	8:0
Fuller	24	*Kirby v. United States,* 174 U. S. 47 (1899)	6:2
Fuller	25	*Jones v. Meehan,* 175 U. S. 1 (1899)	9:0

* Mr. Chief Justice Waite died before the case was heard and was not replaced by Mr. Chief Justice Fuller until after it had been decided.

Under Chief Justice	Recorded Declaration Number	Citation of Case and Year Decided	Vote
Fuller	26	*Fairbank v. United States,* 181 U. S. 283 (1901)	5:4
Fuller	27	*James v. Bowman,* 190 U. S. 127 (1903)	6:2
Fuller	28	*Matter of Heff,* 197 U. S. 488 (1905)	8:1
Fuller	29	*Rassmussen v. United States,* 197 U. S. 516 (1905)	9:0
Fuller	30	*Hodges v. United States,* 203 U. S. 1 (1906)	7:2
Fuller	31	*Employers' Liability Cases,* 207 U. S. 463 (1908)	5:4
Fuller	32	*Adair v. United States,* 208 U. S. 161 (1908)	6:2
Fuller	33	*Keller v. United States,* 213 U. S. 138 (1909)	6:3
Fuller	34	*United States v. Evans,* 213 U. S. 297 (1909)	9:0
White	35	*Muskrat v. United States,* 219 U. S. 346 (1911)	9:0
White	36	*Coyle v. Oklahoma,* 221 U. S. 559 (1911)	7:2
White	37	*Choate v. Trapp,* 224 U. S. 665 (1912)	9:0
White	38	*Butts v. Mer. & Miners' Co.,* 230 U. S. 126 (1913)	9:0
White	39	*United States v. Hvoslef,* 237 U. S. 1 (1915)	8:0
White	40	*Thames & Mersey Mar. Ins. Co. v. U. S.,* 237 U. S. 19 (1915)	8:0
White	41	*Hammer v. Dagenhart,* 247 U. S. 251 (1918)	5:4
White	42	*Knickerbocker Ice Co. v. Stewart,* 253 U. S. 149 (1920)	5:4
White	43	*Eisner v. Macomber,* 252 U. S. 189 (1920)	5:4
White	44	*Evans v. Gore,* 253 U. S. 245 (1920)	7:2
White	45	*United States v. Cohen Grocery Co.,* 255 U. S. 81 (1921)	6:2
White	46	*Weeds, Inc. v. United States,* 255 U. S. 109 (1921)	6:2

Under Chief Justice	Recorded Declaration Number	Citation of Case and Year Decided	Vote
White	47	*Newberry v. United States,* 256 U. S. 232 (1921)	5:4
Taft	48	*United States v. Moreland,* 258 U. S. 433 (1922)	5:3
Taft	49	*Child Labor Tax Case,* 259 U. S. 20 (1922)	8:1
Taft	50	*Hill v. Wallace,* 259 U. S. 44 (1922)	9:0
Taft	51	*Keller v. Potomac Electric Co.,* 261 U. S. 428 (1923)	9:0
Taft	52	*Adkins v. Children's Hospital,* 261 U. S. 525 (1923)	5:3
Taft	53	*Spalding & Bros. v. Edwards,* 262 U. S. 66 (1923)	9:0
Taft	54	*Washington v. Dawson,* 264 U. S. 219 (1924)	7:2
Taft	55	*Miles v. Graham,* 268 U. S. 501 (1925)	8:1
Taft	56	*Trusler v. Crooks,* 269 U. S. 475 (1926)	9:0
Taft	57	*Myers v. United States,* 272 U. S. 52 (1926)	6:3
Taft	58	*Nichols v. Coolidge,* 274 U. S. 531 (1927)	9:0
Taft	59	*Untermyer v. Anderson,* 276 U. S. 440 (1928)	6:3
Taft	60	*National Life Insurance Co. v. United States,* 277 U. S. 508 (1928)	6:3
Hughes	61	*Indian Motorcycle Co. v. United States,* 283 U. S. 570 (1931)	7:2
Hughes	62	*Heiner v. Donnan,* 285 U. S. 312 (1932)	6:2
Hughes	63	*Burnet v. Coronado Oil and Gas Co.,* 285 U. S. 393 (1932)	5:4
Hughes	64	*Booth v. United States,* 291 U. S. 339 (1934)	9:0
Hughes	65	*Lynch v. United States,* 292 U. S. 571 (1934)	9:0
Hughes	66	*Panama Refining Co. v. Ryan et al.,* 293 U. S. 388 (1935)	8:1
Hughes	67	*Perry v. United States,* 294 U. S. 330 (1935)	5:4

Under Chief Justice	Recorded Declaration Number	Citation of Case and Year Decided	Vote
Hughes	68	*Railroad Retirement Bd. v. Alton R. R.,* 295 U. S. 330 (1935)	5:4
Hughes	69	*Schechter Poultry Corp. v. United States,* 295 U. S. 495 (1935)	9:0
Hughes	70	*Louisville Joint Stock Land Bank v. Radford,* 295 U. S. 555 (1935)	9:0
Hughes	71	*United States v. Constantine,* 296 U. S. 287 (1935)	6:3
Hughes	72	*Hopkins Federal Savings and Loan Association v. Cleary,* 296 U. S. 315 (1935)	9:0
Hughes	73	*United States v. Butler,* 297 U. S. 1 (1936)	6:3
Hughes	74	*Rickert Rice Mills v. Fontenot,* 297 U. S. 110 (1936)	9:0
Hughes	75	*Carter v. Carter Coal Co.,* 298 U. S. 238 (1936)	5:4
Hughes	76	*Ashton v. Cameron County Water Improvement District,* 298 U. S. 513 (1936)	5:4
Stone	77	*Tot v. United States,* 319 U. S. 463 (1943)	8:0
None**	78	*United States v. Lovett,* 328 U. S. 303 (1946)	8:0
Vinson	79	*United States v. Cardiff,* 344 U. S. 174 (1952)	8:1
Warren	80	*United States ex rel Toth v. Quarles,* 350 U. S. 11 (1955)	6:3
Warren	81	*Reid v. Covert,* plus *Kinsella v. Singleton, et al.,*** 354 U. S. 1 (1957) and 361 U. S. 234 (1960)	6:2
Warren	82	*Trop v. Dulles,* 356 U. S. 86 (1958)	5:4

** Mr. Chief Justice Stone had died before the case was heard and Mr. Chief Justice Vinson did not take his place on the bench until after it had been decided.

*** See p. 253, *supra,* for elaboration. Also see pp. 170–71 Ch. V, *supra.*

JUDICIAL REVIEW ABROAD

As already indicated, the practice of judicial review is not likely to be found in nonfederal states. Hence the other two major subject-lands of this study either do not, as in the case of Britain, or did not until the adoption of the Constitution of 1958, in the case of France, clothe their courts with the power of judicial review —and in the instance of the French Fifth Republic it is judicial review only in a very limited and tangential sense.

BRITAIN

Here, Parliament is supreme in the sense that *any law* that has been enacted by it and has received the routine approval of the Crown becomes the law of the land and is *ipso facto* beyond over-turning by the British courts. By virtue of the ancient writ of *quo warranto,* the courts do, of course, possess the authority to *interpret* legislation, and particularly administrative action based upon it—for all government officials are potentially accountable to them for their actions—*but they may not strike down the law itself.* In the immortal words of Walter Bagehot, the famous British economist and journalist, "there is nothing the British Parliament cannot do except transform a man into a woman and a woman into a man." Although he expressed this fact of governmental life a century ago, it is still as true today as it was then. The more or less homogeneous people of Britain, deeply steeped in the common experience of centuries, tradition, custom, and a firm, if not uncritical, faith in Westminster and Whitehall, continue to be quite content to entrust their treasured freedoms to the good judgment of their representatives in Parliament assembled—duly checked by the powerful executive arm, the political parties, and public opinion itself. The courts are revered and esteemed as necessary concomitants of the democratic process, but *not* in the role of guardians of the Constitution, be that a written or an unwritten document (the latter in Britain's case).

FRANCE

The French, too, insisting that a law is the expression of the sovereign will, had not endowed their courts with authority to declare laws unconstitutional even in a limited manner until the proclamation of the Constitution of the Fifth Republic in 1958. However, prior to it they did devise a rather interesting safeguard in order to ascertain that suggested legislation of dubious constitutionality did not become law per se short of an amendment to the Constitution. That safeguard was established by the framers of the Constitution of the Fourth Republic in the form of a special 13-member committee known as the *Constitutional Committee* (*Comité Constitutionnel*).

Chaired by the President of the Republic, the Constitutional Committee consisted, in addition to the President of the National Assembly and the President of the Council of the Republic, of three members selected by the latter and seven by the former branch of the legislature. In each instance these ten were chosen from personnel outside the membership of the respective chambers, usually professors of law in general concord with the several political parties represented in Parliament. Whenever it was requested to do so by the President of the Council of the Republic and an absolute majority of its members—and only then!—the committee was empowered to examine a law prior to its final promulgation to determine whether or not it was of such a nature as to require its recasting as a *constitutional amendment* rather than simply pass as a *law*. If the committee concurred that a law did in fact imply an amendment to the Constitution, it was referred back to the National Assembly for appropriate action. Not surprisingly, the Constitutional Committee was hardly a very busy institution; it was called upon in merely a few cases, and only one or two of these gave it an opportunity to perform a significant role. Whatever its performance, the institution was a far cry from bona fide judicial review.

The Constitutional Council. However, France moved a bit closer to it—without actually reaching it—with the adoption of the highly significant provision in the de Gaulle Constitution of 1958 calling for a *Constitutional Council* (*Conseil Constitutionnel*).[12] Not a court at all, it actually lies outside the judicial system of the government; not individual citizens nor groups nor courts of law can appeal to it. The council is composed of all the ex-Presidents of France—regardless of which Republic they may have headed— plus nine other distinguished personages, of whom three each are selected by the President of the Republic, the President of the Senate, and the President of the National Assembly. *M. le président* of the council is chosen from among its membership by the in-

[12] Title VII, Arts. 56–63.

cumbent President of the Republic. The members may hold no public office of any kind, other than already held civil service appointments, for it was the intention of the authors of the institution that its membership be wholly independent, exercising no outside remunerative public activity, whatsoever.

The nine appointive members of the Constitutional Council— usually lawyers who have been active in politics—serve for one nonrenewable, staggered nine-year term of office, whereas all ex-Presidents of France serve for life. In theory, the latter may not resign, but one, the venerable Vincent-Auriol, first President of the Fourth Republic, announced on July 2, 1960, that, in protest against three allegedly unconstitutional actions taken by President de Gaulle, he would no longer participate in the work of *le conseil constitutionnel*. The disputed actions were first, a measure to increase vastly state aid to denominational schools; second, de Gaulle's refusal, in March 1960, to convene Parliament in special session despite a request by a majority of the deputies (who were duly backed by a constitutional provision); and third, the short-cut procedure employed to revise the Constitution on the structure of the French Community. The then 75-year-old popular Socialist, who had done much to bring de Gaulle to power in the dark days of May 1958, concluded his letter of resignation to President Léon Noel of the council as follows:

> This lack of deference for the national sovereignty and our fundamental charter orients the constitutional regime of 1958 toward a system of personal and arbitrary power in opposition to the essential rules and principles of democracy. . . . [T]hus, not wanting to remain powerless and mute before attacks on the national sovereignty, I regret to inform you that I will no longer sit with the Constitutional Council.[13]

The Constitutional Council has the power to declare unconstitutional all *organic laws* (e.g. appointment and removal of high officials; finance bills) and *standing orders* (rules of procedure) of the houses of Parliament; both these categories *must* be submitted to the council prior to their promulgation. It is also empowered to strike down those *ordinary laws, treaties,* and *protocols*

[13] As reported by Robert C. Doty in *The New York Times* (International Edition). July 2, 1960.

which *may* be voluntarily referred to it by the President of the Republic, the Premier, or the Presidents of the two houses of Parliament. Normally, it is expected to hand down a decision within one month, but if the government categorizes a referred measure as "urgent," it must rule on the matter within eight days. Among the other main functions of the council are: supervision of the "regularity" of the elections of the President of the Republic, the members of Parliament—the council, not Parliament, establishes the credentials of the deputies and senators—and of all popular referenda; it may decide disputes between the government (the Ministry) and Parliament regarding the "delimitation of executive and legislative competence"; and it *must* be consulted by the President of the Republic when he is contemplating the assumption of emergency powers under Article 16 of the Constitution, as de Gaulle did in April 1961, both as to the existence of the emergency and the measures he proposes to take under it.

The council cannot itself initiate action in constitutional cases, but it is autonomous regarding the other delimited areas of its power just outlined. A quorum for a valid decision is seven members, but an absolute majority is required to certify Presidential disability—another of its responsibilities. One opinion only is delivered in behalf of the entire body, but all decisions of the council must be written. Its decisions are final and binding and are not appealable to "any jurisdiction whatsoever." Yet it has no power to enforce its decisions, other than the power to persuade.

Given this distinctly limited range of power and authority, it would be highly misleading to characterize the functions of the Constitutional Council as judicial review. There are three main debilitating weaknesses: First, the inability of private individuals and groups to challenge the constitutionality of a law—only the high public officers indicated above possess that right as an adjunct of their official station. Second, a challenge to the constitutionality of a law even by one of the latter—an admittedly unlikely event in and of itself—is possible solely as to the substance of the law and not as to its procedural application (one of the most frequent causes of court review in the United States, for example). Third, the extremely short period of time permitted to the council for its deliberation on a validly challenged measure makes all but a mockery of the concept of an appeal. On the other hand, its record as of the date of this comment (winter 1961–62) indicates a definite inclination to assert itself in the constitutional evaluation of the writing of parliamentary rules. It remains to be seen whether this attitude represents a harbinger of more assertion in other areas of its presumed competence—but this is unlikely, certainly as long as de Gaulle is President. In the opinion of one of the most astute commentators on the French scene, *le conseil constitutionnel* is best thought of as an adjunct to the President of the Republic in his endeavors to ensure respect for the 1958 Constitution.[14] The French Constitutional Council is no Supreme Court of the United States!

Some Other Special Constitutional Tribunals

Several countries have created judicial bodies that approach or even feature some of the manifestations of the power of judicial review, yet they are usually found *outside* or astride the ordinary court structure. Among the most active of these bodies are the constitutional courts of West Germany, Italy, and Austria, all of which practice at least some measure of judicial review. There are other instances, but a brief treatment of these three will suffice to illustrate the point. In each case, these post-World War II states have empowered their special constitutional courts to guard against infringement of their constitutions by simple legislation and other governmental action—e.g. any action that would violate the constitutional guarantee, present in almost identical form in all three lands, that "all persons shall be equal before the law." There has been fairly general acceptance of their purpose and functions.[15]

The most active and most successful among the three is West Germany's *Federal Constitutional Court* (*Bundesverfassungsgericht*), created by the West German Basic Law of 1949, and seated in Karlsruhe. It consists of 16 judges of at least 40 years of age, all with considerable past judicial, legal, professional, or other high public experience and eligible for judicial office as well as for election to the *Bundestag* (though they cannot be members of it).

[14] William Pickles, *The French Constitution, October 4, 1958* (London: Stevens & Co., Ltd., 1960), p. 33.
[15] See the informative article by Taylor Cole, "The Constitutional Courts: A Comparison," in 53 *American Political Science Review* 963–84 (Dec. 1959).

They are elected half by the lower house (*Bundestag*) and half by the upper house (*Bundesrat*) of Parliament by a two-thirds majority. Six members of the Court are chosen for life, the balance for eight-year renewable terms of office; evidently, continuity seems to be considered in order, for of the 20 jurists on the bench in 1961 all but three had served continuously for a decade. The Federal Constitutional Court possesses the extensive power to decide all disputes involving the meaning and effectiveness of the Basic Law (*Grundgesetz*); it decides the constitutional validity of any federal or state (*Land*) statute, whether or not a case involving it has already come before one of the regular courts; and it adjudicates disputes between organs of government at the national level. Out of these powers arise its two most significant functions: jurisdiction over disputes between the Federal Republic and the *Länder* (states) regarding the latter's administration of the former's statutes, and its guardianship over the fundamental rights and privileges of citizens as determined by the Basic Law, both on substantive and procedural grounds—like judicial review in the United States and unlike its restricted practice in France.

The *Bundesverfassungsgericht* has been a busy court, and to the surprise of many a skeptic it has acted with considerable courage and vigor. For example, it braved the wrath and power of Chancellor Konrad Adenauer when, early in 1961, it declared unconstitutional his action to set up a federally controlled, second television network that was to be financed largely through commercials.[16] The decision was particularly remarkable since it resulted from a suit filed some months earlier by four *Länder* dominated by the Chancellor's opposition, the Social Democrats. Two other significant decisions served to declare both the Communist Party in 1956 and in 1952 the Socialist *Reich* Party, a neo-Nazi organization, unconstitutional as detrimental to the constitutional and democratic order of the state.[17] And as another illustration of the Court's virility and assertiveness, it did not hesitate to strike down an executive decree based on what the Court viewed as unconstitutional delegation of legislative power by the *Bundestag* to the Executive.[18] The reasoning employed here was quite similar to that used by the United States Supreme Court in 1935, in the "Hot

[16] Decision of February 28, 1961.
[18] Decision of September 7–9, 1951.

[17] 2B.V.G.E.1 (1952) and 5B.V.G.E.85 (1956).

Oil" case,[19] in declaring unconstitutional, as an illegal delegation of legislative power to the Chief Executive, an important section of the National Industrial Recovery Act which was soon to fall in its entirety.

Another modern special constitutional tribunal is Italy's *Constitutional Court (Corte Costituzionale)*, established under the Italian Constitution of 1948. This 15-member body is staffed with distinguished personages who have had at least 20 years of experience as practicing lawyers, or who are experienced judges or professors of law—once more we note the high esteem in which the professor is held in Europe. The members of the Court are appointed for staggered 12-year terms, five each selected by the President of the Republic of Italy, by a three-fifths vote of Parliament in joint session, and by the Superior Council of the Judicature. The Court is the final interpreter of the Constitution; it has the power to declare laws unconstitutional; and it decides disputes between organs of government at the national level. Access of individuals to it is considerably less readily available than in West Germany and that fact, plus a general tendency to tread much more gingerly, has rendered the *Corte Costituzionale* less of a pacemaker in matters of constitutional checks than its counterpart north of the Alps. Nevertheless, it has asserted itself, and particularly so in the now familiar realm of illegal delegation of legislative power to the executive branch.

Austria, too, has its Constitutional Court, the *Verfassungsgericht*. This 14-member tribunal was reinstituted in 1945, based upon the Austrian Constitution of 1920, as amended in 1925 and 1929. Its members are appointed for life, unlike a majority of the German and all of the Italian justices, by the President of the Republic of Austria from nominees of the federal government and partly on the recommendation of the lower house (National Council) and the upper house (Federal Council) of Parliament. It has the power to review the constitutionality of legislation and to decide jurisdictional disputes between the courts and administrative authorities. Individuals have less ready access to the *Verfassungsgericht* than they do to its German counterpart but more than that of Italy. This center position of the Austrian tribunal applies also to its range of power and conception of functions. But it, too, has

[19] *Panama Refining Co. v. Ryan,* 293 U. S. 388 (1935).

asserted itself and has not been loathe to examine legislation, even extending to the social realm; i.e. it held unconstitutional a section of the Income Tax Law of 1953 that differentiated between the sexes for tax purposes.[20]

Yet of all the issues that have confronted these three constitutional courts of Europe, by far the greatest number has concerned the interpretation and application of respective constitutional provisions in the vexatious areas of delegation of legislative authority, federalism, and equality before the law. The first of these is really no longer a live issue at the bar of the Supreme Court of the United States, but the second and third, the latter particularly since the end of World War II, are very much in the constitutional weather eye.

A HISTORICAL NOTE

The notion that courts, or some other body, should exercise judicial review as the guardian of a basic law or constitution stems primarily from the early European rejection of the idea of the inviolability of an enacted law. One of the first statements clamoring for a type of judicial review in that connection was made in England—oddly enough in view of the subsequent rejection of the concept. It arose out of the famous *Dr. Bonham's Case* in 1610. The King had granted to members of the London College of Physicians the exclusive right to practice medicine in that city. Dr. Bonham was charged with practicing medicine illegally, for he was not a member of that College. When the case came before Sir Edward Coke, he declared the charter void as a violation of the common law. Holding the latter to be supreme, Sir Edward thus simply stated that the courts could declare acts of Parliament null and void; therefore, he held, common law was to be supreme: "When an act of Parliament is against common right and reason—the common law will controul it and adjudge such act to be void."[21] But if Sir Edward's view was ever seriously adopted at all in England, it was promptly superseded when the Glorious Revolution of 1688 established the supremacy of Parliament.

Nevertheless, the concepts of judicial review subsequently found their way across the Atlantic Ocean to the British Colonies, there

[20] Decision of March 29, 1958. [21] 8 Co. 188a.

to be nurtured by several colonial courts. In eight or nine separate early judgments these courts refused to enforce legislative enactments that they deemed to be against "the laws of nature" (shades of Locke and future events) or "the laws of natural equity"—in a sense against the latent, unwritten Constitution.

JUDICIAL REVIEW AT HOME

Yet if the principle of judicial review was imbedded in the minds of the American Founding Fathers, they assuredly failed to spell it out—although the records of the Constitutional Convention in Philadelphia in 1787 prove conclusively that the matter was very much on the minds of the delegates, who after all distrusted unrestrained popular government, and was widely debated. In any event, the evidence is persuasive that a vast majority of the delegates, anti-Federalists as well as Federalists favored it—although for quite different reasons. Such leading constitutional authorities as Professors Beard, Corwin, and Mason are fully agreed on that interpretation of the wishes of the delegates [22] who, with less than a handful of dissenters, concurred in the pronouncement by Gouverneur Morris of Pennsylvania that the courts should decline to give the weight of law to "a direct violation of the Constitution." Morris admitted that such control over the legislature might have "its inconveniences," but that it was nonetheless necessary because even the "most virtuous citizens will often as members of a legislative body concur in measures which afterwards in their private capacity they will be ashamed of." [23]

So prominent a framer as Alexander Hamilton declared in his famous *Federalist* Paper #78 that judicial review was definitely meant to be incorporated into the prerogatives of the judiciary. And the "Father of the Constitution" himself, James Madison, wrote that the:

[22] cf. Charles Beard, "The Supreme Court—Usurper or Grantee?," 27 *Political Science Quarterly* 1 (1912); Max Farrand, *The Framing of the Constitution of the United States* (New Haven: Yale University Press, 1913); and John Schmidhauser, *The Supreme Court as Final Arbiter in Federal-State Relations, 1789–1957* (Chapel Hill: University of North Carolina Press, 1958), especially Chapters I and XI.

[23] As quoted by Alpheus T. Mason and Richard H. Leach, *In Quest of Freedom* (Prentice Hall, Englewood Cliffs, N. J., 1959), p. 124.

Judiciary is truly the only defensive armor of the Federal Government, or rather for the Constitution and laws of the United States. Strip it of that armor and the door is wide open for nullification, anarchy and convulsion.[24]

Despite this solid evidence it is still a matter of considerable academic dispute whether or not the framers intended the power of judicial review to be given to the courts. But there are sundry additional grounds for the conclusion that such doubts as still remain ought to be laid at rest.

FURTHER HISTORICAL ROOTS

The Constitution itself, while admittedly not providing for the power in so many words, assuredly alludes to it by implication. The supremacy clause of Article VI, relating to the duty of state judges, may well be viewed as implying judicial review by federal tribunals over *state actions*. Moreover, that same provision of the Constitution requires acts of Congress to be made "in pursuance thereof," which would seem to call for someone to act as arbiter. It may be well to quote the entire supremacy clause:

> This Constitution, and the laws of the United States which shall be made in pursuance thereof, and all treaties made or which shall be made under the authority of the United States, shall be the supreme law of the land; and the judges in every state shall be bound thereby, anything in the Constitution or laws of any state to the contrary notwithstanding.[25]

Another relevant provision of the basic document is to be found in Article III which states:

> The judicial power shall extend to all cases, in law and equity, arising under this Constitution, the laws of the United States and treaties made or which shall be made, under the authority. . . .[26]

[24] As quoted by Charles Warren in *The Supreme Court in United States History* (Boston: Little Brown, 1937), V. I, p. 740.
[25] Constitution of the United States, Article VI, Sec. 2.
[26] Ibid. Article III, Sec. 2.

If nothing else, this section clearly indicates the authority of the judiciary over cases in a vast area of constitutional interpretation, thus implying its finite power as to their legality.

Moreover, as has already been briefly indicated, it is noteworthy that in the colonial period the British Privy Council had *established* judicial review over acts passed by the colonial legislatures. Furthermore, prior to 1803 the courts in ten of the states had *exercised* that power by declaring state laws to be in conflict with state constitutions.[27] And Section 25 of the Judiciary Act 1789, the law that created the national judiciary, *conferred* on the federal government specific authority to *reverse* provisions of state laws and state constitutions that conflicted with the "Constitution, treaty, statute, or commission of the United States." [28] Still, since neither the Constitution for any level of government, nor the Judiciary Act of 1789 for the national level, specifically provided for judicial review, it remained for the Supreme Court of the United States to do so. This it did in 1803, in *Marbury v. Madison.*[29]

SPELLING IT OUT: MARBURY V. MADISON

With the possible exception of *McCulloch v. Maryland* [30] and, perhaps, *Gibbons v. Ogden* [31] (but for different reasons), no more important case at constitutional law exists than *Marbury v. Madison*—which has been called "the rib of the Constitution." [32] All three were written by that great national constitutionalist, Mr. Chief Justice John Marshall, who had himself been a delegate to the Ratifying Convention of Virginia. The background of the Marbury decision is so colorful, and the decision itself so important, that no treatment of the judicial process would be complete without at least a brief analysis of that fascinating case, which is one that is not only still frequently cited by courts in the United States, but also, and again recently, in other countries, for example, Italy and India!

Prompt enactment of the Judiciary Act of 1789 enabled the na-

---

[27] E.g. *Holmes v. Walton* (New Jersey, 1780) and *Trevett v. Wheeden* (Rhode Island, 1786).

[28] Act of September 24, 1789, c.20, §25, 1 Statutes at Large 73, 87.

[29] 1 Cranch 137.   [30] 4 Wheaton 316 (1819).   [31] 9 Wheaton 1 (1824).

[32] Glendon A. Schubert, *Constitutional Politics* (New York: Holt, Rinehart, & Winston, 1960), p. 178.

tional judiciary to begin to function at once in the fledgling United States, and questions of the existence of the power of judicial review and any possible challenge of it did not arise immediately. However, the issue was simmering. For example, in *Hayburn's Case* two Supreme Court justices riding circuit in Pennsylvania in 1792 had refused to carry out a congressional statute that they deemed contrary to the Constitution. Backed by the full Court, Associate Justices Blair and Wilson ruled that they could not perform certain duties imposed upon them by the law because they were not "judicial in nature." [33] Together with a district judge they were to pass on disputed pension claims of invalid war veterans, with their determination subject to review by the Secretary of War and by Congress! If nothing else this judicial refusal to carry out a legislative act called attention to the constitutional problem. Moreover the Supreme Court had struck down at least two relatively minor *state* enactments [34]— although the second of these decisions was of considerable importance since it held state laws subject to treaties by ruling that the Anglo-American Peace Treaty overrode a Virginia law on the delicate and potentially explosive issue of debts owed to British subjects by Americans.[35] Furthermore, depending upon the historical source, the Supreme Court even held an insignificant *federal* pension claim law unconstitutional in the case of *U. S. v. Yale Todd,* which was decided in 1794 but not reported until it became a footnote almost 60 years later in *U. S. v. Ferreira.*[36] Nevertheless, this was evidently the first instance of the declaration of unconstitutionality of a federal statute. Finally, two years after *Yale Todd* the Court—with three of its six justices not participating—expressly upheld a congressional statute imposing a duty on carriages as not being a "direct tax" and therefore not unconstitutional.[37] Exactly 99 years later (!) the Supreme Court overruled this decision in the *Income Tax Case,*[38] thus precipitating the Sixteenth Amendment. Yet regardless of these aforegone instances of incipient concern with judicial review, it was not until 1803 and *Marbury v. Madison* that matters actually came to a climax.

[33] 2 Dallas 409 (1792).
[34] *Clerke v. Harwood,* 3 Dallas 342 (1797) and *Ware v. Hylton,* 3 Dallas 199 (1796).   [35] *Ware v. Hylton,* loc. cit.   [36] 13 Howard 40 (1851).
[37] *Hylton v. United States,* 3 Dallas 171 (1796).
[38] *Pollock v. Farmers Loan & Trust Co.,* 158 U. S. 601 (1895).

The Factual Setting. The second President of the United States, John Adams, had been defeated in his bid for re-election in 1800 by his arch political rival, Thomas Jefferson. Laboring desperately to salvage something for his now prostrate Federalist party, Adams determined to pack the federal judiciary with as many judgeships as humanly and statutorily possible. With the aid of a more than obliging lame-duck Federalist Congress, which passed both the Circuit Court Act and the District of Columbia Organic Law Act early in 1801, Adams, before leaving office on March 3, 1801, was thus able to nominate, have approved by the Senate, and commission the following into office: 16 new circuit judges (under the Circuit Court Act); 42 new justices of the peace (under the District of Columbia Act); and one Chief Justice of the United States Supreme Court—his own Secretary of State, the staunch Federalist John Marshall. These nominees have often been called "Adams's Midnight Judges" because the President devoted his waning hours in office to signing their commissions of appointment.

It fell to Marshall, as the outgoing premier of the Adams cabinet, to affix to them the Great Seal of the United States and then to deliver the new judgeship commissions to the various appointees. But Marshall, at once fatigued and exhilarated on Inauguration Eve, failed to deliver 17 of the 42 justice-of-the-peace commissions, although, aided by his brother James, he worked until late into the evening. However, he would begin his first full day as Chief Justice in the morning, a post to which he had been appointed almost two months earlier on the resignation of Oliver Ellsworth in favor of a diplomatic position; but Marshall had continued to serve as Secretary of State without pay. As Chief Justice he would have the somewhat less than delightful duty of administering the oath of the Presidency to his avowed political enemy (and distant cousin) Thomas Jefferson. Hence he left the undelivered commissions to his incoming successor as Secretary of State, James Madison.[39] The stage was thus set for a towering battle of three veritable titans of the early days of Constitution and Nation.

[39] For an unusually penetrating analysis of the more technical aspects of *Marbury v. Madison,* see Mr. Justice Harold Burton's article, "The Cornerstone of Constitutional Law: The Extraordinary Case of *Marbury v. Madison,*" 36 *American Bar Association Journal* 805 (Oct. 1950).

Preliminaries. Furious because of the sustained packing of the judiciary with Federalist appointees, Jefferson and Madison were delighted to find the 17 undelivered justice-of-the-peace commissions on the desk of the Secretary of State upon taking office. The two statesmen at once determined not to deliver them, and neither subsequent pleas nor threats by such disappointed office-seekers as William Marbury were to sway them. Marbury and three others—Denis Ramsey, William Harper, and Robert Townsend Howe—subsequently sought aid of counsel and hired Charles Lee, Attorney-General under John Adams, for that purpose.

Lee turned to the law and to the courts. He found what he believed to be the law in a provision of the Judiciary Act of 1789: Section 13 of that important law extended to the Supreme Court of the United States the power to issue *a writ of mandamus,* a writ commanding a public official to perform his official, ministerial, nondiscretionary duty. Invoking that provision, Lee petitioned the Court for appropriate action—and in 1803 *Marbury v. Madison* thus reached the original docket of the highest court of the land, which could have dismissed the petition for want of jurisdiction, leaving Marbury to seek remedy in the lower courts. But, as will become apparent, this would hardly have suited the purposes of the Chief Justice. For presiding over the Supreme Court was Jefferson's mortal political enemy and Adams's staunch supporter, John Marshall, who had issued an order to Madison—promptly ignored by the latter—to show cause why the requested writ of mandamus should not be issued against him. Surely Marshall's decision would be in favor of Marbury, especially in view of the clear language of Section 13!

Marshall, C. J., for the Court. But both the Federalists and the Jeffersonian Republicans had underestimated the boldness and judiciousness, the craftsmanship and shrewd political acumen, the farsightedness and statesmanship, and, above all, the powerful dedication to the Constitution—*as he saw it and wanted to see it* —of the fourth Chief Justice of the United States Supreme Court. And it was John Marshall who spoke for the unanimous Court, despite the fact that he had a direct interest in the case at bar, which today would almost certainly result in self-disqualification from the case. Whatever one may think of his failure to abstain, it is not difficult to agree with Professor Corwin that "his compact presentation of the case marches to its conclusion with all the precision of a demonstration of Euclid." [40]

Marshall's heart, of course, was on the side of Marbury's cause —which happened to be that of his fellow Federalists—and he did not hesitate to chide Jefferson and Madison from the bench, to castigate them for their "rascality." Moreover, he distinctly concurred in the plaintiff's contention that (1) he had a legal right to the commission, and (2) that the laws of the land afforded him a remedy. But as to the remedy, Marshall—an experienced political savant, here confronted with an utterly political situation—announced unmistakably that a writ of mandamus, issued by the Supreme Court under Section 13 of the Judiciary Act, was definitely *not* such a remedy, for it was *unconstitutional!*

It was unconstitutional, explained Marshall for himself and Associate Justices Paterson, Cushing, Chase, Washington, and Moore, because *by incorporating it into the Judiciary Act of 1789 the Congress had added to the original jurisdiction of the Supreme Court by law*—which the verbiage of Article III, the judicial article of the Constitution, does not sanction. And, continued Marshall in an unprecedented display of a combination of judicial self-abnegation and judicial assumption of power—for there is no doubt that judicial review, "the ultimate conservative response to the 'evils of democracy,' " [41] was a goal of the Federalists—in Section 13 Congress had given to the Court a power which it could not legally receive. That section of the act had actually figured in earlier Supreme Court decisions, yet no one had chosen to raise the present constitutional issue. *"An act repugnant to the Constitution is void,"* explained Marshall, thus echoing Hamilton's *Federalist* #78, and, in so stating the matter, he enunciated clearly the doctrine of judicial review.[42] He elaborated:

It is emphatically the province and duty of the judicial department to say what the law is. Those who apply the rule to

---

[40] A lecture at Princeton University, September 1950.

[41] Wallace Mendelson, *Capitalism, Democracy, and the Supreme Court* (New York: Appleton-Century-Crofts, 1960), p. 20.

[42] For a different view, though wholly "pro" judicial review, see Charles L. Black, Jr., *The People and the Court: Judicial Review in a Democracy* (New York: The Macmillan Co., 1960), pp. 25ff. Black contends that judicial review had already been firmly established by then, and he calls a "myth" the usual belief that it was Marshall who gave it authoritative expression.

particular cases, must of necessity expound and interpret that rule. . . . A law repugnant to the Constitution is void; . . . courts as well as other departments are bound by that instrument.[43]

Significance and Summary. In brief, John Marshall—in what his most famous biographer, Senator Albert J. Beveridge of Indiana, perhaps somewhat extravagantly described as "a coup as bold in design and as daring as that by which the Constitution had been framed"[44]—clearly, cogently, and quite emphatically enunciated and interpreted three principles of the utmost significance to the young nation: (1) that the courts have the power of judicial review; (2) that the Constitution of the United States is the supreme law of the land; (3) that the *original* jurisdiction of the Supreme Court cannot be changed by simple law of Congress, since that particular jurisdiction is *specifically* limited by the language of the Constitution—although the *appellate* jurisdiction can be changed by simple legislation plainly because the letter of the Constitution so permits. This, of course, has been done since, with the most famous illustration being the intriguing post-Civil War case of *ex parte McCardle.*[45] Here the Supreme Court had under consideration an already argued appeal in a *habeas corpus* proceeding, in which the constitutionality of one of the Reconstruction Acts was at issue. Fearful that the Court might declare the act at issue unconstitutional, Congress, over President Andrew Johnson's courageous but fruitless veto, amended the statute defining the appellate jurisdiction of the Supreme Court by withdrawing from that jurisdiction appeals in certain classes of *habeas corpus* proceedings, including the present one. Incidentally, the majority of the Court, which had simply postponed action pending the legislative and executive moves, was far from displeased about the congressional victory—although Associate Justices Field and Grier issued a bitter public dissent against what they viewed as an evasion of constitutional responsibility and deliberate procrastination. But the Court was unanimous in upholding the action of Congress— and the Reconstruction Acts were never tested by it.

---

[43] *Marbury v. Madison,* 1 Cranch 137 (1803).
[44] *The Life of John Marshall* (Boston: Houghton Mifflin Co., 1919), vols. I and III, pp. 323, 142, respectively.   [45] 7 Wallace 506 (1869).

The importance of Marshall's decision in *Marbury v. Madison* to American constitutional development can hardly be overestimated. There is no question that judicial review is crucial to the governmental process in the United States under its federal character and its separation of powers principle. Yet it cannot be gainsaid that Marshall strained the judicial process in making *Marbury v. Madison* his vehicle for the announcement of the doctrine of the judicial veto. We have already noted that he should probably have disqualified himself from sitting in the case because of his direct and personal involvement with both its fundamental issue and its personnel—after all, the case in effect arose out of his own negligence or apathy—and that, in any event, he did not really have to accept the case for review. He could readily have dismissed it for want of jurisdiction and directed the petitioner to apply for remedies in a lower federal court. Moreover, based on available precedent, he could easily have interpreted Section 13 and its empowering provision—indeed, he probably should have—in such a manner as to raise no substantial questions regarding statutory additions to the original jurisdiction of the Court. For a good case could be made for the contention, based on the intent of its framers in Congress, headed by the then soon-to-be-Chief Justice of the Supreme Court, Oliver Ellsworth, that Section 13 signified nothing more than that the Court had power to grant writs of mandamus in all instances when such a remedy would be appropriate in the disposition of cases duly and properly brought before it either on its original or its appellate docket. By no means was Section 13 necessarily intended to enlarge the original jurisdiction of the Court!

But none of these suggested alternate courses of action would have suited Marshall's purposes—one of which also was to avoid the potential embarrassment that would have resulted from the almost certain defiance of complying with it by President Jefferson. Having said and recognized that, however, we should acknowledge the genius of that powerful figure in American history and of the great service he performed in expounding the doctrine of judicial review when he did. That debate on the justification and wisdom of the doctrine ensued almost at once, and that it has never really ceased, merely serves to add stature to its progenitor.

VIII

JUDICIAL REVIEW:

II CONTROVERSY AND LIMITATIONS?

JUDICIAL REVIEW IN A DEMOCRATIC STATE:
SAINT OR SINNER?

That no other federal law, or section thereof, was declared unconstitutional by the Supreme Court between *Marbury v. Madison* [1] in 1803 and the *Dred Scott Case*,[2] which was decided fully fifty-four years later, did not lessen the debate on the doctrine of judicial review. That it has remained fresh, indeed, and has lost none of its controversial characteristics, is testified to by the widespread public, often emotion-charged, debate surrounding the unanimous decision for the Court by Mr. Chief Justice Warren in the 1954 *Segregation Cases* [3]—in a sense the grandchildren of the Taney Court's decision in *Dred Scott*. The charge against the Warren Court: in holding compulsory segregation on account of race in the public schools to be a violation of the "equal protection of the laws" clause of the Fourteenth Amendment to the United States Constitution, the Court had not *judged,* not *interpreted,* not *reviewed,* but *legislated*. The indictment of judicial legislation is directly related, of course, to the power and doctrine of judicial review—once characterized as "the people's institutionalized means of self-control." [4]

---

[1] 1 Cranch 137.   [2] *Dred Scott v. Sanford,* 19 Howard 393 (1857).
[3] *Brown v. Board of Education,* 347 U. S. 483 (1954) and *Bolling v. Sharpe,* 347 U. S. 497 (1954).
[4] Charles L. Black, Jr., *The People and the Court: Judicial Review in a Democracy* (New York: The Macmillan Co., 1960), p. 20.

Invoking Authority

Unfortunately, all too few professional observers of the judicial process, and quite naturally even fewer laymen—however informed these may be—are resolutely consistent in their attitude toward either judicial review or the institution that exercises the power. More often than not it has been a case of "it all depends whose ox is being gored," to employ the pungent phrase of Al Smith. Yet it is entirely feasible to determine both articulate and reasonable "con" and "pro" positions regarding the doctrine, without resorting to the more passionate partisans of the controversy. Although a great deal of literature on the subject is available, we may well permit two of America's most honored and most literary governmental personages to speak for the two sides. Had they not lived and functioned considerably more than a century apart, it is fair to say that they would have respected and admired one another and would have made a worthy set of opponents in any public debate on the issue—Thomas Jefferson against and Benjamin Cardozo for! With due allowance for certain deviations, their points of view, even their verbiage, are today very much representative of the two divergent attitudes on the question.

Con: Although evidence contained in at least two letters written from Paris to James Madison is persuasive that Thomas Jefferson had favored some type or degree of direct judicial control at the time of the framing of the Constitution in Philadelphia and even almost two years later,[5] the great Virginian never accepted the notion of judicial review as it was subsequently expounded by his political opponent John Marshall. Jefferson's opposition was based upon two major concepts: first, that the doctrine of judicial review violates that of the constitutionally mandated theory of the separation of powers; and second, that it represents a patent denial of the veritable popular will, the majority will, as expressed by the sovereign people through their duly elected representatives "in Congress assembled" (and in any other properly constituted legislative body). That the second assertion did not, however, blind him to the potential excesses of these representatives, is indicated clearly in one of his letters to Madison, to whom he voiced the

[5] Dec. 20, 1787, and March 15, 1789.

fear that ". . . the tyranny of the legislatures is the most formidable dread at present and will be for many years." [6]

Nonetheless, Jefferson vehemently rejected the contention that the Founding Fathers had intended to give to one of the three branches the right to prescribe rules for the government of the others, "and to that one, too, which is unelected by and independent of the nation." He insisted that each of the three branches, being independent, "has an equal right to decide for itself the meaning of the Constitution in the cases submitted to its action; where it is to act ultimately without appeal." [7] To Jefferson, the doctrine of judicial review was both elitist and *anti*democratic.

This position has been echoed frequently since, but by none better than by a contemporary of Jefferson, Mr. Justice John B. Gibson of the Supreme Court of Pennsylvania. From that bench in 1825, in his now famous dissenting opinion in *Eakin v. Raub,*[8] in which his colleagues upheld the power of Pennsylvania's state courts to declare state statutes unconstitutional, Gibson challenged the Marshallian argument in *Marbury v. Madison* lucidly and forcefully along the lines of the Jeffersonian response. One of his key points was the classic concept of popular democracy—that it is a "postulate in the theory of our government . . . that the people are wise, virtuous, and competent to manage their own affairs." [9] Yet Gibson had apparently modified his viewpoint twenty years later. When an attorney, pleading his case before the Pennsylvania Supreme Court, cited the Gibson dissent in *Eakin v. Raub,* that Justice replied from the bench that he had changed his opinion for two reasons: one, that the Pennsylvania Constitutional Convention of 1838, by remaining silent on judicial review, had "sanctioned the pretensions of the courts to deal freely with the acts of the legislature"; and two, "from experience of the necessity of the case." [10] This does not necessarily connote a change of mind, but it assuredly does indicate at least that Mr. Justice Gibson, true to

---

[6] Letter of March 15, 1789.

[7] From his letter to Judge Spencer Roane of the Virginia Supreme Court, September 6, 1819.

[8] 12 S. & R. (Pa. S. Ct.) 330.   [9] Ibid. at 355.

[10] Cf. *Norris v. Clymer,* 2 Pa. St. 277, at 281 (1845), as reported by Robert E. Cushman and Robert F. Cushman, *Cases in Constitutional Law* (New York: Appleton-Century-Crofts, 1958), pp. 22–3.

his philosophy of the representative legislative function, had accepted the latter's "surrender" to the doctrine.

Pro: Although he greatly admired Jefferson both as a man and as a political philosopher, Benjamin N. Cardozo, who served for many years on the New York State Court of Appeals as well as an Associate Justice of the United States Supreme Court for the regrettably brief period from 1932 to 1938, disagreed strongly with Jefferson's approach to and rejection of judicial review. Cardozo anchored his belief in that doctrine upon the firm conviction that while it must be employed cautiously and sparingly, it serves nonetheless as a necessary and proper check on possible excesses by both the federal and state legislatures. But it would be utterly wrong to label him a "judicial activist." More than a decade prior to his universally hailed appointment to the Supreme Court, where he mounted the seat vacated by Mr. Justice Oliver Wendell Holmes, Jr., Mr. Justice Cardozo advanced his key contention that it is the *restraining influence of its presence* rather than the frequency of its application that renders judicial review so vital to the governmental process in the United States of America. His characteristically beautiful style and language must be quoted directly:

> By conscious or subconscious influence, the presence of this restraining power aloof in the background, but none the less always in reserve, *tends to stabilize and rationalize the legislative judgment,* to infuse it with the glow of principle, to hold the standard aloft and visible for those who must run the race and keep the faith. . . . The restraining power of the judiciary does not manifest its chief worth in the few cases in which the legislature has gone beyond the lines that mark the limits of discretion. Rather shall we find *its chief worth in making vocal and audible the ideals that might otherwise be silenced, in giving them continuity of life and expression, in guiding and directing choice within the limits where choice ranges.* This function should preserve to the courts the power that now belongs to them; if only the power is exercised with insight into social values, and with suppleness of adaption to changing social needs.[11]

[11] *The Nature of the Judicial Process* (New Haven: Yale University Press, 1921), pp. 93—4. Italics added.

The man Cardozo succeeded, who was familiar with the above passage, fully concurred in its sentiment and credo, and he practiced it throughout his three decades on the highest bench of the land. However, although Holmes was willing to grant that the United States would not "come to an end if we lost our power to declare an Act of Congress void," he firmly insisted that "the Union would be imperiled if we could not make that declaration as to the laws of the several states." [12] United States Circuit Court Judge Learned Hand, the great contemporary of Holmes and Cardozo, frequently echoed this Holmesian creed. But he went considerably further than Holmes when, writing several years after his retirement from the bench, he endeavored to set up a test which would provide another modification of the doctrine: While agreeing that the Supreme Court must have the power and authority to review *grants* of power to and by Congress, it should not possess these sanctions regarding "a review of how the power has been *exercised*." [13] It is difficult to see how such an amendment of the doctrine of judicial review would not wound it seriously, if not, in effect, fatally.

The Jefferson and Cardozo viewpoints—and their attempted modifications—have ardent and articulate adherents. Yet there is no longer any doubt that judicial review is a permanent fixture in the American structure and operation of government, notwithstanding the repeated, and presumably continued, frontal and guerilla attacks from both public and private sources.[14]

DRAWING THE LINE— OR ATTEMPTING TO DO SO

Directly related to the controversy over the doctrine of judicial review, and inevitably associated with it intimately, is the frequently voiced charge that the Supreme Court of the United States —and to a somewhat lesser degree the lower rungs of the judi-

[12] Oliver Wendell Holmes, Jr., "Law and the Court," in *Collected Legal Papers* (New York: Harcourt, Brace, 1920), p. 295.

[13] Learned Hand, *The Bill of Rights* (Cambridge: Harvard University Press, 1958), p. 66, pp. 93–4. (Italics supplied.)

[14] For summary analysis of attempted legislative checks on the power, see Sheldon D. Elliott, "Court-Curbing Proposals in Congress," 33 *Notre Dame Lawyer* 597–605 (August, 1958).

ciary—is guilty of *judicial legislating;* in other words, that many of its decisions are tantamount to legislating rather than judging. More often than not, this indictment of the judiciary admits, and indeed grants, that the Court must have the power to *interpret* legislation and, if "absolutely necessary," hold unconstitutional a law that is *clearly* contrary to the Constitution—although no yardstick is provided on the connotation of the modifier "clearly." But this school of thought insists that a line must be drawn between the exercise of judicial *judgment* and the imposition of judicial *will.* The latter is accordingly equated with legislating, presumably reserved to Congress and the legislatures of the 50 states. Like all fine lines, the one between "interpreting" or "judging" and "legislating" is highly tenuous. How is it to be drawn? By whom? Where? Under what circumstances? Clearly there is no simple or single response to these questions so crucial to line-drawing in general, and the line at issue in particular.

JUDICIAL LEGISLATING

The polar extremes in the controversy over the absence or presence of the concept of judicial legislating become readily apparent by the following two quotes, taken from active and honorable participants on both sides of the aisle—institutionally as well as philosophically. Arising on the floor of the United States Senate, of which he constituted one of the finest and most purposeful members for many years, George W. Norris of Nebraska, the "gentle knight of progressive ideals," shouted:

> We have a legislative body, called the House of Representatives, of over 400 men. We have another legislative body, called the Senate, of less than 100 men. We have, in reality, another legislative body, called the Supreme Court, of nine men; and they are more powerful than all the others put together.[15]

The diametrically opposite point of view is represented in a passage from an address to the New York State Bar Association by Mr. Justice David Brewer of the United States Supreme Court:

[15] *Congressional Record,* 71 Cong. 2nd Sess., Vol. 72, Part 4, p. 3566 (Feb. 13, 1930).

They [courts and judges] make no law, they establish no policy, they never enter into the domain of popular action. They do not govern. Their functions in relation to the state are limited to seeing that popular action does not trespass upon right and justice as it exists in written constitutions and natural law.[16]

Both expressions are equally extreme in their thesis as they represent gross oversimplifications, notwithstanding the sincerity and conviction of the two men involved.

Most justices of the highest tribunal do not claim to have a pat answer to the vexatious question presented by the controversy over *the line*. But they have often come to grips with the crux of the matter in recognizing the human element that is so inevitably involved in the judicial process. In the realistic words of Mr. Justice John H. Clarke:

I have never known any judges, no difference how austere of manner, who discharged their judicial duties in an atmosphere of pure, unadulterated reason. Alas! we are all "the common growth of Mother Earth,"—even those of us who wear the long robe.[17]

The blunt-spoken Mr. Justice McReynolds insisted that a judge should not be "an amorphous dummy, unspotted by human emotions." "Judges are men, not disembodied spirits," once remarked Mr. Justice Frankfurter; "as men they respond to human situations. They do not reside in a vacuum." "Our judges are not monks or scientists," wrote Mr. Chief Justice Warren in 1955, "but participants in the living stream of our national life, steering the law between the dangers of rigidity on the one hand and formlessness on the other." [18]

In any event, the justices are agreed that they judge the cases and controversies that reach the Court in accordance with the Constitution and the laws of the land. There is no doubt that the nine justices—judges on all levels of the judicial process—necessarily "legislate" in interpreting constitutional phraseology. The question is how much and how far they are justified in such judicial

[16] Address to the New York State Bar Association, *Proceedings* (1893).
[17] Hoyt L. Warner, *The Life of Mr. Justice Clarke* (Cleveland: Western Reserve University Press, 1959), p. 69.
[18] "The Law and the Future," 52 *Fortune* 106 (November 1955).

legislating. The often-quoted jurist, however apocryphal the story may be, who responded to the question of whether judges make law replied, "Of course we do; made some myself," may sound somewhat extreme—but he is undoubtedly close to the truth of the situation. One of the wisest among the men ever to sit on the bench of the Supreme Court, the revered Mr. Justice Holmes, who has been so well described as the official judicial philosopher for the modern age,[19] also recognized "without hesitation" that judges *do and must* legislate"; but he added that they "can do so only interstitially; they are confined from molar to molecular motions." [20]

Mr. Chief Justice Marshall, however, who was fully aware of the problem at issue, nevertheless insisted on commenting in one case that "judicial power, as contradistinguished from the power of the law, has no existence. Courts are the mere instruments of the law, and can will nothing." [21] Yet this man, who is generally recognized as the most competent and successful of all the Chief Justices to date and ranked among the two or three most powerful and influential jurists ever to sit on the highest bench, was hardly one to be loath to interpret broadly the Constitution and legislation passed under its authority—and in accordance with what Mr. Justice Holmes later referred to as "the felt necessities of the time." After all, had not that same Marshall written, in the great *McCulloch v. Maryland* decision, that our laws were made under a Constitution that was "intended to endure for ages to come and, consequently, to be adapted to the various crises of human affairs"? [22] Probably not a single justice did more of this "adapting," and more incisively, than did Mr. Chief Justice Marshall, who often reminded his countrymen that "we must never forget that it is a *Constitution* we are expounding!" Did he *interpret* or did he *legislate?* Undoubtedly both; but who is to say, who to judge with finality?

More on the Line and on the Goring of Oxen. Marshall's long-term successor, Mr. Chief Justice Roger B. Taney, also troubled

[19] Fred. V. Cahill, Jr., *Judicial Legislation* (New York: The Ronald Press, 1952), p. 32.
[20] *Southern Pacific Co. v. Jensen,* 244 U. S. 205 (1916), at 221. (Italics supplied.)
[21] *Osborn v. United States Bank,* 9 Wheaton 738 (1924).
[22] 4 Wheaton 316 (1819).

by the problem, stared into the heart of the problem when, in rendering the majority opinion in the *Dred Scott* case, he held:

> The Constitution speaks not only in the same words, but with the same meaning and intent with which it spoke when it came from the hands of its framers, and was voted on and adopted by the people of the United States. Any other rule of construction would abrogate the judicial character of this Court and make it the mere reflex of the popular opinion or passion of the day.[23]

But the *Dred Scott* decision has been denounced more often as sheer "legislation" than any other decision of the Court, with the possible exception of the 1954 *Segregation Cases*.[24] When he was informed of the decision in *Dred Scott,* Senator Hale of New Hampshire introduced a resolution to *abolish* the Supreme Court. Yet again depending upon the point of view, those people who hailed the *Dred Scott* judgment as "statesmanlike interpretation" would have violently denounced the *Segregation Cases* as "blatant legislation," whereas the champions of the latter decisions would have roundly denounced the former on reverse grounds! Indeed some of the torrent of linguistic abuse poured upon the Court by *Segregation Cases* critics is almost identical in verbiage to that employed by the enemies of their Southern ancestors, the Radical Republicans of the North, in attacking *Dred Scott!* Could it be that the popular judgment does, indeed, depend upon whose ox is being gored?

Mr. Justice Owen J. Roberts, always searching for, if not inevitably contributing to, a modicum of consistency on the bench, attempted to draw the line once and for all in 1936—"the slot machine theory," commented Roscoe Pound acidly—when he spoke for a majority of six in the significant case of *United States v. Butler,* in which the Court struck down the Agricultural Adjustment Act of 1933:

> When an act of Congress is appropriately challenged in the Courts as not conforming to the constitutional mandate the

[23] *Dred Scott v. Sanford,* 19 Howard 393 (1857).
[24] *Brown v. Board of Education,* 347 U. S. 483 (1954) and *Bolling v. Sharpe,* 347 U. S. 497 (1954).

judicial branch of the Government has only one duty—*to lay the article of the Constitution which is invoked beside the statute which is challenged and to decide whether the latter squares with the former.*[25]

"Bravo," applauded the *opponents* of the New Deal, "great judicial statesmanship, proper and precise interpretation of the Constitution!" "An unwarranted, outrageous assumption of legislative authority," countered the *proponents* of the New Deal, "arrogant disregard of constitutional limitations of judicial power." And President Roosevelt, scarcely one year after *Butler,* moved—unsuccessfully—to pack the Court by statutory provision, setting off one of the most interesting, most heated, and most sustained controversies in the entire history of Court and Nation.[26]

It was in the *Butler* case that the issue was perhaps most nearly faced by Mr. Justice Harlan Fiske Stone, not too many years hence to be the Chief Justice, when he dissented from the opinion of the majority and admonished the members on that side of the decision that

> . . . while unconstitutional exercise of power by the executive and legislative branches is subject to judicial restraint, *the only check on our own exercise of power is our own sense of self-restraint* . . . Courts are not the only agency of government that must be assumed to have capacity to govern. . . . For the removal of unwise laws from the statute books appeal lies not to the courts, but to the ballot and to the processes of democratic government.[27]

This would seem to be as close to the facts of judicial life as is attainable. In a sense, and although he would very likely have disapproved of the comparison, the Stone comment was almost an echo of a famous statement made twenty years earlier by Charles Evans Hughes while he was the Republican presidential nominee in 1916. He had just then become an ex-Associate Justice of the United States Supreme Court; was an ex-Governor of New York; a future Secretary of State in the Administrations of Presidents

[25] 297 U. S. 1 (1936), at 79. (Italics supplied.)
[26] For a timely, engagingly written account, see Joseph Alsop and Turner Catledge, *The 168 Days* (New York: Doubleday, Doran, 1938).
[27] *United States v. Butler,* 297 U. S. 1 (1936). (Italics supplied.)

Harding and Coolidge; and ultimately would ascend the Court for a second time as Chief Justice. While stumping during the campaign, which almost won him election, he stated: *"We are under the Constitution, but the Constitution is what the judges say it is."* That assertion represents both too drastic and too oversimplified an analysis of the complex position of the judiciary and the Court, and it is subject to considerable substantive modification. Surely, in the final analysis, the Constitution is or becomes what the people of the nation want it to be or to become, and it must be considered, as Holmes said, "in the light of our whole experience and not merely in that of what was said a hundred years ago." Moreover, while the Constitution, for the sake of argument, may well be what the judges say it is, that does by no means ascertain appropriate compliance, as has been repeatedly demonstrated. With these essential qualifications in mind, however, the Hughes campaign statement, coupled with the Stone dissent in the *Butler* case, could serve by and large as the definitive view of the Court's attitude. It has frequently been echoed by other articulate members of the highest bench, such as Mr. Justice Frankfurter who, in dissenting in the controversial expatriation case of *Trop v. Dulles,* lectured that:

> All power is, in Madison's phrase, "of an encroaching nature." . . . Judicial power is not immune against this human weakness. It must also be on guard against encroaching beyond its proper bounds, and not the less so since *the only restraint upon it is self-restraint. . . .*[28]

Vast differences about this aspect of the vexatious line exist now and have always existed among the justices themselves, but most, in fact probably all, would in all candor subscribe to the essence of the suggested Stone-Hughes formula, however at variance their interpretation and application of it may be. One thing is clear above all: in the realistic words of Mr. Justice Cardozo, not only one of the most proficient and most beloved justices ever to sit on the Supreme Court but also one of its finest and most haunting stylists, *"The great tides and currents which engulf the rest of men, do not turn aside in their course, and pass the judges*

[28] 356 U. S. 86 (1958). (Italics supplied.)

idly by." [29] In any event, as Mr. Justice Frankfurter again put the matter cogently in the recent past, the Court cannot, in the long run, escape judging; it must adjudicate; it must decide. Not one to judge lightly or hastily—Professor Wallace Mendelson has aptly called him a "humilitarian" among jurists with respect to the legal process—[30] Frankfurter nevertheless thus clearly met the problem in his concurring opinion in a well-known case:

> To be sure, this [opinion] is a conclusion based on a judicial judgment in balancing two contending principles—the right of a citizen to political privacy, as protected by the Fourteenth Amendment, and the right of the State to self-protection. And striking the balance implies the exercise of judgment. This is the inescapable judicial task in giving substantive content, legally enforced, to the Due Process Clause, and it is a task ultimately committed to this Court. It must not be an exercise of whim or will. *It must be an overriding judgment founded on something much deeper and more justifiable than personal preference. As far as it lies within human limitations, it must be impersonal judgment. It must rest on fundamental presuppositions rooted in history to which widespread acceptance may fairly be attributed.* Such a judgment must be arrived at in a spirit of humility when it counters the judgment of the State's highest court. *But, in the end, judgment cannot be escaped— the judgment of this Court.* [31]

That this awesome and even agonizing duty of finding and drawing the line between judicial will and judicial judgment in rendering a necessary decision is not confined to the highest level of the federal judiciary, may be illustrated by a decision of the Supreme Court of Michigan. In a consortium case replete with human factors, the closely divided Court not only reversed a lower court decision but negated precedent of long standing. Speaking for a majority of four, Mr. Justice Talbot Smith recognized that the decision represented a drastic departure from the past and would

---

[29] *The Nature of the Judicial Process,* op. cit. p. 168. (Italics supplied.)

[30] "Mr. Justice Frankfurter—Law and Choice," 10 *Vanderbilt Law Review* 333 (February 1957).

[31] *Sweezy v. New Hampshire, by Wyman, Attorney-General,* 354 U. S. 234 (1957). (Italics supplied.)

surely be viewed as judicial legislating. Yet braving the expected storm, he admitted that the decision to permit the wife of a man seriously injured in an automobile accident to sue for loss of consortium—i.e. marital comfort, affection, and companionship—marked a stride away from the "outworn legal views" derived from old English and Roman law that a wife is merely a "vassal, chattel, and household drudge." He concluded:

> Were we to rule upon precedent alone, we would have no trouble with this case. We would simply tell this woman to be gone, and take her shattered husband with her. . . . Legally today, the wife stands on a par with her husband. . . . *The obstacles to the wife's [court] action were judge-invented and they are herewith judge-destroyed.*[32]

The anticipated critical storm of charges of crass judicial legislating broke over the heads of author and Court at once. Yet perhaps Mr. Justice Smith had simply been unusually frank in writing his opinion as he did—rather than disguising it in judicial semantics. In fine, depending, of course, upon the facts and posture of each individual case, both verbiage and line are very much matters of degree.

JUDGES LIMITED:
THE TAUGHT TRADITION OF THE LAW

Moreover, it must be clearly understood that judges are not free agents in rendering their decisions regardless of the impression given by some—such as the one just discussed. As Mr. Justice Frankfurter once wrote tellingly, "We do not sit like a kadi under a tree, dispensing justice according to considerations of individual expediency." [33] A deplorable tendency exists in the mind of the public to oversimplify the process of judicial decision-making, the area of government obviously least understood by the man on the street, however interested he may be. Although it may perhaps overstate the case somewhat, there is much merit in the contention of the very same Mr. Justice Talbot Smith just cited above that "we are rigidly bound within walls that are unseen" (by the

[32] *Montgomery v. Stephan,* 359 Mich. 33 (1960).
[33] *Terminiello v. Chicago,* 347 U. S. 1 (1949).

layman).[34] These walls are built of the heritage of the law, the spirit of the Anglo-Saxon law, the impact of the cases as they come down through the years—in brief, *the taught tradition of the law.*

Among the vital aspects of this taught tradition are: an abiding sense of judicial integrity; a close and necessary regard for the rules of procedure; considerations of equal treatment before the law; the deference shown to legislative enactments; judicial recognition of the realities of the cultural, ideological, and institutional setting which the judges share with their fellow-citizens, not excluding the political realities; and there is *stare decisis,* the adherence to precedent.

STARE DECISIS

The desirability and, indeed, the need for certainty in planning our affairs, both in their internal (professional) and external aspects, render reliance on precedent an attractive and useful doctrine. Yet be it noted at once that *stare decisis*—"let the decision stand"—is a principle of policy and not a mechanical formula of adherence to the latest decision, "however recent and questionable, when such adherence involves collision with a prior doctrine more embracing in its scope, intrinsically sounder, and verified by experience." [35] The doctrine of *stare decisis* requires a careful weighing in each doubtful case "of the advantages of adherence to precedent and the necessity for judicially planned social and economic progress." [36] The law, as Dean Pound has stated, must be stable and yet it cannot stand still. Or, as Viscount Kilmuir, the Lord High Chancellor of Britain, told a distinguished audience of legal scholars in 1960: "Critics are apt to allege that we treat existing law with such reverence that every antique is replaced unaltered. I believe in an occasional spring cleaning." [37]

Reliance on precedent presents difficult problems to the judge,

---

[34] Statement to author, August 15, 1958.

[35] Mr. Justice Frankfurter, for the Court, in *Helvering v. Hallock,* 309 U. S. 106 (1940), at 110.

[36] Robert A. Sprecher, "The Development of the Doctrine of Stare Decisis and the Extent to Which It Should Be Applied," 31 *American Bar Association Journal* 501–9 (1945).

[37] Speech on the occasion of the dedication ceremony of the University of Chicago Law Center, April 30, 1960.

especially since the question to be resolved comes, normally speaking, to a *choice* of precedents. "Sometimes," commented Mr. Justice Jackson wistfully in his last book, "one is tempted to quote his former self, not only to pay his respects to the author, but to demonstrate the consistency of his views, if not their correctness." [38] Precedents abound and not all precedents are of equal rank; a good many judges generally seem to accord considerably more sanctity to very old and hallowed "precedents," such as most of Mr. Chief Justice John Marshall's decisions, than to those of relatively recent vintage. Progress, in any event, does not stand still, and a precedent may have to be overruled or reversed in time. Indeed, in at least ninety decisions between 1810 and 1957 the Supreme Court of the United States *overruled* its own previous determinations.[39] Many additional cases are *distinguished* from precedent, which is somehow viewed as a less disrespectful device. "From age to age," commented Mr. Justice Douglas in an able treatment of the issue,

> the problem of constitutional adjudication is the same. It is to keep the power of government unrestrained by the social or economic theories that one set of judges may entertain. *It is to keep one age unfettered by the fears or limited vision of another.*[40]

Precedents, in Mr. Justice Talbot Smith's blunt words, being "judge-invented," may thus be "judge-destroyed." The judge must speak and through him society speaks. His function, as a leading student of constitutional law put it so lucidly, is "necessarily something more than to be a grammarian . . . [but] it is decidedly less than to be a zealot." [41] Lord Coke to the contrary, few, if any, judges, would today create a maxim out of whole cloth and then recite, "as the old maxim saith. . . ."

To sum up, the judge is assuredly not a free agent. On the

[38] Robert H. Jackson, *The Supreme Court in the American System of Government* (Cambridge: Harvard University Press, 1955), p. 11.

[39] For a list of these 90 instances and a discussion of the entire "overruling" problem, see A. P. Blaustein and A. H. Field, "Overruling Opinions in the Supreme Court," 57 *Michigan Law Review* 2 (1957).

[40] William O. Douglas, *Stare Decisis* (New York: The Association of the Bar of the City of New York, 1949), p. 31.

[41] Paul A. Freund, *The Christian Science Monitor*, March 26, 1956.

other hand no matter what it may be termed or how it may be styled, of necessity the judge "makes" the law—to some degree, at least. The delicate question will ever be how to aid its development without violating the confines of the constitutional structure. Let Mr. Justice Cardozo state the case:

> . . . [but] no doubt the limits for the judges are narrower. He legislates only between gaps. He fills the open spaces of the law. How far he may go without travelling beyond the walls of the interstices cannot be staked out for him upon a chart. He must learn it for himself as he gains the sense of fitness and proportion that comes with years of the practice of an art . . . None the less, within the confines of those open spaces and those of precedent and traditions, choice moves with a freedom which stamps its action as creative. The law which is the resulting product is not found, but made. The process, being legislative, demands the legislator's wisdom.[42]

Surely, to echo a comment once made by Max Lerner, ". . . judicial decisions are not babies brought by constitutional storks." They are the carefully considered, more or less practical, judgments of the human beings who wield judicial authority.

OTHER LIMITATIONS
ON JUDICIAL POWER AND EFFECTIVENESS

Yet there remain several other qualifying considerations—checks may be a better term—upon judicial authority, even at the highest level of the federal courts. First, the Supreme Court's rulings may be effectively reversed by other participants in the process of government; second, they are almost inevitably responsive to overall policy formulations—sooner or later; third, for enforcement they must look to the executive branch of the government; and fourth, as we have seen in Chapter V, compliance with them is not necessarily automatic.

REVERSING THE COURT

In a variety of ways, and not without some toil and trouble, the Supreme Court of the United States may be reversed by direct or

[42] *The Nature of the Judicial Process,* op. cit. pp. 113–15.

indirect action of other institutions in the political process. Although its decisions unquestionably constitute the supreme law of the land—as they must if government under law is to have any meaning in American society—and are thus final and binding, even that high body "has the last say only for a time." This truth is readily documented by briefly examining the fate of the aforementioned 80-odd cases in which the Court, through its 1960–61 term —and unanimously in almost one-third of these instances—had struck down as unconstitutional 89 provisions of federal laws.

No fewer than 28 times Congress passed legislation that had the effect of reversing the Court either totally or in substantial measure—as it did in passing the Federal Employers' Liability Act of April 22, 1908, designed to replace that of 1906 which the Court had declared unconstitutional 5:4 as an illegal invasion of intrastate commerce in the *First Employers' Liability Cases* [43] earlier in 1908. Since Congress seemed to have corrected the alleged constitutional deficiency of the earlier statute, the Court found no difficulty in upholding it unanimously when the test came in the *Second Employers' Liability Cases* [44] in 1912. In other instances the circumstances or situation of the controversy had either changed or become moot, thus rendering insignificant or totally unimportant the erstwhile decision handed down by the Court— as, for example, the withdrawal of improperly delegated legislative power by action of the legislature or the revocation or amendment of a challenged administrative or executive order, both actions coming prior to the full effect of the Court's decision.[45] In some instances it simply *distinguished* cases from often very similar earlier decisions—as it did when it upheld the second New Deal Agricultural Act of 1938 in *Mulford v. Smith* [46] in 1939, although having struck down the first A.A.A. in *U. S. v. Butler* [47] three years earlier. True, the statutes were not exactly alike, and the personnel of the Court had changed, but the essential features and purposes of the statutes were unchanged. In other cases, the Court itself questioned, reversed, modified, or even negated its earlier judgments—by no means solely due to changes in its personnel— as it did so prominently in the four *Covert-Krueger Cases* between

---

[43] 207 U. S. 463.   [44] 223 U. S. 1.
[45] E.g. *Lewis Publishing Co. v. Wyman,* 228 U. S. 610 (1913).
[46] 307 U. S. 38.   [47] 297 U. S. 1.

1955 and 1960.[48] And in five or six instances—depending upon one's point of view—constitutional amendments were passed in order to reverse the Court: the *Eleventh* (1798), reversing the 1793 decision in *Chisholm v. Georgia*,[49] by amending the original jurisdiction of the Supreme Court to hear certain suits against the several states; the *Thirteenth, Fourteenth,* and *Fifteenth* (the Civil War Amendments, adopted in 1865, 1868, and 1870, respectively), reversing various Supreme Court decisions dealing with suffrage, slavery, and civil rights; and the *Sixteenth* (1913), the Income Tax Amendment, giving Congress power to tax incomes from whatever source derived, thereby effectively reversing the 1895 decisions in *Pollock v. Farmers' Loan and Trust Co.*,[50] which had held various income tax *statutes,* designed to accomplish the same end, unconstitutional as a violation of Article 1, Section 9, Clause 4. Some would include the *Nineteenth* (women suffrage, 1920). The adoption of a constitutional amendment is the most authoritative and most certain method of reversing the Court, but it is also often the most difficult politically to attain, and almost always the most time-consuming.

Going beyond the 89 provisions, between 1937 and 1946 alone, the Supreme Court *overruled* 32 of its decisions between 1937 and 1946 alone—the immediate post "switch-in-time-that-saved-nine" era. Prior thereto, the Court had overruled itself at least 46 times. (These two figures cover not only overrulings of provisions previously held unconstitutional, but also those made on other than constitutional grounds.) [51] Unless it seems to be absolutely necessary, however, the Court is disinclined to resort to the strong concept of *overruling.* Thus, in only six instances among the aforementioned 89 did the Court in subsequent decisions *specifically and literally* acknowledge an overruling—as it did, for example, in upholding the entire federal Fair Labor Standards Act of 1938 in the case of *United States v. Darby* [52] in 1941. There, among others, addressing itself to the child labor provisions of

[48] *Kinsella v. Krueger,* 357 U. S. 470 and *Reid v. Covert,* 351 U. S. 487 (June 11, 1956); 352 U. S. 901 (Nov. 5, 1956); 354 U. S. 1 (June 10, 1957); and *Kinsella v. Singleton et al.,* 361 U. S. 234 (Jan. 18, 1960).
[49] 2 Dallas 419. [50] 158 U. S. 601 and 157 U. S. 429.
[51] For a complete chart of overrulings between 1790 and 1957, see S. Sidney Ulmer, "Lawmaking of the Supreme Court," 8 *Journal of Public Law* 418–23 (1957). [52] 312 U. S. 100.

that statute, it *specifically* overruled its 1918 decision in *Hammer v. Dagenhart*,[53] where it had declared the federal Keating-Owen Child Labor Law of 1916 unconstitutional. Overruling differs from reversing as a matter of definition: technically speaking, a case may be *reversed* only on rehearing; thus, the original decision and the reversing decision are applicable to the *identical case*. An example of that procedure is the Court's decision in *Jones v. Opelika*, 316 U. S. 584, on June 8, 1942, upholding 5:4 an Opelika, Alabama, statute which required payment of the usual license tax or fee even by those groups (here the Jehovah Witnesses) that claimed exemption on grounds of freedom of religion—a decision which the Court *vacated* 5:4 on rehearing less than 11 months later, in *Jones v. Opelika*, 319 U. S. 103, on May 3, 1943.

The various statistics just cited do not take into account the many instances in which the Court overrules precedents *sub silentio*—i.e. when it overrules an earlier decision without saying so, but where the effect is clearly the same as an expressed overruling —as it did on several occasions in the last quarter of the past century and the first quarter of this in the realm of commerce and taxation (and probably for sound policy reasons). Thus, although many of its decisions on questions of constitutionality last, quite a few are ultimately modified or neutralized by the Supreme Court itself or by valid action of other branches of the government, led by Congress. America's system of judicial review, as Professor Freund has noted cogently, indeed produces frustrations, but it has a saving grace of resiliency.

POLICY FORMULATIONS AND CONSIDERATIONS

In any case, the policy views of the Court never remain for long out of line with the policy views of the lawmaking majority— with the probable, but not inevitable, exception of decisions involving the Bill of Rights, particularly between 1940–49 and 1954—57, where the Court on a good number of occasions stood as a veritable bastion against the popular majority viewpoint. Still, on major public policy issues both the Chief Executive and Congress may confidently be expected to succeed—speaking generally and *in the long run,* although in the short run they may well

[53] 247 U. S. 251.

have to bow. If the Court is to thrive, as Professor Wallace Mendelson has said so well, it "must respect the social forces that determine elections and other major political settlements. No court can long withstand the morals of its era." [54] It is the "child of its time."

This judicial alignment with the other two major branches on overriding policy matters may not always follow axiomatically, but it comes very close to reality. Some observers of the scene have even contended that far from representing a dependable means of preventing "legislative tyranny," judicial review of national policy seems to have but marginal value. [55] Whatever the actual merits of this judgment may be, the Court is well aware of the limitations upon its powers. Mr. Justice Frankfurter, the conscience of the Court on this issue during most of his lengthy tenure, once again wisely addressed himself to the question of reversing the Supreme Court in his now well-known separate concurring opinion in the unanimously decided Little Rock School Case, *Cooper v. Aaron,* [56] in which he quoted at length from his concurring opinion in the *United Mine Workers Case* of 1947:

> Even this court has the last say only for a time. Being composed of fallible men, it may err. But revision of its errors must be by orderly process of law. The court may be asked to reconsider its decisions, and this has been done successfully again and again throughout our history. Or, what this court has deemed its duty to decide may be changed by legislation, as it often has been, and, on occasion, by constitutional amendment. [57]

He might have added that one of the major catalysts in revision and reconsideration is the inevitably changing personnel composition of the Court—yet any recognition of that crucial element in judicial decision-making must carefully guard against a pat and oversimplified catch-all analysis of its significance. In any event,

[54] *Justices Black and Frankfurter: Conflict in the Court* (Chicago: University of Chicago Press, 1961), pp. 75–6. On this point see also the excellent article by Robert A. Dahl, "Decision-Making in a Democracy: The Supreme Court as a National Policy-Maker," 6 *Journal of Public Law* 279 (1957).

[55] Cf. S. Sidney Ulmer, "Judicial Review as Political Behavior: A Temporary Check on Congress," 4 *Administrative Science Quarterly* 426 (March 1960).

[56] 358 U. S. 1 (1958).

[57] *United States v. United Mine Workers,* 330 U. S. 258.

reversal of judicial action is possible, and it has frequently been effectuated.

COMPLIANCE AND ENFORCEMENT

But there is more to be said on this point. In Chapter V it was demonstrated at some length that the judgments of the Supreme Court of the United States are not necessarily accepted as automatically binding by those who ought to be bound. A decision may be simply ignored, as was widely proved by the continuation of the practice of "released time" in public secondary schools in situations and settings identical to that struck down as an unconstitutional violation of the principle of separation of state and church in *McCollum v. Board of Education*.[58] Or a decision may be circumvented and even opposed by force, to which the *Segregation Cases* bear ample witness.[59] And there is the already described host of calculated, interminable delays in compliance.[60]

Moreover, with the very few exceptions of the original jurisdiction docket cases, the Court formulates *general* policy. It is the lower federal and state courts, as the case may be, that *apply* it, presumably "not inconsistent with this opinion," as the Supreme Court's mandate normally reads. In so applying the opinion, the lower courts may, and often do, materially modify the Supreme Court's determination. These modifications, moreover, are not at all astonishing in view of the not infrequent habit of Supreme Court justices to mix dogma with dicta. On the other hand, some of the so-called "modifications" or "interpretations" clearly have been little short of outright defiance—especially by state courts.[61]

There is also the obvious fact that, lacking any source of physical power of its own, the Supreme Court depends on the political branches of the government for the enforcement of its mandates, in particular on the Chief Executive. If it fails to obtain that cooperation in those instances where it is vital for compliance, the Court stands helplessly on the sidelines. The most famous case in point is the, perhaps apocryphal, comment by President Andrew

[58] 333 U. S. 203 (1948).   [59] Cf. fn. 3, op. cit.
[60] See Chapter Five, pp. 200–204.
[61] On this general point see the informative article by Walter Murphy, "Lower Court Checks in Supreme Court Power," 53 *American Political Science Review* 1017–31 (December 1959).

Jackson who, according to Mr. Chief Justice Marshall's biographer, once exploded, "John Marshall has made his decision:— *now let him enforce it!*" [62] The outburst reputedly occurred as a result of Marshall's decision in *Worcester v. Georgia*,[63] in which his Court upheld the rights of the Cherokee Indians in a dispute with Georgia, and he strongly implied in his opinion that it was the President's duty to honor and back Worcester's rights under federal law. Apocryphal or not, the Jackson comment illustrates the Court's dependence and its quandary when the necessary executive support is not forthcoming. Its effectiveness in the absence of the executive sword is as limited as its operations in general would be without the necessary appropriations from the legislative purse, and the legislative assent to its jurisdictional and procedural needs. In essence, as Mr. Justice Jackson stated this fact of judicial life starkly, "[the Court] can perform but one function—that of deciding litigations—and can proceed in no manner except by the judicial process." [64]

MACHTKAMPF: THE SUPREME COURT IN THE POLITICAL POWER STRUGGLE

Despite the implications of the preceding paragraphs, the Supreme Court has been a participant in what may be viewed as a continuous struggle for power among the three "separated branches" of the federal government to attain a position of dominance, if not ultimate control, in the American political system. Since it lacks the potent weapons of the other two branches, especially for the purpose of self-protection and for the enforcement of the powers which it exercises, the Court has necessarily been less prominent in this *Machtkampf* (struggle for power); but its own important tool of judicial review has provided it with a genuine measure of authority.

Victory in the *Machtkampf* among the three branches has seen supremacy alternate from branch to branch; sometimes the strug-

[62] Albert J. Beveridge, *The Life of John Marshall,* Vol. 4 (Boston: Houghton Mifflin, 1919), p. 551.

[63] 6 Peters 515 (1832).

[64] *The Supreme Court in the American System of Government* (Cambridge: Harvard University Press, 1955), p. 12.

gle has been featured by a quasi-alliance of two branches against the third over a period of time. A pertinent example is the frustrated and frustrating protracted effort of the closely allied New Deal Legislature and New Deal Executive commencing in 1933, which, on many major issues, had to wait for victory over the Supreme Court until four years later when the famous "switch-in-time-that-saved-nine" of early 1937 took place.

In general, however, the *tone* of dominance has been set by the person and personality of the elected Chief Executive, who, after all, is the sole individual in the American federal governmental process to have a nation-wide constituency, and who, within limits, is in the position of interpreting his powers narrowly or broadly. In other words, whenever the President has been of the category commonly called "active" or "strong"—e.g. Washington, Jackson, Polk, Lincoln, Wilson, and the two Roosevelts—his branch, *in the long run,* has been able to acquire supremacy. Where he has been "passive" or "weak" or simply lacked sufficient support in Congress or by the people—e.g. John Quincy Adams, Pierce, Buchanan, Johnson, Grant, McKinley, Harding, Coolidge, Hoover —supremacy was acquired by Congress or, on occasion, by the Supreme Court. In several instances no clear-cut supremacy can be pinpointed. This is true, for example, of the presidencies of Madison and Monroe—perhaps even Jefferson, although historians and political scientists differ sharply in evaluating his role in office —Hayes, Cleveland, Taft, Truman, and the end of the second Eisenhower term (there is no doubt about the presence of congressional supremacy during Eisenhower's first term in office). Finally, it should be noted that during some presidencies the Executive has tended to dominate in foreign affairs and the Congress in internal matters, e.g. Truman and Eisenhower.

At the risk of some oversimplification and generalization— which inevitably attend categorization and classification—Table IX is designed to indicate periods of American history, some having been necessarily and deliberately omitted (e.g. the Kennedy Administration), in which existed fairly discernible tendencies toward supremacy by one branch or two allied branches against a third. Some periods will be listed in more than one category, for example the first four years of the New Deal era, when presidential supremacy was unquestioned—surrender by Congress to President

TABLE IX
PERIODS OF DISCERNIBLE TENDENCIES TOWARD
SUPREMACY OF BRANCHES OF THE GOVERNMENT

Years	President(s)	Chief Justice(s)	Commentary
A. *Tendencies Toward Legislative Supremacy*			
1809–1829	Madison Monroe J. Q. Adams	Marshall	Supremacy facilitated and advanced by powerful Court.
1837–1845	Van Buren W. H. Harrison Tyler	Taney	Aided by strong Court and passive Presidents.
1849–1861	Taylor Fillmore Pierce Buchanan	Taney	Nadir of Presidency. *Dred Scott* case.
1865–1885	Johnson Grant Hayes Garfield Arthur	S. P. Chase Waite	Partially effective opposition by Johnson and Hayes.
1919–1921	Wilson	White	Defeat of League. President ill.
1921–1933	Harding Coolidge Hoover	Taft Hughes	Co-operative Court. Weak, passive Presidents.
1953–1959	Eisenhower	Warren	Strong Court. Passive President.
B. *Tendencies Toward Executive Supremacy*			
1789–1797	Washington	Jay Rutledge Ellsworth	Co-operative Congress. Weak, docile Court.
1801–1809	Jefferson	Marshall	Some doubt about Executive Supremacy, but tendency.
1829–1837	Jackson	Marshall Taney	President in high form. Last years of Marshall Court.
1845–1849	Polk	Taney	Underrated President.
1861–1865	Lincoln	Taney S. P. Chase	High-water mark of Presidency. Civil War.
1901–1908	T. Roosevelt	Fuller	Assertive Court. Popular President.

Years	President(s)	Chief Justice(s)	Commentary
1913–1919	Wilson	White	President lost control to Republican Congressional majority in 1919.
1933–1947	F. D. Roosevelt Truman	Hughes Stone Vinson	Revolution on Court, 1937. Powerful President: F.D.R.

C. *Tendencies Toward Judicial Supremacy*

1801–1829	Jefferson Madison Monroe J. Q. Adams	Marshall	The greatest Chief Justice at power's peak.
1857	Pierce Buchanan	Taney	The *Dred Scott* case.
1889–1910	B. Harrison Cleveland McKinley	Fuller	Some doubt re Cleveland term (his second).
1935–1936	F. D. Roosevelt	Hughes	13 New Deal Laws declared unconstitutional.

D. *Not Readily Discernible Supremacy Tendencies*

1797–1801	John Adams	Ellsworth	President and Congress shared.
1885–1889	Cleveland	Waite Fuller	Probably President, but . . .
1910–1913	Taft	White	Uncertainty.
1947–1953	Truman	Vinson	Divided foreign and domestic tendencies.
1959–1960	Eisenhower	Warren	Sudden assertion of power by President. Democratic Congressional majority.

Roosevelt is a much more accurate term—but during which time the Supreme Court proved to be a major roadblock to the New Deal program.

There is no doubt that the Supreme Court of the United States has repeatedly *challenged* the authority of both President and Congress. But in spite of the three or four indicated periods of tendencies toward judicial supremacy, the Court has never really actively *bid* for the role of dominant governmental agency of the land—although a good case could be made for such a policy during the era of Mr. Chief Justice Marshall. During that period, as well as during the heyday of the Hughes Anti-New Deal Court, we may speak of periodic "government by judiciary" or "judicial supremacy," yet even then there was never any genuine likelihood that the Court would *in the final analysis* effectively *dominate* the Executive and/or the Legislature. When all is said and done, the Supreme Court of the United States does not possess the political power, the arsenal of potent weapons of government, or the strategic position in the government or in the body politic generally enjoyed by the other two branches.

A Historical Note. If we take a closer look at the Supreme Court's role in the *Machtkampf* on the American political scene we see that the high tribunal began on a very inauspicious note. Its dozen or so pre-Marshall years, during which three Chief Justices came and went—the second of whom, John Rutledge, was not confirmed by the Senate—were characterized by a lack of popular esteem and understanding, little work, and dissatisfied personnel. The first Chief Justice, John Jay, thought so little of his position that he not only spent one year during his tenure in England on a diplomatic mission, but twice ran for Governor of New York, succeeding on the second try, whereupon he happily resigned the Chief Justiceship! And, as already pointed out, the third Chief Justice, Oliver Ellsworth, happily traded a diplomatic post for his august office. The Court did, however, soon make clear that it intended to act as an arbiter in legal disputes between the states and the federal government; and it became quickly apparent that its judicial sympathies lay with the latter.

The Marshall era, of course, brought about a drastic change. The Chief Justice completely dominated the Court—with dissents confined almost solely to Mr. Justice William Johnson. It is quite clear that Marshall, more than any other man in the history of the Court, determined the character of America's federal constitutional system. From its erstwhile lowly, if not discredited, level John Marshall raised the United States Supreme Court to a position of equality with the Executive and the Legislature. He called his constitutional interpretations as he saw them, always adhering to his previously discussed, oft-expressed doctrine that "it is a constitution we are expounding . . . intended to endure for ages to come and, consequently, to be adapted to the various crises of human affairs." [65] Yet, as we know, he hastened to insist that "judicial power, as contradistinguished from the power of law, has no existence. Courts are the mere instruments of the law, and can will nothing." [66] Thus, "willing nothing," Marshall handed down, among many others, four of the most momentous decisions in the history of Court and Country, without which it is doubtful that the nation would have grown and prospered as it has: (1) *Marbury v. Madison* [67] (judicial review, supremacy of the U. S. Constitution); (2) *McCulloch v. Maryland* [68] (implied powers of Congress, reaffirmation of the supremacy of the U. S. Constitution, federal immunity from involuntary state taxation, federal government held to have its powers directly from the people rather than by way of the states); (3) *Gibbons v. Ogden* [69] (plenary federal control over interstate commerce); and (4) *Dartmouth College v. Woodward* [70] (inviolability of contracts). Truly, the Court led and, leading, gave the federal government the means to develop and work.

Whereas the Marshall Court had by its decisions placed the emphasis upon the national commercial-creditor-propertied classes, its successor, the also powerful Taney Court, pursued a different emphasis. The sanctity of property remained a primary consideration of the tribunal, but it devolved upon a different segment of society and, incidentally, of the country. A Southerner from Maryland, the Jackson-appointed Roger B. Taney, a Democrat and a Catholic, the first of his religious persuasion to be on the bench, by his decisions favored "states rights" and *agrarian* property, that is, land and slaves. From a totally different milieu than the great constitutional nationalist who preceded him, Taney, and with him a majority of his Court, demonstrated a faithful attachment to the economic interests of the South and the rapidly developing frontier of the West. But disaster loomed on the horizon: after pursuing the aforementioned policies determinedly, and with little, if any, interference from the other two branches for twenty years, Taney met his, and the Court's, Waterloo in 1857 with his opinion in *Dred Scott v. Sanford*.[71]

This decision by his Southern-dominated Court, with but two

---

[65] *Osborn v. United States Bank,* 9 Wheaton 738 (1824).
[66] *McCulloch v. Maryland,* 4 Wheaton 316 (1819).
[67] 1 Cranch 137 (1803).   [68] Loc. cit.   [69] 9 Wheaton 1 (1824).
[70] 4 Wheaton 518 (1819).   [71] 19 Howard 393.

Justices dissenting (John McLean and Benjamin R. Curtis), and featuring nine separate opinions, including Taney's, that, among other things, no Negro could be a citizen; that the Negro was "a person of an inferior order"; that he was a slave and thus his master's permanent property no matter whether the latter took him to slave or free parts of the country; that the Missouri Compromise was unconstitutional; and that no individual of African descent was "a portion of this American people," permanently tarred Taney's reputation, dragged the Supreme Court of the United States into its lowest depths, and hastened the dawn of the Civil War.

With *Dred Scott,* the Court invited a violent congressional reaction. While that took a while to take concrete form, the influence of the Court declined at once. Far from alleviating the incipient sectional strife, it had promoted it. During and after the Civil War, with Taney's role reduced to one of bitterness and unhappiness, Congress demonstrated its utter contempt of the Supreme Court by *thrice* changing its size in six years: up from nine to ten in 1863; down from ten to seven in 1866; up again from seven to nine in 1869. Quite obviously, all this was done for policy purposes. And, as we have seen earlier in these pages, when in 1868–69 the post-Taney Court indicated a possible declaration of unconstitutionality of some of the military Reconstruction Acts, an angry Congress, acting under its powers derived from the Constitution to limit the Court's appellate jurisdiction, simply deprived it of the power to decide the case.[72] This was the beginning of the Chief Justiceship of Salmon P. Chase (1864–74) and Morrison R. Waite (1874–88), both Northern Republicans, during whose tenure the Court, predictably, was chiefly concerned, in addition to safeguarding property, with maintaining the status quo: state authority over individuals and federal authority over interstate commerce—which represented the two great post-Civil War problems. The former included the Waite Court's nullification of the attempted use of the Fourteenth Amendment by the federal government as a national arm to protect civil rights in the states.[73] The Chase Court, in a burst of judicial activism, did declare ten acts of Congress unconstitutional; but, as explained above, in the final analysis

[72] *Ex parte McCardle,* 7 Wallace 506 (1869).
[73] *Civil Rights Cases,* 109 U. S. 3 (1883).

it bowed before the power of the Radical Republicans in Congress, and it was effectively "packed" by President Grant in 1871, thus nullifying within 15 months its briefly successful attempt to battle for what it had regarded as stable currency in the *Legal Tender Cases*.[74]

But with the long Chief Justiceship of the Cleveland-appointed Melville W. Fuller of Illinois, the Court regained its virility and struck out on a path designed above all to assure the sanctity of property, as the majority of the Court saw it. This majority was composed of a group of highly conservative, property-conscious justices, who, given the opportunity, commenced to strike down as unconstitutional a fair number of federal and state laws in the economic and social sphere. *Laisser faire* seemed secure, indeed. Until roughly this time, state laws, for example, had been held unconstitutional largely because they were viewed as conflicting either with the interstate-commerce or the obligation-of-contract clauses of the Constitution. Of 128 state laws invalidated by the federal courts *before* 1888, 50 involved the former clause, 50 the latter, and only one the taking of property "without due process of law." The Fuller Court, on the other hand, ultimately struck down a large number of state laws on that last ground, holding that the several legislative "experimentations" at issue deprived "persons" of liberty and property without *substantive* due process of law. Substantive due process had truly come of age! And the concept of "persons" now also included *corporations,* thanks to a unanimous Court ruling in the *Santa Clara Case,*[75] a decision invalidating assessments on portions of railroad property. It was featured by a casual *announcement* at the hearing stage by Mr. Chief Justice Waite, who did not even write the opinion: "The Court does not wish to hear argument on the question whether the provision in the Fourteenth Amendment to the Constitution, which forbids a State to deny to any person within its jurisdiction the equal protection of the laws, applies to these Corporations. We are all of the opinion that it does." This was a rather cavalier manner of disposing of a highly significant constitutional issue—one that was neither before the Court nor had been argued in the case at bar!

[74] 12 Wallace 457 (1871) and *Hepburn v. Griswold,* 8 Wallace 603 (1870).
[75] *Santa Clara County v. Southern Pacific Railroad Co.,* 118 U. S. 394 (1886).

The states, however, and—considerably later—the federal government insisted on wishing to pioneer in the realm of economic and social legislation, as they deemed that to be the desire of the majority of the voters. Yet in most areas—viz., maximum hours, minimum wages, working conditions, regulation of woman and child labor, compulsory arbitration, employer liability, and many others—the legislatures ran into the judicial vetoes not only of the Fuller Court, but also those of his successors, the White and Taft and, until 1937, the Hughes Court. Throughout this period the Supreme Court demonstrated again and again a remarkable regard for the protection of *property* under its interpretations of the "liberty and property" phases of the "due process of law" clauses of the Fifth and Fourteenth Amendments to the United States Constitution. Yet, oddly enough, the Court found these clauses no barrier against legislative invasions of the *cultural and political* fields, often referred to as "civil rights" or "civil liberties."

From the turn of the century on, when the great Mr. Justice Oliver Wendell Holmes, Jr., was appointed to what was to be his 30-year tenure on the Court by President Theodore Roosevelt, dissenting voices to the majority's policies were increasingly heard. From 1916 on, Holmes was joined in dissents, although frequently for quite different reasons, by his colleague Louis D. Brandeis, and with the advent of Justices Harlan F. Stone in 1925 and Benjamin N. Cardozo in 1932, the dissenting voices in this area had swelled to just one short of a majority. The previously described switch by Mr. Chief Justice Hughes, and, to a lesser extent, Mr. Justice Owen D. Roberts, ultimately brought on what the eminent American constitutionalist, Edward S. Corwin, has aptly called "a Constitutional Revolution." Having lost the battle of "packing" the Court in February 1937, President F. D. Roosevelt won the "war" when fate, in the form of deaths and resignations, weeded out the remaining four ultra-conservative justices on the bench between 1937 and 1941—Associate Justices Willis Van Devanter, George Sutherland, James C. McReynolds, and Pierce Butler—ultimately allowing him to fill nine vacancies on the Court.[76]

By no means all of these Roosevelt appointees saw the law as

[76] Black, Reed, Frankfurter, Douglas, Murphy, Stone (promotion to Chief Justice), Byrnes, Jackson, and Rutledge.

he had hoped they would, but certainly the New Deal now had clear sailing, and there was no doubt that the new justices rejected outright the "thou-shalt-not-pass" doctrines of their predecessors relative to legislative experimentation in the economic and social sphere. Judicial self-restraint on legislative policy-making in these areas of public life became the avowed policy of the Court—just as the "Old Court" had practiced a similar restraint on legislative policies in the cultural and political realms (e.g. the "separate but equal" concept and abridgement on speech, press, and assembly). Yet, interestingly enough, the "New Court" immediately commenced to complete the cycle of policy reversal by throwing up judicial vetoes in the face of a good many legislative encroachments, as the Court saw these, on civil liberties. When Justices Murphy and Wiley Rutledge joined Mr. Chief Justice Stone and Justices Black and Douglas in the early 1940's, these "libertarian activists" were generally in firm control—certainly until the death of the Chief Justice in April 1946. They briefly relinquished that control during the last four years of the Vinson Court upon the death of Justices Murphy and Rutledge in 1949 and their replacement by Justices Clark and Minton, when the Court tended to side with government rather than the individual in the general field of national security. But they more or less regained it during the first four years of the Warren Court, from 1953 to 1957, Mr. Chief Justice Warren having replaced Mr. Chief Justice Vinson on the latter's death. However, with the Court led by the consistently "non-activist" Mr. Justice Frankfurter, the 1957–58 term of the Court saw a return to greater judicial self-restraint even in that area of public and constitutional policy—some would contend largely as a result of the barrage of congressional and public criticism against the Court as a result of its spate of "pro-civil liberty" decisions in 1956–57. Thus, matters stood as of the 1961–62 term of the Supreme Court of the United States.

If we reflect on these several considerations in this analysis of the *Machtkampf*, the work of the Supreme Court and the force and implications of its decisions come into closer focus. At times the Court has clearly led the country (e.g. the Marshall era); at other times it has more or less held the line (e.g. the Chase-Waite era—with important qualifications); at times it has deliberately stimulated social and economic progress (e.g. the post-1937 Court);

at others it has deliberately delayed it (e.g. the Fuller Court). At times it has looked to majority sentiment, as it were, by following the election returns (e.g. the *Insular* decisions at the turn of the last century); [77] at others it has defied majority sentiment (e.g. some of the 1956-57 term "civil liberties" decisions).[78] At times its decisions have been seemingly motivated by "sectional" or "class" considerations (e.g. *Dred Scott*,[79] proclaiming corporations as "persons," [80] and the 1954 *Segregation Cases*); [81] at others they have been truly "national" in spirit and effect (e.g. the first two major Marshall decisions, cited earlier). In a very real sense, the Court, through the years, has thus been the conscience of the country. In a measure, it has represented the *volonté générale* of the land, in a qualitative rather than a quantitative sense. It has done this through its decisions, speaking through its justices, who—generally of a rather high caliber—have interpreted the Constitution as they saw it, in line with the taught tradition of the law.

Of course, the Supreme Court of the United States is engaged in the political process—but, in Mr. Justice Frankfurter's admonitory prose, it is "the Nation's ultimate judicial tribunal, not a super-legal aid bureau." [82] Of course, the justices consult their own policy preferences. But they do so in an institutional setting that forces responsibility upon them. They must meet and maintain high standards of integrity, intelligence, logic, reflectiveness, and consistency. They have the exciting, yet delicate, task of heeding the "felt necessities of the time"—to employ once again Mr. Justice Holmes's inspired phrase—while holding aloft the banner of constitutional fundamentals.

[77] *Downes v. Bidwell*, 182 U. S. 244 (1901) and *De Lima v. Bidwell*, 182 U. S. 1 (1901).

[78] Cf. *Watkins v. United States*, 354 U. S. 178; *Jencks v. United States*, 353 U. S. 657; *Yates v. United States*, 354 U. S. 298.

[79] *Dred Scott v. Sanford*, loc. cit.

[80] *Santa Clara County v. Southern Pacific Railroad Co.*, loc. cit.

[81] *Brown v. Board of Education*, 347 U. S. 483; *Bolling v. Sharpe*, 347 U. S. 497.

[82] *Uveges v. Pennsylvania*, 335 U. S. 437, at 450 (1948).

IX

CODA:

A REALISTIC BULWARK

If the foregoing analysis of the role of the Supreme Court of the United States in the political process has proved anything at all, it ought to be the acceptance of the need for judicial self-restraint. This acceptance plays an omnipresent and omnipotent part in the judicial composite of the nine members of the highest court in the United States and, from the point of view of effective power in a democratic state, the world. No matter how the judicial record of these nine individuals may appear on a chart or graph, no matter how predictable or unpredictable their position on certain issues may be—a factor that is probably far more of a blessing than a curse—they are fully aware of their role in and responsibility to the democratic body politic which they serve with such dedication. They do so as a collective institution of government; but it is an institution that is characterized more than any other by individual absorption in the tasks at hand, an absorption that calls for more direct personal evaluation and more direct hard work than any other. The one possible exception is the President of the United States at the instance of casting the die of a decision when he is, indeed, at once the most lonely and the most powerful individual in the free world. As has been demonstrated throughout these pages, *each member of the Supreme Court* normally participates in every stage of the consideration of a case—from the review stage through the evaluation of briefs through oral argument through discussion and vote in Conference to the writing of or participation in the ultimate opinion of the Court. At every stage of the life of a case the justices are fully aware of their responsibilities as members of the governmental process, and thus practice much procedural as well as substantive judicial self-restraint—

both in the type of cases they will hear *and* in the kind of decisions they will render. This is a simple, and yet immensely complicated, fact of judicial life—whatever the opinion of expert as well as laymen outsiders on judicial legislating may be. But there is little doubt that the justices believe with Johann Wolfgang von Goethe that "self-limitation is the first mark of the master." *

Throughout the almost two centuries of its existence, the Court has developed a host of unwritten laws, practices, precedents, and attitudes which we may well view as a code of behavior for the highest judicial body in the United States—a series of significant *maxims of judicial self-restraint*. In analyzing the most commonly accepted of these, the reader should be aware that in such an enumeration there will be necessarily some generalization—and that maxims, like rules, are sometimes broken quite deliberately.

THE SIXTEEN GREAT
MAXIMS OF JUDICIAL SELF-RESTRAINT

There is nothing holy about either the number of these maxims or the order in which they will appear below. They are presented roughly in the order in which they would normally confront the several justices as an issue reaches the Court in the form of a case or controversy.

ONE: Before the Court will even glance at a particular issue or dispute, a definite "case" or "controversy" at law or in equity between bona fide adversaries under the Constitution must exist, involving the protection or enforcement of valuable legal rights, or the punishment, prevention, or redress of wrongs directly concerning the party or parties bringing the justiciable suit. Mr. Justice Jackson viewed this maxim as "perhaps the most significant and least comprehended limitation upon the judicial power." [1] The judicial system of the United States is constructed upon specific cases with specific facts. Thus when a group of federal employees endeavored to join one George P. Poole in a suit testing the validity of that portion of the Hatch Act of 1939 which forbids members

*From the sonnet "Was wir bringen," 1802.

[1] Robert H. Jackson, *The Supreme Court in the American System of Government* (Cambridge: Harvard University Press, 1955), p. 11.

of the executive civil service from taking an active part in "political management or in political campaigns," the Supreme Court
disqualified them as appellants since they, unlike Poole, had not
violated the provision in question.[2] Refusing to take jurisdiction,
the Court thereby reiterated its oft-expressed stand against "every
form of pronouncement on abstract, contingent, or hypothetical
issues." [3] Except for Poole's claims, no case or controversy directly
involving the interest of the appellants was involved here in the
face of the Supreme Court's first maxim—regardless of what
lower tribunals might have held.

TWO: Closely related to the need for the presence of a case or
controversy is the logical demand that *the party or parties bringing
suit must have "standing."* There are two major aspects to the difficult and intricate concept of standing. The first, to raise a constitutional issue with proper standing, is a showing that the one who
seeks to challenge the statute or action is personally and substantially injured by it, or is in substantial danger of such injury. The
second is that a petitioner must not only have a personal and
substantial interest infringed by that statute or action, but that he
must also "bring himself, by proper averment and showing, within
the class as to whom the act thus attacked is unconstitutional." [4]
Once properly before it, however, the Court must decide the
dispute in one way or another; it cannot refuse because the task
may be difficult, vexatious, or controversial—as indeed almost all
judgments of the Court necessarily are. The sole action that is not
considered a *decision* by the Court is a *postponement.*

One of the most famous illustrations of a *lack of standing* on
record is the case of a Connecticut physician, who endeavored to
challenge the constitutionality of that state's statutory prohibitions
of "the use of drugs or instruments to prevent conception, and the
giving of assistance or counsel in their use" in the Supreme Court
of the United States, having lost his appeal in the Connecticut
Supreme Court of Errors below. Because of their importance to
the concept of standing, the pertinent sections of the former's *per
curiam* decision are reproduced herewith:

[2] *United Public Workers of America v. Mitchell,* 330 U. S. 75 (1947).
[3] Jackson, loc. cit. p. 12.
[4] *Southern Railroad Co. v. King,* 217 U. S. 524 (1910), at 534.

. . . Appellant [Dr. Tileston] alleged that the statute, if applicable to him, would prevent his giving professional advice concerning the use of contraceptives to three patients whose condition of health was such that their lives would be endangered by childbearing, and that appellees [Ullman and other law enforcement officers of the state], intend to prosecute any offense against the statute and "claim or may claim" that the proposed professional advice would constitute such an offense. The complaint set out in detail the danger to the lives of appellant's patients in the event that they should bear children, but *contained no allegation asserting any claim under the Fourteenth Amendment of infringement of appellant's liberty or his property rights.* The relief prayed was a declaratory judgment [to be explained in the next maxim] as to whether the statutes are applicable to appellant and if so whether they constitute a valid exercise of constitutional power "within the meaning and intent of Amendment XIV of the Constitution of the United States prohibiting a state from depriving any person *of life* without due process of law.". . .

We are of the opinion that the proceedings in the state courts *present no constitutional question which appellant has standing to assert. The sole constitutional attack upon the statutes under the Fourteenth Amendment is confined to their deprivation of life—obviously not appellant's but his patients'.* There is no allegation or proof that appellant's life is in danger. *His patients are not parties to this proceeding* and there is no basis on which we can say that he has standing to secure an adjudication of his patient's constitutional right to life, *which they do not assert in their own behalf.* . . . *No question is raised in the record with respect to the deprivation of appellant's liberty or property in contravention of the Fourteenth Amendment.* . . . Since the *appeal must be dismissed on the grounds that appellant has no standing to litigate the constitutional question which the record presents,* it is unnecessary to consider whether the record shows the existence of a genuine case or controversy essential to the exercise of jurisdiction of this Court. . . . Dismissed.[5]

[5] *Tileston v. Ullman,* 318 U. S. 44 (1943). (Italics supplied.)

In short, Dr. Tileston had no standing to sue: his patients might well have had such, but they did not bring suit; he might have had it, but he brought suit on erroneous grounds. Standing is essential to an orderly and efficacious judicial process; to adhere to its requirements is a small price to pay. (Dividing 5:4, the Court rejected another, and far better planned attack on the Connecticut statute in 1961, Mr. Justice Frankfurter holding for the majority that the controversy was "not fit for adjudication," that no one had been injured, such as by being jailed or fined, and that, consequently, ". . . this Court cannot be umpire to debates concerning harmless, empty shadows." [6])

THREE: The Court does not render advisory opinions, i.e. *judicial rulings upon the constitutionality of governmental action in the absence of a case or controversy requiring such a ruling for its disposition*—nor do the lower federal constitutional courts. Legislative courts may do so, and so may quite a few of the courts of the fifty states—such as Massachusetts and Maine.[7] All courts, however, may render *declaratory judgments*—a device that enables courts generally to enter a final judgment between litigants *in an actual controversy,* defining their respective rights under a statute, contract, will, or other document, *without* attaching to that otherwise binding judgment any consequential or coercive relief. The crucial distinction between a declaratory judgment and an advisory opinion is the presence of an actual controversy in the case of a declaratory judgment, whereas an advisory opinion would deal with an abstract, hypothetical question in so far as the judicial process is concerned. Today, three-quarters of the states, and the federal government under the Federal Declaratory Judgment Act of 1934, permit declaratory judgments. In the words of the federal statute, that judgment—which is reviewable above—in essence thus answers the following question in an actual controversy: ". . . whether or not further relief is or could be prayed." It was for just such a declaratory judgment that Dr. Tileston had pleaded—unsuccessfully because he lacked standing.

The Supreme Court itself has admitted the obvious: that the

[6] *Poe v. Ullman,* 367 U. S. 497 (1961).
[7] In 1961, the courts of the following states—in addition to the two already listed—possessed that power: Alabama, Colorado, Delaware, Florida, North Carolina, New Hampshire, Rhode Island, and South Dakota.

line between advisory opinions and declaratory judgments is a thin one, and that "it would be difficult, if it would be possible, to fashion a precise test for determining in every case whether there is such a controversy [as is demanded by a declaratory judgment]." [8] But it insisted in the *Ashwander* case [9] that the Federal Declaratory Judgment Act "does not attempt to change the essential requisites for the exercise of judicial power," and, on an earlier occasion, that it cannot be invoked to "obtain an advisory decree upon a hypothetical state of facts." [10]

FOUR: Not only must the complainant in federal court expressly declare that he is invoking the Constitution of the United States— "the ultimate touchstone of constitutionality," in Mr. Justice Frankfurter's phrase—*but a specific live rather than dead constitutional issue citing the particular provision on which he relies in that document must be raised by him; the Court will not entertain generalities.* Indeed, it has held specifically that an attack upon a statute as "violative of the Constitution of the United States" is insufficient on its face.[11] Nor will a simple contention that a statute is "in violation of the Fifth or Seventh Amendments to the Constitution" do.[12] Specific, careful, closely reasoned documentation is essential. Moreover, the issue must be raised *seasonably;* that is, timely assertion of the constitutional issue must be made before a tribunal having proper jurisdiction, and it must be reasserted at every opportunity in the course of the litigation. The Court is not, nor can it be, concerned with dead or moot and thus inappropriate problems—as, for example, one caused by the death of an essential party, here the defendant, in an appeal in a criminal action.[13]

FIVE: The Court looks askance at any attempt to have the judicial decision-cake and eat it, too. Thus, *it will not pass upon the constitutionality of a statute at the instance of one who has availed himself of its benefits, but then decides to challenge its legality, anyway.* An illustration is the case of a St. Louis, Missouri, casting

[8] *Maryland Casualty Co. v. Pacific Coal & Oil Co.,* 312 U. S. 270, at 273 (1941).
[9] *Ashwander v. Tennessee Valley Authority,* 297 U. S. 288, at 325 (1936).
[10] *Electric Bond & Share Co. v. Securities & Exchange Commission,* 303 U. S. 419, at 443 (1938).
[11] *Herndon v. Georgia,* 295 U. S. 441 (1935).
[12] *Chapin v. Frye,* 179 U. S. 127 (1900).
[13] *List v. Pennsylvania,* 131 U. S. 396 (1888).

company, in the role of owner of property within a special sewer district who connected his premises with a freshly constructed sewer and availed himself of its benefits. But then he challenged the validity of the statute permitting a tax levy against him as a recipient of the services as an unconstitutional infringement of his property rights under the Fourteenth Amendment.[14] The Supreme Court held unanimously that by accepting and availing himself of the benefits of the construction and zoning involved, the owner was "estopped from maintaining a suit" on the grounds and under the circumstances here involved.

SIX: All remedies in the pertinent lower federal and/or state courts must have been exhausted, and prescribed lower court procedure duly followed, before making application to the United States Supreme Court for review. As Judge Augustus N. Hand of the Second Circuit Court of the United States once observed, "the rule of exhaustion is the only rule which is consistent with orderly government." Thus, the highest court of the land will not review a judgment of a state court unless on the face of the record it affirmatively appears that a *federal question constituting an appropriate ground* for such review was presented in, and expressly or necessarily decided by, such a state court. No matter how vital, inviting, timely, or attractive the issue involved may be, the Supreme Court will not accept a case unless the remedies below have been exhausted; nor does it matter that a lower tribunal might not be "friendly" to the substance of a suit—as has occurred in connection with the integration-segregation controversy and in certain criminal law actions in some states. Orderly procedure is of the very essence of the judicial process; judicial and administrative chaos is the alternative.

SEVEN: Assuming it has been properly raised, *the federal question at issue must be substantial rather than trivial; it must be the pivotal point of the case; and it must be part of the plaintiff's case rather than a part of his adversary's defense.* Whatever the subjective overtones of the term "substantial" may be, it is normally not an overwhelming job to distinguish between a "substantial" and a "trivial" federal question. For example, the controversies

[14] *St. Louis Co. v. Prendergast Co.,* 260 U. S. 459 (1923).

surrounding the extent of the federal government's authority in connection with the Tennessee Valley Authority projects, raised in sundry respects in the famous case of *Ashwander v. T.V.A.*,[15] and the attempt by the State of California to close its borders to a destitute non-citizen traveling in interstate-commerce,[16] are pertinent instances of substantial federal questions. On the other hand, the endeavors of some Greek-letter fraternities on various campuses in New York State to have the Supreme Court review an ordinance by the Trustees of the State University of New York setting a deadline on removing restrictive racial and/or religious clauses from fraternity "constitutions" on pain of revocation of campus privileges, was summarily—and quite predictably—turned aside as not involving a substantial federal question.[17]

EIGHT: Although it would be an oversimplification, if not entirely incorrect, to state that the Supreme Court reviews only questions of law, it is nonetheless generally true that *questions of fact—as distinct from questions of law—are not normally accepted as proper bases for review*. This is especially true of the area of judicial review of administrative construction of statutes, where a *purely* factual question has no chance of a hearing at all, for Congress has statutorily provided for the finality of administrative findings of fact.

However, it is axiomatic that the problem of which questions are of "law," which of "fact," and which "mixtures" is a difficult one. Here again, any attempt to draw a rigid line poses a genuine problem because of the very nature of the two concepts. In any event to cite one example, the Court will not permit administrative procedures—which most frequently are at issue in this particular dichotomy—to fall below what it is prone to regard as a "constitutional minimum," a concept that is clearly a matter of law subject to judicial review.

NINE: While Britain's highest tribunal, the House of Lords, considers itself bound by its own prior decisions, *the Supreme Court of the United States has never held itself absolutely bound by its precedents*. It has often adhered to many of these, of course, and will presumably continue to do so, but it has not permitted itself

[15] 297 U. S. 288 (1936).   [16] *Edwards v. California,* 314 U. S. 160 (1941).
[17] *The New York Times,* November 9, 1954.

to become enslaved by past decisions. Nor could it do so—the law does not stand still; Mr. Justice Holmes's "felt necessities of the times" are ever compelling facts of governmental life. Precedents do indeed abound. The other federal and state courts have brought a generally similar attitude, as they, too, must, to their *own* decisions. But a decision of the Supreme Court is utterly binding *in federal matters* on all courts below, state as well as federal—regardless of occasional foot-dragging and aberrations.[18]

TEN: The Court has been inclined to defer to certain legislative or executive actions by classifying an issue otherwise quite properly before it as a political question—hence refusing to come to grips with it. Depending upon one's point of view—after all, is not every constitutional decision "political" to some extent?—this intriguing practice or formula is either a mere *device* for transferring the responsibility for a decision to another branch of the government, or it is in fact *required* by the realities and necessities of the presence of the separation of powers principle. What really *is* a "political question"? Giving short shrift to this inquiry, Mr. Justice Holmes, as always coming to the core of an issue, once characterized it as ". . . little more than a play on words." [19] He would have no part of the concept as a judicial mechanism—while nevertheless fully recognizing, of course, the realities of the political facts of life.

Professor Edward S. Corwin essayed the following, perhaps not entirely helpful, definition of the vexatious verbiage in his monumental annotation of the Constitution:

> . . . a political question relates to the possession of political power, of sovereignty, of government, the determination of which is vested in Congress and the President, and whose decisions are binding on the courts.[20]

In a different vein, Jack W. Peltason, one of the students of the revered Princeton scholar, preferred to view political questions as "those which judges choose not to decide, and a question becomes

---

[18] See pp. 200–204, 290–92, and 297–8 *supra*.
[19] *Nixon v. Herndon,* 273 U. S. 536, at 540 (1927).
[20] Edward S. Corwin, *The Constitution of the United States,* revised and annotated (Washington, D. C.: United States Government Printing Office, 1953), p. 547.

political by the judges' refusal to decide it." [21] A good many of the Supreme Court's decisions, while not necessarily invalidating Professor Corwin's analysis, would seem to support Professor Peltason's more realistic evaluation. However, judges can, and do, change their minds, depending upon the posture and setting of an issue and what may be rejected or avoided as a political question today may quite conceivably be accepted for review on its merit at a later date—or vice versa, for that matter.

As this maxim is being written (Winter 1961–62) there are signs that one of the more famous areas of the political question, that of legislative districting and redistricting, heretofore inevitably regarded as its very epitome, may be the beneficiary—or the victim—of a change of mind. The Court, after having twice noted probable jurisdiction in the 1960–61 term, heard 3½ hours of oral argument in 1961 in a Tennessee case dealing with state legislative districting problems,[22] with Solicitor-General Cox arguing as *amicus curiae* on the side of the plaintiff. The mere willingness to hear these cases does not, of course, imply an *ipso facto* departure from the political-question stand in this field, but it will at least reopen the problem, one which despite customarily close decisions has been generally regarded as *res adjudicata*.

Thus, the constitutionality of the well-known county unit system of Georgia—a prime example of anti-urban, pro-rural legislative gerrymandering—has been before the Court on several occasions. Under that system, each of the various counties receives a minimum of two and a maximum of six electoral votes for the eight most populous counties, including Fulton County (Atlanta), with each county's electoral vote going to the candidate receiving the highest popular vote therein. The net effect has been that the one million inhabitants of Fulton County—a considerable proportion of whom are registered Negroes—receive but one-third more votes than the handful of residents in numerous small rural counties. In other words a vote in the small counties of Georgia has from 11 to 120 times as much weight as one in Fulton! Yet attempts to have the Supreme Court come to grips with the matter came to

[21] Jack W. Peltason, *Federal Courts in the Political Process* (Garden City, N. Y.: Doubleday, 1955), p. 10.

[22] *Baker v. Carr*, 368 U. S. 804 (1961). An earlier case was *Gomillion v. Lightfoot*, 364 U. S. 339 (1960). The former was argued on Oct. 9, 1961, and was decided in favor of plaintiff, 6:2, on March 26, 1962, as 369 U. S. 186 (1962).

For		Urgent ☐

Date _____ Time _____

While You Were Out

M _____

Of _____

Phone _____

AREA CODE   NUMBER   EXTENSION

Telephoned ☐	Please Call ☐
Came To See You ☐	Will Call Again ☐
Returned Your Call ☐	Wants To See You ☐

Message _____

_____

_____

_____

_____

_____

_____

Signed _____

ADAMS BUSINESS FORMS
9711W

naught as recently as 1950, 1951, 1958, and 1959. The Court preferred to stand by its pronouncement in the 1950 case of *South v. Peters,*[23] that "a state's geographical distribution of electoral strength among its political subdivision" is a political question. The Court hewed to the same general philosophy and tactics in 1946 in a case concerning congressional districts in Illinois. Here, appellants contended that the Illinois law apportioning congressional districts was unconstitutional because the various districts were characterized by rank inequalities. For example, a Chicago congressional district had 914,053 inhabitants, whereas one in Southern Illinois comprised a mere 112,116. But in its decision in *Colegrove v. Green,*[24] the Supreme Court, with only seven justices participating, and these split many ways, nevertheless held that it could not intervene in such a political question, one that was up to the House of Representatives to determine and alleviate. If it did intervene, wrote Mr. Justice Frankfurter, it would be entering into a "political thicket," and that, anyway, it is "hostile to a democratic system to involve the judiciary in the politics of the people." Speaking also for Justices Douglas and Murphy, Mr. Justice Black dissented vigorously, contending that the State of Illinois's failure to redistrict was tantamount to "wilful legislative discrimination" and constituted a denial of the equal protection of the laws presumably guaranteed by the Fourteenth Amendment to the Constitution of the United States.

Another famous example of a political question case in a rather different area of government is *Luther v. Borden,*[25] which arose out of the Rhode Island Dorr Rebellion early in America's history. In brief, the facts of the case were such that the Supreme Court was confronted with the crucial decision as to which of two governments battling for legal supremacy in Rhode Island in 1842 was the legal one. It concluded that this was clearly a "political question" since the President of the United States, in exercising the power conferred upon him by Congress to send federal troops to aid states in suppressing insurrection, had indicated that he regarded the original—the "charter"—government as the lawful one of the two, and that this judgment was binding upon the Court.

If one accepts the concept of the political question at all, the

[23] 339 U. S. 276.   [24] 328 U. S. 549.   [25] 7 Howard 1 (1849).

Luther example is obviously a much more clear-cut one than those involving legislative apportionment. Yet what is a political question remains difficult to determine. However attractive in theory, the "political question" maxim is a treadmill; perhaps to a fatal degree its supporting logic is circular.

ELEVEN: In the event of a validly challenged statute the presumption of its constitutionality is always in its favor. As early as 1827, Mr. Justice Bushrod Washington wrote that:

> It is but a decent respect to the wisdom, integrity, and patriotism of the legislative body, by which any law is passed, to presume in favor of its validity, until its violation of the Constitution is proved beyond a reasonable doubt.[26]

Hence, as the history of the Court shows, if a legislative enactment can be construed to be in reasonable harmony with the Constitution, a majority of the Court will almost always do so. Obviously, the views of the justices have differed somewhat, often drastically, on the meaning of the word "reasonable." Thus, while there is today practically no judicial interference with legislation dealing with economic and social matters, the Court remains seriously divided on what constitutes "reasonable" legislative restrictions in the field of civil liberties, particularly under the First Amendment. There, generally speaking, a hard core of four members of the 1958–61 Warren bench, for example—the Chief Justice himself, Justices Black, Douglas, and Brennan—would brook little, if any, legislative encroachments, whereas an equally hard core of four—Justices Frankfurter, Clark, Harlan, and Whittaker—would exercise more or less judicial self-restraint, with Mr. Justice Stewart more often than not the swing-man.

In any event, the Court will not normally formulate a rule of constitutional law broader than is required by the precise facts to which it is to be applied. "The cardinal principle of statutory construction," wrote Mr. Chief Justice Hughes in a famous case,

> is to save and not to destroy. We have repeatedly held that as between two possible interpretations of a statute, by one of which it would be unconstitutional and the other valid, our

[26] *Ogden v. Saunders,* 12 Wheaton 213 (1827).

plain duty is to adopt that which will save the act. Even to avoid a serious doubt the rule is the same.[27]

On the other hand, Mr. Justice Stone—normally a firm adherent to the philosophy of presumption of constitutionality—implied an important exception to the general rule in his footnote in the otherwise rather unimportant *Carolene Products* case,[28] which became one of the most famous footnotes of all time! It was there that he stated that perhaps there might be occasion for departing from the normal presumption of constitutionality for legislation in cases *where the legislative action in question involved a restriction or curtailment of the ordinary political processes which could generally be expected to be employed to bring about the negation of undesirable legislation,* or *where it appeared to be within "a specific prohibition of the Constitution, such as those of the first ten amendments,* which are deemed equally specific when held to be embraced within the Fourteenth." [29]

TWELVE: In the exercise of what some commentators have been fond of styling "judicial parsimony," *if a case or controversy can be decided upon any other than constitutional grounds—such as by statutory construction, which constitutes the greatest single area of the Court's work, or if it can rest on an independent state ground—the Court will be eager to do so.* For it will not decide questions of a constitutional nature unless absolutely necessary to the decision of the case, and even then it will draw such a decision as narrowly as possible, ever being loath to formulate a rule of constitutional law broader than is clearly required by the precise facts to which it is to be applied. Nor will it anticipate a question of constitutional law in advance of the necessity of deciding it. Mr. Justice Frankfurter succinctly underscored the latter point in an edifying exchange with Thurman Arnold, who was acting as counsel for Dr. J. P. Peters, petitioner in the loyalty-security case of *Peters v. Hobby*.[30] Mr. Arnold pleaded with the Court that he would not like to win the case on the narrow procedural, statutory ground to which a majority of the members of the bench were evidently inclining. Responded Mr. Justice Frankfurter: "The ques-

[27] *N.L.R.B. v. Jones & Laughlin Steel Corporation,* 301 U. S. 1 (1937).
[28] *United States v. Carolene Products Co.,* 304 U. S. 144 (1938), at 152–3, fn. 4.
[29] Ibid. (Italics supplied.)   [30] 349 U. S. 311 (1955).

tion is not whether you want to win the case on that ground or not. This Court reaches constitutional issues last, not first." [31]

The loyalty-security field affords a host of pertinent illustrations of the Court's preference for a resort to statutory construction rather than to constitutional grounds. This delicate and emotion-laden area of public policy is tailor-made for such an approach, which preserves the statute while sometimes smoothing certain ragged edges. Thus the Court effects a gain, however moderate it may be, for individual civil rights, while retaining the generally popular and politically desirable law. To cite just two instances, this is precisely what the Court did in narrowing executive author-ity to dismiss government employees under the Summary Suspen-sion Act of 1950 by holding that the act did not authorize dismissal of employees holding "non-sensitive" positions; [32] and in limiting the power of the Secretary of State to withhold a passport from a citizen "for any substantive reason he may choose," holding that the Immigration and Nationality Act of 1952 did not authorize such sweeping discretionary powers. [33] In both instances, congres-sional reaction was to the effect that "we did *so* intend to authorize what you say we did not," but in the absence of the passage of any clarifying or amplifying amendments the two statutes stood as judicially construed. After all, statutory construction is an act of judgment; and, as Mr. Justice Holmes once observed succinctly, applies to cases "in which there is a fair contest between two readings."

THIRTEEN: The Court will not ordinarily impute illegal motives to the lawmakers. "So long as Congress acts in pursuance of its constitutional power," explained Mr. Justice Harlan in a much-debated decision upholding certain aspects of the investigative authority of the House Committee on Un-American Activities,[34] "the judiciary lacks authority to intervene *on the basis of the motives* which spurred the exercise of that power." And as early as 1810 Mr. Chief Justice Marshall had written that it "may well be doubted how far the validity of a law depends upon the motives

[31] As reported in 23 *U. S. Law Week* 265–6 (1955).
[32] *Cole v. Young,* 351 U. S. 536 (1956).
[33] *Kent and Briehl v. Dulles,* 357 U. S. 116 (1958).
[34] *Barenblatt v. United States,* 360 U. S. 109 (1959). (Italics supplied.)

of its framers." [35] Indeed, the Court is not supposed to consider *motives* at all; but, as Max Radin once put it, that concept is indeed a "transparent and absurd fiction" [36]—to which the decision in the *Child Labor Tax Case* of 1922, for example, bears eloquent witness.

To compound the problem, the Supreme Court *is* expected to, and very frequently does, take legislative *intent* or purpose into account—yet it is no easy task to separate motives and intent, and Mr. Justice Frankfurter, for one, has consistently refused to do so. "I only want to know what the words mean," wrote Mr. Justice Holmes. Still, "words are not crystals," and he found *policy* in those words.[37] The *Steel Seizure Case* [38] of 1952, in which seven separate opinions were written, provided a basis for an opinion for the Court only because a sufficient number of justices was able to agree on the single point that Congress, in enacting the Taft-Hartley Act, had deliberately intended that it *not* provide for presidential authority to seize struck plants. Here the intent of Congress proved to be the basis for the Court's judgment that the Chief Executive had usurped legislative power, with the justices, as is their custom, equating intent with legislative history.

This approach is sometimes styled "psychoanalyzing Congress" by some of the less reverent observers of the governmental scene, who have considerable—and perhaps well-grounded—doubt of the infallibility of the contention, frequently quoted by Mr. Justice Frankfurter, that "a page of history is worth a volume of logic." Yet whatever their merits otherwise, for this purpose at least the *Congressional Record* and the reports of the various committees of Congress are a constant and evidently fertile source of reference for the members of the Supreme Court.

FOURTEEN: If the Court does find that it must hold a law unconstitutional, it will usually try hard to confine the holding to that particular section of the statute which was successfully challenged on constitutional grounds—provided such a course of action is at

---

[35] *Fletcher v. Peck,* 6 Cranch 87.

[36] "Statutory Interpretation," 43 *Harvard Law Review* 863 (April 1930).

[37] See Felix Frankfurter, "Some Reflections on the Readings of Statutes," Sixth Annual Benjamin N. Cardozo Lecture before the Association of the Bar of the City of New York, March 8, 1947. (Reprinted in 47 *Columbia Law Review* 527–46.)   [38] *Youngstown Sheet and Tube Co. v. Sawyer,* 343 U. S. 579.

all feasible. It would not be feasible, of course, if the section at issue constitutes the veritable heart of the legislation. This practice of sectionalized declarations of unconstitutionality is known as *separability,* for which Congress now customarily, and quite specifically, provides in its statutes. A typical separability clause reads:

> If any provision of this Act is declared unconstitutional or the applicability thereof to any person or circumstances is held invalid, the validity of the remainder of the Act and the applicability of such provisions to other persons and circumstances shall not be affected thereby.[39]

This not only serves to save those sections not affected by the Court's particular decision, but it may also act to preserve the law's entire structure for a test involving different litigants.

The series of decisions declaring portions of the Uniform Code of Military Justice Act of 1950 unconstitutional are cases in point; [40] certain powers delegated to the armed services under it are no longer valid, but the balance of the act stands and is enforced. On the other hand, although initially it was merely the "hot oil" provisions of the National Industrial Recovery Act of 1933—standing apart from those provisions of the act dealing with codes of fair competition—that fell as an unconstitutional delegation of legislative power in January 1935,[41] four months later the codes, too, and with them the entire structure of the act, fell on similar grounds.[42]

FIFTEEN: A legislative enactment—or an executive action—may be unwise, unjust, unfair, undemocratic, injudicious, ". . . if you like . . . even tyrannical," [43] or simply stupid, but still be constitutional in the eyes of the Court. Much deference is thus paid to the legislature and justly so under the American system of separation of powers and division of powers. In the clipped language

---

[39] Taken from the *Taft-Hartley Act of 1947.*
[40] Cf. *United States ex rel Toth v. Quarles,* 350 U. S. 11 (1955) and *Reid v. Covert* 354 U. S. 1 (1957), among others.
[41] *Panama Refining Co. v. Ryan,* 293 U. S. 388.
[42] *Schechter v. United States,* 295 U. S. 495.
[43] Mr. Justice Holmes, dissenting in *Lochner v. United States,* 198 U. S. 45 (1905).

of a Holmes opinion: "We fully understand . . . the powerful argument that can be made against the wisdom of this legislation, but on that point we have no concern." [44] Mr. Justice Holmes once stated this constitutional and judicial philosophy in typically colorful fashion to the then 61-year-old Mr. Justice Stone:

> Young man, about 75 years ago I learned that I was not God. And so, when the people . . . want to do something I can't find anything in the Constitution expressly forbidding them to do, I say, whether I like it or not, "Goddamit, let 'em do it." [45]

The man who was appointed to the Holmes seat on the Court after Mr. Justice Cardozo's death in 1938, Mr. Justice Frankfurter, continued to champion that philosophy of judicial self-restraint eloquently, repeatedly, and consistently. Thus, he dissented vigorously from the majority's declaration of unconstitutionality of a section of the Immigration and Nationality Act of 1940 in *Trop v. Dulles:*

> It is not easy to stand aloof and allow want of wisdom to prevail, to disregard one's own strongly held view of what is wise in the conduct of affairs. But it is not the business of this Court to pronounce policy. It must observe a fastidious regard for limitations on its own power, and this precludes the Court's giving effect to its own notions of what is wise or politic. That self-restraint is of the essence in the observation of the judicial oath, for the Constitution has not authorized the justices to sit in judgment on the wisdom of what Congress and the Executive Branch do. . .[46]

But once again much, if not all, depends upon how the justices see the line between self-restraint, which they indubitably all recognize as an essential element in the judicial process, and *ultra vires* legislative and executive actions. If, in drawing this line, some justices, on some issues, are prone to address themselves more to the judicial heart than the judicial mind, who is to say where and

[44] *Noble State Bank v. Haskell,* 219 U. S. 575 (1910).
[45] As quoted by Chârles P. Curtis in his *Lions Under the Throne* (Boston: Houghton Mifflin Co., 1947), p. 281.
[46] 356 U. S. 86 (1958).

how the Founding Fathers of the Constitution of the United States would today distinguish between that document's heart and mind? They too were men, just as judges are men, "not disembodied spirits," in Mr. Justice Frankfurter's words; they are men who "respond to human situations . . . [who] do not reside in a vacuum."

SIXTEEN: The Supreme Court has reiterated time and again that *it is not designed to serve as a check against inept, unwise, emotional, unrepresentative legislators.* Mr. Chief Justice Waite put it well when he wrote in 1876 that for *"protection against abuses by legislatures the people must resort to the polls not the courts."* [47] Some 80 years later, Mr. Justice Douglas reiterated this point of view forcefully: "Congress acting within its constitutional powers, has the final say on policy issues. If it acts unwisely the electorate can make a change." [48] This fundamental truth lies at the very core of the democratic process—which enables the people and their representatives at once to rise to soaring heights of wisdom and magnanimity and to descend to the depths of folly and pettiness. Yet that process, under law, proscribes *unconstitutional* action.

THE BULWARK

The Supreme Court of the United States of America—which Woodrow Wilson viewed as "the balance wheel of our whole constitutional system . . . a vehicle of the Nation's life . . ." [49]—may be steeped in controversy; it may not always have exercised all of its power, or exercised it wisely when it did; it may on occasion have gone beyond that presumed power; it may have deliberately avoided issues that might have proved to be potentially troublesome; it may not always have been able to make its decisions "stick"; and there may well be considerable room for improvement. No institution of government can be devised by human beings that will be satisfactory to all people at all times.

[47] *Munn v. Illinois,* 94 U. S. 113. (Italics supplied.)
[48] *Railway Employees' Department v. Hansen,* 351 U. S. 225 (1956).
[49] *Constitutional Government in the United States* (New York: Columbia University Press, 1907), p. 142.

Paraphrasing Professor Freund, the question is not whether the Court can do everything, but whether it can do something. It can escape neither controversy nor criticism—nor should it.

Yet, when all is said and done, the Court, at the head of the United States judiciary, is not only the most fascinating, the most influential, and the most powerful judicial body in the world, it is also the "living voice of [the] Constitution," as Lord Bryce, who knew America well indeed, once phrased it. As such it is both arbiter and educator and, in essence, represents the sole solution short of anarchy under the American system of government as we know it. And, as Alexander Meiklejohn has observed, no other institution "is more deeply decisive in its effect upon our understanding of ourselves and our government."

Beyond that, moreover, the Supreme Court is the chief protector of the Constitution, of its great system of balances, and of the people's liberties. It may have retreated, even yielded to pressures now and then, but without its viligance our liberties would scarcely have survived. Within the limits of procedure and deference to the presumption of constitutionality of legislation, the Court is the natural forum in our society for the individual and for the small group. It must thus be prepared to say "no" to the government— a role which Madison, the father of the Bill of Rights, hoped fervently it would always exercise. There are many citizens— indeed most, once they have given the problem the careful thought it merits—who will feel far more secure in the knowledge that *that* guardianship is generally characterized by common sense and by a willingness to stand up and be counted, than if it were primarily exercised by the far more easily pressured, more impulsive, and more emotion-charged legislative or executive branches. Far too easily do these two yield to the politically expedient and the popular! The Court is neither engaged nor interested in a popularity contest—should that time ever arrive the supreme judicial tribunal as we now know it will have lost its meaning.

Even if a transfer of that guardianship to other institutions of government were theoretically desirable, which few thoughtful citizens believe, it would be politically impossible. "Do we desire constitutional questions," asked Charles Evans Hughes, then not on the bench, in his fine book on the Court, ". . . to be determined by political assemblies and partisan division?" [50] The response must be a ringing "no!" In the 1955 Godkin Lectures, which he delivered at Harvard University, just before his death, Mr. Justice Jackson expressed this conviction eloquently and ably:

> The people have seemed to feel that the Supreme Court, whatever its defects, is still the most detached, dispassionate, and trustworthy custodian that our system affords for the translation of abstract into concrete constitutional commands.[51]

And we may well agree with Thomas Reed Powell that the logic of American constitutional law is the common sense of the Supreme Court. As a commentary on the point, that distinguished observer of Court and Constitution reported a striking incident that took place in a debate on the floor of the United States Senate after the turn of the century between Senators Spooner of Wisconsin and Tillman of South Carolina. At one juncture of the proceedings, Tillman exclaimed: "I am tired of hearing what the Supreme Court says. What I want to get at is the common sense of the matter." Rejoined Senator Spooner: "I too am seeking the common sense of the matter. But, as for me, I prefer the common sense of the Supreme Court of the United States to that of the Senator from South Carolina." [52]

In the long run common sense has always served the Supreme Court of the United States well in its ceaseless striving to maintain the blend of change and continuity which is the *sine qua non* for a desirable stability in the governmental process of a democracy. In that role it will live in history.

[50] *The Supreme Court of the United States* (New York: Columbia University Press, 1928), p. 236.

[51] Robert H. Jackson, op. cit. p. 23.

[52] "The Logic and Rhetoric of Constitutional Law," 15 *Journal of Philosophy, Psychology, and Scientific Method,* 656 (1918).

SELECTED BIBLIOGRAPHY

I GENERAL WORKS

Abraham, H. J., *Courts and Judges: An Introduction to the Judicial Process* (Oxford, 1959).

Acheson, P. C., *The Supreme Court: America's Judicial Heritage* (Dodd, Mead, 1961).

Administrative Office of the U.S. Courts, *Annual Reports* (U.S. Gov't. Printing Office, 1949 ff.)

Alfange, D., *The Supreme Court and the National Will* (Doubleday, 1937).

Alloway, C. C., *United States Constitutional Law, 1850–1875* (Oceana, 1958).

Alsop, J. and Catledge, T., *The 168 Days* (Doubleday, 1938).

Anderson, W., *The Nation and the States, Rivals or Partners?* (U. of Minnesota, 1955).

Andrews, W. G. (Ed.), *Constitutions and Constitutionalism* (Van Nostrand, 1961).

Annual Report(s) of the Director of the Administrative Office of the U.S. Courts.

Association of American Law Schools, *Selected Essays in Constitutional Law* (1938).

Association of the Bar of the City of New York, *Conflict of Interest and Federal Service* (Harvard, 1960).

Auerbach, C. A., Garrison, L. K., Hurst, W., Mermin, S., *The Legal Process*, rev. ed. (Chandler, 1961).

Aumann, F. R., *The Changing American Legal System* (Ohio State U., 1940).

———, *The Instrumentalities of Justice: Their Forms, Functions and Limitations* (Ohio State U., 1956).

Aycock, W. B. and Wurfel, B. W., *Military Law Under the Uniform Code of Military Justice* (U. of N. Carolina, 1955).

Baldwin, H., *A General View of the Origin and Nature of the Constitution and Government of the United States* (Clark, 1837).

Baldwin, S. E., *The American Judiciary* (Century, 1905).

Bancroft, G., *History of the Formation of the Constitution of the United States of America* (Appleton, 1903).

Barron, W. W. and Holtzoff, A., *Federal Practice and Procedure* (1950) (Thompson, 1950–58).

Bates, E. S., *The Story of the Supreme Court* (Bobbs-Merrill, 1936).

Bauer, E. K., *Commentaries on the Constitution 1790–1860* (Columbia, 1952).

Beard, C. A., *The Supreme Court and the Constitution*, rev. ed. (Prentice-Hall, 1962).

———, *An Economic Interpretation of the Constitution of the United States* (Macmillan, 1913).

———, *The Republic* (Viking, 1943).

Beck, J. M., *The Constitution of the U.S.* (Doran, 1922).

Belli, M. M., *Ready for the Plaintiff* (Holt, 1956).

Benson, G. C. S., *The New Centralization* (Rinehart, 1941).

Binkley, W. E., *President and Congress* (Knopf, 1947).

Black, C. L. Jr., *The People and the Court: Judicial Review in a Democracy* (Macmillan, 1960).

Blaustein, A. D. and Porter, C. O., *The American Lawyer* (Chicago, 1954).

Blix, H., *Treaty-Making Power* (Praeger, 1959).

Bodenheimer, E., *Jurisprudence* (McGraw-Hill, 1947).

Borchard, E. M., *Declaratory Judgments* (Banks-Baldwin, 1941).

Botein, B., *Trial Judge* (Simon & Schuster, 1952).

————, *The Prosecutor* (Simon & Schuster, 1956).

Boudin, L. B., *Government by Judiciary* (Goodwin, 1932).

Bowen, C. D., *The Lion and the Throne: The Life and Times of Sir Edward Coke, 1552–1634* (Little, Brown, 1957).

Braden, G. D., *The Search for Objectivity in Constitutional Law* (*Yale Law Journal*, 1948).

Brandeis, L. D., *Business—A Profession* (Small, 1933).

Brant, I., *Storm Over the Constitution* (Bobbs-Merrill, 1936).

————, *James Madison: Father of the Constitution, 1787–1800* (Bobbs-Merrill, 1950).

Brennan, W. J., *Modernizing the Courts* (Inst. of Jud. Adm., 1957).

Brown, B. (Ed.), *The Natural Law Reader* (Oceana, 1959).

Brown, C. G., *You May Take the Witness* (U. of Texas, 1955).

Brown, R. E., *Charles Beard and the Constitution: A Critical Analysis of an Economic Interpretation of the Constitution* (Princeton, 1956).

Bruce, A. A., *The American Judge* (Macmillan, 1924).

Bunn, C. W., *A Brief Survey of the Jurisdiction and Practice of the Courts of the United States,* rev. ed. (West, 1949).

Burgess, J. W., *Political Science and Comparative Constitutional Law* (Ginn, 1890).

————, *Recent Changes in American Constitutional Theory* (Columbia, 1923).

Burlingame, R., *The American Conscience* (Knopf, 1957).

Butler, C. H., *A Century at the Bar of the Supreme Court* (Putnam, 1942).

Byrd, E. M., Jr., *Treaties and Executive Agreements in the U.S.: Their Separate Roles and Limitations* (Nijhoff, 1960).

Cahill, F. V., *Judicial Legislation: A Study in American Legal Theory* (Ronald, 1952).

———— and Steamer, R. J., *The Constitution: Cases and Comments* (Ronald, 1959).

Cahn, E. (Ed.), *The Sense of Injustice* (New York U., 1951).

————, *Supreme Court and Supreme Law* (Indiana U., 1954).

————, *The Moral Decision: Right and Wrong in the Light of American Law,* 2nd ed. (Indiana U., 1959).

Calhoun, J. C., *A Disquisition on Government* (Poli. Sci. Classics, 1947).

Callender, C. N., *American Courts: Their Organization and Procedure* (McGraw-Hill, 1927).

Callison, I. P., *Courts of Injustice* (Twayne, 1956).

Cardozo, B. N., *The Nature of the Judicial Process* (Yale, 1921).

————, *The Growth of the Law* (Yale, 1924).

————, *The Paradoxes of Legal Science* (Columbia, 1928).

————, *Law and Literature and Other Essays* (Harcourt Brace, 1931).

Carpenter, W. S., *Judicial Tenure in the United States* (Yale, 1918).

————, *Foundations of Modern Jurisprudence* (Appleton, 1958).

Carr, R. K., *Democracy and the Supreme Court* (U. of Oklahoma, 1936).

———, *The Supreme Court and Judicial Review* (Farrar & Rinehart, 1942).

Carson, H. L., *The History of the Supreme Court of the United States* (Yuber, 1891).

Chambers, M. M., *Colleges and the Courts* (Columbia, 1952).

Clark, J. P., *The Rise of a New Federalism* (Columbia, 1938).

Cohen, L. K. (Ed.), *The Legal Conscience: Selected Papers of Felix S. Cohen* (Yale, 1960).

Cohen, M. R., *Reason and Nature* (Harcourt, Brace, 1931).

———, *Law and Social Order* (Harcourt, Brace, 1933).

Collyer, R. (Comp.), *In Defense of the Constitution: Excerpts from Addresses and Opinions of Chief Justices of the United States* (Washington, 1935).

Commager, H. S., *The American Mind* (Yale, 1950).

Cooley, R. M., *Constitutional Limitations* (Putnam, 1868).

Cooper, F. E., *Living and Law* (Bobbs-Merrill, 1958).

Cope, A. H. and Krinsky, F., *Franklin D. Roosevelt and the Supreme Court* (Heath, 1952).

Corwin, E. S., *The Doctrine of Judicial Review* (Princeton, 1914).

———, *The Higher Law Background of American Constitutional Law* (Cornell, 1929).

———, *The Twlight of the Supreme Court: A History of Our Constitutional Theory* (Yale, 1934).

———, *The Commerce Power versus States Rights* (Princeton, 1936).

———, *Court Over Constitution: A Study of Judicial Review as an Instrument of Popular Government* (Princeton, 1938).

———, *Constitutional Revolution, Ltd.* (Claremont, 1941).

———, *The Constitution and World Organization* (Princeton, 1944).

———, *Total War and the Constitution* (Knopf, 1947).

———, *Our Constitutional Revolution and How to Round It Out* (Phila. Brandeis Lawyer Society, 1951).

———, *A Constitution of Powers in a Secular State* (U. of Virginia, 1951).

——— (Ed.), *Constitution of the United States: Analysis and Interpretation* (U.S. Gov't. Printing Office, 1953).

———, *Our Expendable Constitution* (U. of Illinois, 1955).

———, *The President: Office and Powers*, 4th ed. (New York U., 1957).

———, *The Constitution and What It Means Today*, 12th rev. ed (Princeton, 1958).

———, and J. W. Peltason, *Understanding the Constitution*, rev. ed. (Holt, 1958).

Cotter, C. P. and Smith, J. M., *Powers of the President During National Crises* (Public Affairs, 1959).

Cowan, T. (Ed.), *The American Jurisprudence Reader* (Oceana, 1955)

Coxe, B., *Judicial Power and Unconstitutional Legislation* (Kay, 1893).

Coy, H., *The First Book of the Supreme Court* (Watts, 1958).

Cozzens, J. G., *The Just and the Unjust* (Harcourt, Brace, 1942).

Crosskey, W. W., *Politics and the Constitution in the History of the United States* (U. of Chicago, 1953).

Cummings, H. S. and McFarland, C., *Federal Justice* (Macmillan, 1937).

Curtis, C. P., *Lions Under the Throne* (Houghton Mifflin, 1947).

———, *The Bacon Lectures on the Constitution of the U.S., 1940–1950* (Boston U., 1953).

———, *It's Your Law* (Harvard, 1954).

———, *Law as Large as Life* (Simon & Schuster, 1959).

Cushman, R. E., *The Role of the Supreme Court in a Democratic Nation* (Public Affairs Comm., 1938).

————, *The Supreme Court and the Constitution* (Public Affairs Comm., 1940).

————, *The Independent Regulatory Commissions* (Oxford, 1941).

————, *What's Happening to Our Constitution?* (Public Affairs Comm., 1942).

————, *Leading Constitutional Decisions*, 12th ed. (Appleton-Century-Crofts, 1963).

————, and Cushman R. F., *Cases in Constitutional Law* (Appleton-Century-Crofts, 1963).

Davenport, W. H. (Ed.), *Voices in Court* (Macmillan, 1958).

Davis, H. A., *The Judicial Veto* (*Houghton, 1913*).

Davis, J. W., *Selecting Judges* (Andrews, 1933).

Dawson, J. P., *A History of Lay Judges* (Harvard, 1960).

Denning, A., *The Road to Justice* (Stevens (London), 1955).

Desmond, C. S., *Through the Courtroom Window* (West, 1959).

Dietze, G., *The Federalist: A Classic on Federalism and Free Government* (Johns Hopkins, 1960).

Dilliard, I. (Ed.), *The Spirit of Liberty: Papers and Addresses of Learned Hand* (Knopf, 1959).

Dodd, W. F., *Cases and Materials on Constitutional Law* (West, 1954).

Donavan, J. W., *Modern Jury Trials* (Jennings, 1929).

Dougherty, J. W., *The Power of the Federal Judiciary Over Legislation* (Putnam, 1912.

Douglas, W. O., *Being an American* (Way, 1948).

————, *Stare Decises* (Assoc. of Bar of City of N.Y., 1949).

————, *We, the Judges* (Doubleday, 1956).

Dowling, N. T., *Cases on Constitutional Law*, 6th ed. (Foundation Pr., 1959).

————, and Edward, R. A., *American Constitutional Law* (Foundation Pr., 1954).

Dunne, G. T., *Monetary Decisions of the Supreme Court* (Rutgers, 1960).

Edmunds, P. D., *Law and Civilization* (Public Affairs Pr., 1959).

Edwards, M. O. and Decker, C. L., *The Serviceman and the Law* (Stackpole, 1951).

Ehrlich, E., *Fundamental Principles of the Sociology of Law* (Harvard, 1936).

Einaudi, M., *The Physiocratic Doctrine of Judicial Control* (Harvard, 1938).

Elliot, J. (Ed.), *The Debates in the Several State Conventions on the Adoption of the Federal Constitution*, 2nd ed. (Lippincott, 1854).

Elliot, S. D., *Improving Our Courts* (Oceana, 1959).

Evans, L. B., *Cases on American Constitutional Law*, 6th ed. (Callaghan, 1952).

Fainsod, M. and Gordon L., *Government and the American Economy* (Norton. 1948).

Fairman, C., *American Constitutional Decisions* (Holt, 1950).

————, *The Beacon Lectures on the Constitution of the United States, 1940–1950* (Boston U., 1953).

Farrand, M., *The Records of the Federal Convention of 1787* (Yale, 1911).

————, *The Framing of the Constitution of the U.S.* (Yale, 1913).

Fennell, W. G., *The "Reconstructed Court"* (New York U., 1942).

Fenwick, C. G., *Evans Cases on Constitutional Law*, 7th. ed. (Callaghan, 1957).

Flack, H. B., *The Adoption of the Fourteenth Amendment* (Johns Hopkins, 1908).

Fordham, E. W., *Notable Cross-Examinations* (Macmillan, 1957).

Francis, P., *How To Serve on a Jury* (Oceana, 1953).

Frank, J. F., *If Men Were Angels* (Harper, 1942).

———, *Law and the Modern Mind* (Brentano's, 1949).

———, *Courts on Trial: Myth and Reality in American Justice* (Princeton, 1950).

——— and Frank, B., *Not Guilty* (Doubleday, 1957).

Frank, J. P., *Cases and Materials on Constitutional Law,* rev. ed (McGraw-Hill, 1952).

———, *Marble Palace: The Supreme Court in American Life* (Knopf, 1958).

Frank, M. M., *The Diary of a D. A.* (Holt, Rinehart & Winston, 1960).

Frankfurter, F., *The Public and Its Government* (Oxford, 1930).

———, *The Labor Injunction* (with Nathan Greene) (Macmillan, 1930).

———, *The Commerce Clause Under Marshall, Taney and Waite* (U. of N. Carolina, 1937).

———, *Law and Politics* (Harcourt, Brace, 1939).

———, *Of Law and Men: Papers and Addresses* (edited by Philip Elman) (Harcourt, Brace, 1956).

——— and Landis, J. M., *The Business of the Supreme Court* (Macmillan, 1928).

Freund, E., *The Police Power, Public Policy, and Constitutional Rights* (Callaghan, 1904).

Freund, P. A., *On Understanding the Supreme Court* (Little, Brown, 1949).

———, et al., *Constitutional Law* (Little, Brown, 1954).

———, *The Supreme Court of the United States: Its Business, Purposes, and Performance* (Meridian, 1961).

Friedmann, W., *Law in a Changing Society* (U. of California, 1959).

Friedrich, C. J., *The Philosophy of Law in Historical Perspective* (U. of Chicago, 1958).

Fuess, C. M., *Daniel Webster* (Little, Brown, 1930).

Garland, A. H., *Experience in the United States Supreme Court* (Johnson, Phila., 1898).

Gavit, B. C., *The Commerce Clause of the U.S. Constitution* (Principia, 1956).

Gellhorn, W., *Federal Administrative Proceedings* (Johns Hopkins, 1941).

Gierke, O. von, *Natural Law and the Theory of Society* (Cambridge U., 1934).

Gilbert, W. C. (Comp.), *Provisions of Federal Law Held Unconstitutional by the Supreme Court of the United States* (U.S. Gov't. Printing Office, 1936).

Goodhart, A. L., *Five Jewish Lawyers of the Common Law* (Oxford, 1949).

Goodhow, F. J., *Social Reform and the Constitution* (Macmillan, 1911).

Gordon, R. M., *Nine Men Against America* (Devin-Adair, 1958).

Green, L., *Judge and Jury* (Vernon Law Book Co., 1930).

Greenspan, M., *The Modern Law of Land Warfare* (Berkeley, 1959).

Haines, C. G., *A Government of Laws or a Government of Men* (UCLA, 1929).

———, *The Revival of Natural Law Concepts* (Harvard, 1930).

———, *The Role of the Supreme Court in American Government and Politics, 1789–1835* (UCLA, 1944).

——— and Sherwood, F. H., *The Role of the Supreme Court in American Government and Politics, 1835–1864* (Berkeley, 1957).

———, *The American Doctrine of Judicial Supremacy,* 2nd ed., rev. and enl. (Berkeley, 1959).

Hall, J., *Readings in Jurisprudence* (Bobbs-Merrill, 1938).

Hamilton, Jay, and Madison, *The Federalist Papers* (Random House, 1792).

Hamilton, W. H. and Adair, D., *The Power to Govern: The Constitution Then and Now* (Norton, 1937).

334

Harding, A. L. (Ed.), *The Administration of Justice in Retrospect* (Southern Methodist U., 1957).

Harris, J. P., *The Advice and Consent of the Senate: A Study of the Confirmation of Appointment by the United States Senate* (Berkeley, 1953).

Harris, R. J., *The Judicial Power of the United States* (La. State Univ., 1940).

Hart, H. M. Jr. and Wechsler, H., *The Federal Court and the Federal System* (Foundation Pr., 1953).

——, *The Judicial Code and Rules of Procedure in the Federal Courts* (Foundation Pr. 1954).

Hartman, P. J., *State Taxation of Interstate Commerce* (Dennis, 1953).

Haynes, E., *The Selection and Tenure of Judges* (Nat'l. Conf. of Judicial Councils, 1944).

Hazlitt, H., *A New Constitution Now* (McGraw-Hill, 1942).

Heller, F. H., *Introduction to American Constitutional Law* (Harper, 1952).

Henderson, G. C., *The Position of Foreign Corporations in American Constitutional Law* (Harvard, 1918).

Hendrick, B. J., *Bulwark of the Republic* (Little, Brown, 1939).

Henry, J. M., *Nine Above the Law: Our Supreme Court* (Lewis, 1936).

Henson, R. D. (Ed.), *Landmarks of Law: Highlights of Legal Opinion from 1890 to the Present* (Harper, 1960).

Hine, R. L., *Confessions of an Un-Common Attorney* (Macmillan, 1945).

Hockett, H. C., *The Constitutional History of the United States* (Macmillan, 1939).

Holcombe, A. N., *Our More Perfect Union: From 18th Century Principles to 20th Century Practice* (Harvard, 1950).

Holmes, O. W., *The Common Law* (Little, Brown, 1881).

Horton, J. T., *James Kent: A Study in Conservatism* (Appleton, Century, 1939).

Horwill, H. W., *The Usages of the American Constitution* (Oxford, 1925).

Hughes, C. E., *The Supreme Court of the United States* (Columbia, 1928).

Hunt, C. and Scott, J. B. (Eds.), *The Debates in the Federal Convention of 1787* (Oxford, 1920).

Hurst, J. W., *The Growth of American Law: The Lawmakers* (Little, Brown, 1950).

Jackson, R. H., *The Struggle for Judicial Supremacy* (Knopf, 1941).

——, *Full Faith and Credit: The Lawyer's Clause in the Constitution* (Columbia U., 1945).

——, *The Supreme Court in the American System of Government* (Harvard, 1955).

Jacobs, C. E., *Law Writers and the Courts* (Berkeley, 1954).

Jaffe, L. and Nathanson N., *Administrative Law: Cases and Materials* (Little, Brown, 1961).

Jahr, A. D., *The Law of Eminent Domain—Valuation and Procedure* (C. Boardman, 1953).

James, J. B., *The Framing of the Fourteenth Amendment* (U. of Illinois, 1956).

Journal of Public Law (Symposium), "Policy-Making in a Democracy: The Role of the United States Supreme Court" (1957).

Kallenbach, J. E., *Federal Cooperation with the States under the Commerce Clause* (U. of Michigan, 1942).

Karlen D., *Primer of Procedure* (Campus Park Co., 1950).

Kauper, P. G., *Frontiers of Constitutional Liberty* (U. of Michigan, 1956).

Kelly, A. H. and Harbison, W., *The American Constitution—Its Origin and Development,* rev. ed (Norton, 1955).

Kelsen, H., *General Theory of Law and State* (Harvard, 1945).

——, *What Is Justice?* (Berkeley, 1957).

Kendrick, B. J., *Journal of the Joint Committee of Fifteen on Reconstruction* (Scribner, 1914).

Kent, J., *Commentaries on American Law*, 5th ed. (Little, Brown, 1830).

Kilpatrick, J. J., *The Sovereign States* (Regnery, 1957).

Knox, J. C., *A Judge Comes of Age* (Scribner's, 1940).

Koenig, L. W., *The President and the Crises: Powers of the Office from the Invasion of Poland to Pearl Harbour* (Kings Crown, 1944).

Kurland, P. (Ed.), *The Supreme Court Review* (U. of Chicago, 1960 ff).

Landis, J. M., *The Administrative Process* (Yale, 1938).

Laski, H. J., *The American Democracy* (Viking, 1948).

Laurent, F. W., *The Business of a Trial Court* (U. of Wisconsin, 1959).

Lawson, J. F., *The General Welfare Clause* (The Author, 1934).

Leach, R. H. and Sugg, R. S. Jr., *The Administration of Interstate Compacts* (Louisiana State U., 1959).

Lerner, M., *The Supreme Court and American Capitalism* (*Yale Law Journal*, 1933).

Levy, B. H., *Our Constitution: Tool or Testament* (Ryerson, 1941).

Levy, L. W., *The Law of the Commonwealth and Chief Justice Shaw* (Harvard, 1957).

Lewinson, J. L., *Limiting Judicial Review* (Parker, Stone & Baird, 1937).

Lewis, W. D. (Ed.), *Great American Lawyers* (Winston, 1907).

Llewellyn, K. N., *The Bramble Bush: On Our Law and Its Study* (Oceana, 1957).

——, *The Common Law Tradition: Deciding Appeals* (Little, Brown, 1960).

——, *Essays in Jurisprudence* (Chicago, 1962).

Lloyd, D. (Ed.), *Introduction to Jurisprudence* (Praeger, 1960).

Loewenstein, K., *Political Power and the Governmental Process*, Ch. VIII (U. of Chicago, 1956).

London, E., *The World of Law* (Simon & Schuster, 1960).

Lord Macmillan, *Law and Other Things* (Cambridge U., 1937).

Lummus, H. T., *The Trial Judge* (Foundation, 1937).

Mahany, M. M., *Commerce Clause Tax Problems* (Wilkinson, 1940).

Maine, Sir H., *Ancient Law* (Murray, 1917).

Mason, A. T., *The Supreme Court: Instrument of Power or of Revealed Truth, 1930–1937* (Boston U., 1953).

——, *The Supreme Court from Taft to Warren* (Louisiana St. U., 1958).

—— and Beaney, W. M., *The Supreme Court in a Free Society* (Prentice-Hall, 1959).

—— and Beaney, W. M., *American Constitutional Law: Introductory Essays and Selected Cases*, 3rd ed. (Prentice-Hall, 1959).

—— and Leach, R. H., *In Quest of Freedom: American Political Thought and Practice* (Prentice-Hall, 1959).

Mathews, J. M., *The American Constitutional System* (McGraw-Hill, 1940).

Maverick, M., *In Blood and Ink* (Modern Age, 1939).

Maxwell, J. A., *Fiscal Impact of Federalism in the United States* (Harvard, 1946).

May, E. R. (Ed.), *The Ultimate Decision: The President as Commander in Chief* (Braziller, 1960).

Mayers, L., *The American Legal System* (Harper, 1955).

McBain, H. L., *The Living Constitution* (Macmillan, 1927).

McCloskey, R. G., *Essays in Constitutional Law* (Knopf, 1957).

——, *American Conservatism in the Age of Enterprise* (Harvard, 1957).

————, *The American Supreme Court* (U. of Chicago, 1960).

McClure, W., *International Executive Agreements* (Columbia, 1941).

McCollum, V., *One Woman's Fight*, rev. ed (Beacon, 1961).

McConnell, G., *The President Seizes the Steel Mills* (U. of Alabama, 1960).

McCormick, C. T., *Handbook of the Law of Evidence* (West, 1954).

McCune, W., *The Nine Young Men* (Harper, 1947).

McDonald, F., *We the People: The Economic Origins of the Constitution* (U. of Chicago, 1958).

McFarland, C., *Judicial Control of the F. T. C. and the I. C. C.* (Harvard, 1933).

McHargue, D., *Appointments to the Supreme Court* (Unpublished Ph.D. Dissertation UCLA, 1949).

McIlwain, C. H., *The American Revolution: A Constitutional Interpretation* (Macmillan, 1928).

————, *Constitutionalism and the Changing World* (Macmillan, 1939).

————, *Constitutionalism, Ancient and Modern*, rev. ed. (Cornell, 1958).

McKay, R. B. (Ed.), *The American Constitutional Law Reader* (Oceana, 1958).

McLaughlin, A. C., *The Courts, The Constitution and Parties* (U. of Chicago, 1912).

————, *A Constitutional History of the United States* (Appleton-Century, 1935).

McRuer, J. C., *The Evolution of the Judicial Process* (Clarke, Irwin, 1957).

McWhinney, E., *Judicial Review in the English-Speaking World*, 2nd ed. (U. of Toronto, 1961).

Meigs, W. M., The *Relation of the Judiciary to the Constitution* (Neale, 1919).

Mendelson, W., *The Constitution and the Supreme Court* (Dodd, Mead, 1959).

————, *Capitalism, Democracy, and the Supreme Court* (Appleton-Century-Crofts, 1960).

Merriam, C. E., *The Written Constitution and the Unwritten Attitude* (R. R. Smith, 1931).

Miller, J. C., *Origins of the American Revolution* (Little, Brown, 1943).

Millis, W., *The Constitution and the Common Defense* (Fund for the Republic, 1959).

Moore, B. F., *The Supreme Court and Unconstitutional Legislation* (Columbia, 1913).

Moreland, C. C., *Equal Justice Under Law* (Oceana, 1957).

Morris, C. (Ed.), *The Great Legal Philosophers; Selected Readings in Jurisprudence* (U. of Penna., 1959).

Munro, W. B., *The Makers of the Unwritten Constitution* (Macmillan, 1930).

Munsterberg, H., *On the Witness Stand* (Boardman, 1923).

Murphy, W. F. and Pritchett, C. H. (Eds.), *Courts, Judges, and Politics* (Random House, 1961).

Musmanno, M. M., *Verdict* (Doubleday, 1958).

Meyers G., *History of the Supreme Court of the United States*, (Kerr, 1912).

Northrup, F. C. S., *Complexity of Legal and Ethical Experience* (Little, 1959).

Notre Dame Lawyer (Symposium) "The Role of the Supreme Court in the American Constitutional System" (Notre Dame Law School, 1959).

Oceana Publications, Inc. (Eds.), The Legal Almanac Series (1955 ff.).

Orfield, L. B. *The Amending of the Federal Constitution* (Callaghan, 1942).

Padover, S. K., *The Living U.S. Constitution* (New Amer. Library, 1953).

Paton, G. W., *A Textbook of Jurisprudence* (Clarendon, 1951).

Patterson, C. P., *Constitutional Principles of Thomas Jefferson* (U. of Texas, 1953).

Paul, J., *The Legal Realism of Jerome N. Frank: A Study of Fact-Scepticism and the Judicial Process* (Nijhoff, 1959).

Pearson, D. and Allen, R. S., *The Nine Old Men* (Doubleday, 1936).

Peltason, J. W., *Federal Courts in the Political Process* (Doubleday, 1955).

Pekelis, A. H., *Law and Social Action* (Cornell, 1950).

Pennock, J. R., *Administration and the Rule of Law* (Rinehart, 1941).

Petrazycki, L. J., *Law and Morality* (Harvard, 1955).

Pollock, Sir F., *A First Book in Jurisprudence*, 4th ed. (Macmillan, 1918).

———, *Essays in the Law* (Macmillan, 1922).

Post, C. G., *The Supreme Court and Political Questions* (Johns Hopkins, 1936).

Pound, R., *Interpretations of Legal History* (Macmillan, 1923).

———, *Law and Morals* (U. of North Carolina, 1924).

———, *The Spirit of the Common Law* (Marshall Jones, 1931).

———, *The Future of the Common Law* (Harvard, 1937).

———, *The Formative Era of American Law* (Little, Brown, 1938).

———, *Organization of Courts* (Little, Brown, 1940).

———, *Contemporary Juristic Theory* (Claremont, 1940).

———, *Appellate Procedure in Civil Cases* (Little, Brown, 1941).

———, McIlwain, C. H., and Nichol, R. F., *Federalism as a Democratic Process* (Rutgers, 1942).

———, *Administrative Law: Its Growth, Procedure, Significance* (U. of Pittsburgh, 1942).

———, *Social Control Through Law* (Yale, 1942).

———, *The Task of the Law* (Franklin & Marshall, 1944).

———, *Interpretations of Legal History* (Harvard, 1946).

———, *New Paths of the Law* (U. of Nebraska, 1950).

———, *Justice According to Law* (Yale, 1951).

———, *The Lawyer from Antiquity to Modern Times* (West, 1953).

———, *An Introduction to the Philosophy of Law*, rev. ed. (Yale, 1959).

———, *Law Finding through Experience and Reason* (U. of Georgia, 1960).

Powell, T. R., *Vagaries and Varieties in Constitutional Interpretations* (Columbia, 1956).

Pritchett, C. H., *The Roosevelt Court: A Study in Judicial Politics and Values, 1937–1947* (Macmillan, 1948).

———, *The American Constitution* (McGraw-Hill, 1959).

———, *Congress versus the Supreme Court* (Minnesota, 1961).

Pusey, M. J., *The Supreme Court Crises* (Macmillan, 1937).

Raby, R. C., *Fifty Famous Trials* (Washington Law Books, 1937).

Radin, M., *The Law and Mr. Smith* (Bobbs-Merrill, 1938).

———, *The Law as Logic and Experience* (Yale, 1940).

———, *The Law and You* (Mentor, 1948).

Ramaswamy, M., *Commerce Clause in the Constitution of the United States* (Longmans, Green, 1948).

———, *The Creative Role of the Supreme Court of the U.S.* (Stanford, 1956).

Randall, J. G., *The Civil War and Reconstruction* (Heath, 1937).

———, *Constitutional Problems Under Lincoln*, rev. ed., (U. of Delaware, 1956).

Read, C. (Ed.), *The Constitution Reconsidered* (Columbia, 1938).

Rich, B. N., *The President and Civil Disorder* (Brookings, 1941).

Roberts, O. J., *The Court and the Constitution* (Harvard, 1951).

Robertson, R., *Jurisdiction of the Supreme Court of the U.S.* (Bender, 1951).

Robson, W. A., *Civilization and the Growth of Law* (Macmillan, 1935).

———, *Justice and Administrative Law* (Stevens, 1947).

Rodell, F., *Nine Men: A Political History of the Supreme Court from 1790–1955* (Random House, 1955).

Rodick, B. C., *American Constitutional Custom: A Forgotten Factor in the Founding* (Philosophical Lib., 1953).

Roettinger, R., *The Supreme Court and State Police Power: A Study in Federalism* (Public Affairs Pr., 1957).

Rogers, H. W. (Ed.), *Constitutional History of the U.S. as Seen in the Development of American Law* (Bender, 1890).

Rose, J. C., *Jurisdiction and Procedure of Federal Courts* (Bender, 1938).

Rosenblum, V. G., *Law as a Political Instrument* (Doubleday, 1955).

Ross, A., *Towards A Realistic Jurisprudence* (Munksgaard, 1946).

————, *On Law and Justice* (Stevens, 1959).

Rossiter, C., *Constitutional Dictatorship* (Princeton, 1948).

————, *The Supreme Court and the Commander-in-Chief* (Cornell, 1951).

————, *Seedtime of the Republic* (Harcourt, Brace, 1953).

Rottschaefer, H., *Constitutional Law* (West, 1939).

————, *The Constitution and Socio-Economic Change* (U. of Michigan Law School, 1949).

Roe, G. E., *Our Judicial Oligarchy* (Huebesch, 1912).

Rutherford, M. L. S., *The Influence of the American Bar Association on Public Opinion and Legislation* (Unpublished Ph.D. Dissertation, U. of Penna., 1937).

Rutledge, W. B., *The Declaration of Legal Faith* (U. of Kansas, 1947).

Schmidhauser, J. R., *The Supreme Court as Final Arbiter of Federal-State Relations* (U. of N. Carolina, 1958).

————, *The Supreme Court: Its Politics, Personalities, and Procedures* (Holt, 1960).

Schubert, G. A., *The Presidency in the Court* (U. of Minnesota, 1957).

————, *Constitutional Politics* (Holt, Rinehart, Winston, 1960).

————, *Quantitative Analysis of Judicial Behavior* (Free Press, 1960).

Schwartz, B., *The Supreme Court: Constitutional Revolution in Retrospect* (Ronald, 1954) .

————, *American Constitutional Law* (Cambridge, 1955).

————, *The Code Napoleon and the Common Law World* (New York U., 1956).

Scigliano, R. G., *The Michigan One-Man Grand Jury* (Michigan State U., 1957).

Scott, J. B., *Judicial Settlement of Controversies between States of the American Union* (Clarendon, 1918).

Seagle, W., *The Quest for Law* (Knopf, 1941).

————, *Law, the Science of Inefficiency* (Macmillan, 1952).

Senior, M. R., *The Supreme Court: Its Power of Judicial Review with Respect to Congressional Legislation* (George Washington U., 1937).

Shartel, B., *Our Legal System and How It Operates* (U. of Michigan Law School, 1950).

Shientag, B. L., *Moulders of Legal Thought* (Viking, 1943).

Silver, D. M., *Lincoln's Supreme Court* (U. of Illinois, 1956).

Simpson, S. P. and Stone, J., *Cases and Readings on Law and Society* (West, 1948).

Smith, F. A., *Judicial Review of Legislation in New York, 1906–1938* (Columbia, 1952).

Smith, J. M. and Murphy, P. L., *Liberty and Justice* (Knopf, 1958).

———— and Cotter, C. P., *Powers of the President During Crises* (Public Affairs Pr., 1960).

Smith, L., *American Democracy and Military Power: A Study of Civil Control of the Military Power in the United States* (U. of Chicago, 1951).

Sommer, F. H., *Reforming the Supreme Court* (New York U., 1951).

Stannard, H., *The Two Constitutions: A Comparative Study of British and American Constitutional Systems* (Van Nostrand, 1959).

Starr, I., *The Federal Judiciary* (Oxford Social Studies, 1957).

Stern, R. L. and Gressman, E., *Supreme Court Practice*, 3rd ed. (Bureau of Nat'l. Affairs, 1962).

Stevens, C. E., *Sources of the Constitution of the U. S.* (Macmillan, 1894).

Stone, J., *The Province and Function of Law* (Associated General Publications, 1946).

Story, J., *Commentaries on the Constitution of the United States* (Little, 1833).

———, *A Familiar Exposition on thè Constitution of the U.S.: Containing a Brief Commentary* (Petersburg, 1840).

Stryker, L. P., *The Art of Advocacy* (Simon & Schuster, 1954).

Sunderland, E. R., *Judicial Administration* (Callaghan, 1939).

Surrency, E., Field, B., and Crea J., *A Practical Guide to Legal Research*, 2nd ed. (Oceana, 1959).

Sutherland, A. E., *The Law and One Man Among Many* (U. of Wisconsin, 1956).

——— (Ed.), *Government Under Law* (Harvard, 1956).

Swisher, C. B., *The Growth of Constitutional Power in the United States* (U. of Chicago, 1946).

———, *American Constitutional Development*, 2nd ed. (Houghton Mifflin, 1954).

———, *Historic Decisions of the Supreme Court* (Toronto, 1958).

———, *The Supreme Court in Modern Role* (New York U., 1958).

Syracuse Law Review, *Controversy Over the Supreme Court* (A Symposium) (Spring 1959).

Taft, W. H., *Our Chief Magistrate and His Powers* (Columbia, 1916).

Tenbroek, J., *Anti-Slavery Origins of the Fourteenth Amendment* (Berkeley, 1951).

Thayer, J. B., *Cases on Constitutional Law* (Sever, 1895).

———, *Legal Essays* (Boston Book Co., 1908).

Thursby, V. B., *Interstate Cooperation: A Study of the Interstate Compact* (Public Affairs Pr. 1953).

Timasheff, N. S., *An Introduction to the Sociology of Law* (Harvard, 1938).

Tocqueville, A. de, *Democracy in America* (H. G. Langley, 1845).

Tompkins, D. C., *The Supreme Court of the United States: A Bibliography* (Berkeley, 1959).

Tresolini, R. J., *American Constitutional Law* (Macmillan, 1959).

Twiss, B. R., *Lawyers and the Constitution: How Laissez Faire Came to the Supreme Court* (Princeton, 1942).

Ulman, J. N., *A Judge Takes the Stand* (Knopf, 1933).

United States Code, Title 28 (comprising the *Federal Judicial Code*).

United States Senate, Committee on the Judiciary, *Composition and Jurisdiction of the U.S. Supreme Court* (1954).

University of Michigan Law School 1955 Conference, *Aims and Methods of Legal Research* (U. of Michigan, 1958).

Vanderbilt, A. T., *Men and Measures in the Law* (Knopf, 1949).

———, *Minimum Standards of Judicial Administration* (New York U., 1949).

———, *The Doctrine of Separation of Powers and Its Present-Day Significance* (U. of Nebraska, 1953).

———, *The Challenge of Law Reform* (Princeton, 1955).

————, *Judges and Jurors: Their Functions, Qualifications, and Selection* (Boston U., 1956).

Van Doren, C. C., *The Great Rehearsal: The Story of the Making and Ratifying of the Constitution of the U.S.* (Viking, 1948).

Vinogradoff, P., *Outlines of Historical Jurisprudence* (Oxford, 1920).

————, *Common Sense in Law*, 3rd ed., rev. by H. G. Hanbury (Oxford, 1959).

Wagner, W. J., *Federal States and their Judiciary: Comparative Study in Constitutional Law and Organization of Courts in Federal States* (Mouton, 1959).

Wallace, H. A., *Whose Constitution?* (Reynal & Hitchcock, 1936).

Warren, C., *History of the American Bar* (Little, Brown, 1911).

————, *The Supreme Court and Sovereign States* (Princeton, 1924).

————, *The Supreme Court in United States History*, rev. ed. (Little, Brown, 1937).

————, *Congress, The Constitution and the Supreme Court* (Little, Brown, 1935).

————, *The Making of the Constitution* (Little, Brown, 1937).

————, *The Supreme Court and Disputes Between States* (William & Mary, 1940).

Warren, E., *The Law in the Future* (Fortune, 1955).

Wasserstrom, R. A., *The Judicial Decision: Toward a Theory of Legal Justification* (Stanford, 1961).

Weaver, S. P., *Constitutional Law and Its Administration* (Callaghan, 1946).

Wechsler, H., *Principles, Politics, and Fundamental Law* (Harvard, 1961).

Welch, J., *The Constitution* (Houghton Mifflin, 1956).

Wellman, F. L., *Day in Court* (Macmillan, 1910).

————, *Gentlemen of the Jury* (Macmillan, 1924).

————, *The Art of Cross-Examination*, 4th ed. (Macmillan, 1936).

Wendell, M., *Relations Between the Federal and State Courts*, rev. ed. (Columbia, 1953).

Westin, A. F., *Anatomy of a Constitutional Law Case* (Macmillan, 1958).

————, *The Supreme Court: Views from Inside* (Norton, 1961).

Wheare, K., *Modern Constitutions* (Oxford, 1951).

————, *Federal Government* (Oxford, 1953).

White, L. D., *The States and the Nation* (Louisiana St. U., 1956).

Whitney, H. C., *Life on the Circuit with Lincoln* (Estes-Lauriat, 1892).

Wigmore, J. H., *Wigmore on Evidence*, 3rd ed. (Little, Brown, 1942).

Willistron, S. *Law and Life* (Little, Brown, 1941).

Willoughby, W. W., *Principles of Judicial Administration* (Brookings Inst., 1929).

————, *The Constitutional Law of the United States* (Baker, 1929).

Wilson, R. R., *U.S. Commercial Treaties and International Law* (Hauser, 1959).

Wilson, W., *Congressional Government* (Houghton Mifflin, 1885).

————, *Constitutional Government in the United States* (Columbia, 1908).

Winters, G. R., *Selection of Judges in New York and in Other States* (Lawyer Com., 1943).

————, *Bar Association Organization and Other Activities* (Am. Judicature, 1954.)

Wormuth, F. D., *The Origins of Modern Constitutionalism* (Harper, 1949).

Wright, B. F., *American Interpretation of Natural Law* (Harvard, 1931).

————, *The Contract Clause of the Constitution* (Harvard, 1938).

————, *The Growth of American Constitutional Law* (Reynal & Hitchcock, 1942).

————, *Consensus and Continuity, 1776–1787* (Boston U., 1958).

Wu, J. C. H., *Fountain of Justice* (Sheed & Ward, 1959).

Zeisel, H., Kalvern, H. Jr., and Buchholz, B., *Delay in the Court* (Little, Brown, 1959).

II BIOGRAPHIES AND AUTOBIOGRAPHIES OF
JUSTICES OF THE SUPREME COURT OF THE UNITED STATES

Adams, J. S. (Ed.), *An Autobiographical Sketch by John Marshall* (U. of Michigan, 1937).

Barbar, J., *The Honorable Eighty-eight* (Vanguard, 1957).

Barry, R., *Mr. Rutledge of South Carolina* (Duell, Sloan, & Pearce, 1942).

Bent, S., *Justice Oliver Wendell Holmes* (Vanguard, 1932).

Beveridge, A. J., *The Life of John Marshall* (Houghton, 1916).

Bickel, A. M., *The Unpublished Opinions of Mr. Justice Brandeis: The Supreme Court at Work* (Harvard, 1957).

Biddle, F., *Mr. Justice Holmes* (Scribner, 1942).

Binney, H., *Bushrod Washington* (Sherman, 1858).

Blaisdell, D., *Mr. Justice James Clark McReynolds* (Unpublished Ph.D. Dissertation, U. of Wisconsin, 1948).

Bowen, C. D., *A Yankee from Olympus* (Little, Brown, 1944).

Bradley, C. (Ed.), *Miscellaneous Writings of Joseph P. Bradley* (Hardham, 1901).

Brown, F. J., *The Social and Economic Philosophy of Pierce Butler* (Catholic U., 1945).

Brown, J. M., *Through These Men* (Harper, 1956).

Brown, W. G., *The Life of Oliver Ellsworth* (Macmillan, 1905).

Byrnes, J. F., *All in One Lifetime* (Harper, 1958).

Campbell, T. W., *Four-Score Forgotten Men* (Pioneer, 1950).

Cate, W. A., *Lucius Q. C. Lamar* (U. of N. Carolina, 1935).

Christman, H. M. (Ed.), *The Public Papers of Chief Justice Earl Warren* (Simon & Schuster, 1959).

Clark, F. B., *The Constitutional Doctrines of Justice Harlan* (Johns Hopkins, 1915).

Clifford, P. G., *Nathan Clifford, Democrat* (Putnam, 1922).

Connor, H. G., *John A. Campbell, Associate Justice of the United States Supreme Court, 1853–1861* (Houghton, 1920).

Corwin, E. S., *John Marshall and the Constitution: A Chronicle of the Supreme Court* (Yale, 1921).

Cotton, J. P., Jr. (Ed.), *The Constitutional Decisions of John Marshall* (Putnam, 1905).

Countryman, V., (Ed.), *Douglas of the Supreme Court: A Selection of His Opinions* (Doubleday, 1959).

Curtis, B. R., *A Memoir of Benjamin Robbins Curtis, LL.D.* (Little, Brown, 1879).

DeHaas, J., *Louis W. Brandeis* (Bloch, 1929).

Delaplaine, E. S., *The Life of Thomas Johnson* (Hitchcock, 1927).

Dilliard, I. (Ed.), *Mr. Justice Brandeis: Great American* (Modern View Pr., 1941).

Dillon, J. M. (Ed.), *John Marshall: Complete Constitutional Decisions* (Callaghan, 1903).

Dunham, A., and Kurland, P. B. (Eds.), *Mr. Justice* (U. of Chicago, 1956).

Early, S. T. Jr., *James Clark McReynolds and the Judicial Process* (Unpublished Ph. D. Dissertation, U. of Virginia, 1954).

Ewing, C. A. M., *Judges of the Supreme Court, 1789–1938* (U. of Minnesota, 1938).

Fairman, C., *Mr. Justice Miller and the Supreme Court, 1862–1890* (Harvard, 1939).

Fitzgerald, M. J., *Justice Reed: A Study of a Center Judge* (Unpublished Ph.D. Dissertation, U. of Chicago, 1950).

Flanders, H., *The Lives of the Chief Justices of the U.S. Supreme Court* (Lippincott, 1855).

Frank, J. P., *Mr. Justice Black: The Man and His Opinions* (Knopf, 1949).

Fraenkel, O.K. (Ed.), *The Curse of Bigness: Miscellaneous Papers of Louis D. Brandeis* (Viking, 1934).

Frankfurter, F. and others, *Mr. Justice Holmes* (Coward-McCann, 1931).

——, *Mr. Justice Brandeis* (Yale, 1932).

——, *Mr. Justice Holmes and the Constitution* (Harvard, 1938).

——, *Mr. Justice Holmes and the Supreme Court* (Harvard, 1939).

Gerhart, E. C., *America's Advocate: Robert H. Jackson* (Bobbs-Merrill, 1958).

Goldman, S. (Ed.), *The Words of Mr. Justice Brandeis* (Schuman, 1953).

Gregory, C. N., *Samuel Freeman Miller* (State Hist. Soc. of Iowa, 1907).

Hall, M. E. (Ed.), *Selected Writings of B. N. Cardozo* (Fallon, 1947).

Hart, A. B., *Salmon P. Chase* (Houghton, 1899).

Hellman, G. S., *Benjamin N. Cardozo—American Judge* (Whittlesey, 1940).

Hendel, S., *Charles Evans Hughes and the Supreme Court* (Columbia, 1951).

Hendricks, B. J., *Bulwark of the Republic: A Biography of the Constitution* [re: P. V. Daniel] (Little, Brown, 1957).

Hill, A. B., *The Constitutional Doctrine of Chief Justice White* (Unpublished J. D. Dissertation, U. of Calif., 1922).

Holmes, O. W., *Speeches* (Little, Brown, 1913).

——, *Collected Legal Papers* (A. Harcourt, 1920).

Howe, M. de W. (Ed.), *The Holmes-Pollock Letters, 1874–1932* (Harvard, 1941).

—— (Ed.), *The Holmes-Laski Letters, 1916–1935* (Harvard, 1953).

——, *Justice Oliver Wendell Holmes: The Shaping Years, 1841–1870* (Harvard 1957).

Iowa Law Review, Symposium, "Wiley B. Rutledge" (Summer 1950).

Jay, W., *The Life of John Jay* (Harper, 1833).

Johnston, H. P. (Ed.), *Correspondence of John Jay* (Putnam, 1890).

Jones, W. M. (Ed.), *Chief Justice John Marshall: A Reappraisal* (Cornell, 1956).

Kent, C. A., *Memoir of Henry Billings Brown* (Duffield, 1915).

Kentucky Law Journal, Symposium, "John Marshall Harlan, 1833–1911" (Spring 1958).

King, W. L., *Melville Weston Fuller* (Macmillan, 1950).

Klinkhamer, Sister Marie Carolyn, *Edward Douglas White, Chief Justice of the United States* (Unpublished Ph.D. Dissertation, Catholic U., 1943).

Konefsky, S. J., *Chief Justice Stone and the Supreme Court* (Macmillan, 1946).

—— (Ed.), *The Constitutional World of Mr. Justice Frankfurter* (Macmillan, 1949).

——, *The Legacy of Holmes and Brandeis: A Study in the Influence of Ideas* (Macmillan, 1956).

Lamar, C. P., *The Life of Joseph Rucker Lamar, 1857–1916* (Putnam, 1926).

Lawrence, A. A., *James Moore Wayne: Southern Unionist* (U. of N. Carolina, 1943).

Lerner, M. (Ed.), *The Mind and Faith of Justice Holmes* (Little, Brown, 1943).

Levy, B. H., *Cardozo and Legal Thinking* (Oxford, 1938).

Lief A., Brandeis: *The Personal History of an American Ideal* (Stackpole, 1936).

—— (Ed.), *The Dissenting Opinions of Mr. Justice Holmes* (Vanguard, 1943).

Livingston, E. B., *The Livingstons of Livingston Manor* (Knickerbocker, 1910).

Loth, D., *Chief Justice: John Marshall and the Growth of the Republic* (Norton, 1949).

MacLeish, A. and Prichard, E. F. (Eds.), *Law and Politics: Occasional Papers of Mr. Justice Frankfurter* (Harcourt, Brace, 1939).

Marke, J. (Ed.), *The Holmes Reader* (Oceana, 1955).

Mason, A. T., *Brandeis: Lawyer and Judge in the Modern State* (Princeton, 1933).

——, *Brandeis: And the Modern State* (Nat'l. Home Library, 1936).

——, *The Brandeis Way* (Princeton, 1938).

——, *Brandeis—A Free Man's Life* (Viking, 1946).

——, *Harlan Fisk Stone: Pillar of the Law* (Viking, 1956).

Mayes, E., *Lucius W. C. Lamar* (Barbee, 1895).

McDevitt, M., *Joseph McKenna* (Catholic U., 1946).

McHale, F., *President and Chief Justice: The Life and Public Services of William Howard Taft* (Dorrance, 1931).

McLean, J. E., *William Rufus Day, Supreme Court Justice From Ohio* (Johns Hopkins, 1947).

McRee, G. F. (Ed.), *The Life and Correspondence of James Iredell* (Peter Smith, 1949).

Mendelson, W., *Justices Black and Frankfurter* (U. of Chicago, 1961).

Merrill, H. S., *Bourbon Leader* [re: L. Q. J. Lamar] (Little, Brown, 1957).

Michigan Law Review, Symposium, "Mr. Justice Frank Murphy" (April 1950).

Monoghan, F., *John Jay* (Bobbs-Merrill, 1935).

Morgan, D. G., *Justice William Johnson: The First Dissenter* (U. of S. Carolina, 1954).

O'Brien, F. W., *Justice Reed and the First Amendment: the Religion Clauses* (Georgetown U., 1958).

Palmer, B. W., *Marshall and Taney: Statesmen of the Law* (U. of Minnesota, 1939).

Paschal, J. F., *Mr. Justice Sutherland: A Man Against the State* (Princeton, 1951).

Perkins, D., *Charles Evans Hughes and American Democratic Statesmanship* (Little, Brown, 1956).

Phillips, H. B. (Ed.), *Felix Frankfurter Reminisces* (Reynal, 1960).

Pollack, E. H. (Ed.), *The Brandeis Reader* (Oceana, 1956).

Pollard, J. P., *Mr. Justice Cardozo: A Liberal Mind in Action—American Lawyer* (Yorktown, 1940).

Pringle, H., *The Life and Times of William Howard Taft* (Farrar & Rinehart, 1939).

Pusey, M. J., *Charles Evans Hughes* (Macmillan, 1951).

Roberts, O. J., "In Memoriam" in *University of Pennsylvania Law Review* (December, 1955).

Schuckers, J. W., *The Life and Public Services of Salmon Portland Chase* (Appleton, 1874).

Schwartz, M. D. and Hogan, J. C., *Joseph Story: A Collection of Writings By and About an Eminent American Jurist* (Oceana, 1959).

Scott, W. W., *History of Orange County* [re: P. P. Barbour] (Waddey, 1907).

Seagle, W., *Men of Law: From Hammurabi to Holmes* (Macmillan, 1947).

Servies, J. A., *A Bibliography of John Marshall* (U. S. Commission for Celebration of 200th Anniv. of Birth of John Marshall, 1956).

Shiras, G. 3rd (Ed.), *Justice George Shiras, Jr. of Pittsburgh* (U. of Pittsburgh, 1953).

Smith, C. P., *James Wilson, Founding Father* (U. of N. Carolina, 1956).

Smith, C. W., *Roger B. Taney: Jacksonian Jurist* (U. of N. Carolina, 1936).

Stanford Law Review, Symposium, "Mr. Justice Jackson," (December 1955).

Steamer, R. J., *The Constitutional Doctrines of Mr. Justice Robert H. Jackson* (Unpublished Ph.D. Dissertation, Cornell U., 1954).

Steiner, B. C., *The Life of Roger Brooke Taney* (Norman, Remington, 1922).

Story, W. W. (Ed.), *Life and Letters of Joseph Story* (Little, 1851).

Surrency, E. (Ed.), *The Marshall Reader* (Oceana, 1955).

Sutherland, A. E., *Government Under Law* [re: J. Marshall] Harvard, 1956).

Swayne, N. W. (Comp.), *The Descendants of Francis Swayne and Others* (Lippincott, 1921).

Swisher, C. B., *Stephen J. Field: Craftsman of the Law* (Brookings, 1930).

———, *Roger B. Taney* (Macmillan, 1935).

Thomas, H. S., *Felix Frankfurter: Scholar on the Bench* (Johns Hopkins, 1960).

Trimble, B. R., *Chief Justice Waite: Defender of the Public Interest* (Princeton, 1938).

Umbreit, K. B., *Our Eleven Chief Justices: A History of the Supreme Court in Terms of Their Personalities* (Harper, 1938).

University of Chicago Law Review, "Justices Frankfurter and Douglas," (Autumn 1958).

Vanderbilt Law Review, Symposium, "Studies in Judicial Biography," Vol. X, No. 2 (1957).

Van Santvoord, G., *Sketches of the Lives and Judicial Services of the Chief Justices of the Supreme Court of the U.S.* (Scribner, 1854).

Warner, H. L., *The Life of Mr. Justice Clarke: A Testimony to the Power of Liberal Dissent in America* (Western Reserve U., 1959).

Weisenburger, F. P., *The Life of John McLean: A Politician on the Supreme Court* (Ohio State, 1937).

Wiener, F. B., *The Life and Judicial Career of William Henry Moody* (Harvard, 1937).

Williams, C., *Hugo L. Black: A Study in the Judicial Process* (Johns Hopkins, 1950).

Wood, G. S., *William Paterson of New Jersey, 1745–1806* (Fair Lawn Pr., 1933).

Woodbury, C. L. (Ed.), *Writings of Levi Woodbury* (Little, Brown, 1852).

Wyman, T. B., *Genealogy of the Name and Family of Hunt* (Wilson, 1862).

Yale Law Journal, Symposium, "Mr. Justice Black," (February 1956).

———, Symposium, "Mr. Justice Felix Frankfurter," (December 1957).

Yale Law Library, *Louis Dembitz Brandeis, 1856–1941: A Bibliography* (New Haven, 1958).

III COMPARATIVE

CONSTITUTIONAL AND ADMINISTRATIVE LAW

Allen, C. K., *Law in the Making,* 6th ed. (Oxford, 1958).

———, *Law and Orders: An Inquiry into the Nature and Scope of Delegated Legislative and Executive Powers in England,* 2d ed. (Stevens, 1957).

Amos, Sir M. S. and Walton, F. P., *Introduction to French Law* (Oxford, 1935).

Archer, P., *Queen's Courts* (Penguin, 1956).

Bagehot, W., *The English Constitution*, 2nd ed. (World's Classics, 1928).

Banerjee, D. N., *Our Fundamental Rights: Their Nature and Extent (As Judicially Determined)* (World Pr., 1960).

Barker, Sir E., *Church, State, and Education* (U. of Michigan, 1957).

Bedford, S., *The Faces of Justice: A Traveller's Report* (Simon & Schuster, 1961).

Berman, H. J., *Justice in Russia: An Interpretation of Soviet Law* (Harvard, 1950).

Boutmy, E. G., *Studies in Constitutional Law: France, England, United States*, 2nd ed. (Macmillan, 1891).

Carr, Sir T., *Concerning English Administrative Law* (Columbia, 1941).

Castberg, F., *Freedom of Speech in the West* (Oceana, 1960).

Cowen, Z., *Federal Jurisdiction in Australia* (Oxford, 1959).

David R. and de Vries, H. P., *The French Legal System: An Introduction to Civil Law Systems* (Oceana, 1958).

Denning, Sir A., *The Changing Law* (Stevens, 1953).

Devlin, P., *The Criminal Prosecution in England* (Yale, 1958).

Dicey, A. V., *Law and Public Opinion in England During the 19th Century* (Torch, 1958).

Ensor, R. C. K., *Courts and Judges in France, Germany, and England (Oxford, 1933).

Flecher, J. K., *The British Courts: Traditions and Ceremonial* (Cassell, 1953).

Fouilee, A., et al., *Modern French Legal Philosophy* (Macmillan, 1921).

Freedeman, C. E., *The Conseil d'État in Modern France* (Columbia, 1961).

Friedmann, W., *Law in a Changing Society* (Berkeley, 1959).

Geldart, W. M., *Elements of English Law*, 6th ed. (Holt, 1959).

Giles, F. T., *The Criminal Law* (Penguin, 1955).

Ginsberg, M. (Ed.), *Law and Opinion in England in the 20th Century* (Berkeley, 1959).

Gsovsky, V. and Grzybowski, K. (Eds.), *Government, Law, and the Courts in the Soviet Union and Eastern Europe* (Praeger, 1960).

Hamson, C. J., *Executive Discretion and Judicial Control: An Aspect of the French Conseil d'État* (Stevens, 1954).

Hanbury, H. G., *English Courts of Law*, 2nd ed. (Oxford, 1953).

Hawgood, J. A., *Modern Constitutions since 1787* (Macmillan, 1939).

Hazard, J. N., *Settling Disputes in Soviet Society: The Formative Years in Legal Institutions* (Columbia, 1954).

Heuss, Th., *Verfassungsrecht und Verfassungspolitik* (Scherpe Verlag, 1950).

Jackson, R. M., *The Machinery of Justice in England*, 3rd ed. (Cambridge U., 1960).

Jenks, C. W., *The Common Law of Mankind* (Praeger, 1959).

Jennings, Sir W. I., *The Law and the Constitution*, 4th ed. (U. of London, 1958).

Jones, A. H. M., *Studies in Roman Government and Law* (Praeger, 1960).

Keir, Sir D. L. and Lawson, F. H. (Eds.), *Cases in Constitutional Law*, 4th ed. (Oxford, 1954).

Kelson, H., *The Communist Theory of Law* (Praeger, 1960).

Kiralfy, A. K., *The English Legal System*, 3rd ed. (Sweet & Maxwell, 1960).

Lawson, F. H., *A Common Lawyer Looks at the Civil Law* (Oxford, 1955).

———, *The Rational Strength of English Law* (Stevens, 1951).

McWhinney, E., *Judicial Review in the English-Speaking World*, 2nd ed. (Toronto, 1961).

———— (Ed.), *Canadian Jurisprudence: The Civil Law and the Common Law in Canada* (Toronto, 1958).

Mueller, G. O. W. (Ed.), *The French Penal Code* (Rothman, 1960).

Parker, J., *Some Aspects of French Law* (Scribner 1929).

Peaslee, A. J., *Constitutions of Nations*, 2nd ed. (Nijhoff, 1956).

Pollard, R. S. W. (Ed.), *Administrative Tribunals at Work: A Symposium* (Stevens, 1950).

Potter, H., *An Historical Introduction to English Law and Its Institutions*, 3rd ed. (Sweet & Maxwell, 1948).

Rice, W. G., *Law Among States in Federacy: A Survey of Decisions of the Swiss Federal Tribunal in Intercantonal Controversies* (Nelson, 1959).

Robson, W. A., *Justice and Administrative Law: A Study of the English Constitution*, 3rd ed. (Stevens, 1951).

Schlesinger, R., *Comparative Law*, 2nd ed. (Foundation Pr., 1959).

————, *Soviet Legal Theory* (Humanities, 1951).

Schwartz, B., *French Administrative Law and the Common Law World* (New York U., 1954).

————, *Law and the Executive in Britain* (New York U., 1949).

de Smith, S. A., *Judicial Review of Administrative Action* (Oceana, 1959).

Smith, M., *The Development of European Law* (Columbia, 1928).

Stephenson, C. and Marcham, F. G. (Eds.), *Sources of English Constitutional History* (Harper, 1937).

Stevens, R. B., *Questions and Answers on Constitutional Law and Legal History*, 7th ed. (Sweet & Maxwell, 1959).

St. John-Stevas, N., *Life, Death, and the Law: Law and Christian Morals in England and the U.S.* (Indiana U., 1961).

Street, H., *Governmental Liability: A Comparative Study* (Cambridge, 1953).

Szirmai, Z. (Ed.), *Law in Eastern Europe* (Hillary, 1959).

Szladits, C., *A Guide to Foreign Legal Materials—French, German, Swiss* (Oceana, 1959).

————, *Bibliography of Foreign and Comparative Law Books and Articles in English* (Oceana, 1955).

The Inns of Court, *Rule of Law: A Study by the Inns of Court* (Conservative and Unionist Central Office, 1955).

Von Mehren, A. T., *The Civil Law Systems: Cases and Materials for the Comparative Study of Law* (Little, Brown, 1957).

Vyshinsky, A. Y., *Law of the Soviet State* (Macmillan, 1948).

Wade, E. C. S., *Dicey's Introduction to the Study of the Law of the Constitution*, 10th ed. (Macmillan, 1961).

———— (Ed.), and Phillips, G. G., *Constitutional Law*, 6th ed. (Longmans, Green, 1960).

Wagner, W. J., *Federal States and their Judiciary: Comparative Study* (Mouton, 1959).

Walker, D. M., *The Scottish Legal System* (W. Green, 1959).

Wheare, K. C., *The Constitutional Structure of the Commonwealth* (Oxford, 1961).

————, *Modern Constitutions* (Oxford, 1951).

Zurcher, A. J., *Constitutions and Constitutional Trends since World War II*, 2nd ed. (New York U., 1955).

IV CIVIL RIGHTS AND LIBERTIES

Abernathy, G., *The Right of Assembly and Association* (South Carolina, 1961).

Abrams, C., *Forbidden Neighbors* (Harper, 1955).

Alexander, N., *The Rights of Aliens Under the Federal Constitution* (Capital, 1931).

Allport, G. W., *The Nature of Prejudice* (Doubleday, 1960).

Almond, G. A., *The Appeals of Communism* (Princeton, 1954).

American Civil Liberties Union, *Annual Report*(s) (ACLU).

American Jewish Committee, *Assault upon Freedom of Association* (Amer. Jew. Comm., 1957).

Andrews, B., *Washington Witch Hunt* (Random House, 1948).

Anthony, J. G., *Hawaii Under Army Rule* (Stanford, 1955).

Ashmore, H. S., *The Negro and the Schools*, rev. ed. (U. of North Carolina, 1954).

———, *An Epitaph for Dixie* (Norton, 1957).

———, *The Other Side of Jordan: Negroes Outside the South* (Norton, 1960).

Association of the Bar of the City of New York, *The Federal Loyalty-Security Program* (Dodd, Mead, 1956).

———, *Freedom to Travel: Report of the Special Committee to Study Passport Procedures* (Dodd, Mead, 1958).

———, *Equal Justice for the Accused* (Dodd, Mead, 1959).

Auerbach, F. L., *Immigration Laws of the United States* (Bobbs-Merrill, 1955).

Avins, A., *The Law of AWOL* (Oceana, 1957).

Bachrach, P., *Problems in Freedom* (Stackpole, 1953).

Baldwin, R. N., *Civil Liberties and Industrial Conflict* (Harvard, 1938).

Barker, Sir E., *Church, State, and Education* (U. of Michigan, 1957).

Barrett, E. L. Jr., *The Tenney Committee: Legislative Investigation of Subversive Activities in California* (Cornell, 1951).

Barth, A., *Loyalty of Free Men* (Viking, 1951).

———, *Government by Investigation* (Viking, 1955).

———, *When Congress Investigates Loyalty and Security in a Democracy* (Public Affairs Comm., 1956).

Bay, C., *The Structure of Freedom* (Stanford, 1958).

Beaney, W. M., *The Right to Counsel in American Courts* (U. of Michigan, 1955).

Beck, C., *Contempt of Congress* (Hauser, 1959).

Becker, C. L., *Freedom and Responsibility in the American Way of Life* (Knopf, 1945).

———, *et al.*, *Safeguarding Civil Liberty Today* (Cornell, 1945).

Beisel, A. R., *Control Over Illegal Enforcement of the Criminal Law: Role of the Supreme Court* (Boston U., 1955).

Berger, M., *Equality by Statute* (Columbia, 1952).

Bernard, W. S. (Ed.), *American Immigration Policy: A Reappraisal* (Harper, 1950).

Berns, W., *Freedom, Virtue, and the First Amendment* (Louisiana State U., 1957).

Beth, L. P., *The American Theory of Church and State* (U. of Florida, 1958).

Bibby, C., *Race, Prejudice, and Education* (Heinemann, 1960).

Biddle, F., *The Fear of Freedom* (Doubleday, 1951).

Black, A., *Who's My Neighbor?* (Public Affairs Comm., 1956).

Blanshard, P., *Communism, Democracy, and Catholic Power* (Beacon, 1951).

———, *The Right To Read: The Battle Against Censorship* (Beacon, 1955).

———, *American Freedom and Catholic Power*, rev. ed (Beacon, 1958).

———, *God and Man in Washington* (Beacon, 1960).

Blaustein, A. P. and Ferguson, C. C., Jr., *Desegregation and the Law* (Rutgers, 1956.

Blossom V., *It Has Happened Here* (Harper, 1959).

Blumer, H. and Hauser, P., *Movies, Delinquency and Crime* (Macmillan, 1933).

Bok, C., *Star Wormwood* (Knopf, 1959).

Boles, D. E., *The Bible, Religion, and the Public Schools* (Iowa State, 1961).

Bontecou, E., *The Federal Loyalty-Security Program* (Cornell, 1953).

——— (Ed.), *Freedom in the Balance: Opinions of Judge Henry W. Edgeton Relating to Civil Liberties* (Cornell, 1960).

Bouscaren, A. T., *The Security Aspects of Immigration Work* (Marquette U., 1959).

Brewster, S. F., *Twelve Men in a Box* (Callaghan, 1934).

Brookes, E. H. and Macaulay, J. B., *Civil Liberty in South Africa* (Oxford, 1959).

Brookings Institution, *Suggested Standards for Determining Un-American Activities,* 1945).

Brown, N. C. (Ed.), *The Study of Religión in the Public Schools: An Appraisal* (Amer. Council on Education, 1958).

Brown, R. R., *Bigger Than Little Rock* (Seaberg, 1958).

Brown, R. S., Jr., *Loyalty and Security: Employment Tests in the United States* (Yale, 1958).

Bruce, J. C., *The Irony of Our Immigration Policy* (Random House, 1954).

Brucker, H., *Freedom of Information* (Macmillan, 1949).

Buckley, W. F. Jr., *God and Man at Yale* (Regnery, 1951).

Buranelli, V. (Ed.), *The Trial of Peter Zenger* (New York U., 1957).

Burlingham, C. C. and Flexner, B. (Eds.), *The Sacco-Vanzetti Case: Transcript of the Trial of Nicola Sacco and Bartolomeo Vanzetti in the Courts of Massachusetts and Subsequent Proceedings, 1920–1927* (Holt, 1928).

Burstein, A., *Law Concerning Religion* (Oceana, 1950).

Butts, R. F., *The American Tradition in Religion and Education* (Beacon, 1950).

Byse, C. and Joughin, L., *Tenure in American Higher Education* (Cornell, 1959).

Cable, G. W., *The Negro Question: A Selection of Writings on Civil Rights in the South* (Doubleday, 1890) [Edited by Arlin Turner in 1959].

Cable, J. L., *Loss of Citizenship; Denaturalization—the Alien in Wartime* (Nat'l. Law Book Co., 1943).

Cahn, E., *The Sense of Injustice* (New York U., 1949).

———, *Can the Supreme Court Defend Civil Liberties?* (Sidney Hillman Fund, 1956).

Campbell, E. Q. and Pettigrew, T. F., *Christians in Racial Crisis: A Study of Little Rock's Ministry* (Public Affairs Pr., 1959).

Cantey, R. C., *The Law of Search and Seizure* (U. of Georgia, 1957).

Carmichael, O. and James W., *The Louisville Story* (Simon & Schuster, 1957).

Carr, R. K., *Federal Protection of Civil Rights: Quest for a Sword* (Cornell, 1947).

———, *The House Committee on Un-American Activities 1945–1950* (Cornell, 1952).

————, *The Constitution and Congressional Investigating Committees* (Cornell, 1954).

Carter, H., *Southern Legacy* (Louisiana State U., 1950).

————, *The Angry Scar: The Story of Reconstruction* (Doubleday, 1959).

Carter, H., III, *The South Strikes Back* (Doubleday, 1959).

Cash, W. J., *The Mind of the South* (Knopf, 1956).

Castberg, F., *Freedom of Speech in the West* (Oceana, 1960).

Catterall, H. H. (Ed.), *Judicial Cases Concerning American Slavery and the Negro* (Carnegie Inst., 1926–37).

Caughey, J. W., *In Clear and Present Danger: The Critical State of Our Freedoms* (U. of Chicago, 1958).

————, *Their Majesties the Mob* (U. of Chicago, 1960).

Chafee, Z., *Freedom of Speech* (Harcourt, 1920).

————, *Watchman, What of the Night?* (University, 1942).

————, *Government and Mass Communication* (U. of Chicago, 1947).

————, *Thirty-five Years with Freedom of Speech* (Harvard, 1952).

————, *How Human Rights Got into the Constitution* (Boston U., 1952).

————, *Documents on Fundamental Human Rights* (Harvard, 1952).

————, *Free Speech in the United States* (Harvard, 1954).

————, *Freedom of Speech and Press* (Harvard, 1955).

————, *Three Human Rights in the Constitution of 1787* (U. of Kansas, 1956).

————, *The Blessings of Liberty* (Lippincott, 1956).

Chalmers, A. K., *They Shall Be Free* (Doubleday, 1951).

Chamberlain, L. H., *Loyalty and Legislative Action: A Survey of Activity by the New York State Legislature, 1919–1949* (Cornell, 1952).

Chambers W., *Witness* (Random House, 1956).

Chase, H. W., *Security and Liberty: The Problem of Native Communists, 1947–1955* (Doubleday, 1955).

Chenery, W. L., *Freedom of the Press* (Harcourt, Brace, 1955).

Chessman, C., *Cell 2455 Death Row* (Prentice-Hall, 1954).

Chute, C. L., *Crime, Courts, and Probation* (Macmillan, 1956).

Clark, J. P., *The Deportation of Aliens from the United States* (Columbia, 1931).

Cogan, J. J., *Law of Search and Seizure* (Oceana, 1950).

Cogley, J., *Report on Blacklisting* Vol. I: Movies; Vol. II: Radio-TV (Fund for the Republic, 1956).

Collins, C. W., *The Fourteenth Amendment and the States* (Little, Brown, 1912).

Commager, H. S., *Majority Rule and Minority Rights* (Oxford, 1943).

————, Carr, R. K., Chafee, Z., Gellhorn, W., Bok, C., and Baxter, J. P., *Civil Liberties Under Attack* (U. of Pennsylvania, 1951).

————, *Freedom, Loyalty, Dissent* (Oxford, 1954).

Commission on the Freedom of the Press, *A Free and Responsible Press: A General Report on Mass Communications* (1947).

Cook, F. J., *The Unfinished Story of Alger Hiss* (Morrow, 1958).

Cook, T. I., *Democratic Rights versus Communist Activity* (Doubleday, 1954).

Cooper, K., *The Right To Know: An Exposition of the Evils of News Suppression and Propaganda* (Farrar, Straus, & Cudahy, 1956).

Cornell University Study, *The Tenney Committee: Study of Legislative Investigations of Subversive Activities in California* (1952).

Corwin, E. S., *Total War and the Constitution* (Knopf, 1947).

————, *Liberty Against Government: The Rise, Flowering and Decline of a Famous Juridical Concept* (Louisiana State U., 1948).

Countryman, V., *Un-American Activities in the State of Washington* (Cornell, 1951).

Cousins, R. E., et al., *South Carolinians Speak: A Moderate Approach to Race Relations* (U. of South Carolina, 1957).

Cuniggim, M., et al., *Free Man Versus His Government* (Southern Methodist U., 1958).

Curtis, C. P., *The Oppenheimer Case* (Simon & Schuster, 1955).

Cushman, R. E. (Ed.), *Safeguarding Civil Liberty Today* (Cornell, 1945).

———, *Civil Liberties in the United States: A Guide to Current Problems and Experience* (Cornell, 1956).

Dabbs, J. M., *The Southern Heritage* (Knopf, 1958).

Darrow, C. S., *The Story of My Life* (Scribner, 1958).

Dash, S., Schwartz, R., and Knowlton, R. E., *The Eavesdroppers* (Rutgers, 1959).

Davidson, I. D., and Gehman, R., *The Jury Is Still Out* (Harper, 1959).

Davis, A., Gardner, B. B., and Gardner, M. R., *Deep South: A Social Anthropological Study of Caste and Class* (U. of Chicago, 1954).

Davis, E., *But We Were Born Free* (Bobbs-Merrill, 1954).

Davis, J., *Character Assassination* (Philosophical Library, 1951).

Dawson, J. M., *Separate Church and State Now* (R. R. Smith, 1948).

Day, E. E., *The Defense of Freedom* (Cornell, 1941).

Dean, J., *Hatred, Ridicule, or Contempt: A Book of Libel Cases* (Constable, 1953).

De Haas, E., *Antiquities of Bail: Origin and Historical Development in Criminal Cases to the Year 1275* (Columbia, 1940).

Deutsch, A., *The Trouble with Cops* (Crown, 1955).

Deutsch, M., *Interracial Housing* (U. of Minnesota, 1951).

Dexter, H. H., *What's Right with Race Relations* (Harper, 1959).

Dienstein, W., *Are You Guilty?* (Thomas, 1954).

Divine, R. A., *American Immigration Policy, 1924–52* (Yale, 1957).

Donner, F. J., *The Un-Americans* (Ballantine, 1961).

Douglas, W. O., *An Almanac of Liberty* (Doubleday, 1954).

———, *The Right of the People* (Doubleday, 1958).

———, *America Challenged* (Princeton, 1960).

———, *A Living Bill of Rights* (Doubleday, 1961).

Dowell, E. F., *A History of Criminal Syndicalism Legislation in the U.S.* (Johns Hopkins, 1939).

Downs, R. B. (Ed.), *The First Freedom: Liberty and Justice in the World of Books and Reading* (A.L.A., 1960).

Draper, T., *The Roots of American Communism* (Viking, 1957).

Drinker, H. S., *Some Observations on the Freedoms of the First Amendment* (Boston U., 1957).

Dumbauld, E., *The Bill of Rights and What It Means Today* (U. of Oklahoma, 1957).

Dykeman, W., and Stokely, J., *Neither Black nor White* (Rinehart, 1957).

Eberling, E. J., *Congressional Investigations* (Columbia, 1928).

Ebersole, L., *Church Lobbying in the Nation's Capitol* (Macmillan, 1951).

Edwards, R. A., *The Fourteenth Amendment and Civil Liberty* (Catt Mem. Fund, 1955).

Ehirch, A. A., *The Decline of American Liberalism* (Longmans, Green, 1955).

Ehler, S. Z. and Morral, J. B., *Church and State through the Centuries* (Newman Pr., 1954).

Ehrmann, H. B., *The Untried Case: The Sacco-Vanzetti-Case and the Morelli Gang* (Vanguard, 1933; rev. ed. 1960).

Emerson, T. I. and Haber, D., *Political and Civil Rights in the United States*, 2nd ed. (Dennis, 1959).

English, R. (Ed.), *The Essentials of Freedom* (Kenyon, 1960).

Ernst, M. L. and Loth, D., *Report on the American Communist* (Holt, 1952).

Ernst, M. L., *The First Freedom* (Macmillan, 1946).

Ernst, M. L. and Lindley, A., *The Censor Marches On* (Doubleday, Doran, 1940).

Fairman, C., *The Law of Martial Rule* (Callaghan, 1943).

Faulkner, W., Mays, B., and Sims, C., *The Segregation Decisions: Three Views* (Southern Reg. Council, 1956).

Fellman, D., *The Censorship of Books* (Hauser, 1957).

———, *The Defendant's Rights* (Rinehart, 1958).

———, *The Limits of Freedom* (Rutgers, 1959).

——— (Ed.), *The Supreme Court and Education* (Columbia, 1960).

Fenton, J. H., *The Catholic Vote* (Hauser, 1960).

Fiske, M., *Book Selection and Censorship* (Berkeley, 1959).

Flack, H. E., *The Adoption of the Fourteenth Amendment* (Johns Hopkins, 1908).

Fleming, H. C. and Constable, J., *What's Happening in School Integration* (Public Affairs Comm., 1956).

Fletcher, J. L. Jr., *The Segregation Case and the Supreme Court* (Boston U., 1958).

Forster, A. and Epstein, B. H., *The Trouble-Makers* (Doubleday, 1952).

Foster, A., *A Measure of Freedom* (Doubleday, 1950).

Fraenkel, O. K., *The Sacco-Vanzetti Case* (Knopf, 1931).

———, *Our Civil Liberties*, 2nd ed. (Viking, 1944).

———, *The Supreme Court and Civil Liberties* (Oceana, 1963).

Frankfurter, F., *The Case of Sacco and Vanzetti: A Critical Analysis for Lawyers and Laymen* (Little, Brown, 1927).

Frankfurter, M. D. and Jackson, G., *The Letters of Sacco and Vanzetti* (Viking, 1928).

Franklin, J. H., *From Slavery to Freedom: A History of American Negroes*, 2nd ed., rev. & enl. (Knopf, 1956).

Frazier, E. F., *The Negro in the United States*, rev. ed. (Macmillan, 1957).

Friedrich, C. J. (Ed.), *Authority* (Harvard, 1958).

Fund for the Republic, *Bibliography on the Communist Problem in the United States* (Fund for the Rep., 1955).

Gabel, R. J., *Public Funds for Church and Private Schools* (Catholic U., 1937).

Gardiner, H. C., *Catholic Viewpoints on Censorship* (Hanover House, 1958).

Garfinkel, H., *When Negroes March* (Free Press, 1959).

Gates, J., *The Story of an American Communist* (Nelson, 1958).

Gellhorn, W., *Security, Loyalty and Science* (Cornell, 1950).

——— (Ed.), *The States and Subversion* (Cornell, 1952).

———, *Individual Freedom and Governmental Restraints* (Louisiana State U., 1956).

———, *American Rights: The Constitution in Action* (Macmillan, 1960).

Gerald, J. E., *The Press and the Constitution, 1931–1947* (U. of Minnesota, 1948).

Gettys, C. L., *The Law of Citizenship in the United States* (U. of Chicago, 1934).

Giles, H. H., *The Integrated Classroom* (Basic Books, 1959).

Gillmor, D., *Fear the Accusor* (Abelard-Schuman, 1954).

Ginger, R., *Six Days or Forever? Tennessee v. John Thomas Scopes* (Beacon, 1958).

Ginzberg, E., *The Negro Potential* (Columbia, 1956).

Gittler, J. P., *Understanding Minority Groups* (Wiley, 1956).

Goldbloom, M., *American Security and Freedom* (Amer. J. Comm., 1955).

Grant, J. A. C., *Our Common Law Constitution* (Boston U., 1960).

Grebstein, S. H. (Ed.), *Monkey Trial: The State of Tennessee vs. John Thomas Scopes* (Houghton Mifflin, 1960).

Greenberg, J., *Race Relations and American Law* (Columbia, 1959).

Greene, E. B., *Religion and the State: The Making and Testing of an American Tradition* (Cornell, 1959).

Gregory, C. O., *Labor and the Law* (Norton, 1958).

Griswold, E. N., *The Fifth Amendment Today* (Harvard, 1955).

Grodzins, M., *Americans Betrayed: Politics and the Japanese Evacuations* (U. of Chicago, 1949).

————, *The Loyal & the Disloyal: Social Boundaries of Patriotism & Treason* (U. of Chicago, 1956).

Guerin, D., *Negroes on the March* (Weissman, 1956).

Gwaltney, F. I., *The Numbers of Our Days* (Random House, 1959).

Haight, A. L., *Banned Books* (Bowker, 1956).

Hale, R. L., *Freedom through Law* (Columbia, 1952).

Hand, L., *The Bill of Rights* (Harvard, 1958).

————, *The Spirit of Liberty: Papers and Addresses of Learned Hand*, 3rd ed. (Knopf, 1960).

Handlin, O., *The Uprooted* (Little, Brown, 1951).

————, *Race and Nationality in American Life* (Little, Brown, 1957).

————, *The Newcomers: Negroes and Puerto Ricans in a Changing Metropolis*.

Haney, R. W., *Comstockery in America* (Beacon, 1960).

Hanely, T. O. B., S. J., *Their Rights and Liberties* (Newman Pr., 1959).

Hansen, M. L., *The Immigrant in American History* (Harvard, 1940).

Harding, A. L. (Ed.), *Fundamental Law in Criminal Prosecutions* (S. Methodist U., 1959).

Harlan, L. R., *Separate and Unequal* (U. of N. Carolina, 1958).

Harris, R. J., *The Quest for Equality: The Constitution, Congress, and the Supreme Court* (Louisiana State U., 1960).

Hawkins, C., *Communism: Challenge to Americans* (Michigan State, 1953).

Hays, A. C., *Let Freedom Ring* (Boni & Liveright, 1937).

Hays, B. A., *A Southern Moderate Speaks* (U. of N. Carolina, 1959).

Heely, A. V., *Why The Private School?* (Harper, 1951).

Heller, F. H., *The Sixth Amendment to the Constitution of the United States: A Study in Constitutional Development* (U. of Kansas, 1951).

Herberg, W., *Protestant—Catholic—Jew*, rev. ed. (Doubleday, 1960).

Herring, P., *The Impact of War* (Farrar & Rinehart, 1941).

Higham, J., *Strangers in the Land: Patterns of American Nativism, 1860–1929* (Rutgers, 1955).

Hill, H. and Greendberg, S., *Citizen's Guide to De-Segregation* (Beacon, 1955).

Hiss, A., *In the Court of Public Opinion* (Knopf, 1957).

Hocking, W. E., *Freedom of the Press: A Framework of Principle* (U. of Chicago, 1947).

Hofstader, R. and Metzger, W. P., *The Development of Academic Freedom in the U.S.* (Columbia, 1955).

Hofstadter, S. H., *The Fifth Amendment* (Fund for the Rep., 1955).

Holcombe, A. N., *Human Rights in the Modern World* (New York U., 1948).

Hook, S., *Heresy, Yes—Conspiracy, No!* (Day, 1953).

————, *Common Sense and the Fifth Amendment* (Criterion, 1957).

————, *Political Power & Personal Freedom: Critical Studies in Democracy, Communism, and Civil Rights* (Criterion, 1959).

Hoover, J. E., *Masters of Deceit* (Holt, 1958).

Hopkins, E., *Our Lawless Police* (Viking, 1931).

Hopkins, V. C., *Dred Scott's Case* (Fordham, 1951).

Horn, R. A., *Groups and the Constitution* (Stanford, 1956).

Howe, I. and Coser, L., *The American Communist Party: A Critical History 1919–1957*, rev. ed. (Praeger, 1962).

Howe, M. de W., *Cases on Church and State in the United States* (Harvard, 1952).

Hunt, R. N. C. (Ed.), *Books on Communism* (Amperstand, 1959).

Huntington, S. P., *The Soldier and the State: The Theory and Politics of Civil Military-Relations* (Harvard, 1957).

Hurst, J. W., *Law and the Conditions of Freedom in the Nineteenth Century United States* (U. of Wisconsin, 1956).

Hutchins, R. M., *The Bill of Rights Yesterday, Today and Tomorrow* (Fund for the Rep., 1956).

Hutchinson, E. P., *Immigrants and their Children, 1850–1950* (Wiley, 1956).

Hyman, H. H., *To Try Men's Souls: Loyalty Tests in American History* (Berkeley, 1959).

Ickes, H. L., *Freedom of the Press Today* (Vanguard, 1941).

Inbau, F. E., *Self-Incrimination* (Thomas, 1950).

Inglis, R. A., *Freedom of the Movies* (U. of Chicago, 1947).

Irwin, L. B., *Minorities in the United States* (Oxford, 1951).

Iversen, R. W., *The Communists and the Schools* (Harcourt, Brace, 1959).

James, J. B., *The Framing of the Fourteenth Amendment* (U. of Illinois, 1956).

Javits, J. K., *Discrimination—U.S.A.* (Harcourt, Brace, 1960).

Johnsen, J. E., *Investigating Powers of Congress* (H. W. Wilson, 1951).

Johnson, A. W. and Yost, F., *Separation of Church and State in the U.S.* (U. of Minnesota, 1948).

Johnson, C. S., *Patterns of Negro Segregation* (Harper, 1943).

Johnson, F. E. (Ed.), *American Education and Religion: The Problem of Religion in the Schools* (Harper, 1952).

Johnson, G. W., *Peril and Promise: An Inquiry Into Freedom of the Press* (Harper, 1958).

Jones, H. M. (Ed.), *Primer of Intellectual Freedom* (Harvard, 1949).

Jones, M. A., *American Immigration* (U. of Chicago, 1960).

Joughin, G. L. and Morgan, E. M., *The Legacy of Sacco and Vanzetti* (Harcourt, Brace, 1948).

Kahn, J., *The Threat to Academic Freedom* (Horizon, 1956).

Kallen, H. M., *The Lamont Case: History of a Congressional Investigation* (Horizon, 1957).

————, *A Study of Liberty* (Antioch, 1959).

Kansas, S., *U.S. Immigration, Exclusion and Deportation, and Citizenship*, rev. ed. (Bender, 1940).

Kauper, P. G., *Frontiers of Constitutional Liberty* (U. of Michigan, 1957).

Kefauver, E., *Crime in America* (Doubleday, 1951).

Kelly, A. H., *Where Constitutional Liberty Came From* (Catt Mem. Fund, 1954).

—— (Ed.), *Foundations of Freedom in the American Constitution* (Harper, 1958).

Kephart, W. M., *Racial Factors and Urban Law Enforcement* (U. of Pennsylvania, 1958).

Kerwin, J. G., *Catholic Viewpoint on Church and State* (Doubleday, 1960).

Kesselman, L. C., *The Social Politics of the FEPC: A Study in Reform Pressure Movement* (U. of N. Carolina, 1948).

Kilpatrick, J. J., *The Smut Peddlers* (Doubleday, 1960).

King, M. L., *Stride Toward Freedom: The Montgomery Story* (Harper, 1958).

Knauff, E. R., *The Ellen Knauff Story* (Norton, 1952).

Koestler, A., *Reflections on Hanging* (Macmillan, 1957).

Konvitz, M. R., *The Alien and Asiatics in American Law* (Cornell, 1946).

——, *The Constitution and Civil Rights* (Columbia, 1946).

——, *Civil Rights in Immigration* (Cornell, 1953).

——, *Fundamental Liberties of a Free People: Religion, Speech, Press, Assembly* (Cornell, 1957).

—— and Rossiter, C. (Eds.), *Aspects of Liberty: Essays Presented to Robert E. Cushman* (Cornell, 1958).

——, *Bill of Rights Reader: Leading Constitutional Cases*, 2nd ed. (Cornell, 1960).

—— and Leskes, J., *A Century of Civil Rights* (Columbia, 1961).

Kronhausen, E. & P., *Pornography and the Law* (Ballantine, 1959).

Lacy, D., *Freedom and Communication* (Illinois Univ., 1961).

Lamont, C., *Freedom Is as Freedom Does: Civil Liberties Today* (Horizon, 1956).

——, *The Right to Travel* (Basic Pamphets, 1957).

Laponce, J. A., *The Protection of Minorities* (UCLA, 1960).

Laski, H., *Liberty in the Modern State* (Viking, 1930).

Lasson, N. B., *The History of the Development of the Fourteenth Amendment* (Johns Hopkins, 1937).

Lasswell, H. D., *National Security and Individual Freedom* (McGraw-Hill, 1950).

Lattimore, O., *Ordeal by Slander* (Little, Brown, 1950).

Laurenti, Luigi, *Property Values and Race: Studies in Seven Cities* (Berkeley, 1960).

Lieberman, E., *Unions Before the Bar* (Harper, 1950).

Leopold, N. F., *Life Plus 99 Years* (Doubleday, 1958).

Levy, L. W., *Legacy of Suppression: Freedom of Speech & Press in Early American History* (Harvard, 1960).

Lewis, J., *An Atheist Manifesto* (Harvard, 1958).

Lien, A. J., *Concurring Opinion: The Privileges or Immunities Clause of the Fourteenth Amendment* (Washington U., 1957).

Logan, R. W., *The Negro in the United States* (Van Nostrand, 1957).

Longaker, R. P., *The Presidency and Individual Liberties* (Cornell, 1961).

Loth, D. and Fleming, H., *Integration North and South* (Fund for the Rep., 1956).

Lowenthal, M., *The Federal Bureau of Investigation* (Sloane, 1950).

Lowenstein, E. (Ed.), *The Alien and the Immigration Law* (Oceana, 1958).

Lustgarten, E., *The Murder and the Trial* (Scribner, 1958).

Lyons, E., *The Life and Death of Sacco and Vanzetti* (Never, 1927).

MacIver, R. M., *Conflict of Loyalties* (Harper, 1952).

——, *Academic Freedom in our Time* (Columbia, 1955).

MacLeish, A., *Freedom is the Right to Choose* (Beacon, 1951).

Madden, W., *Religious Values in Education* (Harper, 1951).

Mangum, C. S., *The Legal Status of the Negro* (U. of N. Carolina, 1940).

Mannheim, H., *Criminal Justice and Social Reconstruction* (Paul, French, Teubner & Co., 1946).

Martin, J. B., *The Deep South Say Never* (Ballantine, 1957).

Mason, A. T., *Security Through Freedom: American Political Thought and Practice* (Cornell, 1955).

Mason, L., *The Language of Dissent* (World, 1959).

Maston, T. B., *Segregation and Desegregation: A Christian Approach* (Macmillan, 1959).

Matusow, H., *False Witness* (Cameron & Kahn, 1955).

Mayer, M. (Ed.), *The Tradition of Freedom* (Oceana, 1960).

Mayers, L., *Shall We Amend the Fifth Amendment?* (Harper, 1959).

McCauley, P. and Ball, E. D. (Eds.), *Southern Schools: Progress and Problems* (So. Educ. Rep. So., 1959).

McCluskey, N. G, *Catholic Viewpoint on Education* (Hanover House, 1959)

McEntire, D., *Residence and Race* (Berkeley, 1960).

McGeary, M. N., *The Development of Congressional Investigative Power* (Columbia, 1940).

McGill, R., *A Church, A School* (Abingdon, 1959).

McKeown, R., Merton, R. D., and Gellhorn, W., *The Freedom To Read: Perspective and Program* (Bowker, 1957).

McKernan, M., *The Amazing Crime and Trial of Leopold and Loeb* (New Amer. Lib., 1958).

McWilliams, C., *Prejudice—Japanese-American—Symbols of Racial Intolerance* (Little, Brown, 1944).

———, *A Mask for Privilege* (Little, Brown, 1948).

———, *Witch Hunt: The Revival of Heresy* (Little, Brown, 1950).

Medina, H. R., *The Anatomy of Freedom* (Holt, 1959).

Meiklejohn, A., *Free Speech and Its Relation to Self-Government* (Harper, 1948).

———, *Political Freedom: The Constitutional Powers of the People* (Harper, 1960).

Merson, M., *The Private Diary of a Public Servant* (Macmillan, 1955).

Michael, J. and Wechsler, H. (Eds.), *Criminal Law and Its Administration: Cases, Statutes, and Commentaries* (Foundation Pr., 1940).

Mill, J. S., *On Liberty* (Appleton-Century-Crofts, 1851).

Miller, A. S., *Racial Discrimination and Private Education* (U. of N. Carolina, 1957).

Miller, J. C., *Crisis in Freedom* (Little, Brown, 1951).

Miller, M., *The Judges and the Judged* (Doubleday, 1952).

Miller, W. L., et al., *Religion and the Free Society* (Fund for the Rep., 1958).

Millis, H. A. and Brown, E. C., *From the Wagner Act to Taft-Hartley* (U. of Chicago, 1950).

Millis, W., *Individual Freedom and the Common Defense* (Fund for the Rep., 1957).

——— et al., *Arms and the State: Civil–Military Elements in National Policy* (20th Century Fund, 1958).

Milton J., *Areopagitica* (Dent, 1925).

Moehlman, C., *Wall of Separation Between Church and State* (Beacon, 1951).

Monnerot, J., *Sociology and Psychology of Communism* (Beacon, 1953).

Montgomery, R. H., *Sacco-Vanzetti: The Murder and the Myth* (Devin-Adair, 1960).

Moos, M. and Rourke, F., *The Campus and the State* (Johns Hopkins, 1959).

Morison, S. E., *Freedom in Contemporary Society* (Little, Brown, 1956).

Morley, F., *Freedom and Federalism* (Regnary, 1961).

Morris, R. B., *Fair Trial: Fourteen Who Stood Accused from Anne Hutchinson to Alger Hiss* (Knopf, 1952).

Mott, R. L., *Due Process of Law* (Bobbs-Merrill, 1926).

Murray, R. K., *Red Scare: A Study in National Hysteria 1919–1920* (U. of Minnesota, 1955).

Muse, B., *Virginia's Massive Resistance* (Indiana U., 1961).

Musmanno, M. A., *After Twelve Years: The Sacco-Vanzetti Case* (Knopf, 1939).

Myers, G. A., *History of Bigotry in the United States* (Random House, 1943).

Myrdahl, G., *An American Dilemma: The Negro Problem and Modern Democracy* (Harper, 1946).

Nelson, H. L., *Libel in News of Congressional Investigating Committees* (U. of Minnesota, 1961).

Newman, E. S. (Ed.), *The Freedom Reader* (Oceana, 1955).

———, *The Law of Civil Rights and Civil Liberties* (Oceana, 1958).

Nicholls, W. H., *Southern Tradition and Regional Progress* (U. of N. Carolina, 1960).

Nichols, L., *Breakthrough on the Color Front* (Random House, 1954).

Nock, A. J., *Our Enemy, the State* (Capton, 1946).

O'Brian, J. L., *National Security and Individual Freedom* (Harvard, 1955).

O'Brien, F. W., *Justice Reed and the First Amendment: The Religion Clauses* (Georgetown, 1958).

Odegard, P. H., *Religion and Politics* (Oceana, 1960).

Ogden, A. R., *The Dies Committee,* 2nd ed. (Catholic U., 1946).

Ogden, F. D., *The Poll Tax in the South* (U. of Alabama, 1958).

O'Neill, J. M., *Religion and Education Under the Constitution* (Harper, 1949).

———, *Catholicism and American Freedom* (Harper, 1952).

Orfield, L. B., *Criminal Appeals in America* (Little, Brown, 1939).

———, *Criminal Procedure from Arrest to Appeal* (New York U., 1947).

Orton, W. A., *The Liberal Tradition: Social and Spiritual Conditions of Freedom* (Oxford, 1945).

Overstreet, H. and B., *What We Must Know About Communism* (Norton, 1958).

Oxnam, G. B., *I Protest: My Experience with the House Committee on Un-American Activities* (Harper, 1954).

Palmer, E. E. (Ed.), *The Communist Problem in America* (Crowell, 1951).

Parker, R., *A Guide to Labor Law* (Praeger, 1961).

Parsons, W. P., S. J., *The First Freedom: Considerations on Church and State in the United States* (McMullen, 1948).

Patterson, B. B., *The Forgotten Ninth Amendment* (Bobbs-Merrill, 1955).

Patterson, G., *Free Speech and a Free Press* (Little Brown, 1939).

Patterson, H., *Scottsboro Boy* (Doubleday, 1950).

Paul, J. C. N. and Schwartz, M. L., *Federal Censorship* (Free Press, 1959).

Peltason, J., *Constitutional Liberty and Seditious Activity* (Catt Mem. Fund, 1954).

Pennock, J. R., *Liberal Democracy* (Rinehart, 1950).

Penrose, W. O., *Freedom Is Ourselves* (U. of Delaware, 1952).

Perry, R. L. (Ed.), *Sources of Our Liberties: Documentary Origins of Individual Liberties in the U.S. Constitution and Bill of Rights* (Amer. Bar Found., 1959).

Peters, W., *The Southern Temper* (Doubleday, 1959).

Pfeffer, L., *Church, State, and Freedom* (Beacon, 1953).

———, *The Liberties of An American: The Supreme Court Speaks* (Beacon, 1956).

———, *Creeds in Competition* (Harper, 1959).

Pike, J. A., *A Roman Catholic in the White House* (Doubleday, 1960).

Pike, R., *Jehovah's Witnesses* (Phil. Lib., 1954).

Ploscowe, M., *The Truth About Divorce* (Hawthorn, 1955).

Polsky, S. (Ed.), *The Medico-Legal Reader* (Oceana, 1956).

Post, L. F., *The Deportation Delirium of Nineteen-twenty* (Kerr, 1923).

Pound, R., *Criminal Justice in America* (Holt, 1945).

———, *The Development of Constitutional Guarantees of Liberty* (Yale, 1957).

Powell, T., *The School Bus Law: A Case Study in Education, Religion, and Politics* (Wesleyan, 1961).

President's Commission on Immigration and Naturalization, *Whom Shall We Welcome?* (Simon & Schuster, 1947).

President's Committee on Civil Rights, To Secure These Rights (Simon & Schuster, 1947).

Price, H. D., *The Negro in Southern Politics* (New York U., 1957).

Pritchett, C. H., *Civil Liberties and the Vinson Court* (U. of Chicago, 1954).

———, *The Political Offender and the Warren Court* (Boston U., 1958).

Putkammer, E. W., *Administration of Criminal Law* (U. of Chicago, 1953).

Quint, H. H., *Profile of Black and White: A Frank Portrait of South Carolina* (Public Affairs Pr., 1958).

Race Relations Law Reporter (Published bi-monthly since 1956 by the Vanderbilt U. School of Law).

Rankin, R. S., *When Civil Law Fails: Martial Law and Its Legal Basis in the U.S.* (Duke, 1939).

Raymond, A., *The People's Right To Know: A Report on Government News Suppression* (A.C.L.U., 1955).

Record, W. and Record, J. C. (Eds.), *Little Rock, U.S.A.* (Chandler, 1960).

———, *The Negro and the Communist Party* (U. of N. Carolina, 1951).

Reddick, L. D., *Crusader Without Violence* (Harper, 1959).

Redding, J. S., *On Being Negro in America* (Bobbs-Merrill, 1951).

———, *The Lonesome Road: The Story of the Negro's Past in America* (Doubleday, 1958).

Reel, A. F., *The Case of General Yamashita* (U. of Chicago, 1949).

Reid, I. (Ed.), *Racial Desegregation and Integration* (Amer. Acad., 1956).

Reik, T., *The Compulsion To Confess* (Farrar, Straus & Cudahy, 1959).

Reppy, A., *Civil Rights in the United States* (Central Books, 1951).

Reynolds, Q., *Courtroom* (Farrar, Straus, 1950).

Robin, E. F. and Hirsch, J. G., *The Pursuit of Equality* (Crown, 1957).

Roelofs, H. M., *The Tension of Citizenship: Private Man and Public Duty* (Rinehart, 1957).

Rogge, O. J., *Why Men Confess* (Nelson, 1959).

———, *The First and the Fifth* (Nelson, 1960).

Rose, A., *The Negro in America* (Beacon, 1956).

Ross, M., *All Manner of Men* (Reynal & Hitchcock, 1948).

Rossiter, C., *Seedtime of the Republic: The Origin of the American Tradition of Political Liberty* (Harcourt, Brace, 1953).

Rourke, F. E., *Secrecy and Publicity: Dilemmas of Democracy* (Johns Hopkins, 1961.

Rowan, C., *South of Freedom* (Knopf, 1952).

358

———, *Go South to Sorrow* (Random House, 1957).

Roy, R. L., *Communism and the Churches* (Harcourt, Brace, 1960).

———, *Apostles of Discord* (Beacon, 1953).

Royal Commission on the Press, *Report of the Royal Commission on the Press, 1947–1949* (H.M.G.P.O., 1949).

Rubin, L. D. Jr. and Kilpatrick, J. J. (Eds.), *The Lasting South* (Regnery, 1957).

Ruchames, L., *Race, Jobs, and Politics: The Story of F.E.P.C.* (Columbia, 1953).

Russell, B., *Authority and the Individual* (Simon & Schuster, 1949).

Rutland, R. A., *The Birth of the Bill of Rights: The Background and Consequences, 1776–1791* (U. of N. Carolina, 1955).

Savage, H. Jr., *The Seeds of Time: The Background of Southern Thinking* (Holt, 1959).

Schaar, J. H., *Loyalty in America: The Background and Consequences* (UCLA, 1957).

Scheiber, H. N., *The Wilson Administration & Civil Liberties* (Cornell, 1960).

Schultz, H. E., *Religious Education and the Public Schools* (UCLA, 1955).

Schwartzman, R. and Stein, J., *The Law of Personal Liberties* (Oceana, 1955).

Seagle, W., *Acquitted—of Murder* (Regnery, 1958).

Seldes, G., *Freedom of the Press* (Bobbs-Merrill, 1935).

———, *"We Hold These Truths . . ."* (League of Amer. Writers, 1939).

———, *Witch Hunt* (Modern Age Books, 1940).

———, *The People Don't Know* (Gaer Assoc., 1949).

Sellin, H. (Ed.), *Practice and Procedure under the Immigration and Nationality Act* (McCarran-Walter Act) (New York U., 1954).

Shannon, D. A., *The Decline of American Communism: A History of the Communist Party of the U.S. Since 1945* (Harcourt, Brace, 1959).

Shapiro, H. H., *Federal Enforcement of the Criminal Civil Rights Statutes* (Rutgers, 1960).

Shaver, E. L., The *Weekday Church School* (Pilgrim, 1956).

Shields, C., *Democracy and Catholicism in America* (McGraw-Hill, 1958).

Shils, E. A., *The Torment of Secrecy: American Security Policies* (Free Press, 1956).

Shoemaker, D. (Ed.), *With All Deliberate Speed* (Harper, 1957).

Sibley, M. Q. and Jacob, P. E., *Conscription of Conscience: The American State and the Conscientious Objector, 1940–1947* (Cornell, 1952).

Silving, H., *Immigration Laws of the U.S.* (Oceana, 1949).

Smead, E. E., *Freedom of Speech by Radio and Television* (Public Affairs Br., 1958).

Smith, B., *Police Systems in the United States,* rev. ed. (Harper, 1949).

Smith, J. M., *Freedom's Fetters: The Alien and Sedition Laws and American Civil Liberties* (Cornell, 1956).

Smith, L., *American Democracy and Military Power* (U. of Chicago, 1951).

———, *Now Is the Time* (Viking, 1955).

Smith, T. V., *The Bill of Rights and Our Individual Liberties* (Catt Mem. Fund, 1954).

Snow, C. P., *The Affair* (Scribner, 1960).

———, *Science and Government* (Harvard, 1961).

Somerville, J., *The Communist Trials and the American Tradition: Expert Testimony on Force and Violence* (Cameron, 1956).

Southern Education Reporting Service, *Southern Schools: Progress and Problems* (Nashville, 1959).

Southern Regional Council, *Intimidation, Reprisal and Violence in the South's Racial Crisis* (So. Reg. Council, 1959).

Spencer, H., *Man versus the State* (Appleton, 1884).

Spicer, G. W., *The Supreme Court and Fundamental Freedom* (Appleton-Century-Crofts, 1959).

Spitz, D., *Democracy and Challenge of Power* (Columbia, 1958).

Spring, S., *Risks and Rights in Publishing, Television, Radio, Motion Pictures, Advertising, and the Theatre* (Allen & Unwin, 1952).

Spurlock, C., *Education and the Supreme Court* (U. of Illinois, 1955).

Stark, L., *We Saw It Happen* (Simon & Schuster, 1939).

St. John-Stevas, N., *Obscenity and the Law* (Secker & Warburg, 1956).

————, *Life, Death, and the Law* (Indiana U., 1961).

Stewart, G. R., *The Year of the Oath: The Fight for Academic Freedom at the University of California* (Doubleday, 1950).

Stokes, A. P., *Church and State in the United States*, 3 vols. (Harper, 1950).

Stouffer, S. A., *Communism, Conformity and Civil Liberties: A Cross-Section of the Nation Speaks Its Mind* (Doubleday, 1955).

Stryker, L. P., *Courts and Doctors* (Macmillan, 1932).

Superintendent of Documents, *The Report of the U.S. Commission on Civil Rights* (1959–   ).

Sutherland, A. E., *Two Reference Volumes on Communism in the United States* (Harvard, 1956).

Talmadge, H. E., *You and Segregation* (Vulcan, 1955).

Tawney, R. H., *Equality*, 5th ed. (Putnam's, 1961).

Taylor, T., *Grand Inquest: The Story of Congressional Investigations* (Simon and Schuster, 1955).

Tenbroek, J., et al., *Japanese-American Evacuation and Resettlement* (Berkeley, 1944).

————, Barnhart, E. N., and Matson, F. W., *The Anti-Slavery Origins of the Fourteenth Amendment*, (Berkeley, 1951).

————, et al., *Prejudice, War, and the Constitution* (Berkeley, 1954).

Thayer, F., *Legal Control of the Press* (Foundation Pr., 1944).

Thomas, D. S. and Nishimito, R. S., *The Spoilage* (Berkeley, 1946).

Thomas, N., *The Test of Freedom* (Norton, 1954).

Thoreau, H. D., *On the Duty of Civil Disobedience* (Yale, 1849).

Thorp, W., *A Southern Reader* (Knopf, 1955).

Torpey, W. G., *Judicial Doctrines of Religious Rights in America* (U. of N. Carolina, 1948).

Tumin, M. M., *Desegregation: Readiness and Resistance* (Princeton, 1958).

Tussman, J., *Obligation and the Body Politic* (Oxford, 1960).

Uhr, L. and Miller, J. G. (Eds.), *Drugs and Behavior* (Wiley, 1960).

University of North Carolina Press, *When a City Closes Its Schools* (U. of N. Carolina, 1960).

Vanderbilt Univ. School of Law, *The Race Relations Law Reporter* (current).

Virginia Senate Committee for Courts of Justice, *The Doctrine of Interposition: Its History and Application* (1957).

Vose, C. E., *Caucasians Only: The Supreme Court, the NAACP, and the Restrictive Covenant Cases* (Berkeley, 1959).

Wahlke, J. C., *Loyalty in A Democratic State* (Heath, 1952).

Wakefield, D., *Revolt in the South* (Grove, 1960).

Walter, E. A. (Ed.), *Religion and the State University* (U. of Michigan, 1958).

Warren, R. P., *Segregation: The Inner Conflict in the South* (Random House, 1956).

Wechsler, J. A., *The Age of Suspicion* (Random House, 1953).

Weinberg, A., *Attorney for the Damned* (Simon & Schuster, 1957).

Weinstein, S. and Brown, H. S. Jr., *Personnel Security Programs of the Federal Government* (Fund for the Rep., 1954).

Weintraub, R. G., *How Secure These Rights* (Doubleday, 1949).

Westin, A., *The Constitution and Loyalty Programs* (Catt Mem. Fund, 1954).

————, *The Miracle Case* (U. of Alabama, 1961).

Weyl, N., *Treason: The Story of Disloyalty and Betrayal in American History* (Public Affairs Pr., 1950).

————, *The Battle Against Disloyalty* (Crowell, 1951).

————, *The Negro in American Civilization* (Public Affairs Pr., 1960).

Wheeler, K., *Peaceable Lane* (Simon & Schuster, 1960).

Whipple, L., *The Story of Civil Liberty in the United States* (Vanguard, 1927).

————, *Our Ancient Liberties* (H. W. Wilson, 1927).

White, L., *The American Radio* (U. of Chicago, 1947).

White, W., *How Far the Promised Land?* (Viking, 1955).

Whitehead, D., *The F.B.I. Story: A Report to the People* (Random House, 1956).

Wiggins, J. R., *Freedom or Secrecy?* (Oxford, 1956).

Wigmore, Sir J. H., *A Treatise on the Anglo-American System of Evidence in Trials at Common Law* (Little, Brown, 1940).

Wilcox, C. (Ed.), *Civil Liberties Under Attack* (U. of Pennsylvania, 1952).

Williams, B., *Due Process* (Morrow, 1960).

Williams, F., *Press, Parliament, and People* (Heinemann, 1946).

Williams, R. J. and Ryan, M. W. (Eds.), *Schools in Transition: Community Experiences in Desegregation* (U. of N. Carolina, 1954).

Wilson, H. H. and Glickman, H., *The Problem of Internal Security in Great Britain, 1948–1953* (Doubleday, 1954).

Wittenberg, P. (Ed.), *The Lamont Case: History of a Congressional Investigation* (Horizon, 1957).

————, *Dangerous Words: A Guide to the Law of Libel* (Columbia, 1960).

Wood, V., *Due Process of Law 1932–1949* (Louisiana St. U., 1951).

Woodward, C. V., *The Strange Career of Jim Crow*, rev. ed. (Oxford, 1957).

Woofter, T. J., *Southern Race Progress: The Wavering Color Line* (Public Affairs Pr., 1957).

Workman, W. D., Jr., *The Case for the South* (Devin-Adair, 1960).

Yarmolinsky, A. (Ed.), *Case Studies in Personnel Security* (Bureau of Nat'l. Affairs, 1955).

Yeager, P. B. and Stark, J. R., *Your Inalienable Rights* (Public Affairs Pr., 1960).

Zabel, O. H., *God and Caesar in Nebraska: A Study of the Legal Relationship of Church and State, 1854–1954* (U. of Nebraska, 1955).

Zelermyer, W., *Invasion of Privacy* (Syracuse U., 1959).

Ziegler, B. M. (Ed.), *Immigration: An American Dilemma* (Heath, 1953).

————, *Desegregation and the Supreme Court* (Heath, 1958).

————, *The Supreme Court and American Economic Life* (Row, Peterson, 1962).

I. GENERAL INDEX

A

Abraham, H. J., 73n, 236n
accusation, 126
Acheson, D., 212
Act of Settlement of 1701 (Eng.), 44
Adams, J., 42, 49, 61, 272, 273
Adams, J. Q., 49, 77, 80
Adenauer, K., 265
administering the federal judiciary (U.S.), 153–5
Administration of Justice (Miscellaneous Provisions) Act of 1933 (Eng.), 97, 100
Administrative Courts, 229, 234–7, 241; England, 236–7; France, 237–40; U.S., 236–7
Administrative Office of the United States Courts, 153–5
adversary proceeding, 96–7, 123–7
advisory opinion, 313–14
Agricultural Adjustment Act of 1933 (U.S.), 188, 285, 293
Agricultural Adjustment Act of 1938 (U.S.), 293
Alaska Plan, 34, 38
Alcibiades, 98
Alien Property Custodian (U.S.), 148
Alien and Sedition Law (U.S.), 41
Allen, F., 56–7
Alsop, J., 286n
American Bar Association (A.B.A.), 210; Committee on the Federal Judiciary, 28–9

American Civil Liberties Union (A.C.L.U.), 210
American Federation of Labor–Congress of Industrial Organizations (A.F. of L.–C.I.O.), 210
American Jewish Congress (A.J.C.), 210
American Legion, 210
amicus curiae, brief, 205, 209–12
Anglo-American Peace Treaty, 271
appeal, writ of, 158–60
Appellate Jurisdiction Act of 1876 (Eng.), 226
appellant, 124
appellee, 124
apprehension, 125
Archbald, R. W., 42
Argentina, 141–2
Arnold, T., 321
arraignment, 126
Arthur, C. A., 49
Assize of Clarendon, 100
Assize of Novel Disseisin of 1166 (Eng.), 11
Athenians, 97–9
Attorney-General (Eng.), 221
Attorney-General (U.S.), 27, 30, 150, 175, 180
Atwell, W. H., 201
Austin, J., 7
Australia, 13, 227, 251
Austria, 264, 266–7
avocat, 87
avouet, 87

361

II. COURT CASES

This book may be kept

FOURTEEN DAYS

A fine will be charged for each day the book
is kept over time.

MAY 9 MAY 0 4 1990			
APR 4 '73			
74 APR 22 1982			
MAR 6 '80 NOV 24 1982			
OCT 28 '80 APR 07 1993			
FEB 20 '81 APR 20 1995			
12-1-83 OCT 18 1993			
MAR 28 '84 DEC 04 1995			
MAR 06 1986 NOV 09 1995			
MAR 19 1986			
APR 02 1986			
APR 28 1986			
MAY 5 1986			
DEC 02 1987			
MAR 04 1988			
APR 04 1988			

bd   CAT. NO. 23 159   PRINTED IN U.S.A.